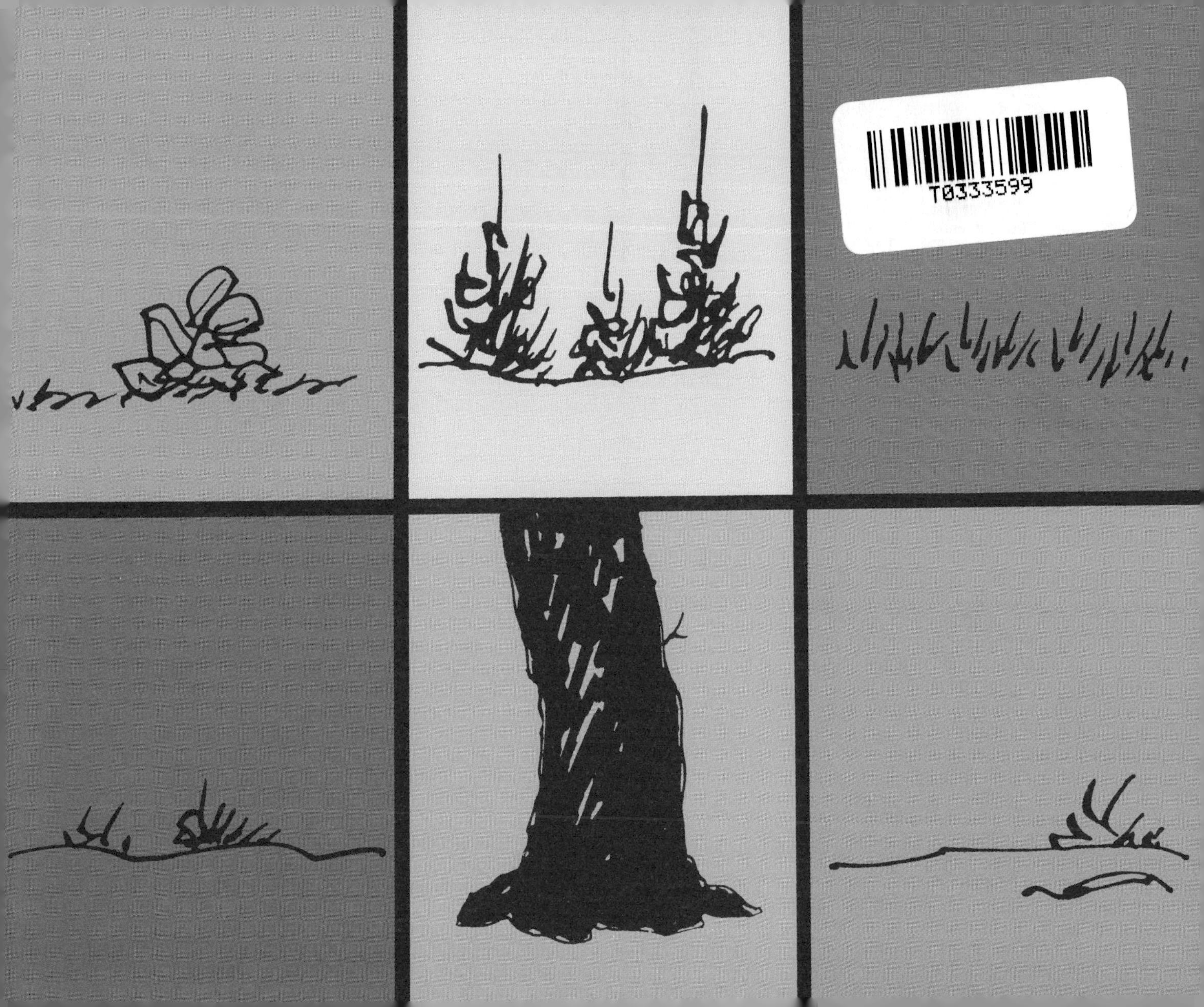

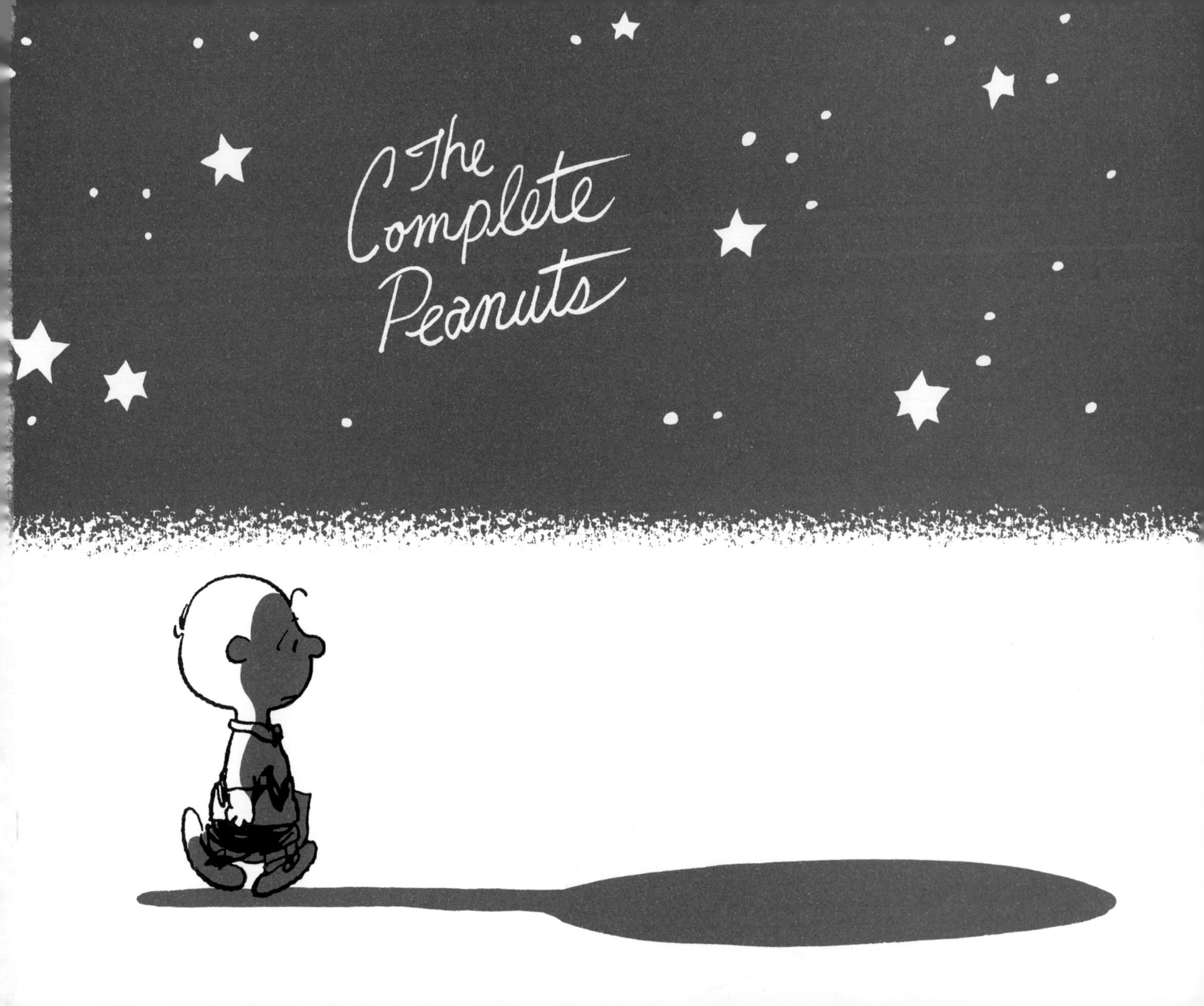
The Complete Peanuts

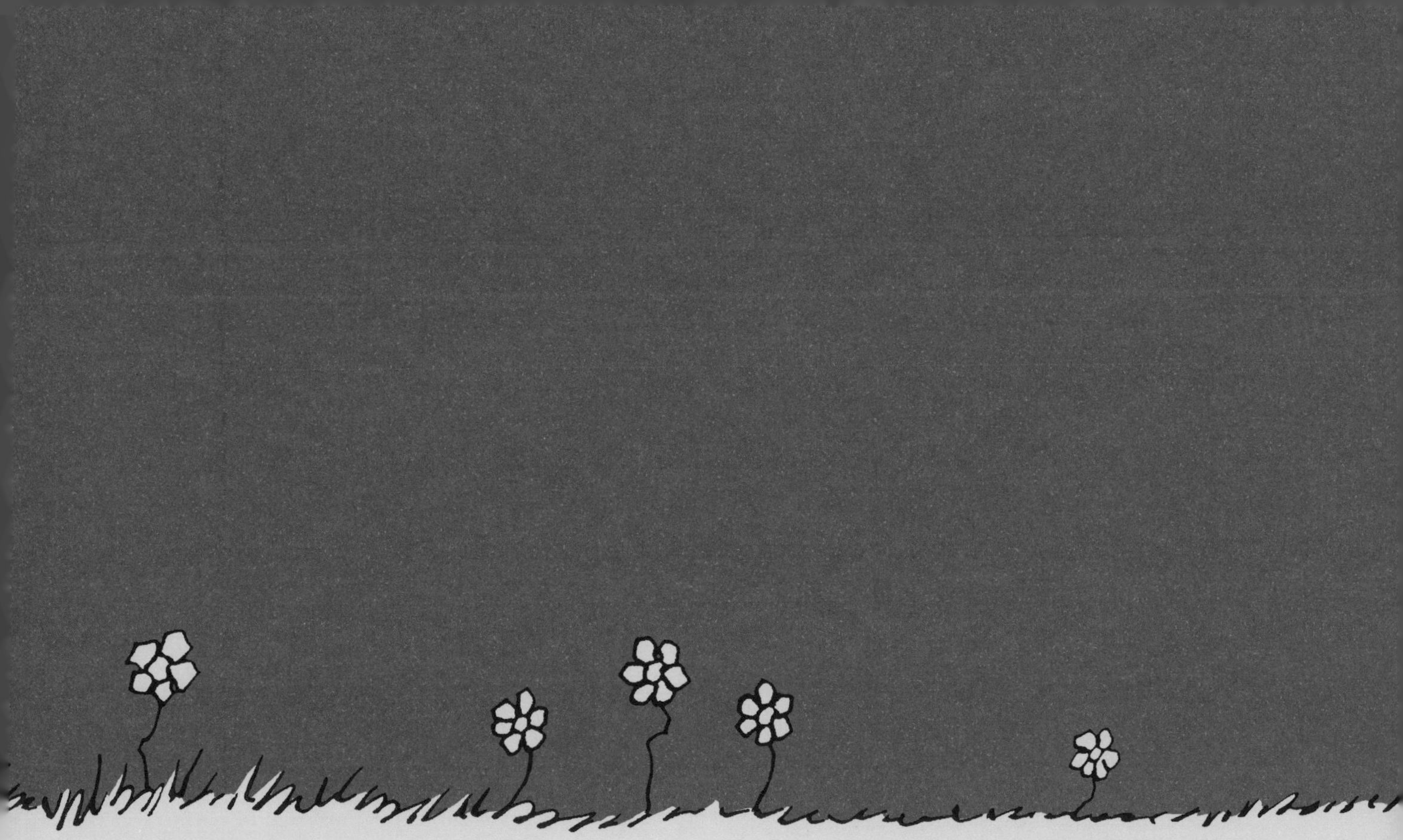

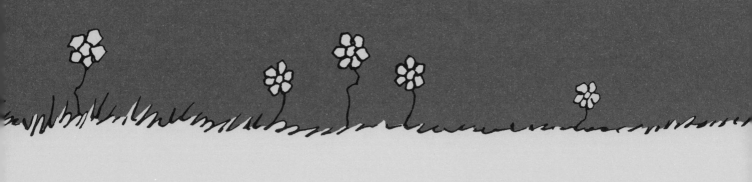

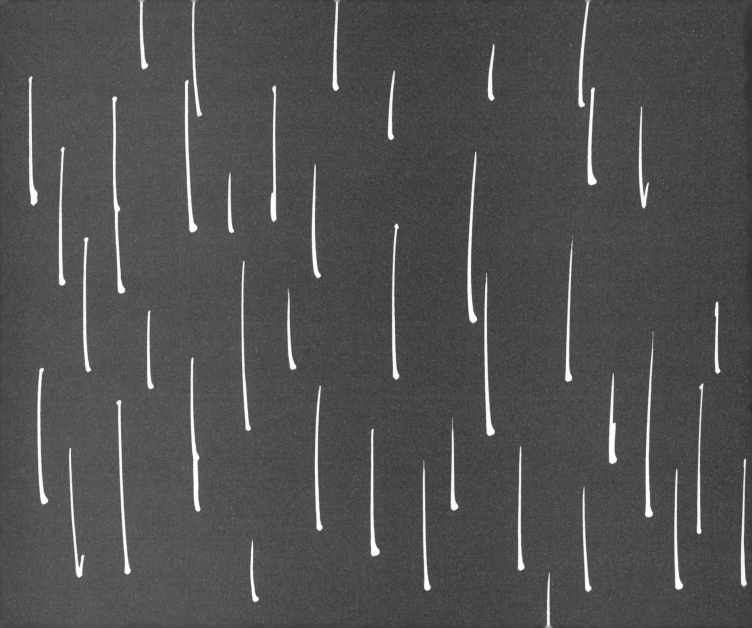

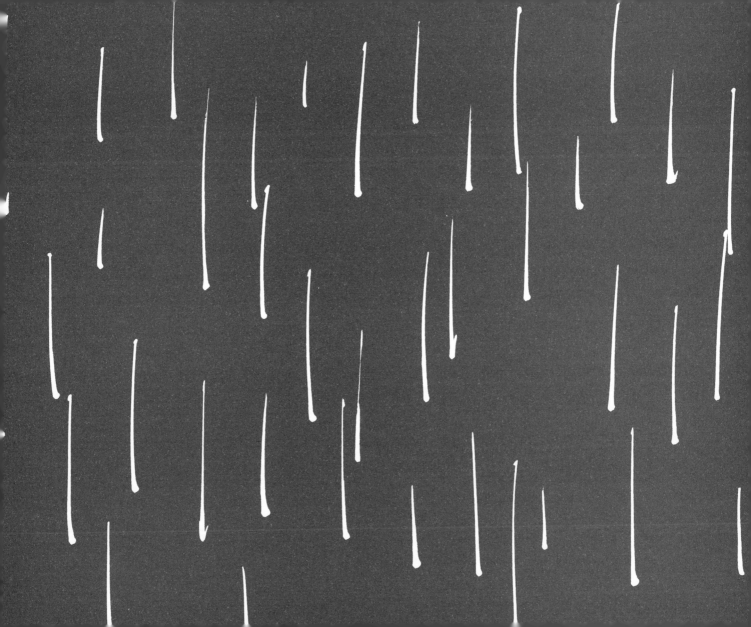

THE COMPLETE PEANUTS
by Charles M. Schulz

Editor: Gary Groth
Designer: Seth
Production, assembly, and restoration: Paul Baresh
Archival assistance: Marcie Lee
Index compiled by Elaine Lin and Lucy Kiester
Associate Publisher: Eric Reynolds
Publisher: Gary Groth

Thanks to: Karen Green, Secret Headquarters, Eduardo Takeo "Lizarkeo" Igarashi, John DiBello,
Ted Haycraft, Andy Koopmans, Juan Manuel Domínguez, Paul van Dijken, Nick Capetillo, Randall Bethune,
Kevin Czapiewski, Thomas Eykemans, Christian Schremser, Thomas Zimmermann, Kurt Sayenga, Anne Lise
Rostgaard Schmidt, Coco and Eddie Gorodetsky, Big Planet Comics, Nevdon Jamgochian, Dan Evans III, Scott
Fritsch-Hammes, Black Hook Press (Japan), Mungo van Krimpen-Hall, Philip Nel, Jason Aaron Wong,
Vanessa Palacios, and Mathieu Doublet.

Special thanks to Jeannie Schulz, without whom this project would not have come to fruition.

First published in America in 2014 by Fantagraphics Books,
7563 Lake City Way, Seattle, WA, 98115, USA.

First published in Great Britain in 2015 by Canongate Books,
14 High Street, Edinburgh, EH1 1TE

3

British Library Cataloguing-in-Publication Data
A catalogue record for this book is available on request from the British Library.

ISBN: 978 1 78211 519 9
Printed and bound in Malaysia
canongate.co.uk

CHARLES M. SCHULZ

THE COMPLETE PEANUTS

1993 TO 1994

" I LOVE TO COME OUT HERE TO
MY SNOW COVERED PITCHER'S
MOUND AND RELIVE ALL
THOSE GOOD MEMORIES.."

CANONGATE BOOKS

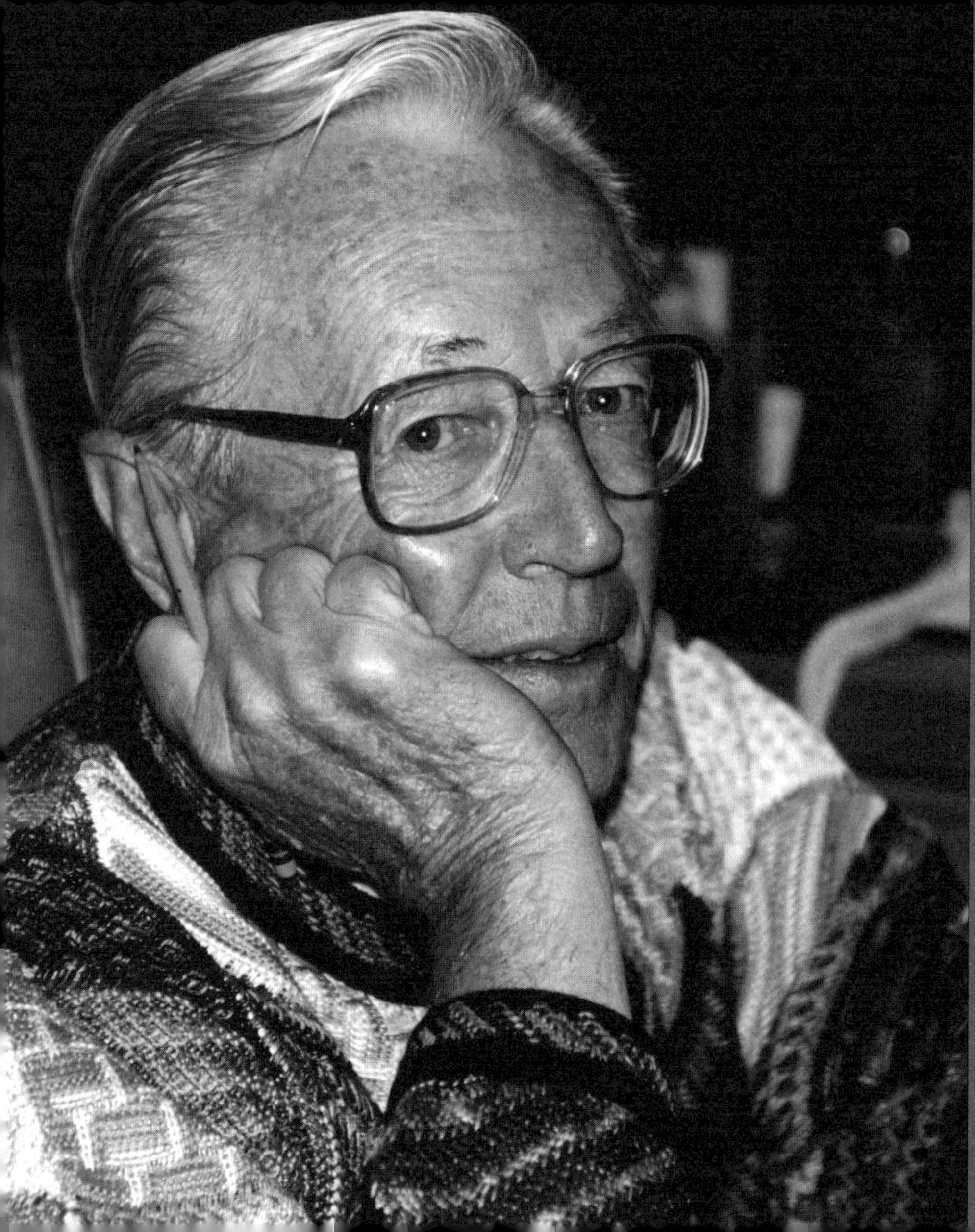

Charles M. Schulz in his home studio at the drawing board, Santa Rosa, California, mid-1990s: courtesy of the Charles M. Schulz Museum.

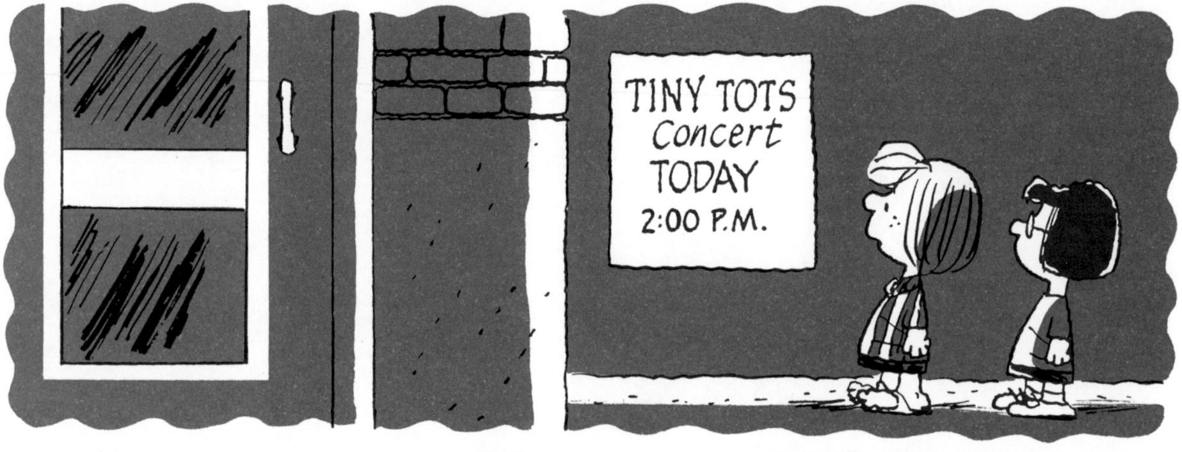
TINY TOTS
Concert
TODAY
2:00 P.M.

FOREWORD by JAKE TAPPER

When I was a little boy, my mother worried about how much I loved *Peanuts*. Specifically, she fretted that I identified too closely with Charlie Brown.

In retrospect, my *Peanuts* preoccupation was mostly motivated by a love of cartooning and my appreciation for Charles "Sparky" Schulz's sense of humor and graphic skill. But I don't want to dismiss my mother's concerns, because they weren't without merit.

While other cartoon characters' "humor" was rooted in gluttony (Garfield, Hagar the Horrible) or mischief (Dennis the Menace), Charlie Brown's defining characteristic has been for decades his insecurity.

And that, yes, I could relate to. I suspect most of us can, even though insecurity is something we all so rarely discuss.

It's hardly an original observation to suggest that *Peanuts* is so popular not because Charlie Brown is a loser whom we all deride, but rather because he's someone to whom we can all relate. Whose life has not included an unattainable love like the little red-haired girl? Who does not have a kite-eating tree lurking, existentially? Who does not return, on blind faith, time after time, to try to kick that football?

But the thing about Charlie Brown: he's not a loser.

Charlie Brown, when all is said and done, is a winner. Yes, he has struggles and insecurities, disappointments and dark voices in the middle of the night, as do we all. And yes, he's a C-student (not unlike some Presidents.) But Charlie Brown has a good life and a loving family. He has friends. A sister who adores him. A fun dog who depends upon him. He's the manager of his baseball team. And while he might be either blissfully unaware or not interested, there are plenty of girls who seem to dig him.

Charles Schulz himself was a winner, though how much he let himself enjoy his tremendous bounty is debatable. Interviews with him are a mix of confidence and doubts. The man revealed is both assured of his achievements in the popular culture, while also longing for Olympian heights he cannot reach as well as his own metaphorical "Rosebud" sleds from his past.

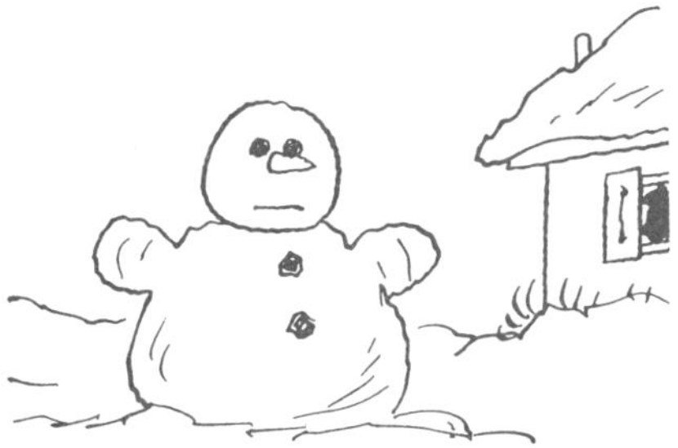

Schulz's farewell to his mother, on her cancer death bed in 1943, was a heartbreak that never healed. Then just 20, a soldier shipping to Europe but home with a day pass from Fort Snelling, Sparky visited his mom and before he left heard her say "Goodbye, Sparky. We'll probably never see each other again." He would later suggest that he never fully recovered from that moment.

For all the talk of his loneliness and anxiety, Schulz was not without ego; he fully understood what he had accomplished. Some have portrayed this as a contradiction, but it isn't. The ghosts that haunt us from our past — bullies, a parent's sudden and early death, rejections romantic and professional — do not vanish upon success. Making the *Forbes* list did not bring Schulz's mother back to life. High ratings for his TV specials did not make Donna Mae Johnson, the actual little red-haired girl, accept his marriage proposal.

"I can think of no more emotionally damaging loss than to be turned down by someone whom you love very much," Schulz told one biographer. "A person who not only turns you down, but almost immediately will marry the victor. What a bitter blow that is."

Of course one has to wonder how much Schulz nurtured that red-haired loss for the sake of his art. After all, as Schulz once quipped to the actual Shermy, "I got my money's worth out of that relationship."

It is indeed this laying bare the disappointments of life upon the page that makes *Peanuts* so resonant. We tend not to discuss our feelings of inadequacy, our fears of others' distaste for us. To do so, we are taught, is weak. And so the charade continues.

And, though I confess that I'm happy that my son identifies more with Snoopy than with his owner, this is why the notion that Charlie Brown is indeed a winner is so important for *Peanuts* fans. Because he, and Sparky, are us.

"The poetry of these children is born from the fact that we find in them all the problems, all the sufferings of the adults, who remain offstage," Umberto Eco wrote in his introduction to the first *Peanuts* collection in Italian.

The very first cartoon in this volume occurs on New Year's Day. Peppermint Patty is calling Charlie Brown to ask if he loves her. His response is hardly satisfying, and a reminder that Charlie Brown is not the only one who suffers unrequited love: when one factors in goals such as defeating the Red Baron, returning to the happy days of the Daisy Hill Puppy Farm or witnessing an appearance by the Great Pumpkin, virtually all the characters pine for something or someone out of reach. Sally loves Linus, Lucy loves Schroeder, Peppermint Patty and Marcie compete for Charlie Brown's affection. Within these pages, we are also introduced to another young girl who takes a fancy to our hero, one who claims to be Roy Hobbs' great-granddaughter — despite the continued reminders to the girl that Malamud's *The Natural* was a work of fiction.

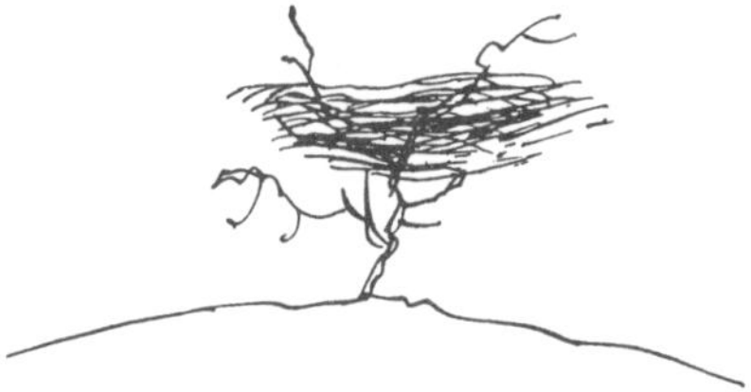

A few of the strips in this volume contain zeitgeist-y references that may now date them — Peppermint Patty confusing Snow White with Vanna White, Snoopy as Joe Grunge, a discussion of Snoopy facing then-Sen. Joe Biden, chair of the Judiciary Committee in 1993. But for the most part they land in the timeless suburb that enables *Peanuts* to continue in syndication today. Most of the cultural references are similarly timeless: Mickey Mouse, Alice in Wonderland, and Willy Loman.

Leo Tolstoy continues to be a frequent *Peanuts* touchstone; Schulz thought *War and Peace* the greatest novel ever written, and he could relate to the author's demons. "He sure went through a lot of turmoil," Schulz told *The Comics Journal* in 1997. "And he also had what Scott Fitzgerald talked about once, 'the dark side of the soul,' didn't he…I think perhaps a lot of us have gone through that in different ways. And I don't even know if it can be explained."

In a Summer strip, on page 77, Linus asks Charlie Brown which he would rather do, write *War and Peace* like Tolstoy, or be the first to hit more than 60 home runs in a single season like Roger Maris.

After striking out, Charlie Brown says, "I probably won't write 'War and Peace,' either."

Don't be so sure that you didn't, Mr. Schulz.

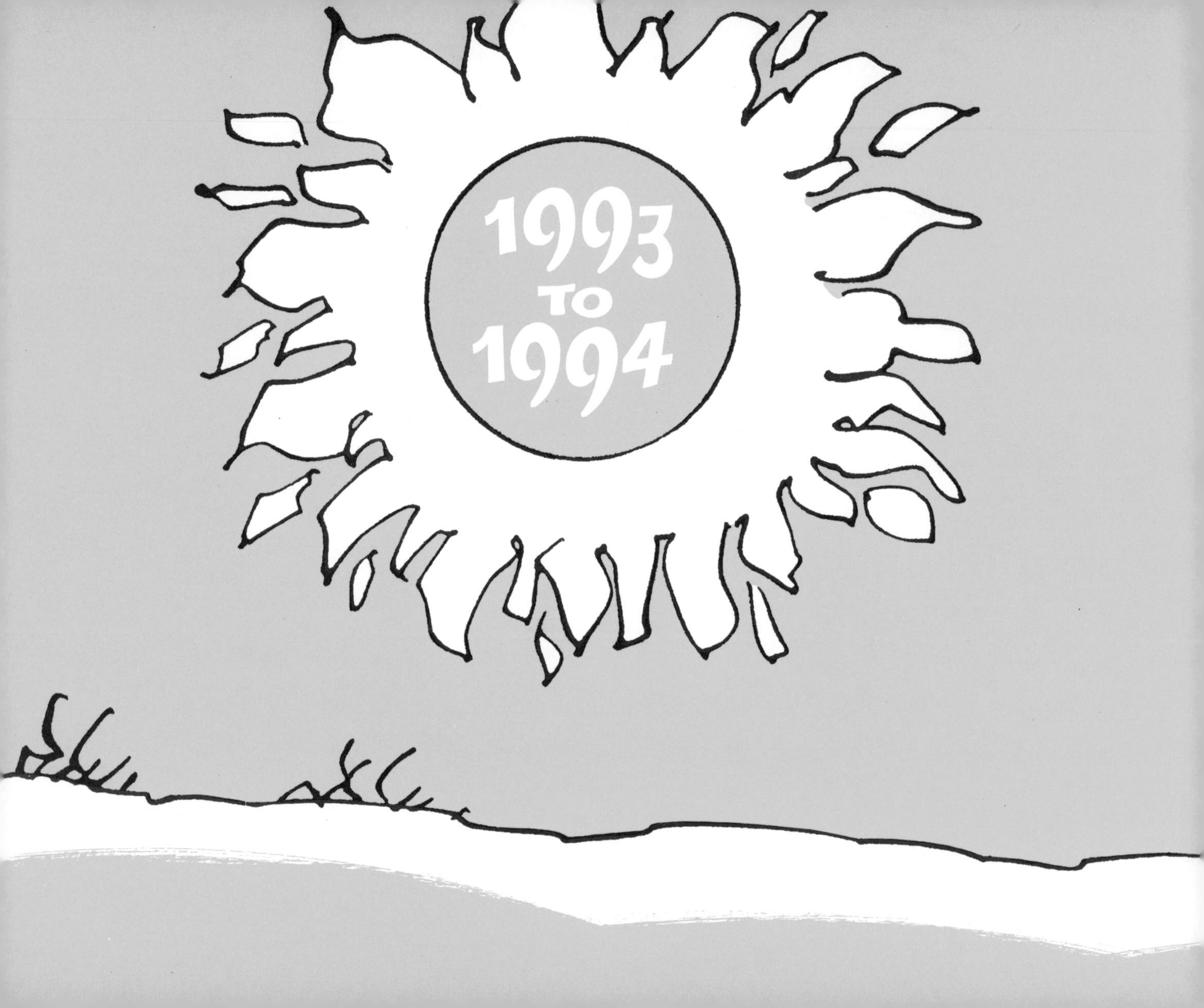
1993
TO
1994

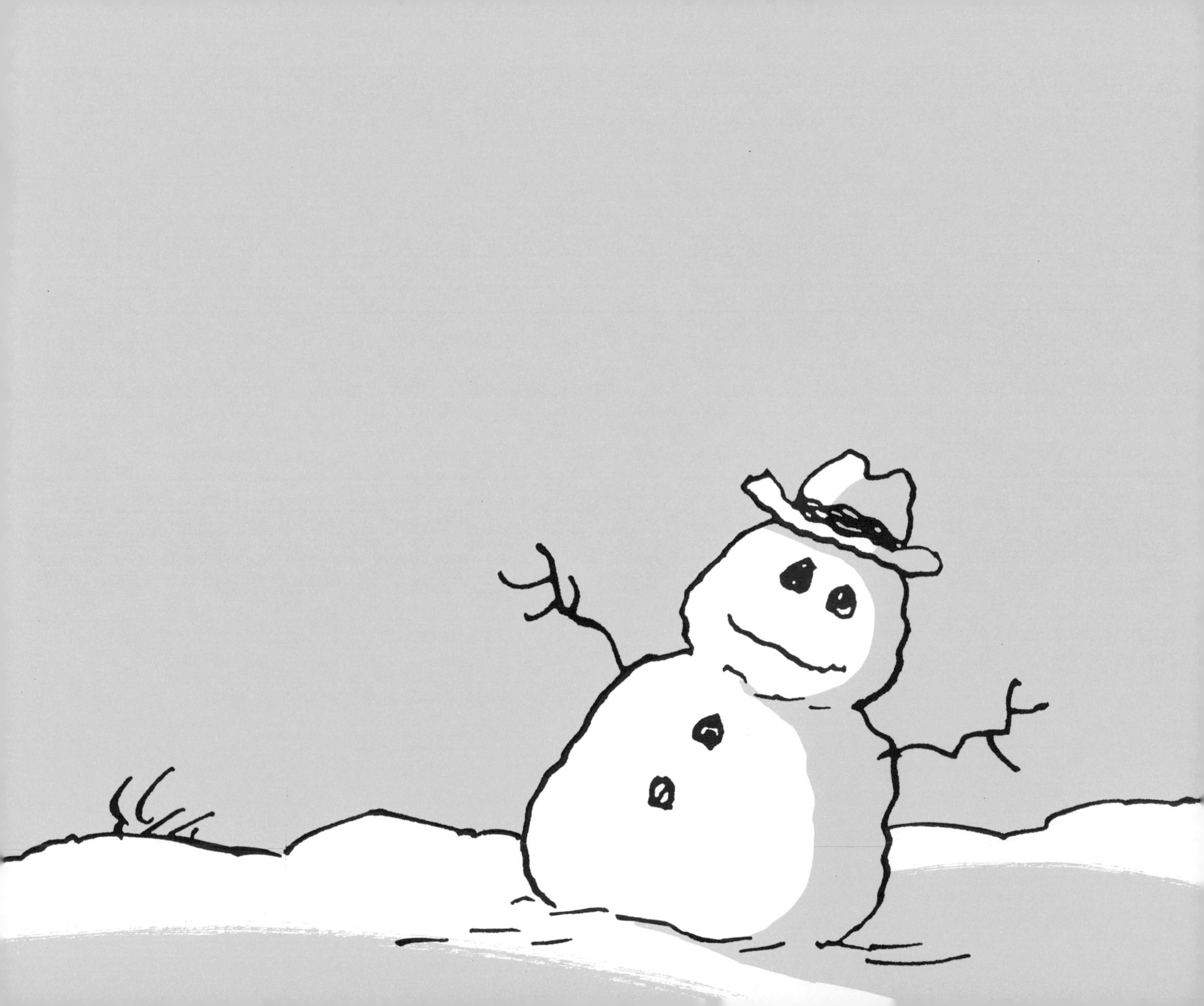

HI, CHUCK..JUST CALLING TO WISH YOU A HAPPY NEW YEAR...
DO YOU LOVE ME, CHUCK?
1-1-93
I'M SORRY, BUT YOUR CALL CANNOT GO THROUGH..PLEASE HANG UP, AND DO NOT DIAL AGAIN..
SCHULZ

I'M THINKING MAYBE WHEN I GROW UP, I'LL BE A BEAUTY QUEEN..
1-2-93
DO YOU HAVE TO BE REALLY BEAUTIFUL?
PROBABLY
DO THEY HAVE A SORT OF FAIRLY, KIND OF, YOU KNOW, CUTE QUEEN?
SCHULZ

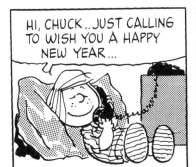

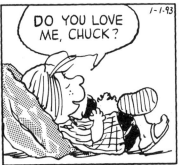

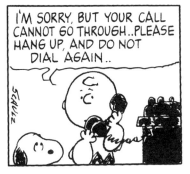

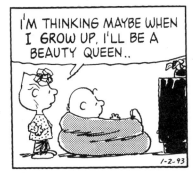

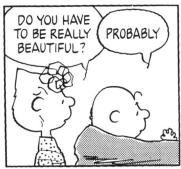

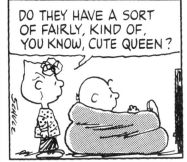

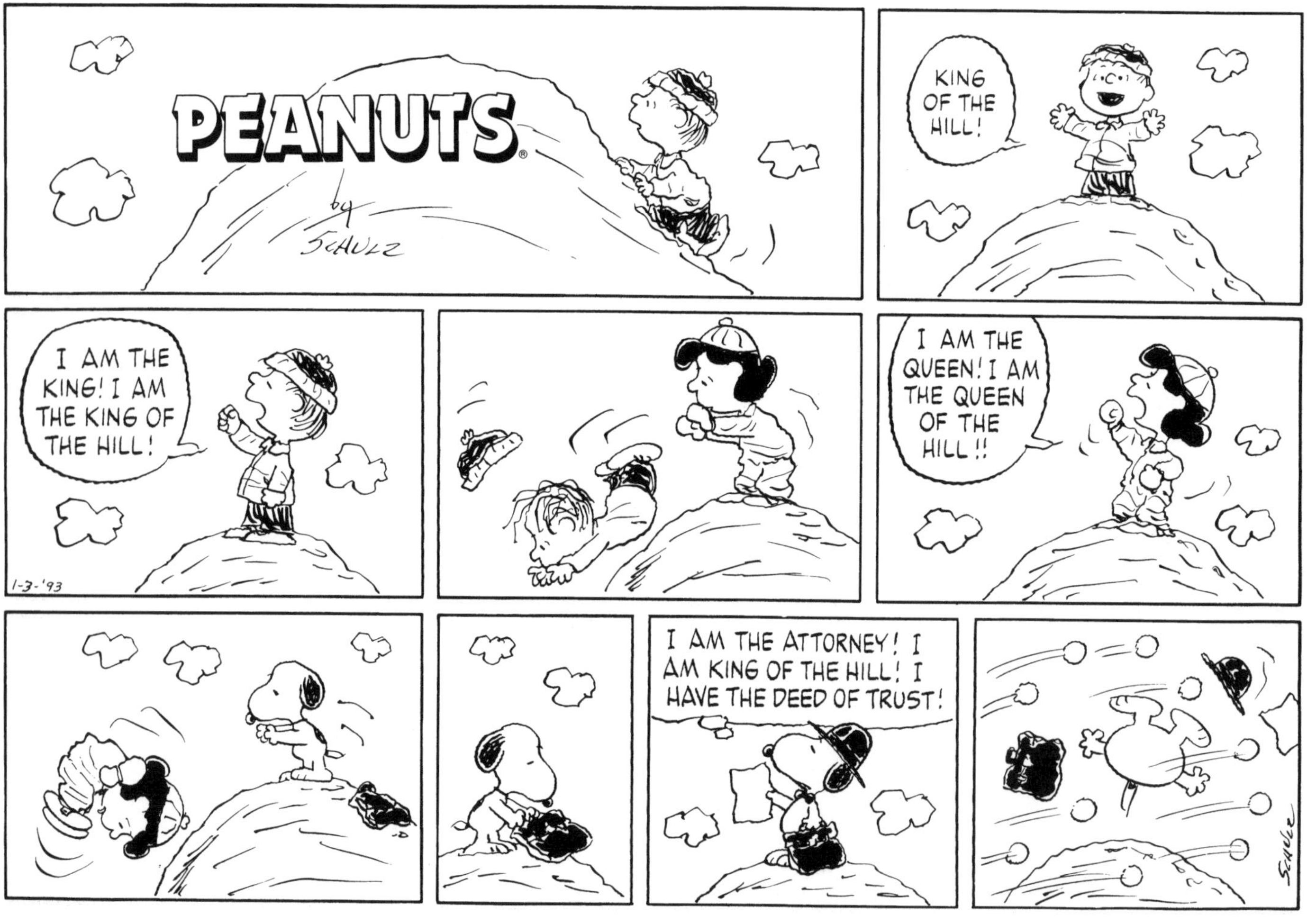
PEANUTS
by SCHULZ
KING OF THE HILL!
I AM THE KING! I AM THE KING OF THE HILL!
1-3-'93
I AM THE QUEEN! I AM THE QUEEN OF THE HILL!!
I AM THE ATTORNEY! I AM KING OF THE HILL! I HAVE THE DEED OF TRUST!
SCHULZ

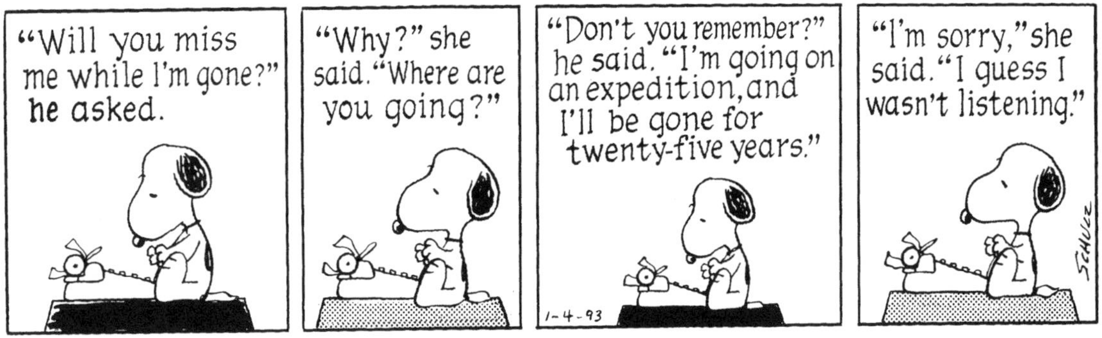
"Will you miss me while I'm gone?" he asked.
"Why?" she said. "Where are you going?"
"Don't you remember?" he said. "I'm going on an expedition, and I'll be gone for twenty-five years."
1-4-93
"I'm sorry," she said. "I guess I wasn't listening."
SCHULZ

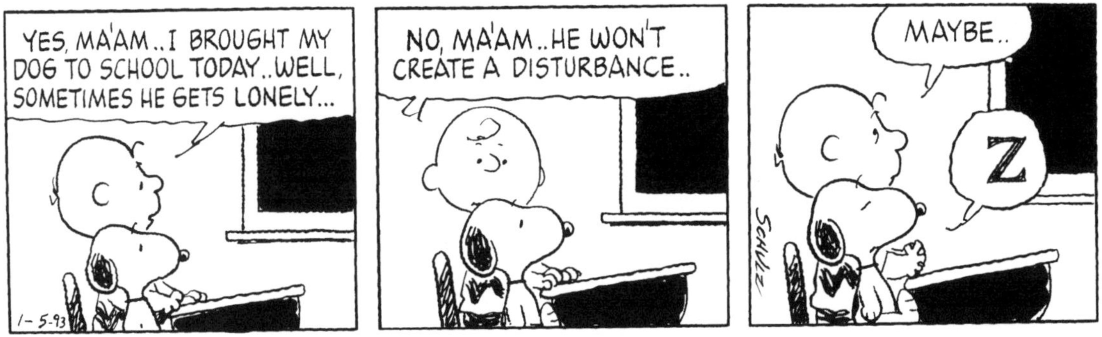
YES, MA'AM.. I BROUGHT MY DOG TO SCHOOL TODAY.. WELL, SOMETIMES HE GETS LONELY...
1-5-93
NO, MA'AM.. HE WON'T CREATE A DISTURBANCE..
MAYBE..
Z
SCHULZ

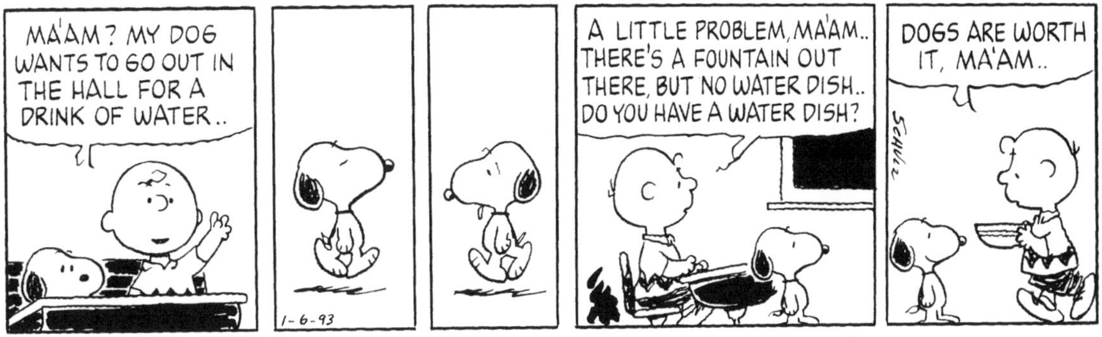
MA'AM? MY DOG WANTS TO GO OUT IN THE HALL FOR A DRINK OF WATER..
1-6-93
A LITTLE PROBLEM, MA'AM.. THERE'S A FOUNTAIN OUT THERE, BUT NO WATER DISH.. DO YOU HAVE A WATER DISH?
DOGS ARE WORTH IT, MA'AM..
SCHULZ

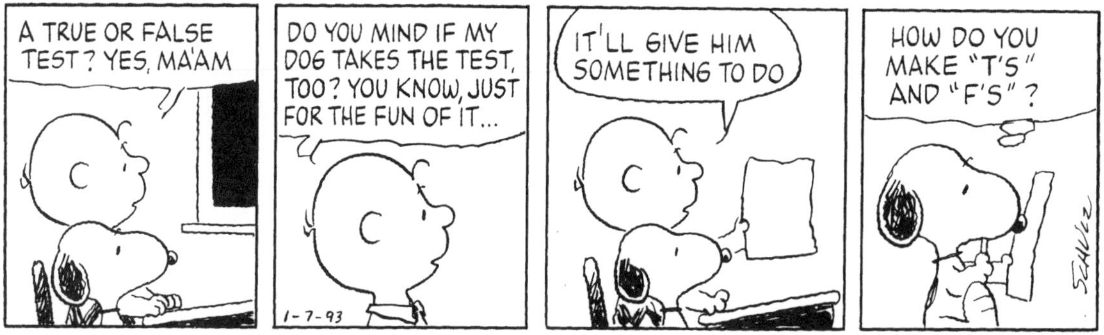
A TRUE OR FALSE TEST? YES, MA'AM
DO YOU MIND IF MY DOG TAKES THE TEST, TOO? YOU KNOW, JUST FOR THE FUN OF IT...
1-7-93
IT'LL GIVE HIM SOMETHING TO DO
HOW DO YOU MAKE "T'S" AND "F'S"?
SCHULZ

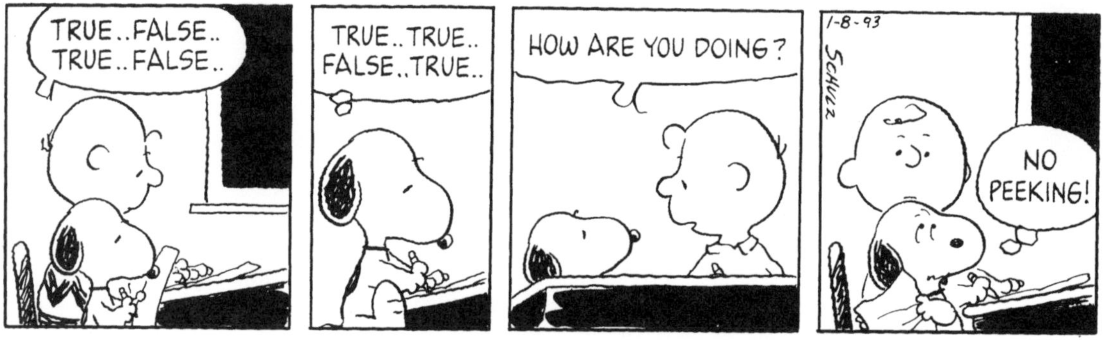
TRUE..FALSE.. TRUE..FALSE..
TRUE..TRUE.. FALSE..TRUE..
HOW ARE YOU DOING?
1-8-93
SCHULZ
NO PEEKING!

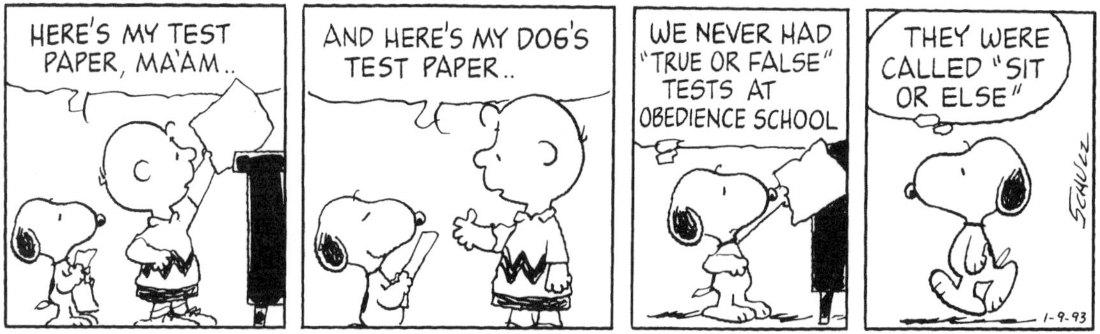
HERE'S MY TEST PAPER, MA'AM..
AND HERE'S MY DOG'S TEST PAPER..
WE NEVER HAD "TRUE OR FALSE" TESTS AT OBEDIENCE SCHOOL
THEY WERE CALLED "SIT OR ELSE"
SCHULZ
1-9-93

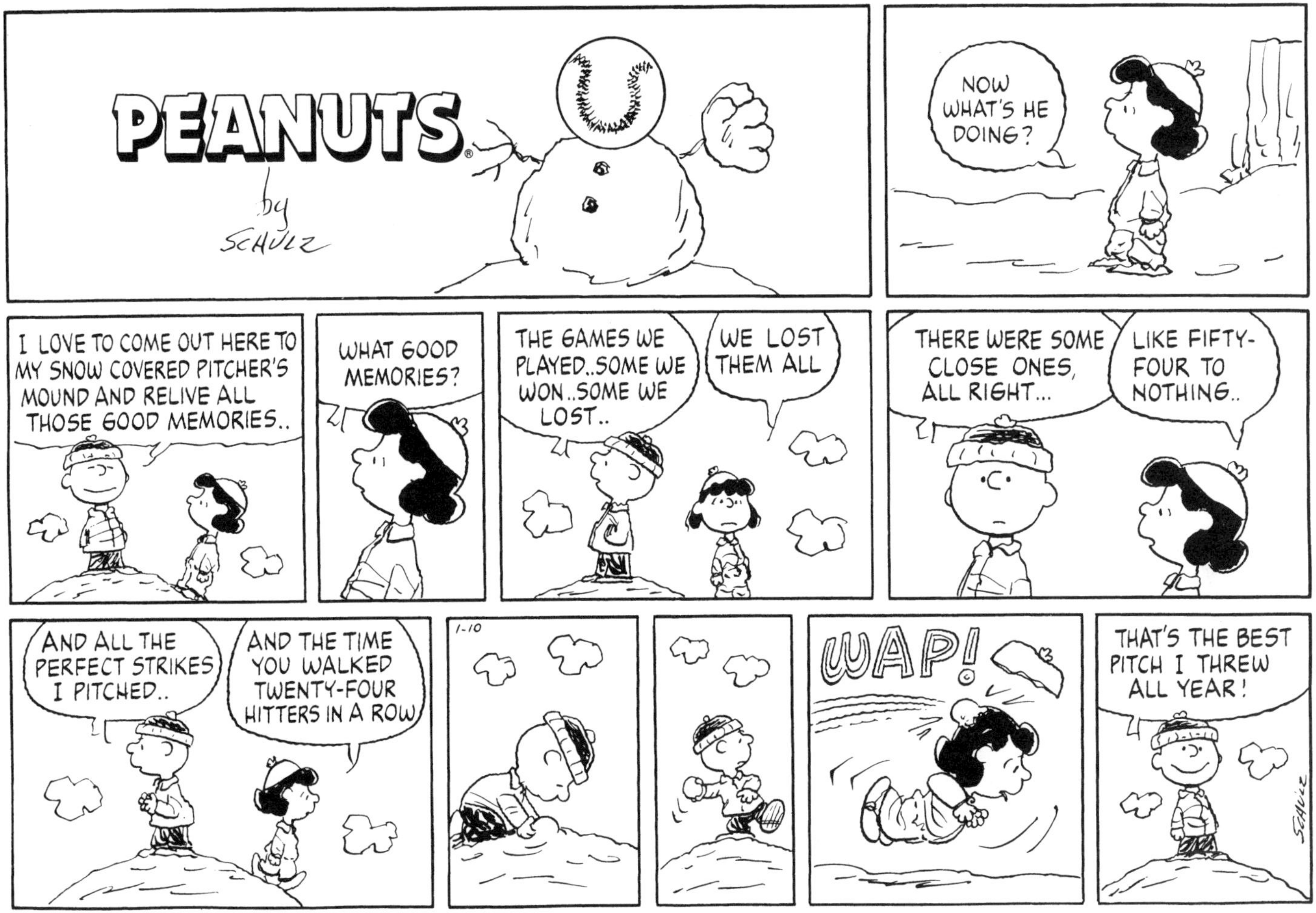
PEANUTS
by SCHULZ
NOW WHAT'S HE DOING?
I LOVE TO COME OUT HERE TO MY SNOW COVERED PITCHER'S MOUND AND RELIVE ALL THOSE GOOD MEMORIES..
WHAT GOOD MEMORIES?
THE GAMES WE PLAYED..SOME WE WON..SOME WE LOST..
WE LOST THEM ALL
THERE WERE SOME CLOSE ONES, ALL RIGHT...
LIKE FIFTY-FOUR TO NOTHING..
AND ALL THE PERFECT STRIKES I PITCHED..
AND THE TIME YOU WALKED TWENTY-FOUR HITTERS IN A ROW
1-10
WAP!
THAT'S THE BEST PITCH I THREW ALL YEAR!
SCHULZ

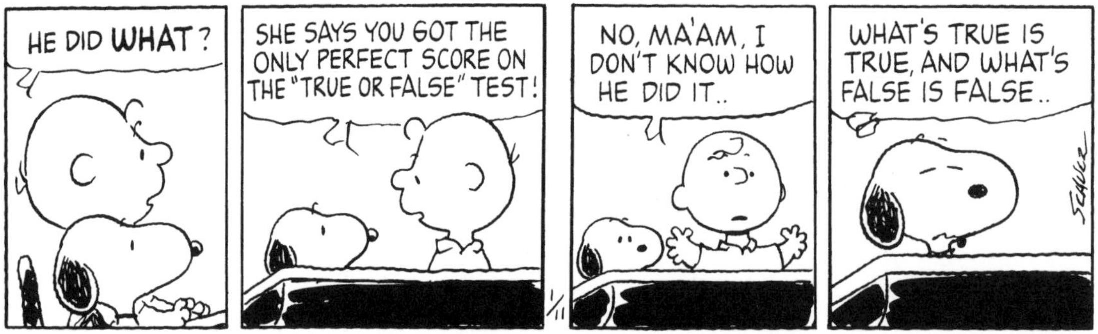
HE DID WHAT?
SHE SAYS YOU GOT THE ONLY PERFECT SCORE ON THE "TRUE OR FALSE" TEST!
1/11
NO, MA'AM, I DON'T KNOW HOW HE DID IT..
WHAT'S TRUE IS TRUE, AND WHAT'S FALSE IS FALSE..
SCHULZ

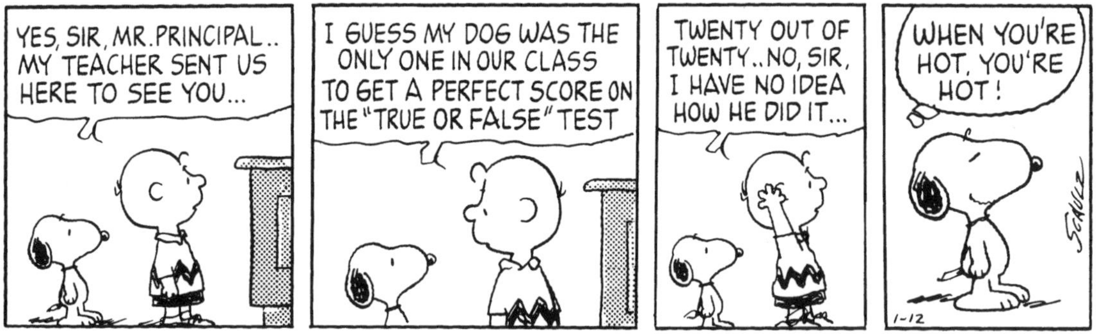
YES, SIR, MR. PRINCIPAL.. MY TEACHER SENT US HERE TO SEE YOU...
I GUESS MY DOG WAS THE ONLY ONE IN OUR CLASS TO GET A PERFECT SCORE ON THE "TRUE OR FALSE" TEST
TWENTY OUT OF TWENTY.. NO, SIR, I HAVE NO IDEA HOW HE DID IT...
WHEN YOU'RE HOT, YOU'RE HOT!
SCHULZ
1-12

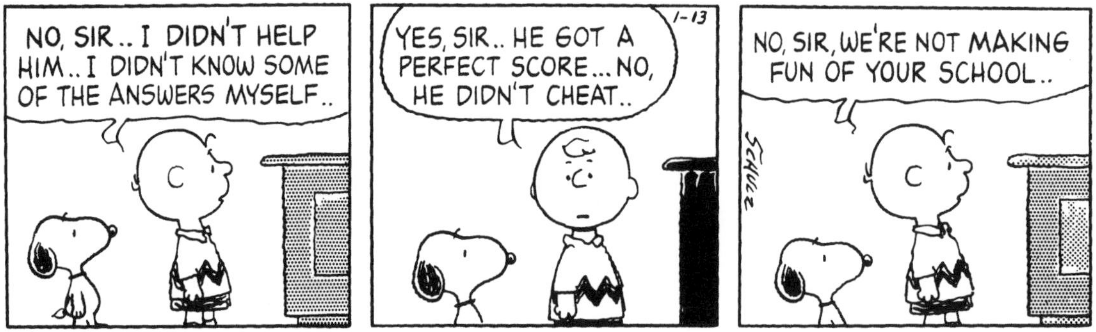
NO, SIR.. I DIDN'T HELP HIM.. I DIDN'T KNOW SOME OF THE ANSWERS MYSELF..
1-13
YES, SIR.. HE GOT A PERFECT SCORE... NO, HE DIDN'T CHEAT..
SCHULZ
NO, SIR, WE'RE NOT MAKING FUN OF YOUR SCHOOL..

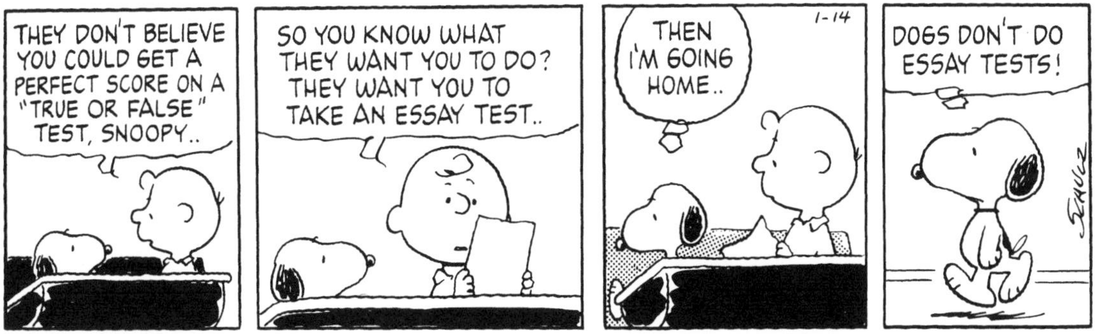
THEY DON'T BELIEVE YOU COULD GET A PERFECT SCORE ON A "TRUE OR FALSE" TEST, SNOOPY..
SO YOU KNOW WHAT THEY WANT YOU TO DO? THEY WANT YOU TO TAKE AN ESSAY TEST..
1-14
THEN I'M GOING HOME..
DOGS DON'T DO ESSAY TESTS!
SCHULZ

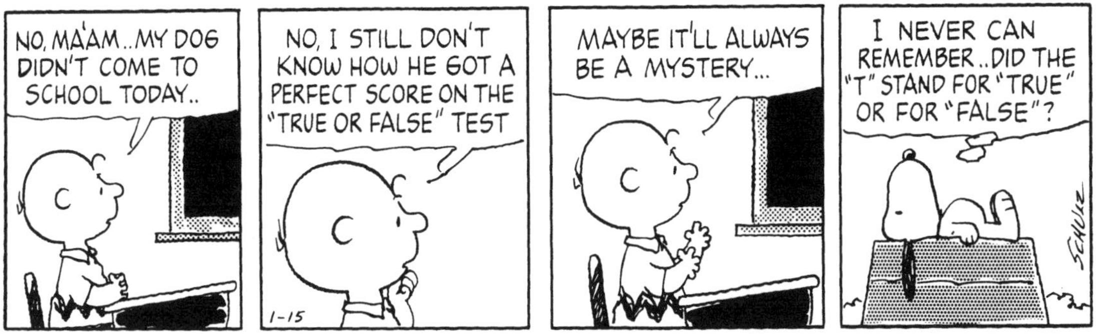
NO, MA'AM..MY DOG DIDN'T COME TO SCHOOL TODAY..
NO, I STILL DON'T KNOW HOW HE GOT A PERFECT SCORE ON THE "TRUE OR FALSE" TEST
1-15
MAYBE IT'LL ALWAYS BE A MYSTERY...
I NEVER CAN REMEMBER..DID THE "T" STAND FOR "TRUE" OR FOR "FALSE"?
SCHULZ

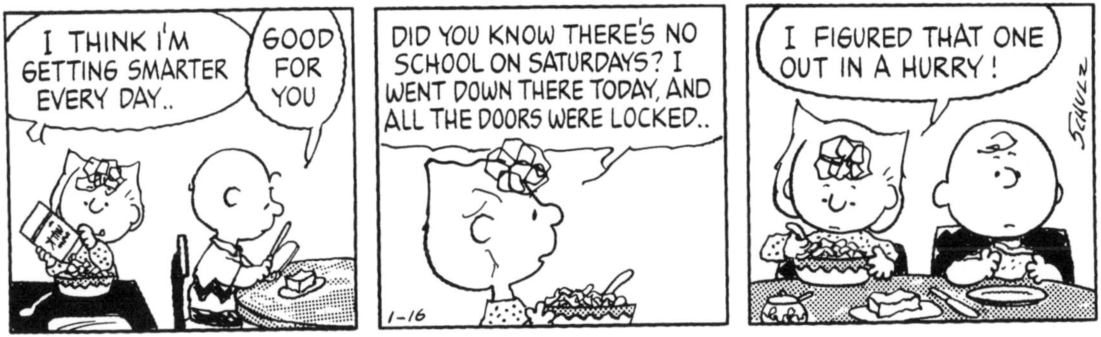
I THINK I'M GETTING SMARTER EVERY DAY..
GOOD FOR YOU
DID YOU KNOW THERE'S NO SCHOOL ON SATURDAYS? I WENT DOWN THERE TODAY, AND ALL THE DOORS WERE LOCKED..
1-16
I FIGURED THAT ONE OUT IN A HURRY!
SCHULZ

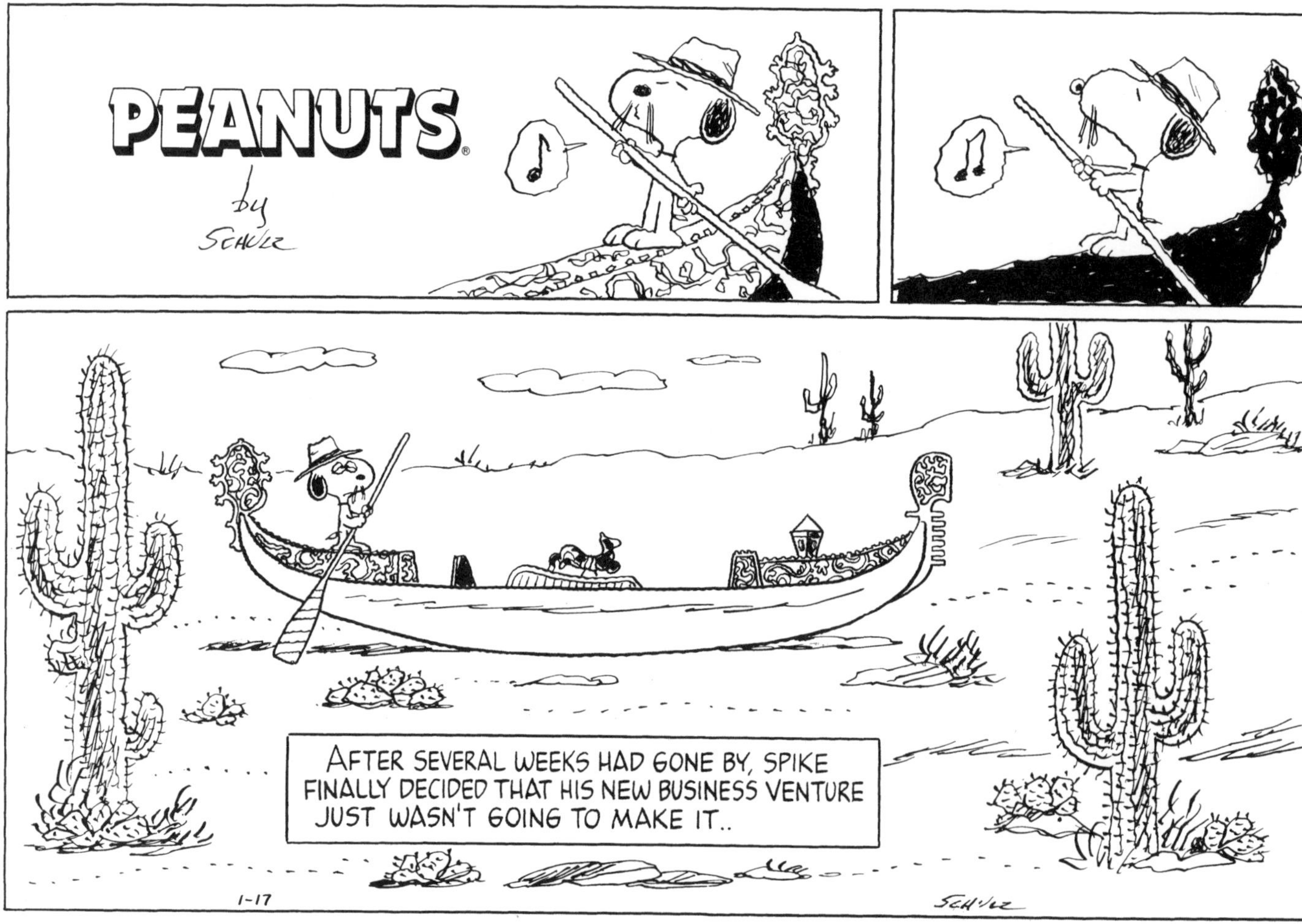
PEANUTS®
by SCHULZ
AFTER SEVERAL WEEKS HAD GONE BY, SPIKE FINALLY DECIDED THAT HIS NEW BUSINESS VENTURE JUST WASN'T GOING TO MAKE IT..
1-17
SCHULZ

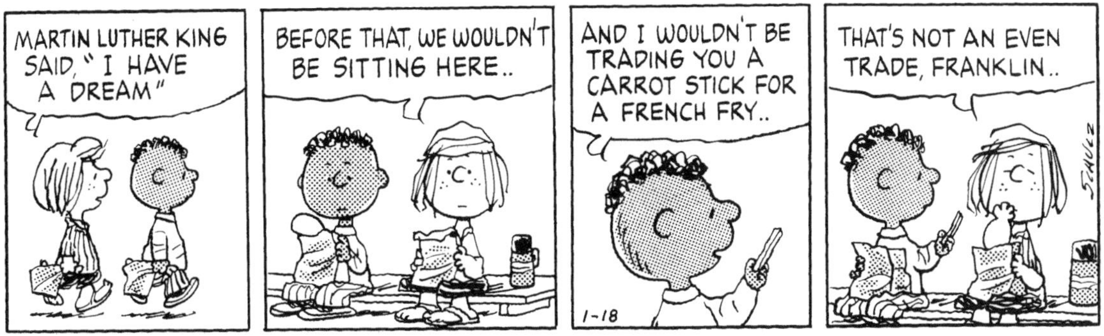
MARTIN LUTHER KING SAID, "I HAVE A DREAM"
BEFORE THAT, WE WOULDN'T BE SITTING HERE..
AND I WOULDN'T BE TRADING YOU A CARROT STICK FOR A FRENCH FRY..
THAT'S NOT AN EVEN TRADE, FRANKLIN..
SCHULZ
1-18

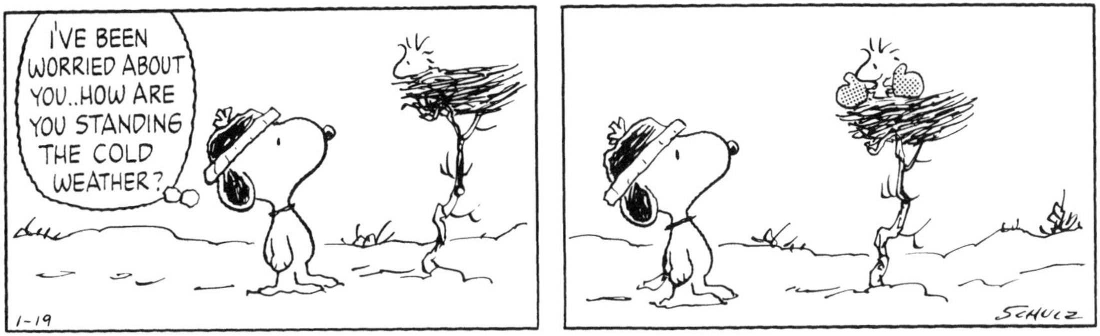
I'VE BEEN WORRIED ABOUT YOU..HOW ARE YOU STANDING THE COLD WEATHER?
1-19
SCHULZ

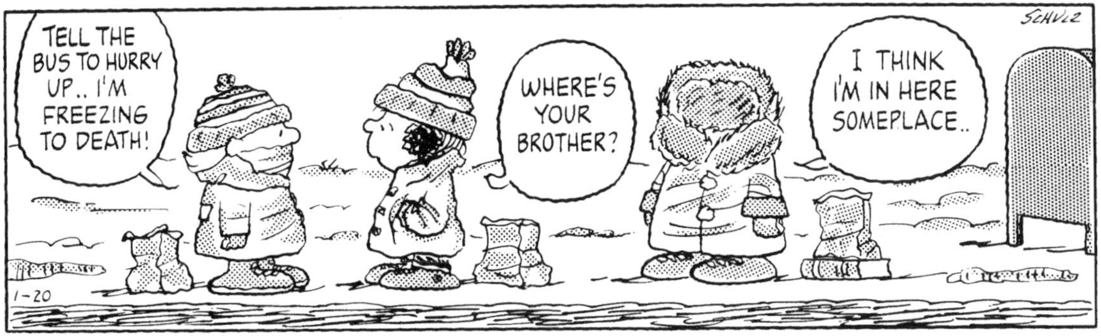
SCHULZ
TELL THE BUS TO HURRY UP.. I'M FREEZING TO DEATH!
WHERE'S YOUR BROTHER?
I THINK I'M IN HERE SOMEPLACE..
1-20

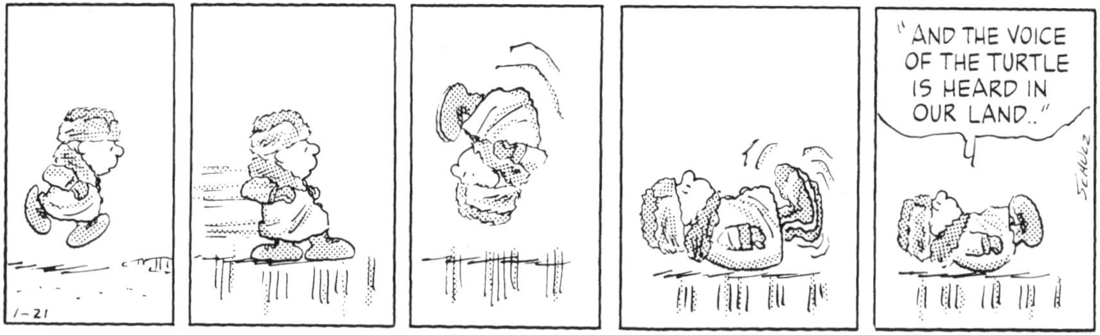
"AND THE VOICE OF THE TURTLE IS HEARD IN OUR LAND.."

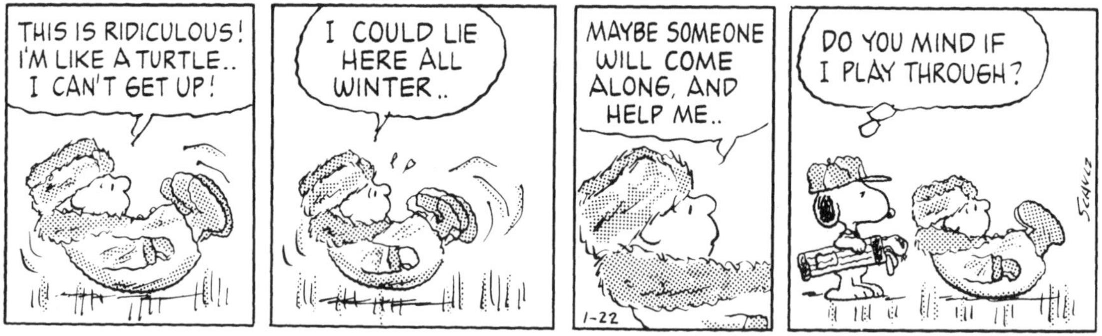
THIS IS RIDICULOUS! I'M LIKE A TURTLE.. I CAN'T GET UP!
I COULD LIE HERE ALL WINTER..
MAYBE SOMEONE WILL COME ALONG, AND HELP ME..
DO YOU MIND IF I PLAY THROUGH?

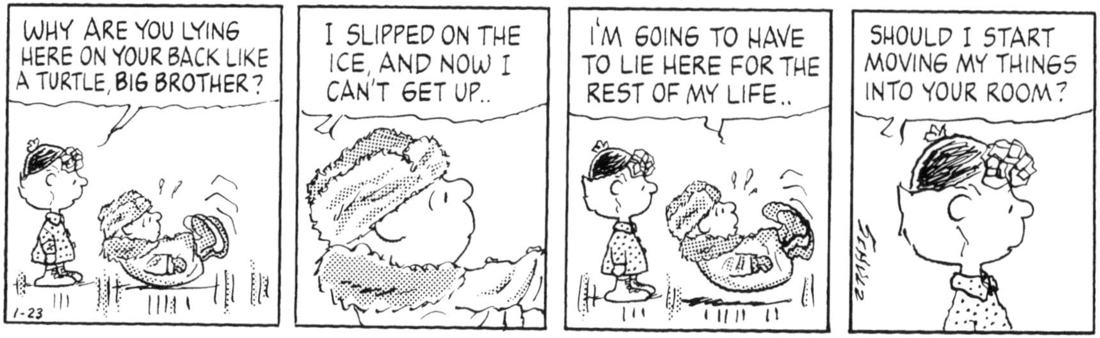
WHY ARE YOU LYING HERE ON YOUR BACK LIKE A TURTLE, BIG BROTHER?
I SLIPPED ON THE ICE, AND NOW I CAN'T GET UP..
I'M GOING TO HAVE TO LIE HERE FOR THE REST OF MY LIFE..
SHOULD I START MOVING MY THINGS INTO YOUR ROOM?

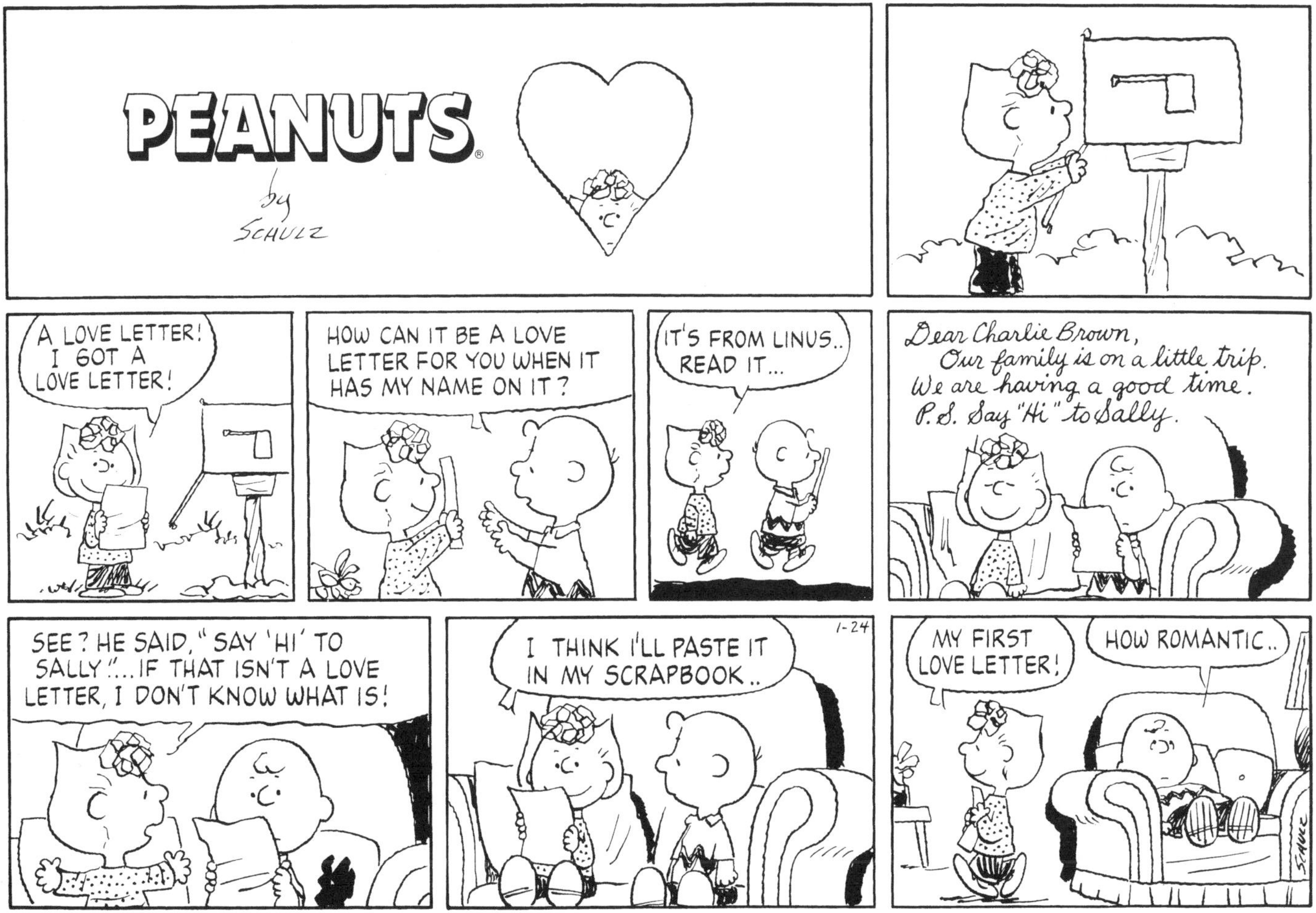
PEANUTS
by SCHULZ
A LOVE LETTER! I GOT A LOVE LETTER!
HOW CAN IT BE A LOVE LETTER FOR YOU WHEN IT HAS MY NAME ON IT?
IT'S FROM LINUS.. READ IT...
Dear Charlie Brown,
Our family is on a little trip. We are having a good time.
P.S. Say "Hi" to Sally.
SEE? HE SAID, "SAY 'HI' TO SALLY!"... IF THAT ISN'T A LOVE LETTER, I DON'T KNOW WHAT IS!
1-24
I THINK I'LL PASTE IT IN MY SCRAPBOOK..
MY FIRST LOVE LETTER!
HOW ROMANTIC..
SCHULZ

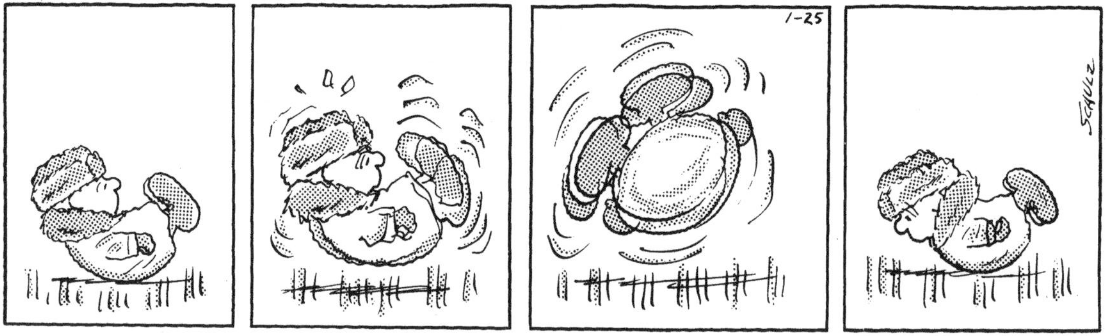
1-25
SCHULZ

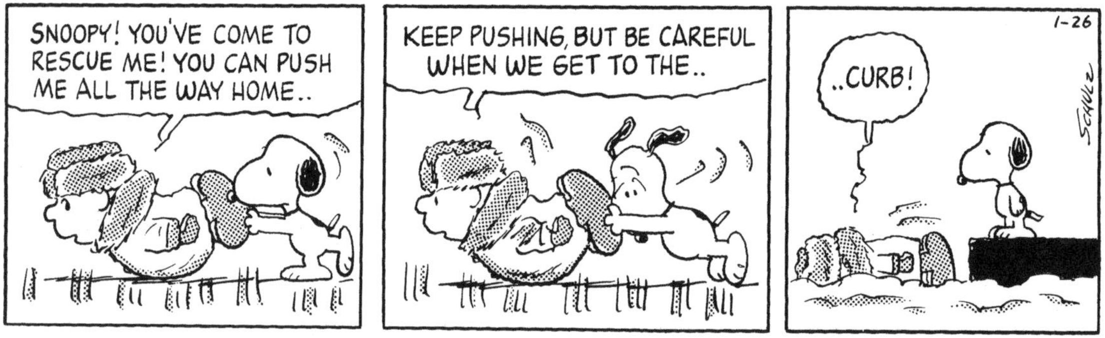
SNOOPY! YOU'VE COME TO RESCUE ME! YOU CAN PUSH ME ALL THE WAY HOME..
KEEP PUSHING, BUT BE CAREFUL WHEN WE GET TO THE..
1-26
..CURB!
SCHULZ

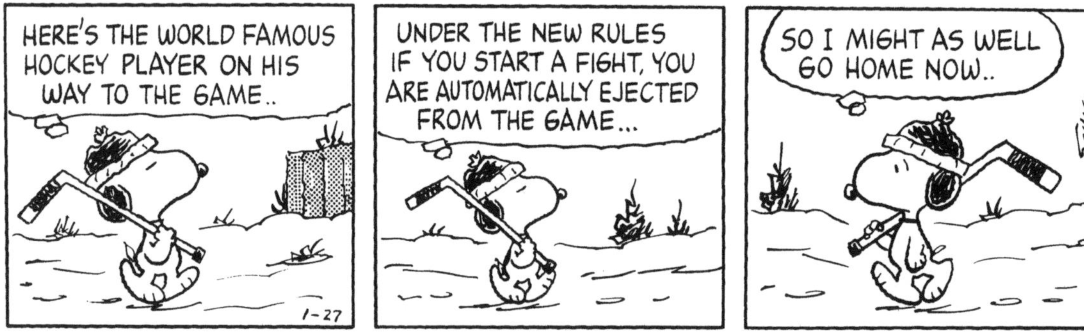
HERE'S THE WORLD FAMOUS HOCKEY PLAYER ON HIS WAY TO THE GAME..
1-27
UNDER THE NEW RULES IF YOU START A FIGHT, YOU ARE AUTOMATICALLY EJECTED FROM THE GAME...
SO I MIGHT AS WELL GO HOME NOW..
SCHULZ

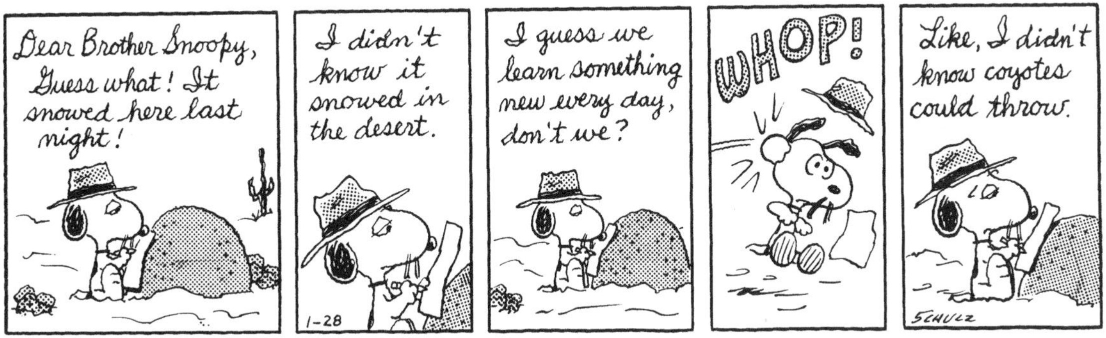

Dear Brother Snoopy, Guess what! It snowed here last night!
I didn't know it snowed in the desert.
1-28
I guess we learn something new every day, don't we?
WHOP!
Like, I didn't know coyotes could throw.
SCHULZ

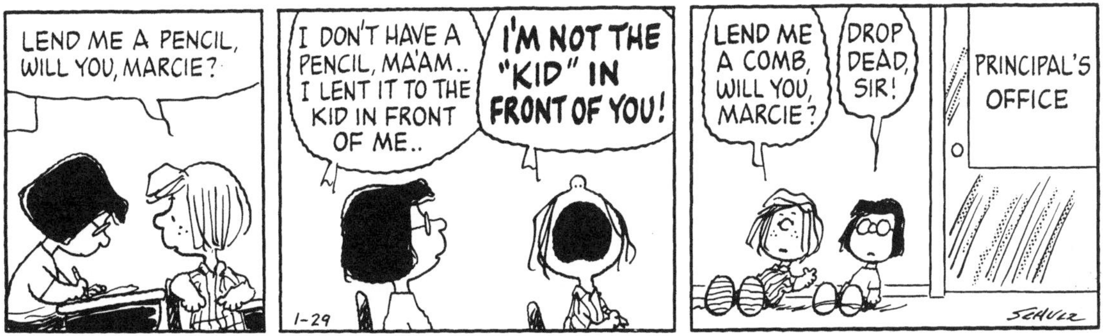

LEND ME A PENCIL, WILL YOU, MARCIE?
I DON'T HAVE A PENCIL, MA'AM.. I LENT IT TO THE KID IN FRONT OF ME..
I'M NOT THE "KID" IN FRONT OF YOU!
1-29
LEND ME A COMB, WILL YOU, MARCIE?
DROP DEAD, SIR!
PRINCIPAL'S OFFICE
SCHULZ

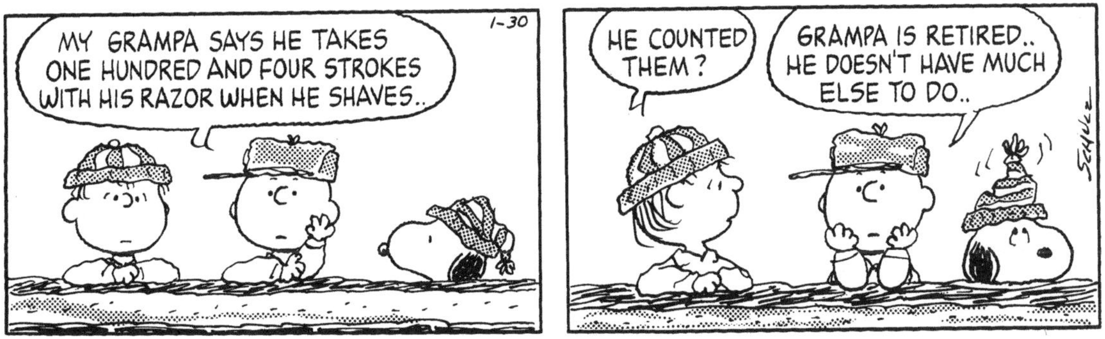

1-30
MY GRAMPA SAYS HE TAKES ONE HUNDRED AND FOUR STROKES WITH HIS RAZOR WHEN HE SHAVES..
HE COUNTED THEM?
GRAMPA IS RETIRED.. HE DOESN'T HAVE MUCH ELSE TO DO..
SCHULZ

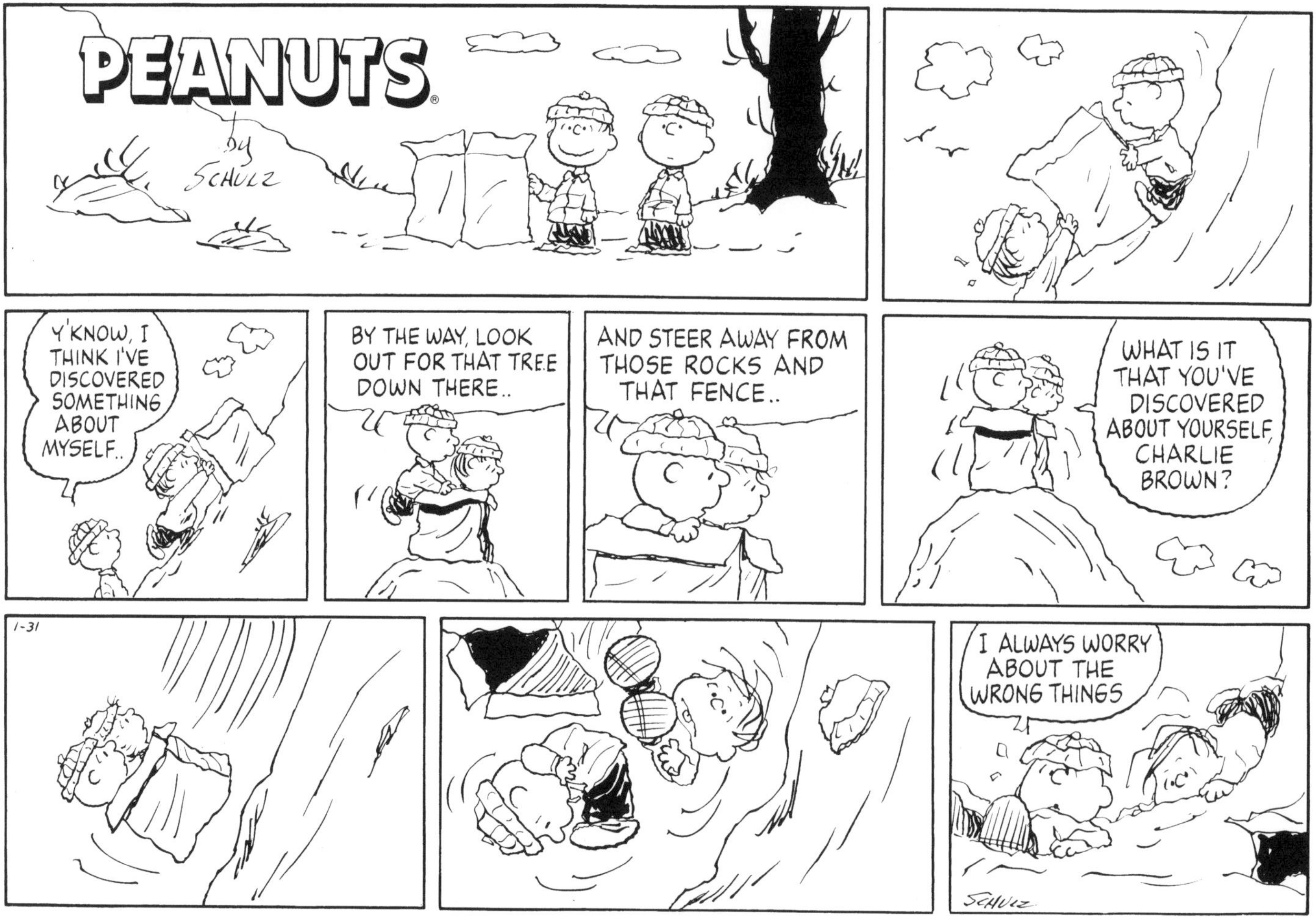
PEANUTS
BY SCHULZ
Y'KNOW, I THINK I'VE DISCOVERED SOMETHING ABOUT MYSELF..
BY THE WAY, LOOK OUT FOR THAT TREE DOWN THERE..
AND STEER AWAY FROM THOSE ROCKS AND THAT FENCE..
WHAT IS IT THAT YOU'VE DISCOVERED ABOUT YOURSELF, CHARLIE BROWN?
1-31
I ALWAYS WORRY ABOUT THE WRONG THINGS
SCHULZ

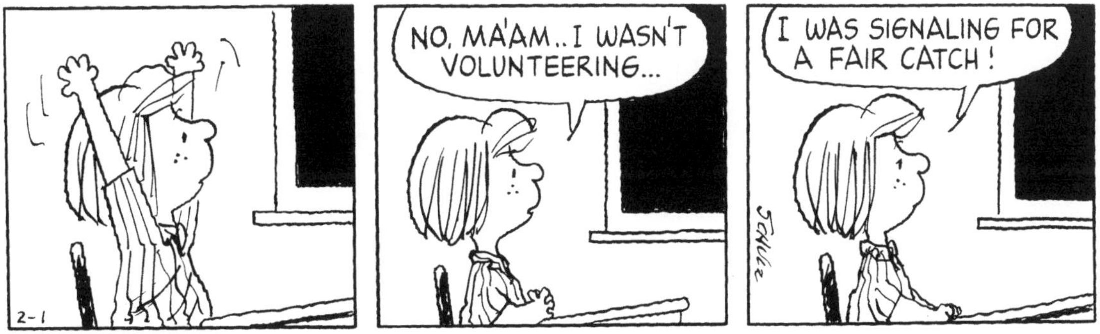
NO, MA'AM..I WASN'T VOLUNTEERING...
I WAS SIGNALING FOR A FAIR CATCH !

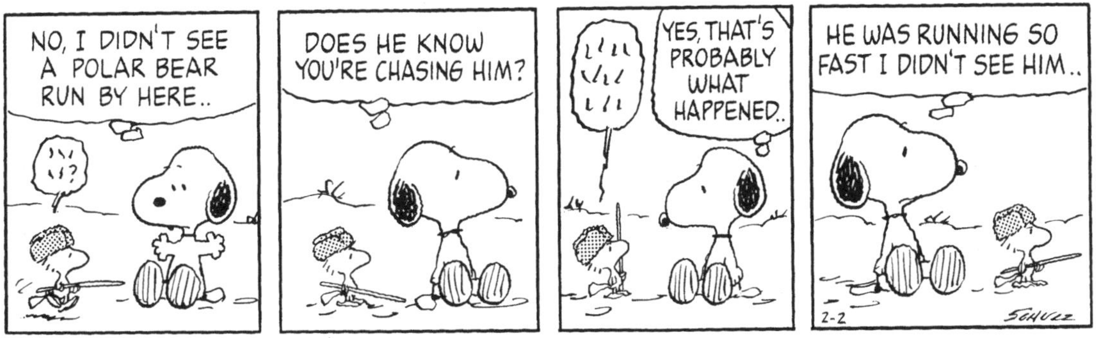
NO, I DIDN'T SEE A POLAR BEAR RUN BY HERE..
DOES HE KNOW YOU'RE CHASING HIM?
YES, THAT'S PROBABLY WHAT HAPPENED..
HE WAS RUNNING SO FAST I DIDN'T SEE HIM..

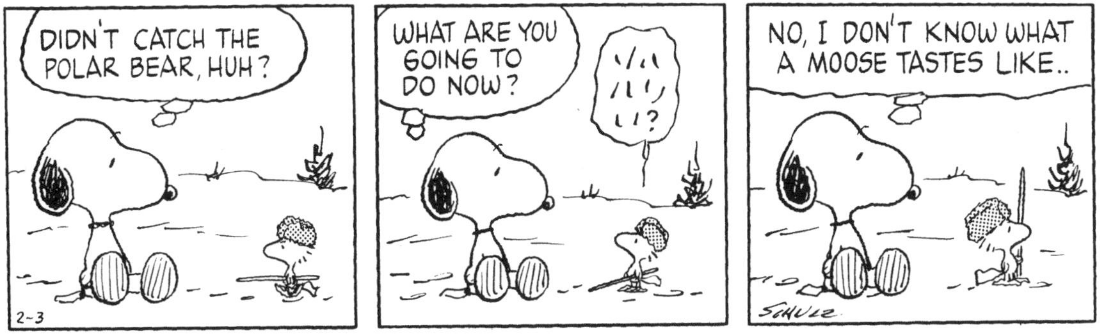
DIDN'T CATCH THE POLAR BEAR, HUH?
WHAT ARE YOU GOING TO DO NOW?
NO, I DON'T KNOW WHAT A MOOSE TASTES LIKE..

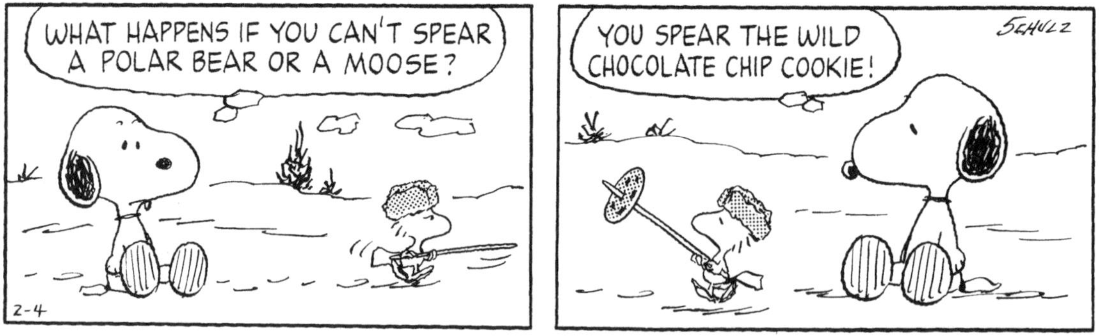
WHAT HAPPENS IF YOU CAN'T SPEAR A POLAR BEAR OR A MOOSE?
2-4
SCHULZ
YOU SPEAR THE WILD CHOCOLATE CHIP COOKIE!

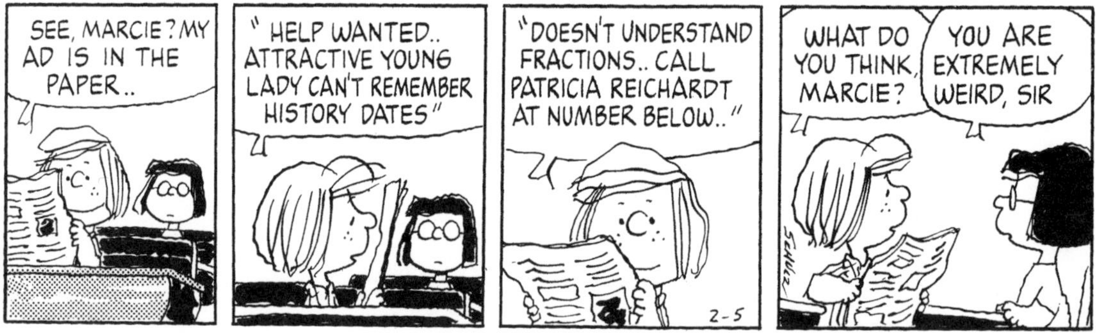
SEE, MARCIE? MY AD IS IN THE PAPER..
" HELP WANTED.. ATTRACTIVE YOUNG LADY CAN'T REMEMBER HISTORY DATES"
"DOESN'T UNDERSTAND FRACTIONS.. CALL PATRICIA REICHARDT AT NUMBER BELOW.."
2-5
SCHULZ
WHAT DO YOU THINK, MARCIE?
YOU ARE EXTREMELY WEIRD, SIR

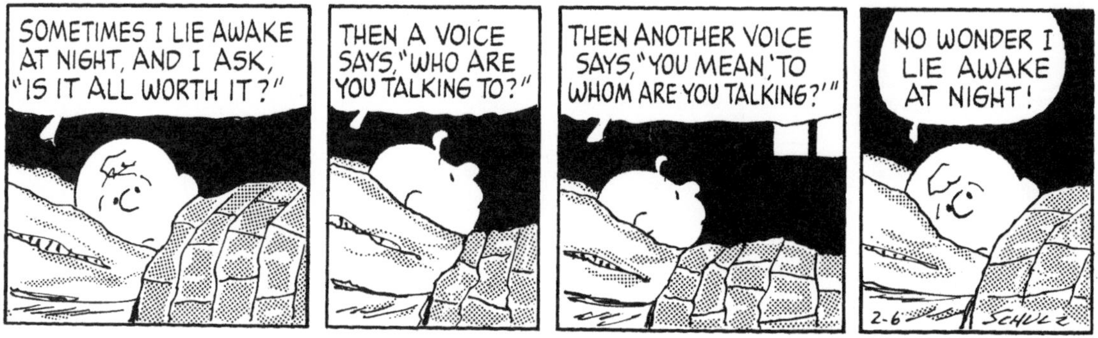
SOMETIMES I LIE AWAKE AT NIGHT, AND I ASK, "IS IT ALL WORTH IT?"
THEN A VOICE SAYS, "WHO ARE YOU TALKING TO?"
THEN ANOTHER VOICE SAYS, "YOU MEAN, 'TO WHOM ARE YOU TALKING?'"
NO WONDER I LIE AWAKE AT NIGHT!
2-6
SCHULZ

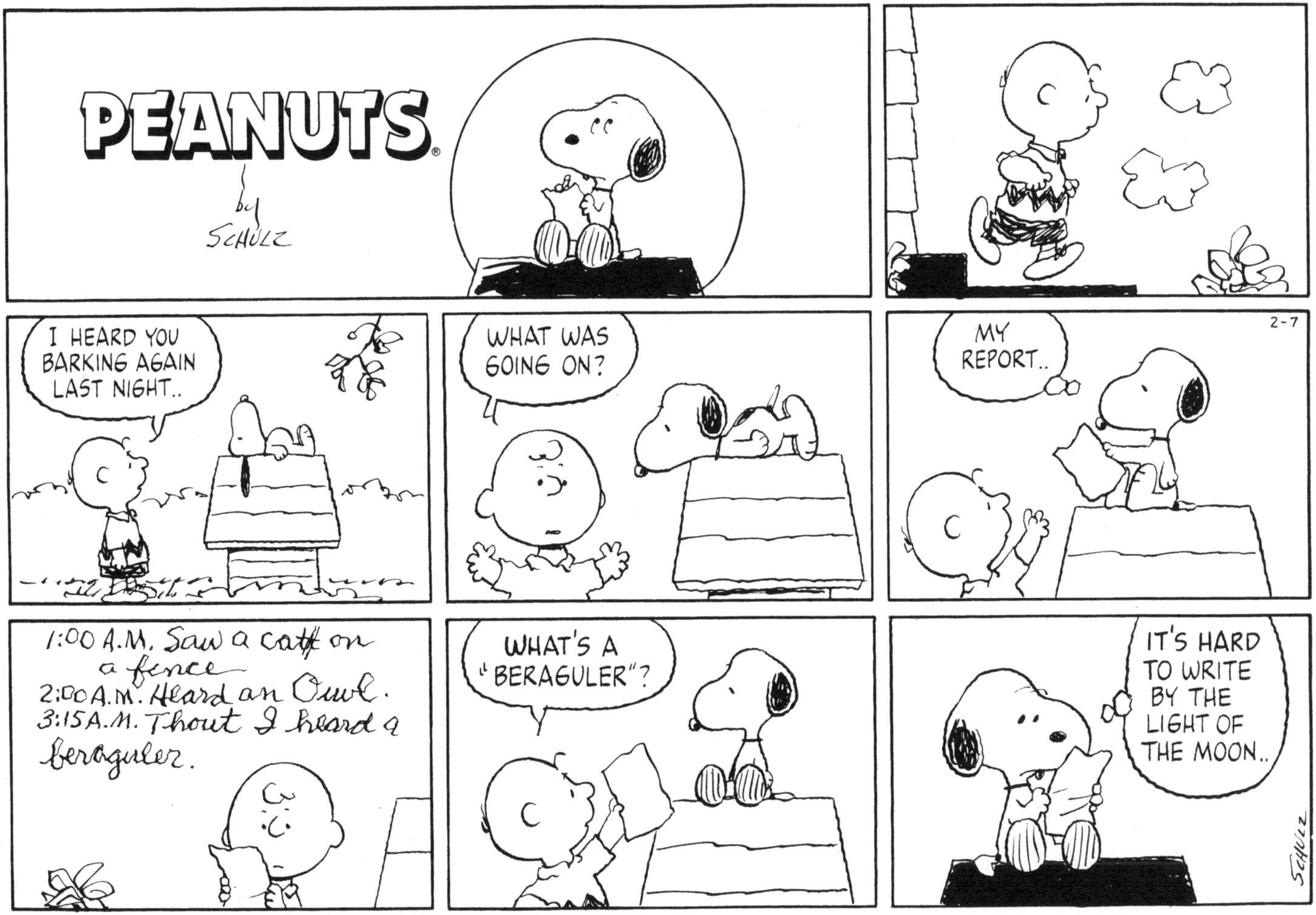
PEANUTS
by SCHULZ
I HEARD YOU BARKING AGAIN LAST NIGHT..
WHAT WAS GOING ON?
MY REPORT..
2-7
1:00 A.M. Saw a catt on a fence
2:00 A.M. Heard an Owl.
3:15 A.M. Thout I heard a beraguler.
WHAT'S A "BERAGULER"?
IT'S HARD TO WRITE BY THE LIGHT OF THE MOON..
SCHULZ

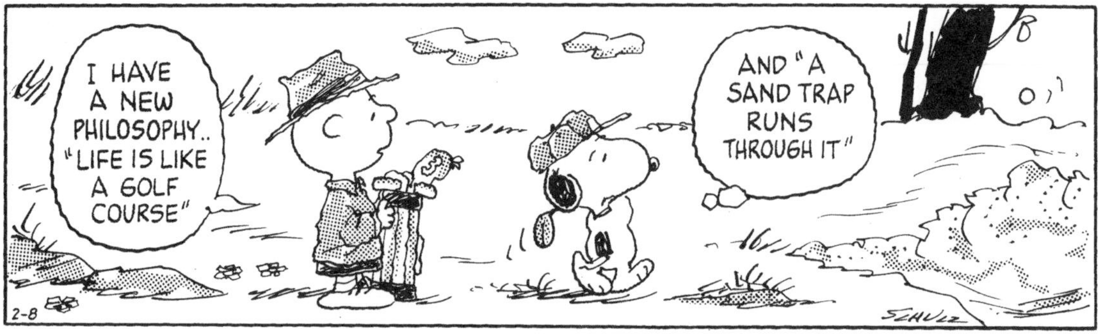
I HAVE A NEW PHILOSOPHY.. "LIFE IS LIKE A GOLF COURSE"
AND "A SAND TRAP RUNS THROUGH IT"
2-8
SCHULZ

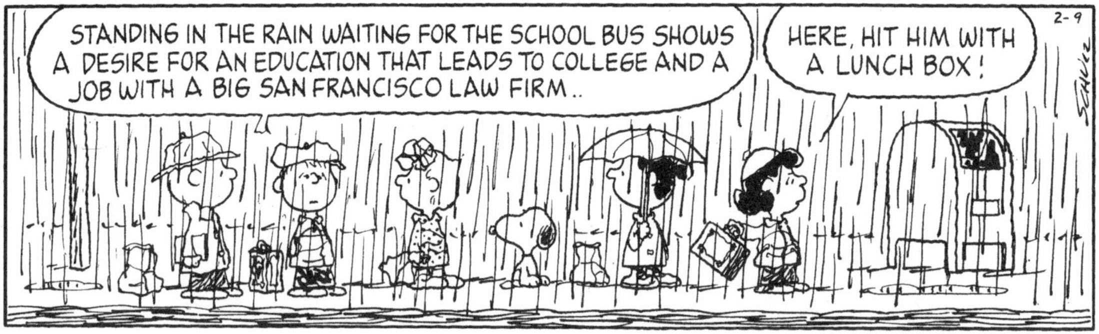
STANDING IN THE RAIN WAITING FOR THE SCHOOL BUS SHOWS A DESIRE FOR AN EDUCATION THAT LEADS TO COLLEGE AND A JOB WITH A BIG SAN FRANCISCO LAW FIRM..
HERE, HIT HIM WITH A LUNCH BOX!
2-9
SCHULZ

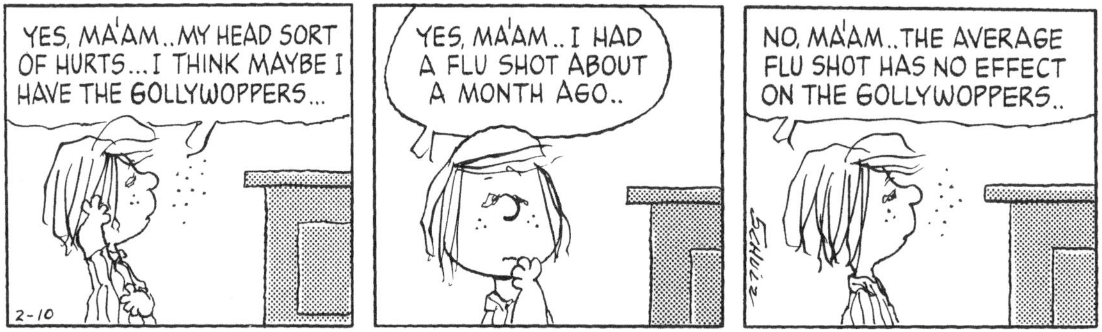
YES, MA'AM..MY HEAD SORT OF HURTS...I THINK MAYBE I HAVE THE GOLLYWOPPERS...
YES, MA'AM..I HAD A FLU SHOT ABOUT A MONTH AGO..
NO, MA'AM..THE AVERAGE FLU SHOT HAS NO EFFECT ON THE GOLLYWOPPERS..
2-10
SCHULZ

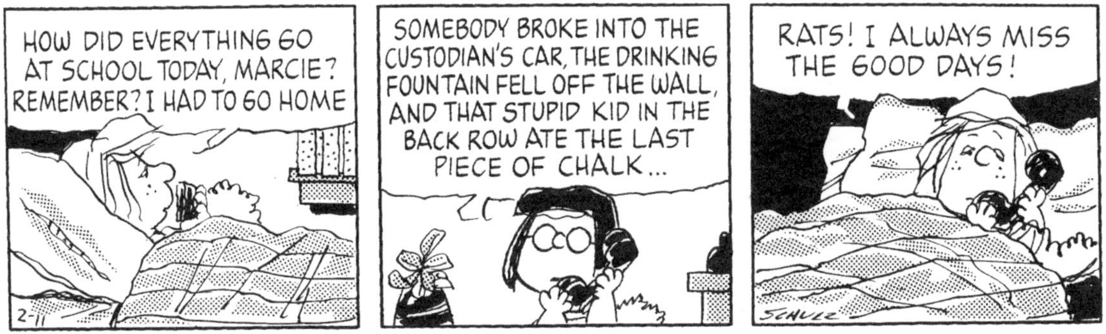
HOW DID EVERYTHING GO AT SCHOOL TODAY, MARCIE? REMEMBER? I HAD TO GO HOME
2-11
SOMEBODY BROKE INTO THE CUSTODIAN'S CAR, THE DRINKING FOUNTAIN FELL OFF THE WALL, AND THAT STUPID KID IN THE BACK ROW ATE THE LAST PIECE OF CHALK...
RATS! I ALWAYS MISS THE GOOD DAYS!
SCHULZ

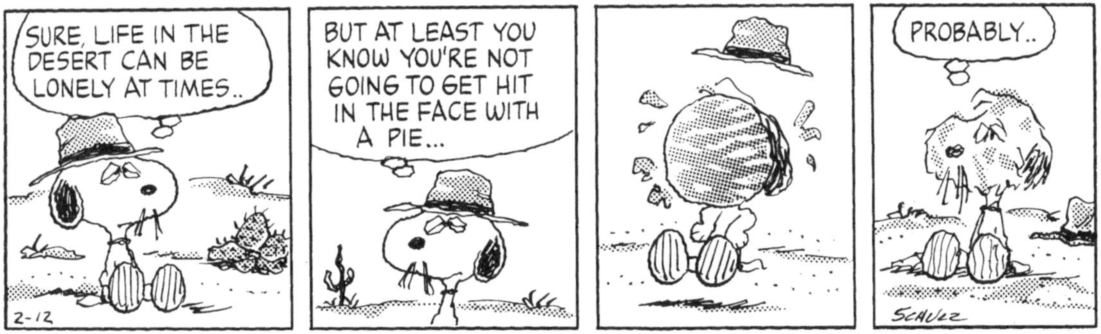
SURE, LIFE IN THE DESERT CAN BE LONELY AT TIMES..
2-12
BUT AT LEAST YOU KNOW YOU'RE NOT GOING TO GET HIT IN THE FACE WITH A PIE...
PROBABLY..
SCHULZ

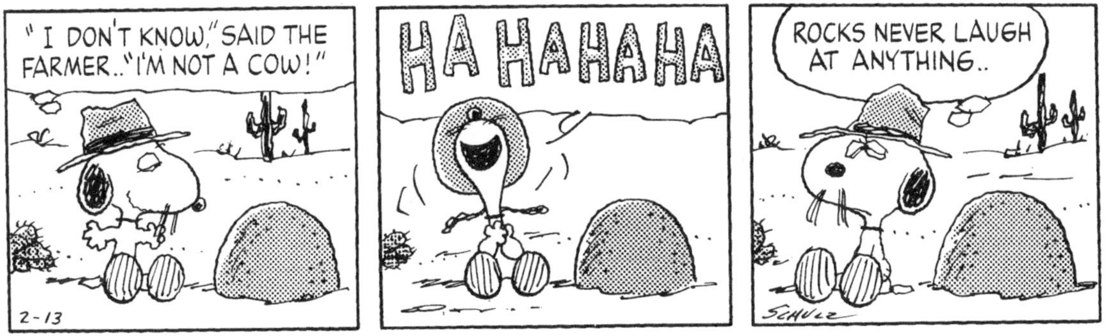
"I DON'T KNOW," SAID THE FARMER.."I'M NOT A COW!"
2-13
HA HA HA HA HA
ROCKS NEVER LAUGH AT ANYTHING..
SCHULZ

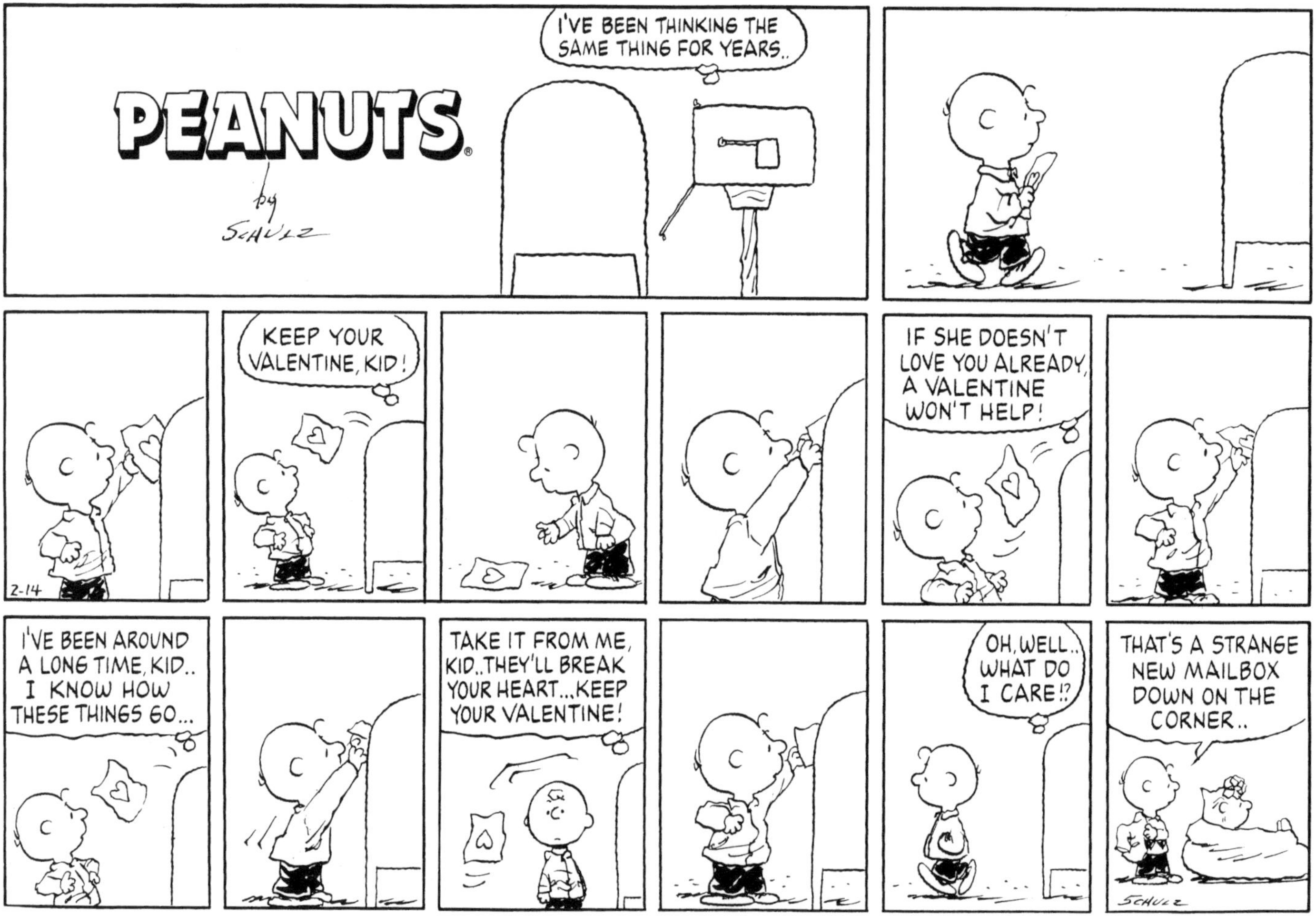
PEANUTS
by SCHULZ
I'VE BEEN THINKING THE SAME THING FOR YEARS..
2-14
KEEP YOUR VALENTINE, KID!
IF SHE DOESN'T LOVE YOU ALREADY, A VALENTINE WON'T HELP!
I'VE BEEN AROUND A LONG TIME, KID.. I KNOW HOW THESE THINGS GO...
TAKE IT FROM ME, KID..THEY'LL BREAK YOUR HEART...KEEP YOUR VALENTINE!
OH, WELL.. WHAT DO I CARE!?
THAT'S A STRANGE NEW MAILBOX DOWN ON THE CORNER..
SCHULZ

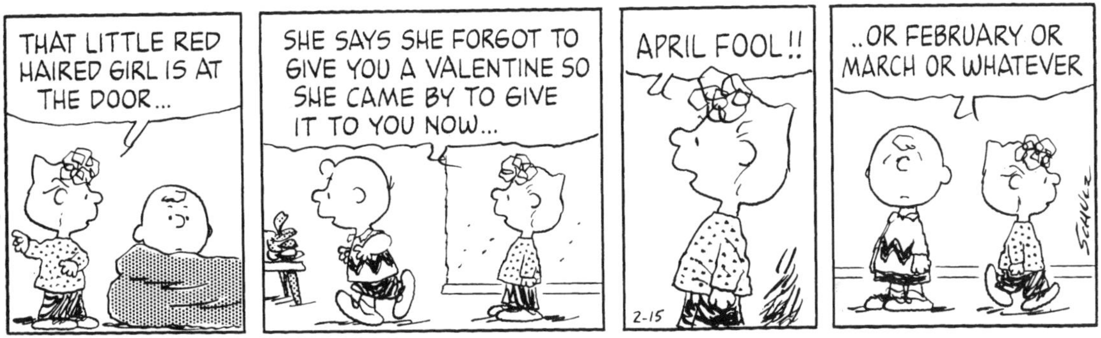
THAT LITTLE RED HAIRED GIRL IS AT THE DOOR...
SHE SAYS SHE FORGOT TO GIVE YOU A VALENTINE SO SHE CAME BY TO GIVE IT TO YOU NOW...
APRIL FOOL!!
2-15
..OR FEBRUARY OR MARCH OR WHATEVER
SCHULZ

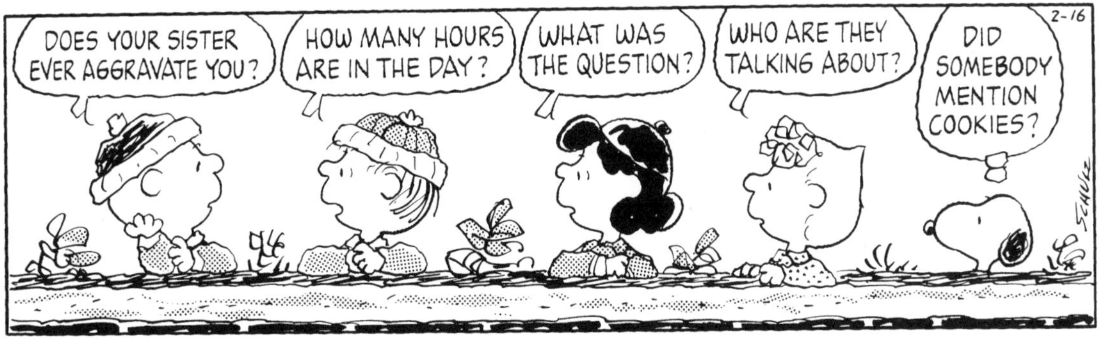
2-16
DOES YOUR SISTER EVER AGGRAVATE YOU?
HOW MANY HOURS ARE IN THE DAY?
WHAT WAS THE QUESTION?
WHO ARE THEY TALKING ABOUT?
DID SOMEBODY MENTION COOKIES?
SCHULZ

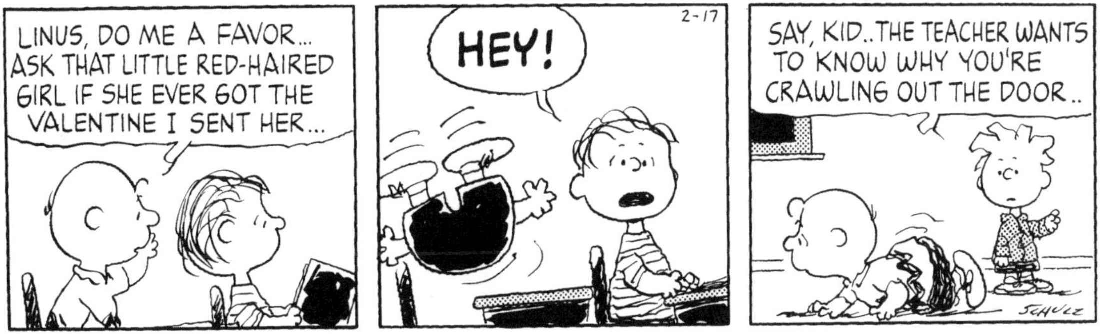
LINUS, DO ME A FAVOR... ASK THAT LITTLE RED-HAIRED GIRL IF SHE EVER GOT THE VALENTINE I SENT HER...
2-17
HEY!
SAY, KID..THE TEACHER WANTS TO KNOW WHY YOU'RE CRAWLING OUT THE DOOR..
SCHULZ

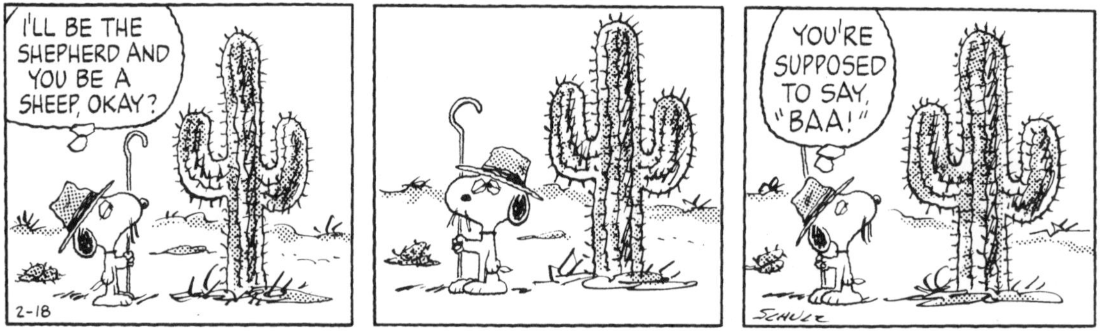
I'LL BE THE SHEPHERD AND YOU BE A SHEEP, OKAY?
YOU'RE SUPPOSED TO SAY, "BAA!"
2-18
SCHULZ

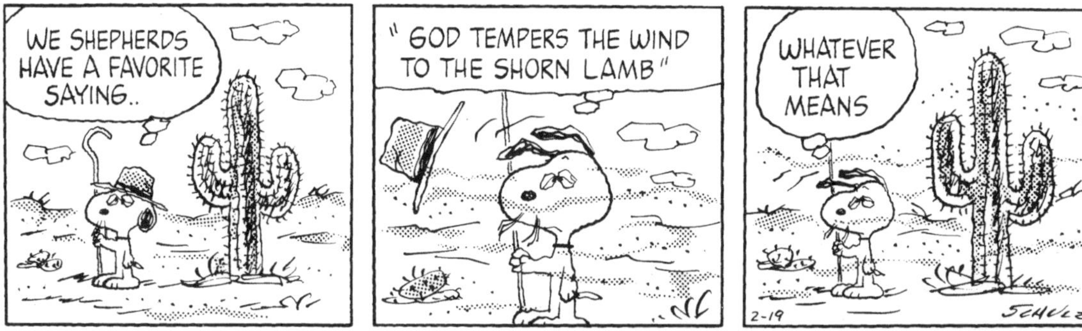
WE SHEPHERDS HAVE A FAVORITE SAYING..
" GOD TEMPERS THE WIND TO THE SHORN LAMB "
WHATEVER THAT MEANS
2-19
SCHULZ

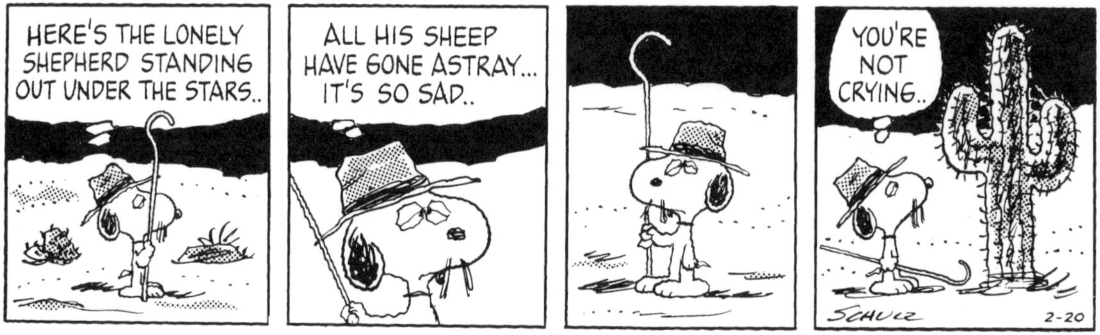
HERE'S THE LONELY SHEPHERD STANDING OUT UNDER THE STARS..
ALL HIS SHEEP HAVE GONE ASTRAY... IT'S SO SAD..
YOU'RE NOT CRYING..
SCHULZ
2-20

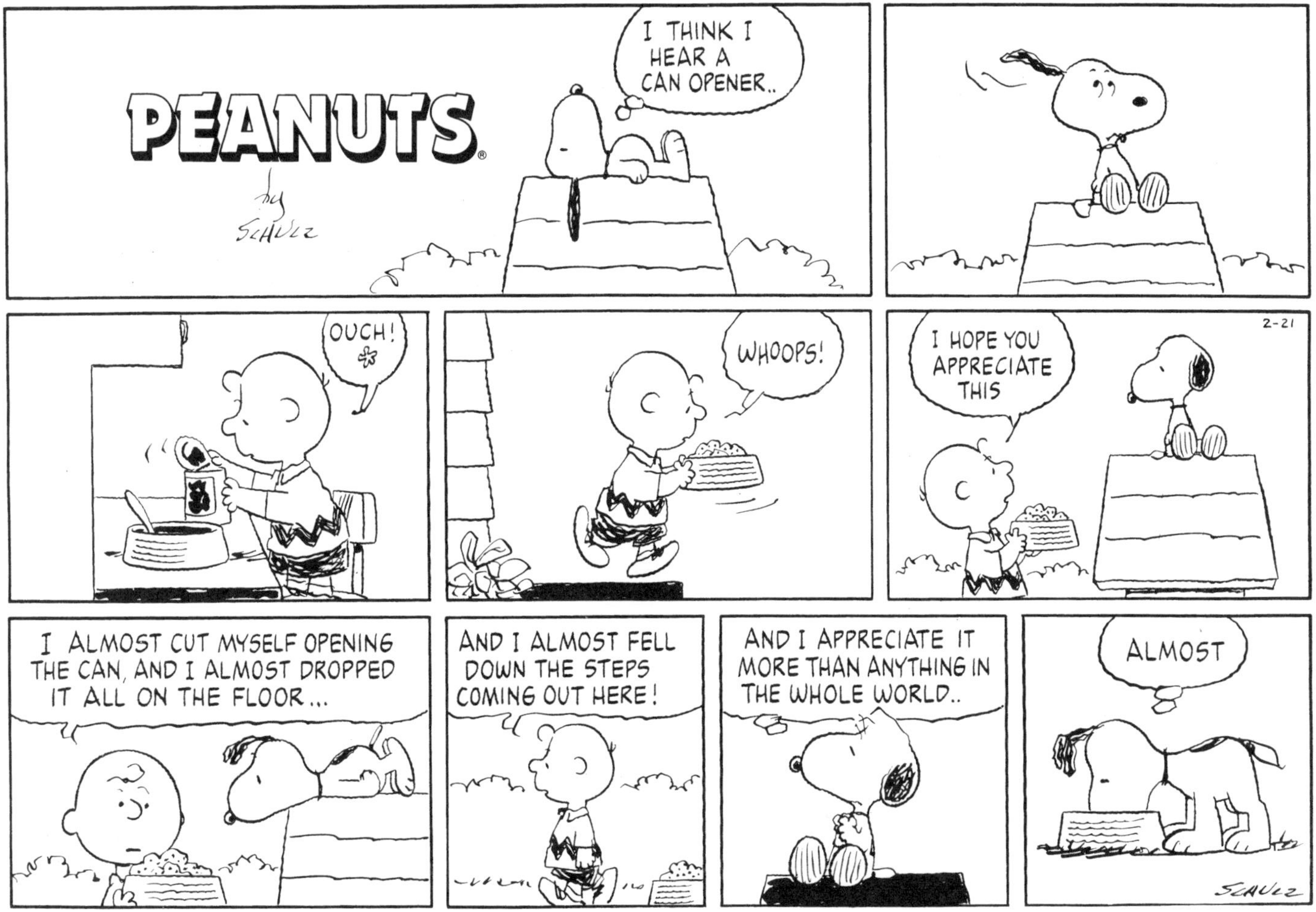
PEANUTS
by SCHULZ
I THINK I HEAR A CAN OPENER..
OUCH!
WHOOPS!
I HOPE YOU APPRECIATE THIS
2-21
I ALMOST CUT MYSELF OPENING THE CAN, AND I ALMOST DROPPED IT ALL ON THE FLOOR...
AND I ALMOST FELL DOWN THE STEPS COMING OUT HERE!
AND I APPRECIATE IT MORE THAN ANYTHING IN THE WHOLE WORLD..
ALMOST
SCHULZ

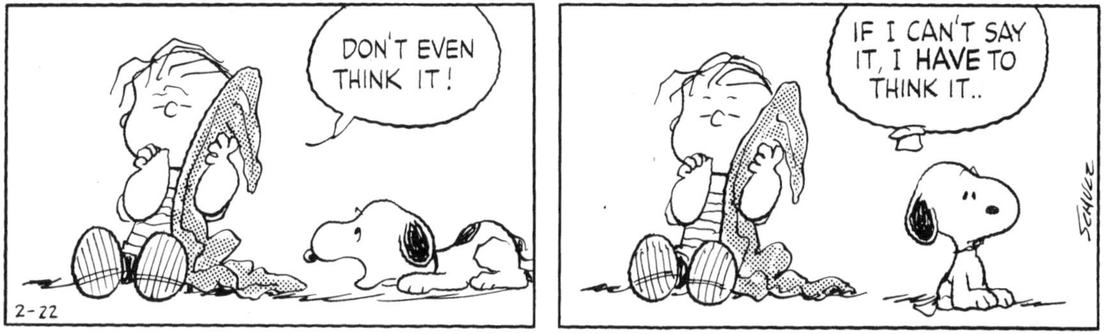
DON'T EVEN THINK IT!
IF I CAN'T SAY IT, I **HAVE** TO THINK IT..
2-22
SCHULZ

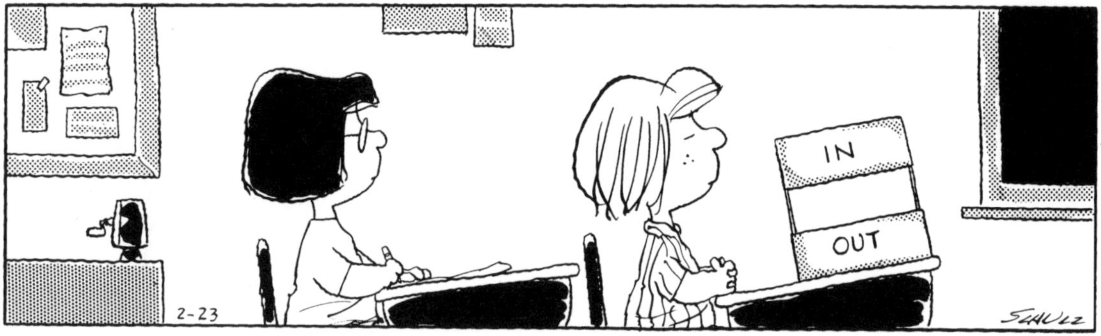
IN
OUT
2-23
SCHULZ

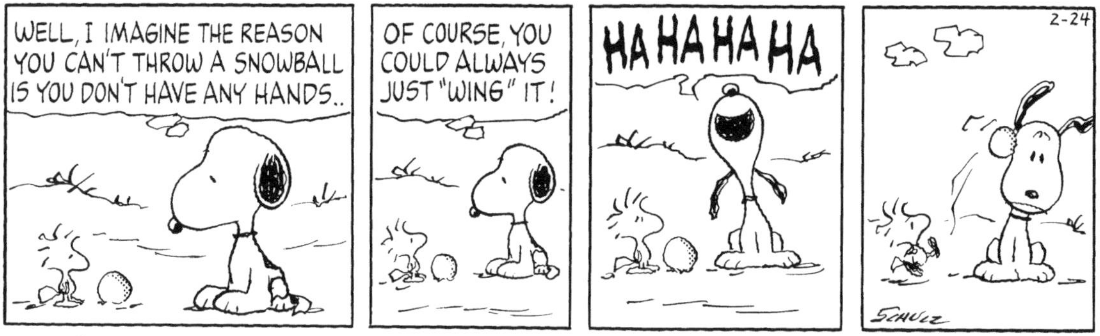
WELL, I IMAGINE THE REASON YOU CAN'T THROW A SNOWBALL IS YOU DON'T HAVE ANY HANDS..
OF COURSE, YOU COULD ALWAYS JUST "WING" IT!
HA HA HA HA HA
2-24
SCHULZ

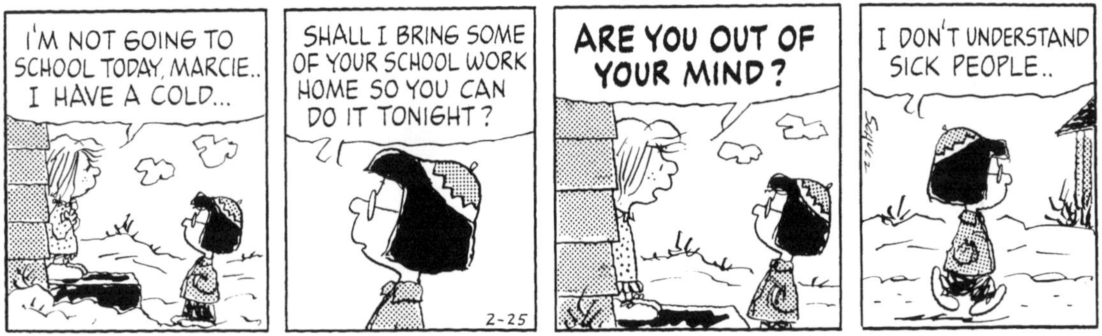
I'M NOT GOING TO SCHOOL TODAY, MARCIE.. I HAVE A COLD...
SHALL I BRING SOME OF YOUR SCHOOL WORK HOME SO YOU CAN DO IT TONIGHT?
2-25
ARE YOU OUT OF YOUR MIND?
I DON'T UNDERSTAND SICK PEOPLE..
SCHULZ

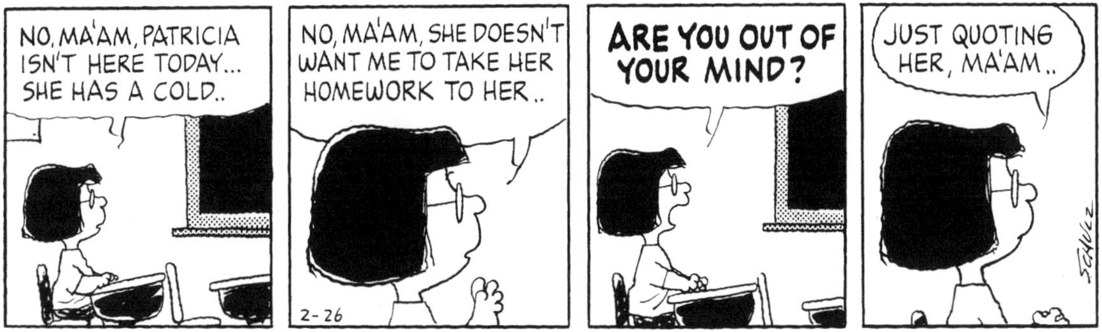
NO, MA'AM, PATRICIA ISN'T HERE TODAY... SHE HAS A COLD..
NO, MA'AM, SHE DOESN'T WANT ME TO TAKE HER HOMEWORK TO HER..
2-26
ARE YOU OUT OF YOUR MIND?
JUST QUOTING HER, MA'AM..
SCHULZ

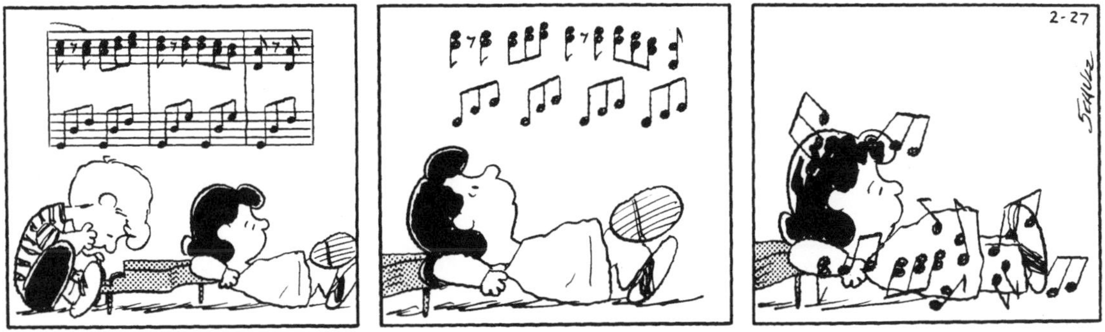
2-27
SCHULZ

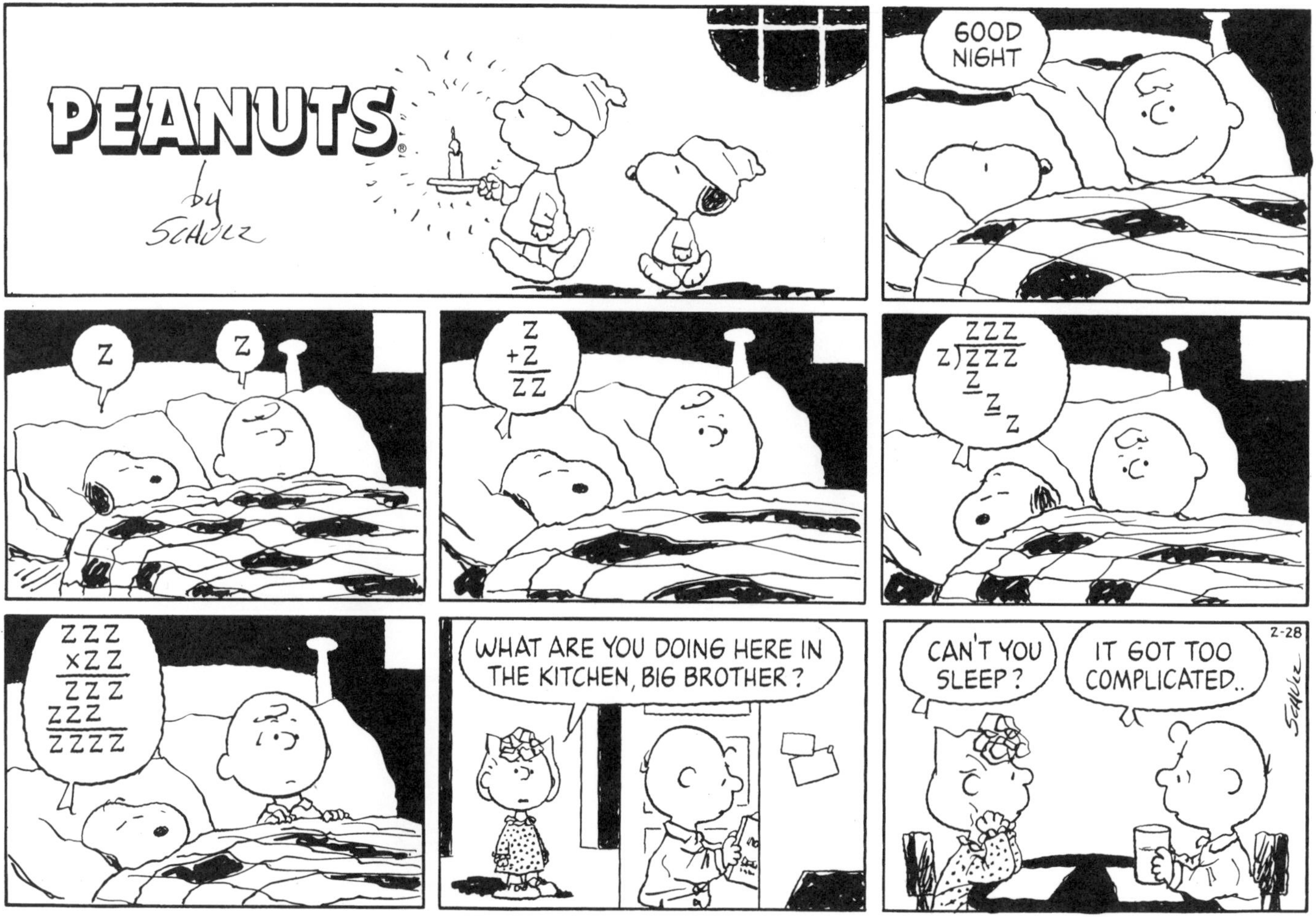
PEANUTS
by SCHULZ
GOOD NIGHT
Z
Z
Z
+Z
ZZ
ZZZ
Z)ZZZ
Z
Z
Z
ZZZ
×ZZ
ZZZ
ZZZ
ZZZZ
WHAT ARE YOU DOING HERE IN THE KITCHEN, BIG BROTHER?
2-28
CAN'T YOU SLEEP?
IT GOT TOO COMPLICATED..
SCHULZ

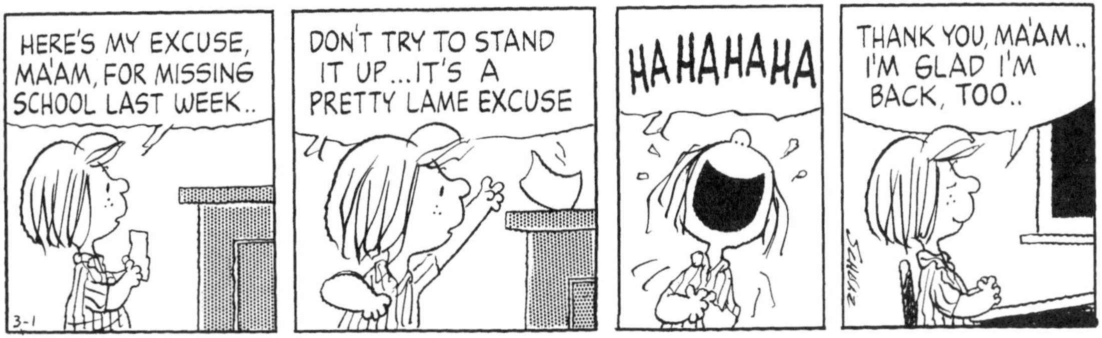
HERE'S MY EXCUSE, MA'AM, FOR MISSING SCHOOL LAST WEEK..
DON'T TRY TO STAND IT UP...IT'S A PRETTY LAME EXCUSE
HAHAHAHA
THANK YOU, MA'AM.. I'M GLAD I'M BACK, TOO..

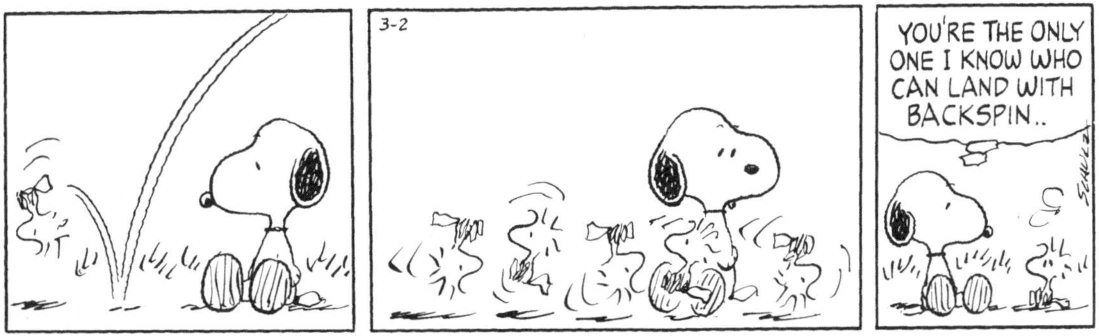
YOU'RE THE ONLY ONE I KNOW WHO CAN LAND WITH BACKSPIN..

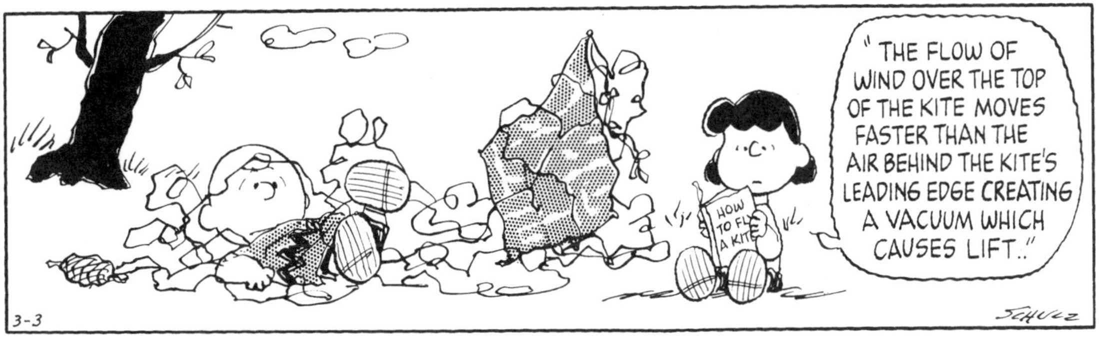
HOW TO FLY A KITE
" THE FLOW OF WIND OVER THE TOP OF THE KITE MOVES FASTER THAN THE AIR BEHIND THE KITE'S LEADING EDGE CREATING A VACUUM WHICH CAUSES LIFT.."

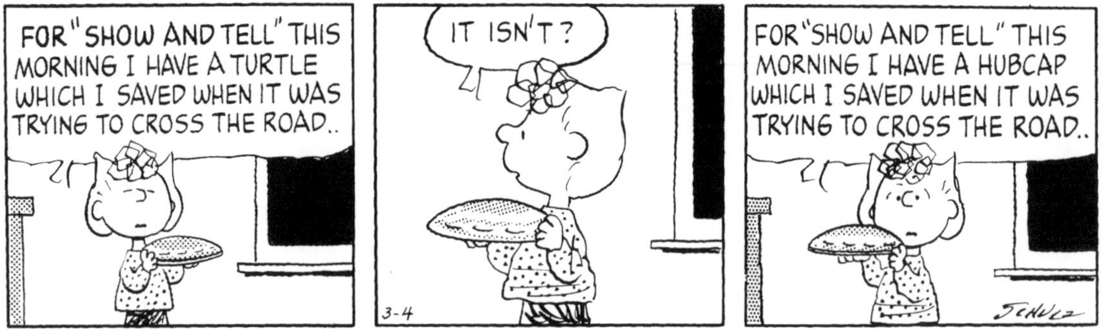
FOR "SHOW AND TELL" THIS MORNING I HAVE A TURTLE WHICH I SAVED WHEN IT WAS TRYING TO CROSS THE ROAD..
IT ISN'T?
3-4
FOR "SHOW AND TELL" THIS MORNING I HAVE A HUBCAP WHICH I SAVED WHEN IT WAS TRYING TO CROSS THE ROAD..
SCHULZ

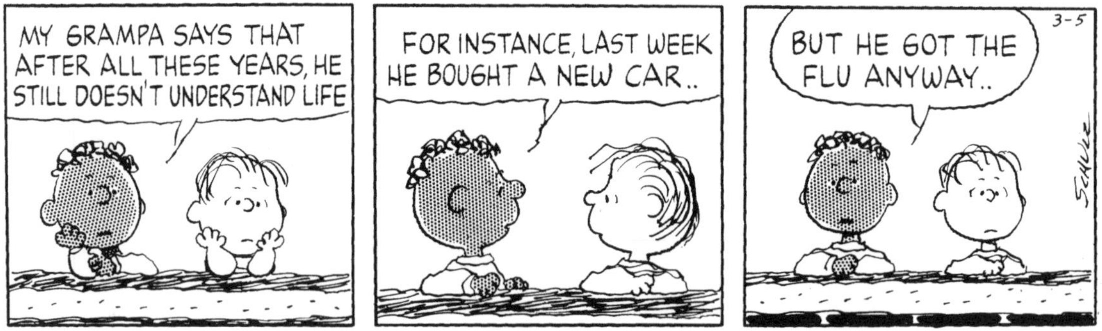
MY GRAMPA SAYS THAT AFTER ALL THESE YEARS, HE STILL DOESN'T UNDERSTAND LIFE
FOR INSTANCE, LAST WEEK HE BOUGHT A NEW CAR..
3-5
BUT HE GOT THE FLU ANYWAY..
SCHULZ

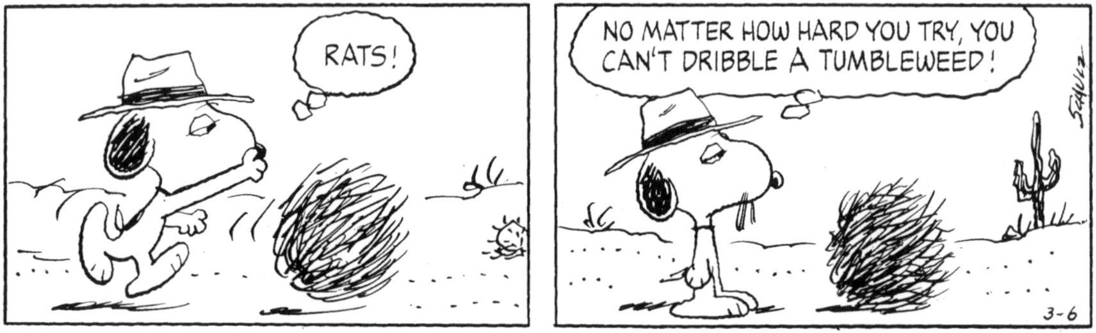
RATS!
NO MATTER HOW HARD YOU TRY, YOU CAN'T DRIBBLE A TUMBLEWEED!
SCHULZ
3-6

PEANUTS®
by SCHULZ
THE DOCTOR IS IN
PSYCHIATRIC HELP 5¢
?!
THE DOCTOR IS IN
3-7
THE DOC IS IN
THE DOCT IS IN
YOU'RE A BLOCKHEAD! FIVE CENTS, PLEASE..
SCHULZ

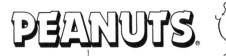

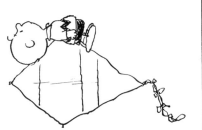

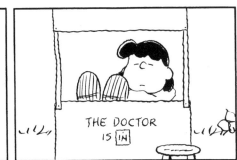

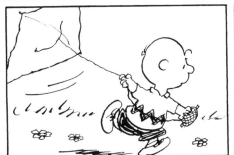

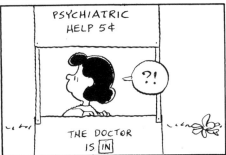

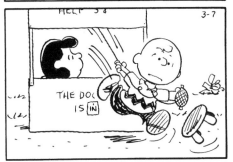

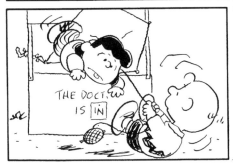

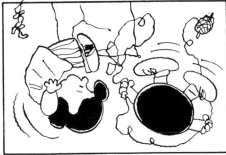

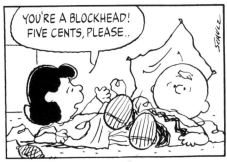

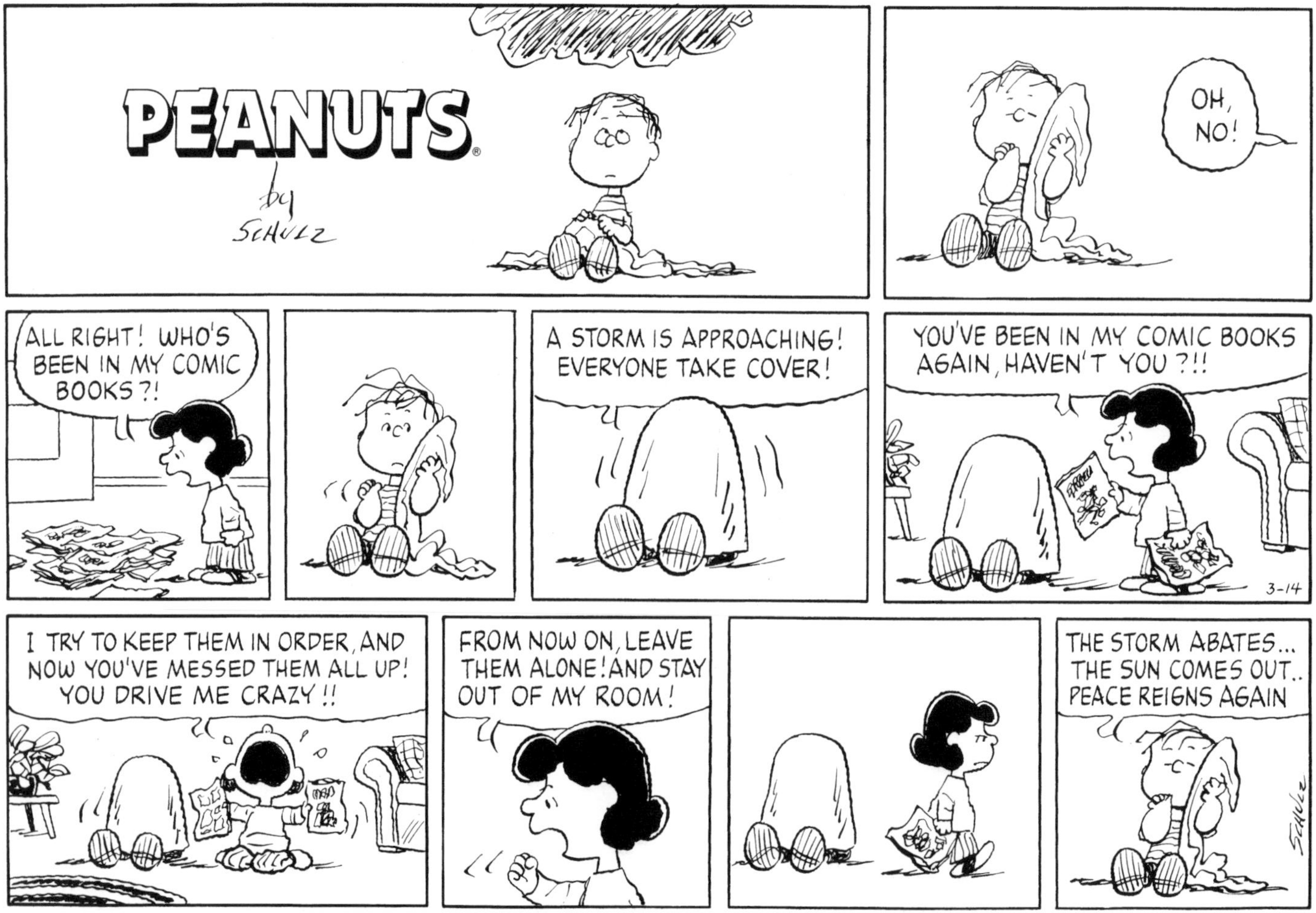
PEANUTS
by SCHULZ
OH, NO!
ALL RIGHT! WHO'S BEEN IN MY COMIC BOOKS?!
A STORM IS APPROACHING! EVERYONE TAKE COVER!
YOU'VE BEEN IN MY COMIC BOOKS AGAIN, HAVEN'T YOU?!!
3-14
I TRY TO KEEP THEM IN ORDER, AND NOW YOU'VE MESSED THEM ALL UP! YOU DRIVE ME CRAZY!!
FROM NOW ON, LEAVE THEM ALONE! AND STAY OUT OF MY ROOM!
THE STORM ABATES... THE SUN COMES OUT.. PEACE REIGNS AGAIN
SCHULZ

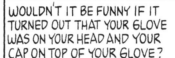

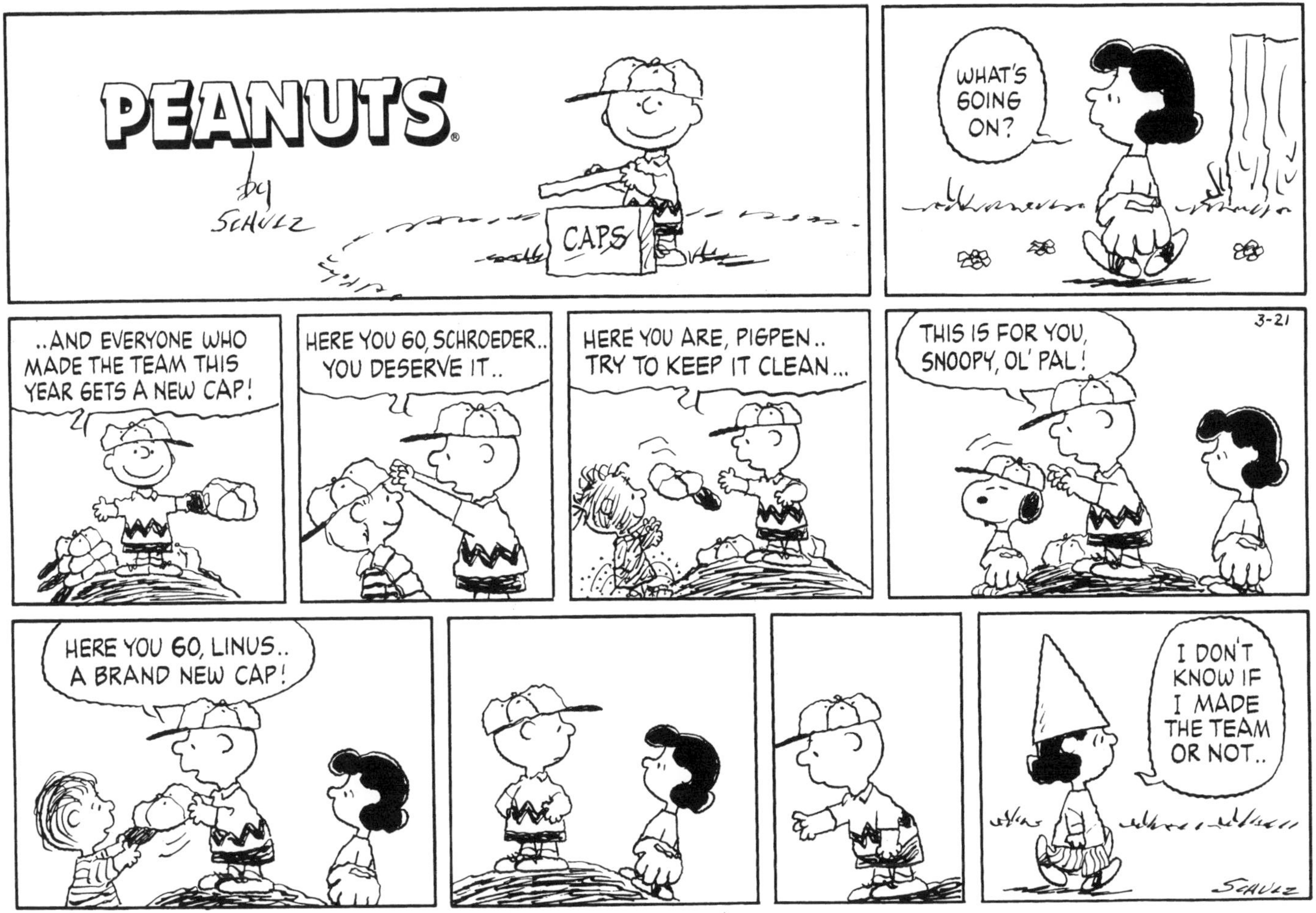
PEANUTS
by SCHULZ
CAPS
WHAT'S GOING ON?
..AND EVERYONE WHO MADE THE TEAM THIS YEAR GETS A NEW CAP!
HERE YOU GO, SCHROEDER.. YOU DESERVE IT..
HERE YOU ARE, PIGPEN.. TRY TO KEEP IT CLEAN...
3-21
THIS IS FOR YOU, SNOOPY, OL' PAL!
HERE YOU GO, LINUS.. A BRAND NEW CAP!
I DON'T KNOW IF I MADE THE TEAM OR NOT..
SCHULZ

I FEEL UP FOR THE GAME TODAY! I REALLY THINK WE CAN WIN!

I FEEL GOOD MENTALLY, AND I FEEL GOOD PHYSICALLY.. THIS IS THE MOST CONFIDENT I'VE EVER FELT...

3-25

YOU'VE GOT GRAPE JELLY ON YOUR SHIRT..

ONE FINGER WILL MEAN YOUR FAST BALL WHICH ISN'T VERY FAST ANYWAY..

TWO FINGERS WILL BE YOUR CURVE WHICH DOESN'T CURVE AT ALL..

THREE FINGERS WILL BE YOUR CHANGE-UP WHICH HASN'T FOOLED ANYONE YET...

FOUR FINGERS WAS FOR A PITCH-OUT, BUT WE WON'T USE THAT ONE

WHY NOT?

3-26

EVERYTHING YOU THROW LOOKS LIKE A PITCH-OUT!

3-27

HELLO? OH, HI! HOW ARE YOU?

OH, NOTHING.. JUST PLAYING IN THIS STUPID BALL GAME..YEAH, RIGHT FIELD..

SHE DID? SHE WORE THE PINK ONE AGAIN? I CAN'T BELIEVE IT! SHE...

BONK!

SORRY.. WE WERE CUT OFF..

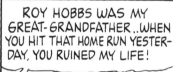

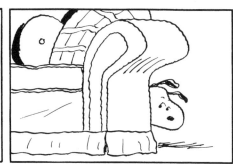

HOW ABOUT SHARING YOUR UMBRELLA?

IT'S HARD TO BE A SHEPHERD WITHOUT ANY SHEEP..

OF COURSE, THERE WAS LITTLE BO-PEEP WHO HAD SOME SHEEP, BUT THEN SHE LOST THEM

BUT MAYBE IT'S BETTER TO HAVE LOST YOUR SHEEP THAN NEVER TO HAVE HAD ANY SHEEP AT ALL..

I THINK I'M CRACKING UP

YOU SHOULD WRITE A SELF-HELP BOOK..

YOU KNOW, TO HELP THOSE WHO ARE LONELY AND CAN'T GO ANYPLACE..

How to be Happy Even Though You're Stuck in the Back Yard.

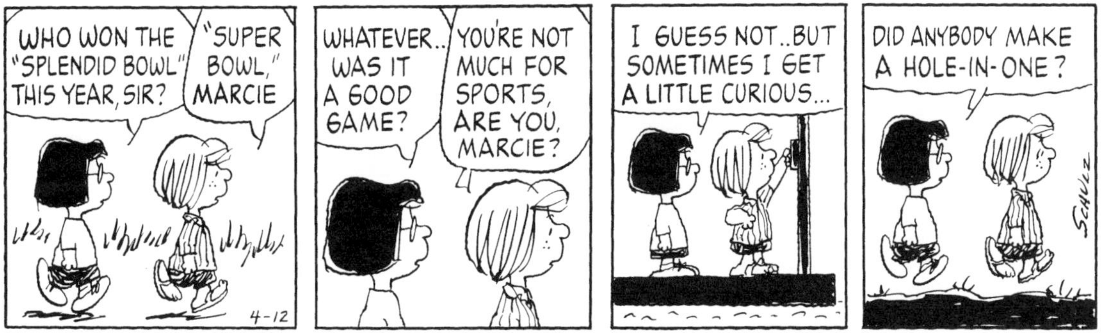
WHO WON THE "SPLENDID BOWL" THIS YEAR, SIR?
"SUPER BOWL," MARCIE
WHATEVER.. WAS IT A GOOD GAME?
YOU'RE NOT MUCH FOR SPORTS, ARE YOU, MARCIE?
I GUESS NOT..BUT SOMETIMES I GET A LITTLE CURIOUS...
DID ANYBODY MAKE A HOLE-IN-ONE?
4-12
SCHULZ

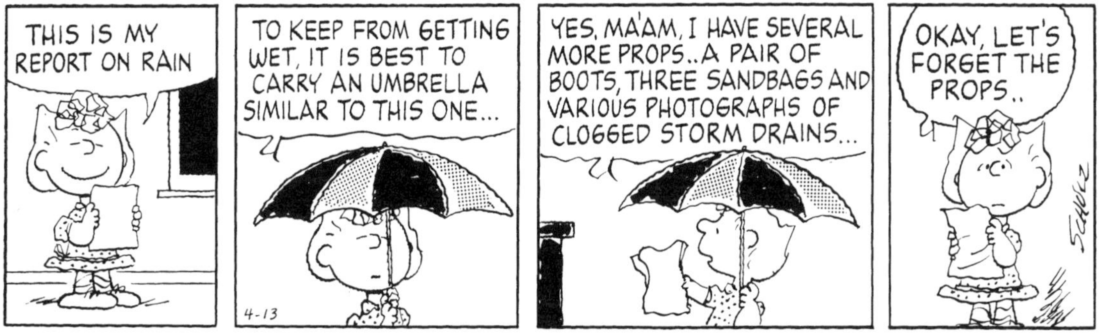
THIS IS MY REPORT ON RAIN
TO KEEP FROM GETTING WET, IT IS BEST TO CARRY AN UMBRELLA SIMILAR TO THIS ONE...
YES, MA'AM, I HAVE SEVERAL MORE PROPS..A PAIR OF BOOTS, THREE SANDBAGS AND VARIOUS PHOTOGRAPHS OF CLOGGED STORM DRAINS...
OKAY, LET'S FORGET THE PROPS..
4-13
SCHULZ

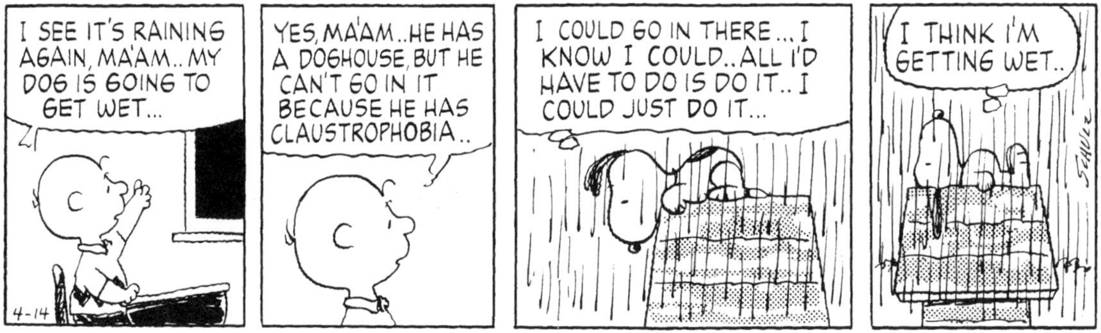
I SEE IT'S RAINING AGAIN, MA'AM.. MY DOG IS GOING TO GET WET...
YES, MA'AM..HE HAS A DOGHOUSE, BUT HE CAN'T GO IN IT BECAUSE HE HAS CLAUSTROPHOBIA..
I COULD GO IN THERE... I KNOW I COULD..ALL I'D HAVE TO DO IS DO IT.. I COULD JUST DO IT...
I THINK I'M GETTING WET..
4-14
SCHULZ

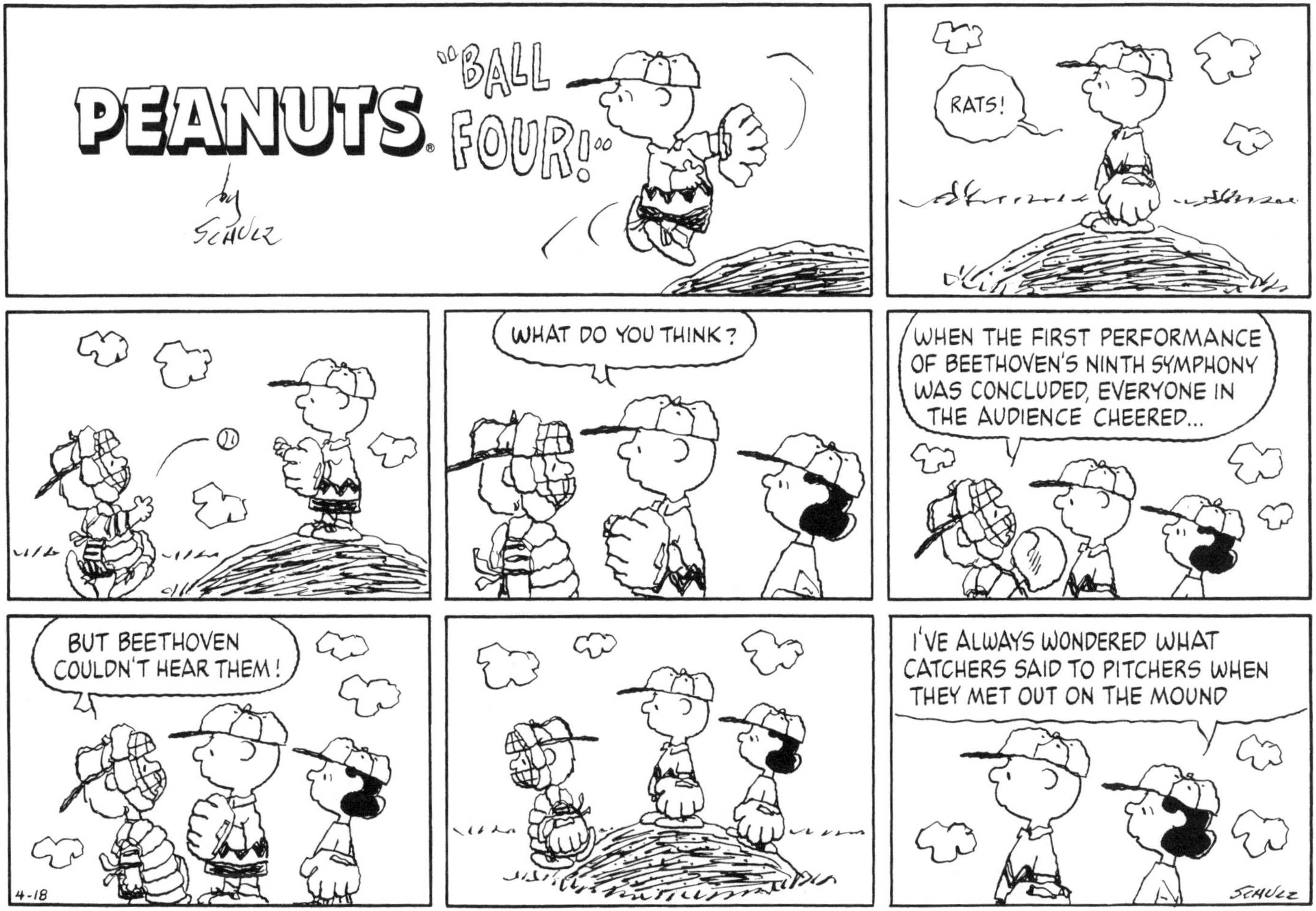
PEANUTS
by SCHULZ
"BALL FOUR!"
RATS!
WHAT DO YOU THINK?
WHEN THE FIRST PERFORMANCE OF BEETHOVEN'S NINTH SYMPHONY WAS CONCLUDED, EVERYONE IN THE AUDIENCE CHEERED...
BUT BEETHOVEN COULDN'T HEAR THEM!
I'VE ALWAYS WONDERED WHAT CATCHERS SAID TO PITCHERS WHEN THEY MET OUT ON THE MOUND
4-18
SCHULZ

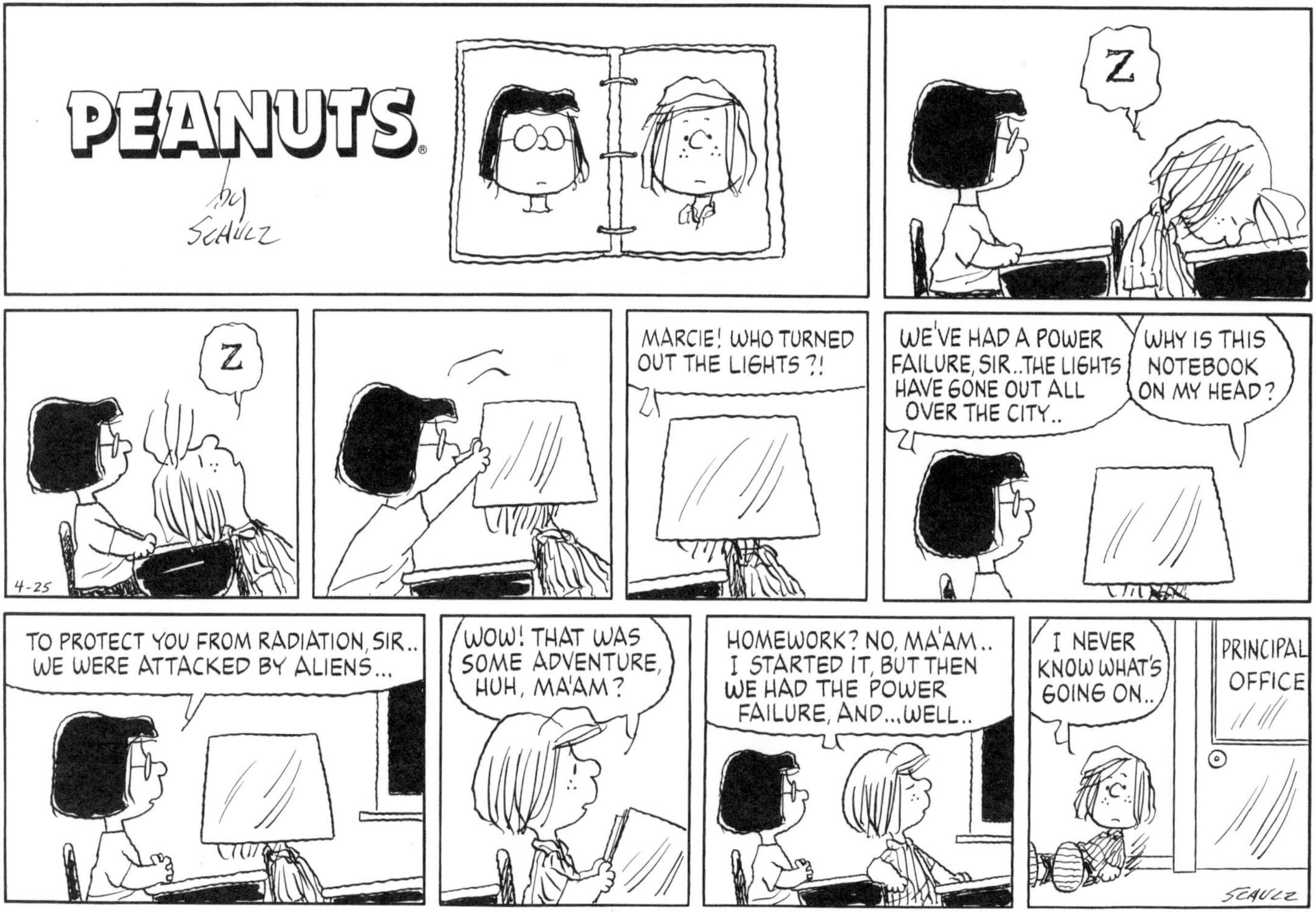
PEANUTS
by SCHULZ
Z
Z
4-25
MARCIE! WHO TURNED OUT THE LIGHTS?!
WE'VE HAD A POWER FAILURE, SIR..THE LIGHTS HAVE GONE OUT ALL OVER THE CITY..
WHY IS THIS NOTEBOOK ON MY HEAD?
TO PROTECT YOU FROM RADIATION, SIR.. WE WERE ATTACKED BY ALIENS...
WOW! THAT WAS SOME ADVENTURE, HUH, MA'AM?
HOMEWORK? NO, MA'AM.. I STARTED IT, BUT THEN WE HAD THE POWER FAILURE, AND...WELL..
I NEVER KNOW WHAT'S GOING ON..
PRINCIPAL OFFICE
SCHULZ

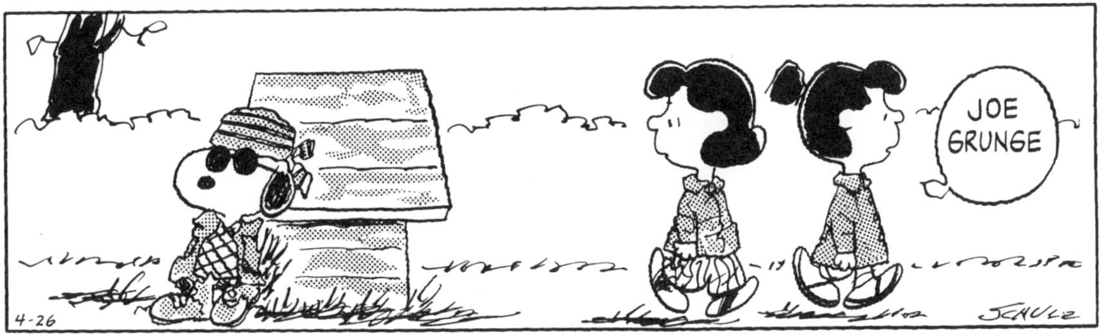
JOE GRUNGE

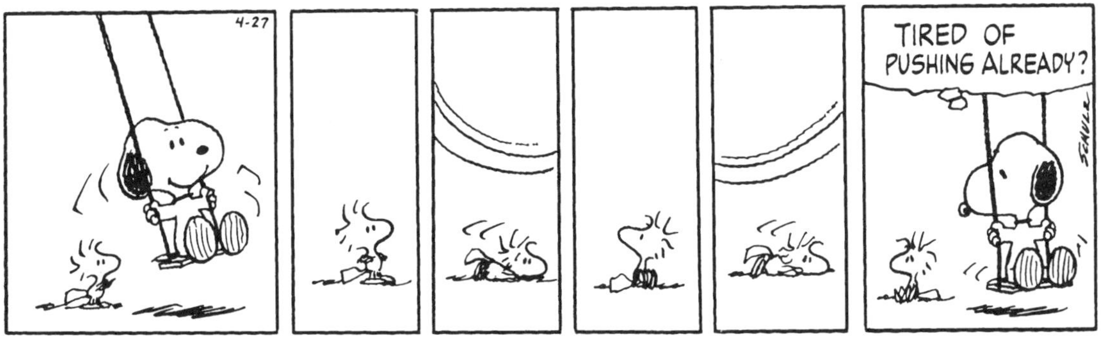
TIRED OF PUSHING ALREADY?

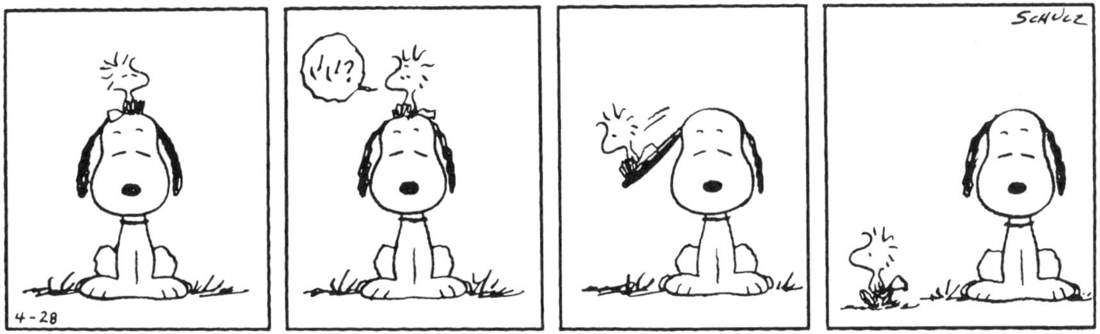

THIS SHOULD BE A GOOD "TINY TOTS" CONCERT, SIR..

I HATE BEING CALLED A "TINY TOT"

WHAT ARE THEY PLAYING?

"TALES FROM THE VIENNA WOODS"

WHERE ARE THE ICE SKATERS?

1993

GRAMPA SAYS HE WENT TO SCHOOL FOR TWELVE YEARS, AND WAS NEVER ALLOWED TO DRAW ON THE BLACKBOARD

5-3

HE SAYS HE WAS DEPRIVED OF ONE OF THE GREAT JOYS OF LIFE..

HE SAYS SOME NIGHT AFTER A PTA MEETING, HE'S GOING TO DRAW ALL OVER ONE OF THE BLACKBOARDS..

CAN HE DRAW PRETTY WELL?

NO, ALL HE EVER DRAWS IS MICKEY MOUSE..

I'M NOT GOING TO SCHOOL ANYMORE BECAUSE I ALREADY KNOW EVERYTHING I'LL EVER NEED TO KNOW..

HOW FAR AWAY IS THE MOON, WHEN WAS GEORGE WASHINGTON BORN AND WHAT'S THE FRENCH WORD FOR TOOTHPASTE?

I HOPE I HAVE A CUPCAKE IN MY LUNCH TODAY..

5-4

WHAT ARE YOU WATCHING?

I DON'T KNOW

5-5

I MEAN, I KNOW WHAT I'M WATCHING, BUT I DON'T KNOW WHAT'S GOING ON

WELL, ACTUALLY, I KNOW WHAT'S GOING ON, BUT I'VE SORT OF LOST TRACK..

WHY IS BARNEY PURPLE?

I'VE GOT THE NUMBERS FIGURED OUT, BUT WHO ARE THESE PEOPLE WITH THE FUNNY CLOTHES, AND WHAT GAME ARE WE PLAYING, ANYWAY?

I'VE GOT THE NUMBERS FIGURED OUT, BUT WHO ARE THESE PEOPLE WITH THE FUNNY CLOTHES, AND WHAT GAME ARE WE PLAYING, ANYWAY?

COOKIES

5-6

5-7

FIRST-TIME CARD PLAYERS, SNOOPY AND RERUN, QUICKLY DISCOVER THAT THE GAME IS MORE FUN WHEN PLAYED WITH A DOUBLE DECK!

TAKE A LETTER..

5-8

I'VE ALWAYS WANTED TO SAY THAT..

PEANUTS

by SCHULZ

SUPPERTIME!

JUST WHAT YOU LIKE, AND RIGHT ON TIME..

I'LL SET IT RIGHT HERE..

I EVEN BROUGHT YOU A NAPKIN

NOW YOU DON'T HAVE A THING TO COMPLAIN ABOUT

NO NAPKIN RING..

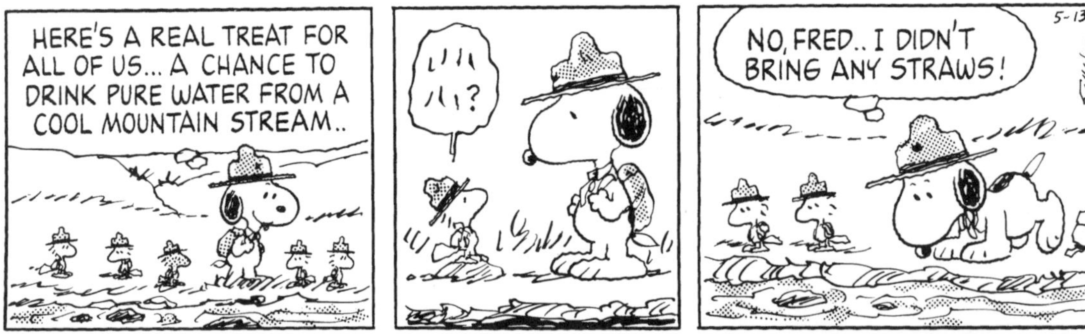
HERE'S A REAL TREAT FOR ALL OF US... A CHANCE TO DRINK PURE WATER FROM A COOL MOUNTAIN STREAM..
5-13
NO, FRED.. I DIDN'T BRING ANY STRAWS!

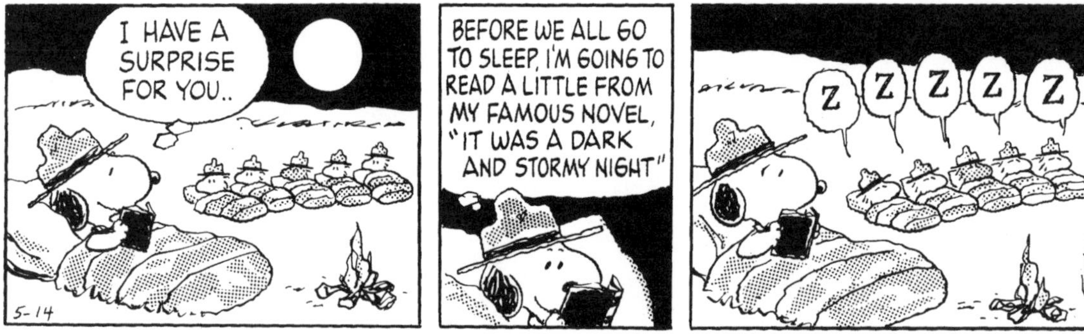
I HAVE A SURPRISE FOR YOU..
5-14
BEFORE WE ALL GO TO SLEEP, I'M GOING TO READ A LITTLE FROM MY FAMOUS NOVEL, "IT WAS A DARK AND STORMY NIGHT"
Z Z Z Z Z

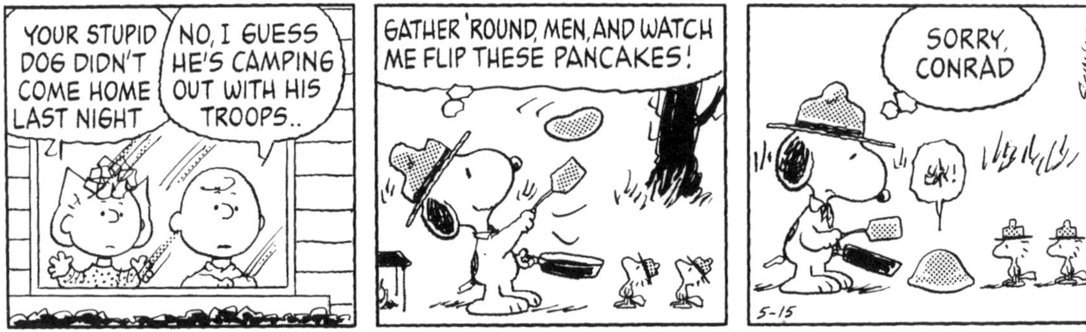
YOUR STUPID DOG DIDN'T COME HOME LAST NIGHT
NO, I GUESS HE'S CAMPING OUT WITH HIS TROOPS..
GATHER 'ROUND, MEN, AND WATCH ME FLIP THESE PANCAKES!
SORRY, CONRAD
5-15

WELL, I SEE YOU'RE BACK FROM YOUR CAMPING TRIP..

I HOPE YOU ENJOYED IT AS MUCH AS THE BIRDS..

I DON'T KNOW.. I HATE CHIRPING AROUND THE CAMPFIRE..

5-17

LEND ME YOUR PEN, WILL YOU, MARCIE?

THEN LET ME HAVE YOUR PENCIL..

5-18

TIME OUT, MA'AM, FOR AN EQUIPMENT CHANGE!

AS A WORLD FAMOUS ATTORNEY, WOULD YOU EVER BE INTERESTED IN BECOMING A MEMBER OF THE SUPREME COURT?

WHY NOT?

5-19

OF COURSE, YOU'D HAVE TO MOVE TO WASHINGTON..

WHERE'S THAT?

1993

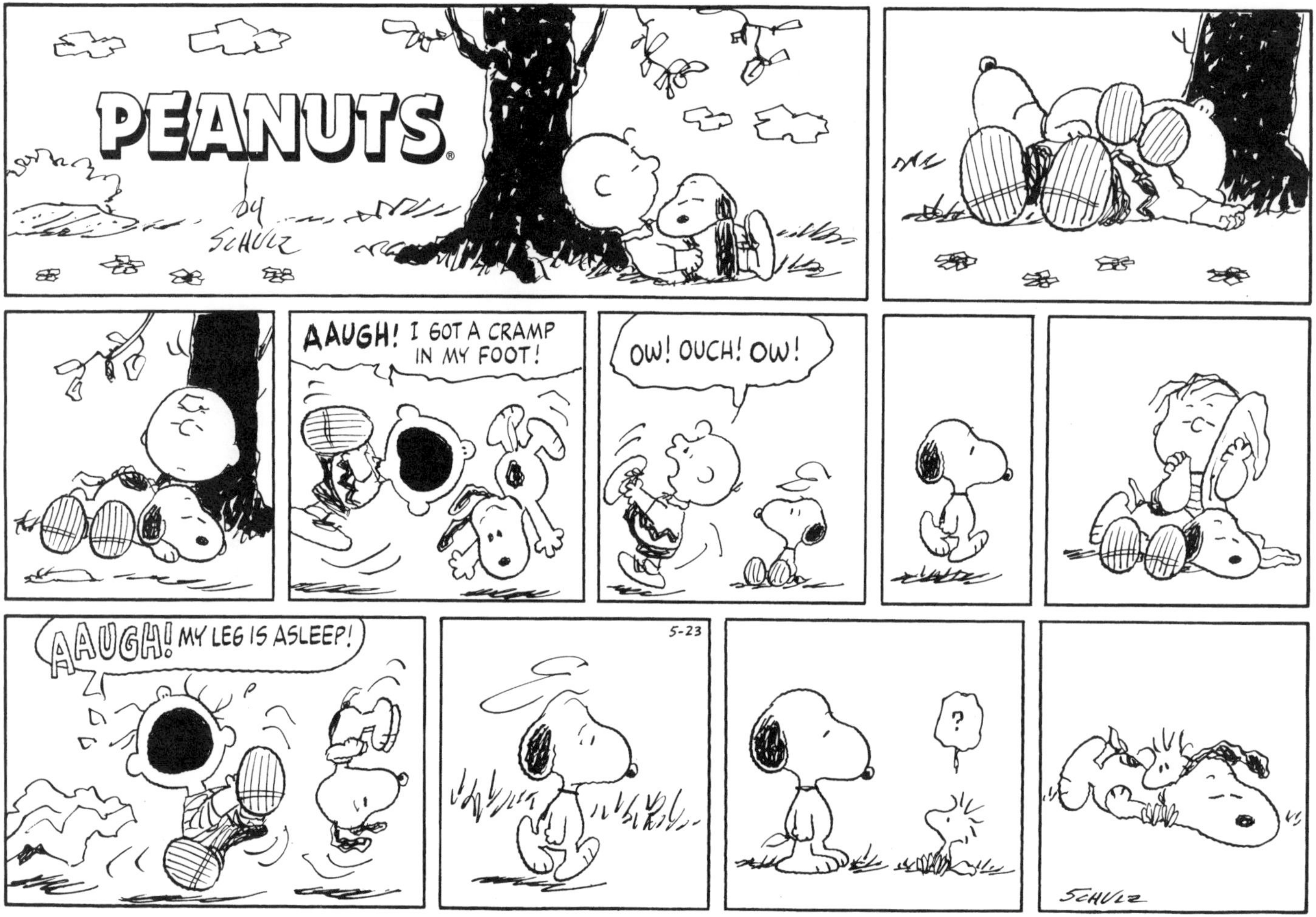
PEANUTS
by SCHULZ
AAUGH! I GOT A CRAMP IN MY FOOT!
OW! OUCH! OW!
AAUGH! MY LEG IS ASLEEP!
5-23
?
SCHULZ

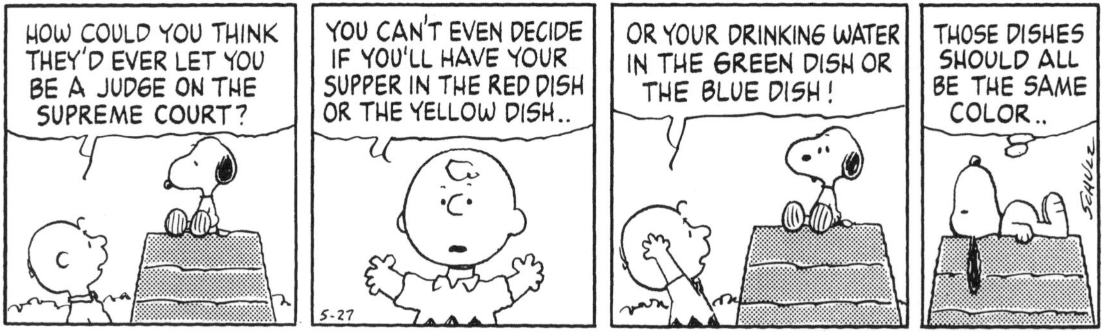
HOW COULD YOU THINK THEY'D EVER LET YOU BE A JUDGE ON THE SUPREME COURT?
YOU CAN'T EVEN DECIDE IF YOU'LL HAVE YOUR SUPPER IN THE RED DISH OR THE YELLOW DISH..
OR YOUR DRINKING WATER IN THE GREEN DISH OR THE BLUE DISH!
THOSE DISHES SHOULD ALL BE THE SAME COLOR..
5-27
SCHULZ

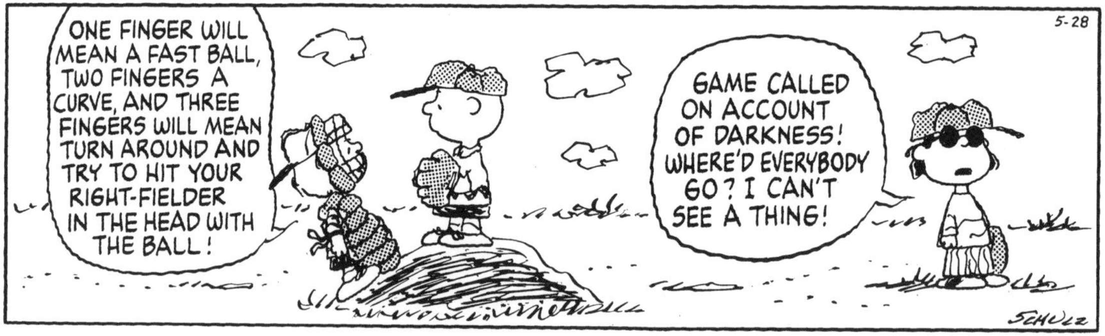
ONE FINGER WILL MEAN A FAST BALL, TWO FINGERS A CURVE, AND THREE FINGERS WILL MEAN TURN AROUND AND TRY TO HIT YOUR RIGHT-FIELDER IN THE HEAD WITH THE BALL!
GAME CALLED ON ACCOUNT OF DARKNESS! WHERE'D EVERYBODY GO? I CAN'T SEE A THING!
5-28
SCHULZ

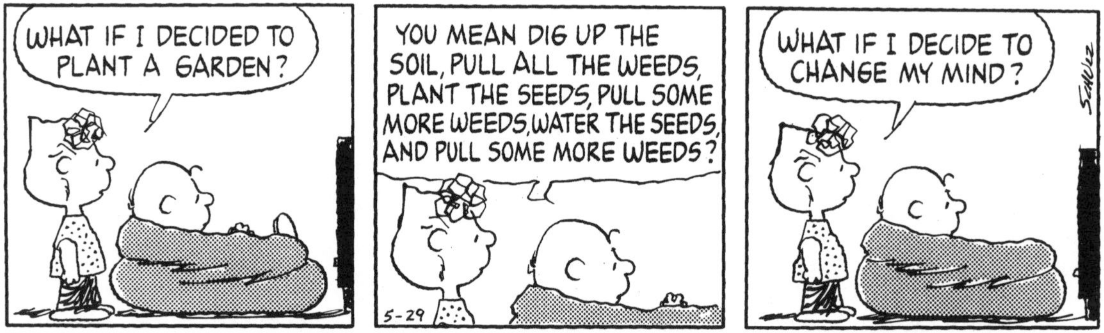
WHAT IF I DECIDED TO PLANT A GARDEN?
YOU MEAN DIG UP THE SOIL, PULL ALL THE WEEDS, PLANT THE SEEDS, PULL SOME MORE WEEDS, WATER THE SEEDS, AND PULL SOME MORE WEEDS?
WHAT IF I DECIDE TO CHANGE MY MIND?
5-29
SCHULZ

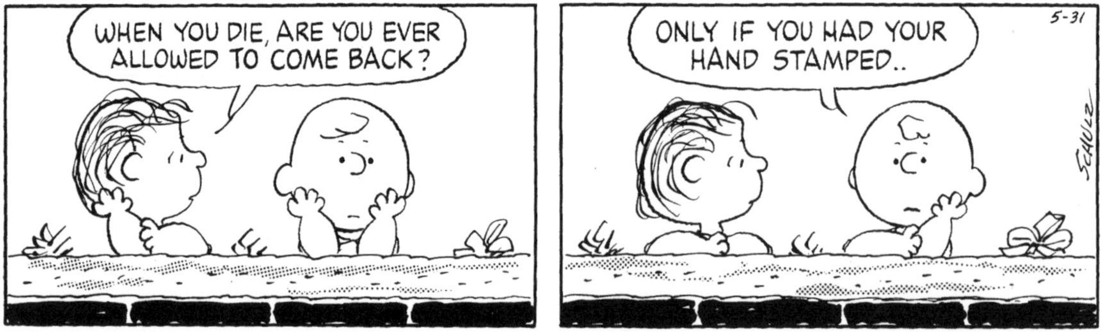
WHEN YOU DIE, ARE YOU EVER ALLOWED TO COME BACK?
5-31
ONLY IF YOU HAD YOUR HAND STAMPED..
SCHULZ

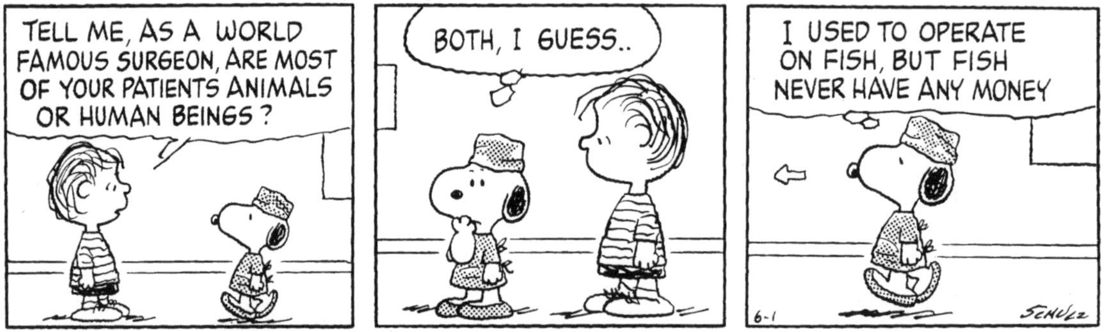
TELL ME, AS A WORLD FAMOUS SURGEON, ARE MOST OF YOUR PATIENTS ANIMALS OR HUMAN BEINGS?
BOTH, I GUESS..
I USED TO OPERATE ON FISH, BUT FISH NEVER HAVE ANY MONEY
6-1
SCHULZ

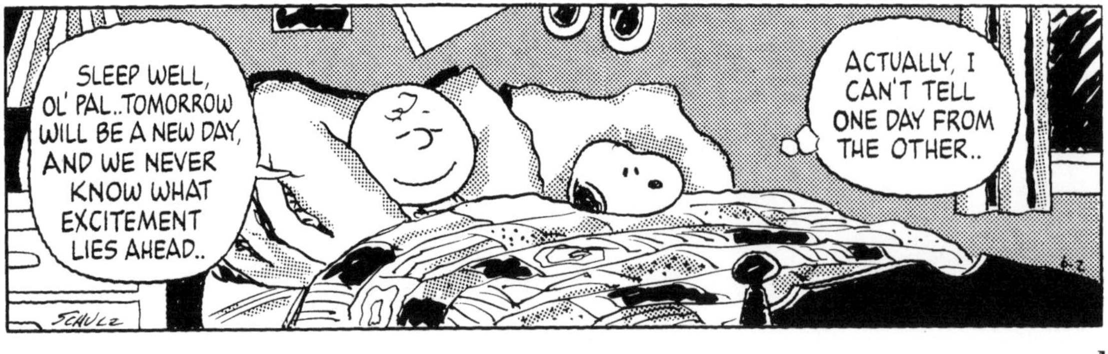
SLEEP WELL, OL' PAL..TOMORROW WILL BE A NEW DAY, AND WE NEVER KNOW WHAT EXCITEMENT LIES AHEAD..
ACTUALLY, I CAN'T TELL ONE DAY FROM THE OTHER..
SCHULZ

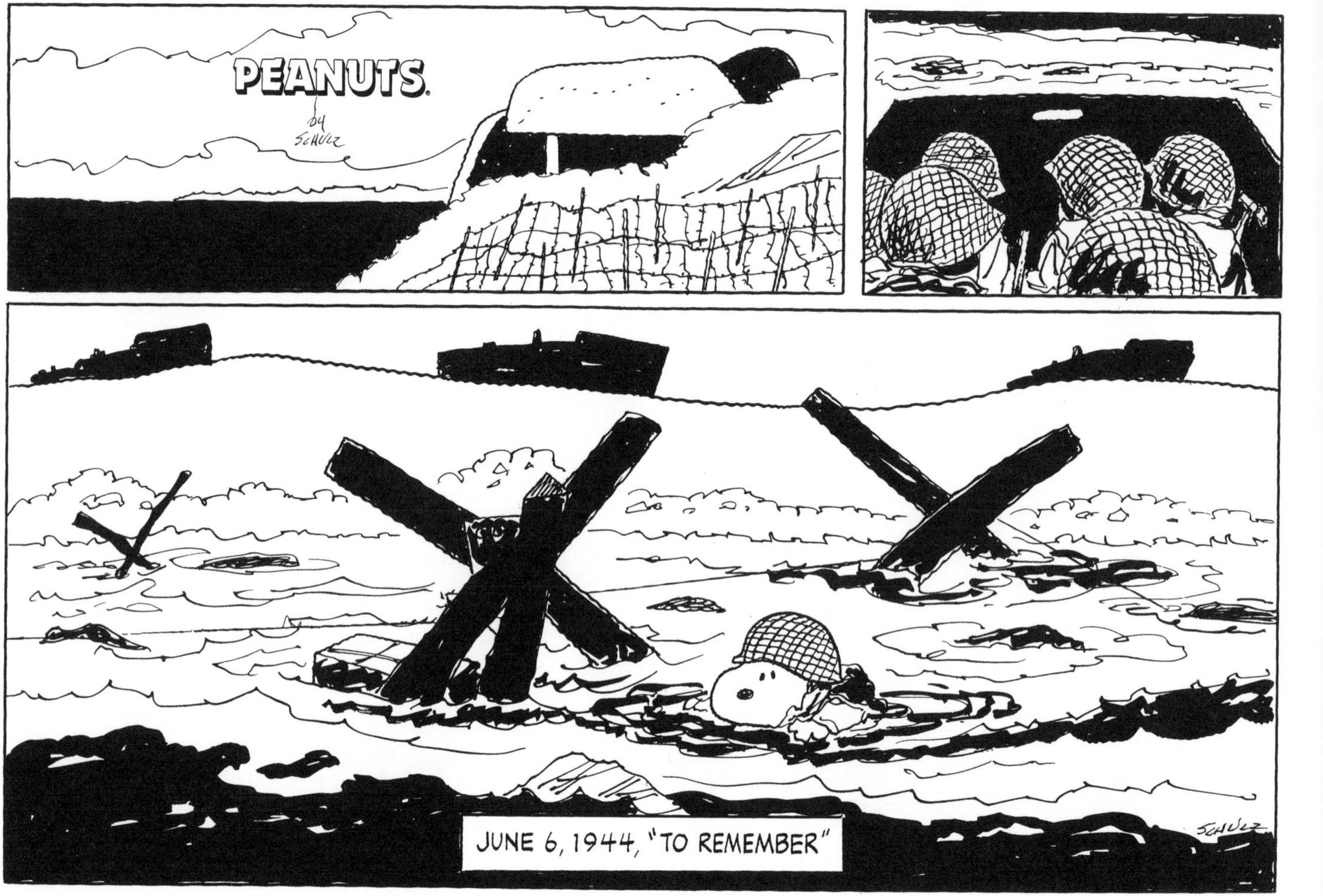
PEANUTS
by SCHULZ
JUNE 6, 1944, "TO REMEMBER"
SCHULZ

I'M SORRY I'M LATE WITH YOUR SUPPER.. I STOPPED TO ADMIRE THE SUNSET..

THERE WAS A GLOW IN THE SKY LIKE I'VE NEVER SEEN BEFORE..

6-10

I DON'T THINK THERE'S A WORD THAT DESCRIBES HOW IT CAN MAKE YOU FEEL...

HUNGRY!

SO HERE I AM RIDING ON THE BACK OF MY MOM'S BICYCLE..

THIS SHOULD BE A GOOD TRIP IF SHE STEERS STRAIGHT...

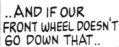

..AND IF OUR FRONT WHEEL DOESN'T GO DOWN THAT..

6-11

..GRATE!

ALL RIGHT, TROOPS..BEFORE YOU GO TO SLEEP, I WANT TO HEAR SOME BEDTIME PRAYERS..

6-12

I DIDN'T KNOW THEY HAD THEOLOGICAL DIFFERENCES..

BONK

LUCY, YOU'RE THE WORST PLAYER IN THE HISTORY OF THE GAME!

YOU CAN'T PROVE THAT! YOU SHOULD NEVER SAY THINGS THAT YOU CAN'T PROVE!

IN ALL PROBABILITY, YOU ARE THE WORST PLAYER IN THE HISTORY OF THE GAME!

I CAN ACCEPT THAT..

DID YOU KNOW THAT BLACKBEARD, THE PIRATE, BURIED ALL HIS GOLD HERE IN THE DESERT?

AND THAT BLACKBEARD ONCE SPENT THE NIGHT IN A MOTEL IN NEEDLES? THAT'S WHAT SOMEONE TOLD ME..

YOU DON'T BELIEVE ANYTHING, DO YOU?

Dear Pen Pal, How have you been?

WHY DO YOU HAVE A PEN PAL?

TO LEARN ABOUT OTHER CULTURES... HE TELLS ME ABOUT HIMSELF, AND I TELL HIM ABOUT ME..

WHY WOULD ANYONE WANT TO HEAR ABOUT YOU?

Some days I feel like I'm writing uphill.

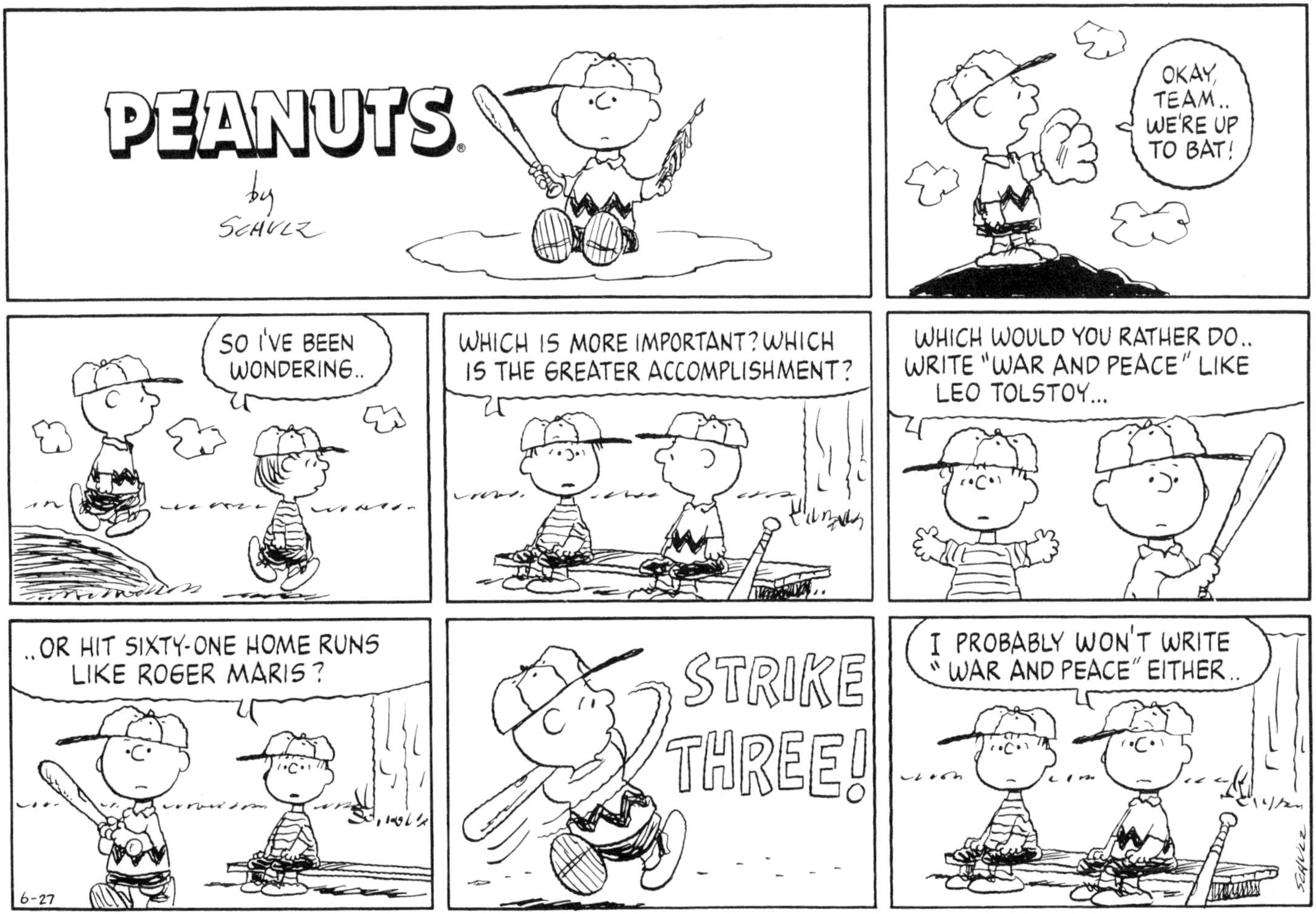
PEANUTS
by SCHULZ
OKAY, TEAM.. WE'RE UP TO BAT!
SO I'VE BEEN WONDERING..
WHICH IS MORE IMPORTANT? WHICH IS THE GREATER ACCOMPLISHMENT?
WHICH WOULD YOU RATHER DO.. WRITE "WAR AND PEACE" LIKE LEO TOLSTOY...
..OR HIT SIXTY-ONE HOME RUNS LIKE ROGER MARIS?
6-27
STRIKE THREE!
I PROBABLY WON'T WRITE "WAR AND PEACE" EITHER..
SCHULZ

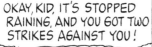

OKAY, KID, IT'S STOPPED RAINING, AND YOU GOT TWO STRIKES AGAINST YOU!

TIME OUT! ONE OF MY PLAYERS WANTS TO TALK TO ME...

THEY'RE HAVING A CONFERENCE, AREN'T THEY? THEY'RE PLANNING SOME CLEVER STRATEGY.. I JUST FEEL IT...

6-28

NO, LAST NIGHT YOU HAD YOUR SUPPER IN THE RED DISH AND WATER IN THE YELLOW DISH..

CRACK!

6-29

HE HIT IT! CHARLIE BROWN HIT IT! THE BALL IS GOING TO THE FENCE! RUN, CHARLIE BROWN! RUN!

OH, NO! THE WORLD IS COMING TO AN END! I ALWAYS KNEW IT WOULD END THIS WAY!

CHARLIE BROWN IS ROUNDING FIRST! HE'S ROUNDING SECOND! HE'S ROUNDING THIRD...

BUT ROY HOBBS' GREAT-GRANDDAUGHTER HAS THE BALL!! SHE'S BLOCKING THE PLATE!!!

6-30

SLIDE, CHARLIE BROWN, SLIDE!!

7-1

YOU DID IT, CHARLIE BROWN! YOU HIT ANOTHER HOME RUN, AND WE WON THE GAME!

YOU MEAN I WAS SAFE?

I'M ROY HOBBS' GREAT-GRANDDAUGHTER.. WHERE AM I? WHAT HAPPENED?

YOU WERE BLOCKING THE PLATE, SWEETIE.. HERE, I COULD ONLY FIND ONE SHOE..

7-2

WELL, YOU DID IT AGAIN, DIDN'T YOU? YOU HIT ANOTHER HOME RUN, AND RUINED MY LIFE!

I WAS LUCKY

YOU ALMOST KILLED ME WHEN YOU SLID INTO HOME..

YOU WERE BLOCKING THE PLATE, SWEETIE..

I STILL CAN'T FIND MY OTHER SHOE...

I'M SORRY

7-3

I HATE GOING THE REST OF MY LIFE WEARING ONLY ONE SHOE

1993

Page 79

1993

YES, I AGREE..IT TAKES COURAGE TO SAIL IN UNCHARTED WATERS..

7-8

I'M NOT SURE I WANT TO GO TO CAMP..

WELL,YOU'D BETTER MAKE UP YOUR MIND...THE BUS LEAVES IN FIVE MINUTES!

7-9

I'LL BE THERE IN SIX MINUTES..

NO, SIR.. MY SISTER WON'T BE COMING TO CAMP THIS YEAR..SHE MISSED THE BUS...BUT I'M HERE!

YES, SIR .. A YEAR AGO.. LAST PLACE IN THE SACK RACE..UH HUH.. THAT WAS ME..

7-10

NO, I UNDERSTAND...YOU HAVE A LOT OF CAMPERS COME THROUGH HERE..

CALLING HOME, CHARLIE BROWN?

I THOUGHT I'D LET EVERYONE KNOW THAT I GOT HERE TO CAMP SAFELY..

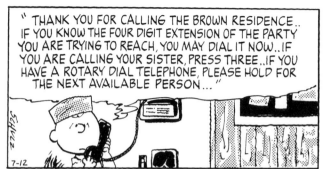

" THANK YOU FOR CALLING THE BROWN RESIDENCE.. IF YOU KNOW THE FOUR DIGIT EXTENSION OF THE PARTY YOU ARE TRYING TO REACH, YOU MAY DIAL IT NOW..IF YOU ARE CALLING YOUR SISTER, PRESS THREE..IF YOU HAVE A ROTARY DIAL TELEPHONE, PLEASE HOLD FOR THE NEXT AVAILABLE PERSON..."

7-12

HELLO? OH, IS THIS YOU, BIG BROTHER?

7-13

YOU'RE AT CAMP, AND I'M NOT! HA HA HA HA HA!!

NEVER CALL HOME!

HI! MY NAME IS ETHAN.. I JUST GOT BACK FROM "CRAFTS"

WE'VE BEEN LEARNING HOW TO MAKE BOWS AND ARROWS LIKE THE INDIANS..

7-14

THIS IS THE ARROW I MADE..

THAT'S AN INDIAN ARROW?

SURE, WITHOUT IT, THEY WOULDN'T KNOW WHICH WAY THEY WERE GOING..

WHAT DO YOU WANT TO BE WHEN YOU GROW UP, ETHAN?

A NEWSPAPER COLUMNIST..

I HAVE VERY STRONG OPINIONS ABOUT EVERYTHING

7-15

THAT'S A STUPID LOOKING SHIRT YOU'RE WEARING..

CARL SAGAN SAYS THERE ARE A HUNDRED BILLION STARS IN OUR GALAXY, AND THERE ARE A HUNDRED BILLION GALAXIES, AND EACH GALAXY CONTAINS A HUNDRED BILLION STARS! SORT OF PUTS THINGS IN PERSPECTIVE, DOESN'T IT CHARLIE BROWN?

7-16

I MISS MY DOG..

HI, SALLY.. I'M COMING HOME THIS AFTERNOON...

HAS MY DOG MISSED ME?

7-17

OH, YES.. HE'S BEEN WAITING FOR YOU...

WELCOME HOME, ROUND-HEADED KID!

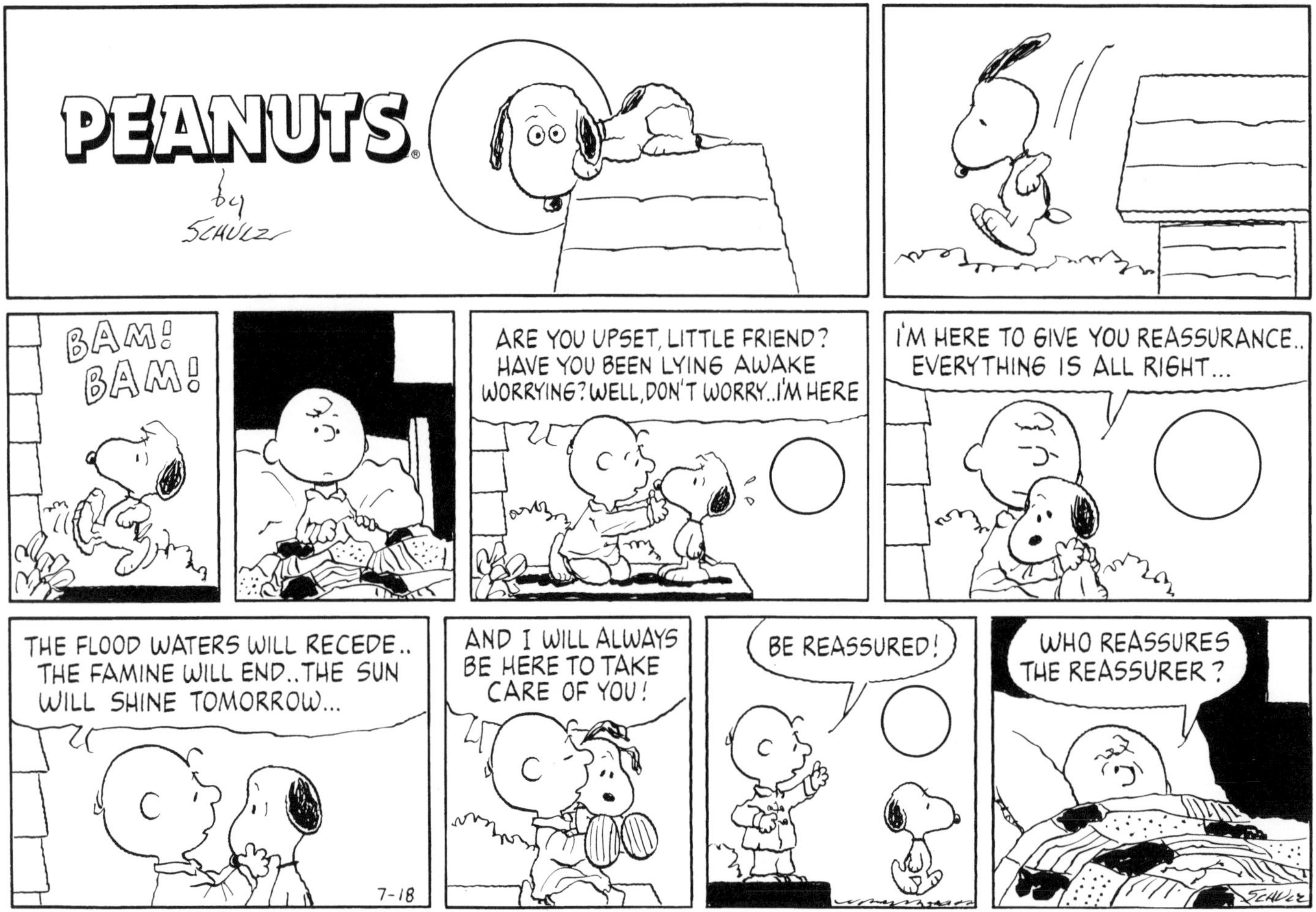
PEANUTS®
by SCHULZ
BAM! BAM!
ARE YOU UPSET, LITTLE FRIEND? HAVE YOU BEEN LYING AWAKE WORRYING? WELL, DON'T WORRY..I'M HERE
I'M HERE TO GIVE YOU REASSURANCE.. EVERYTHING IS ALL RIGHT...
THE FLOOD WATERS WILL RECEDE.. THE FAMINE WILL END..THE SUN WILL SHINE TOMORROW...
7-18
AND I WILL ALWAYS BE HERE TO TAKE CARE OF YOU!
BE REASSURED!
WHO REASSURES THE REASSURER?
SCHULZ

I KNOW IT'S HOT, MEN, BUT LET'S KEEP GOING..

NOT TOO FAR AHEAD IS AN OASIS WHERE THERE'LL BE LOTS OF WATER...

7-19

7-20

IT IS SAID THAT WHEN DOGS DRINK FROM THE RIVER NILE, THEY DO IT WHILE RUNNING SO AS NOT TO BE SEIZED BY CROCODILES..

I FEEL RIDICULOUS

JUST SPIT THEM OUT..

7-21

THOSE ARE BUTTONS..THEY KEEP THE WATERMELON FROM FALLING APART..

HE NEVER BELIEVES ANYTHING I TELL HIM

7-22

FALLING ROCK

FALLING THINGS

SO HERE I AM LEFT TO GUARD THE CAR WHILE THE FAMILY GOES SHOPPING..

7-23

ANYONE WHO COMES NEAR THIS VEHICLE WILL MEET A SNARLING TORNADO!

ON THE OTHER HAND, FOR TWO COOKIES THEY CAN HAVE THE CAR..

7-24

PEANUTS by SCHULZ

THIS IS KIND OF INTERESTING

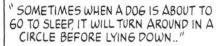

"SOMETIMES WHEN A DOG IS ABOUT TO GO TO SLEEP, IT WILL TURN AROUND IN A CIRCLE BEFORE LYING DOWN.."

"THIS HABIT GOES BACK TO THE DOG'S WILD ANCESTORS WHO STAMPED DOWN THE GRASS TO FORM A NESTLIKE BED.."

7-25

WHAT DOES IT SAY ABOUT WAKING UP?

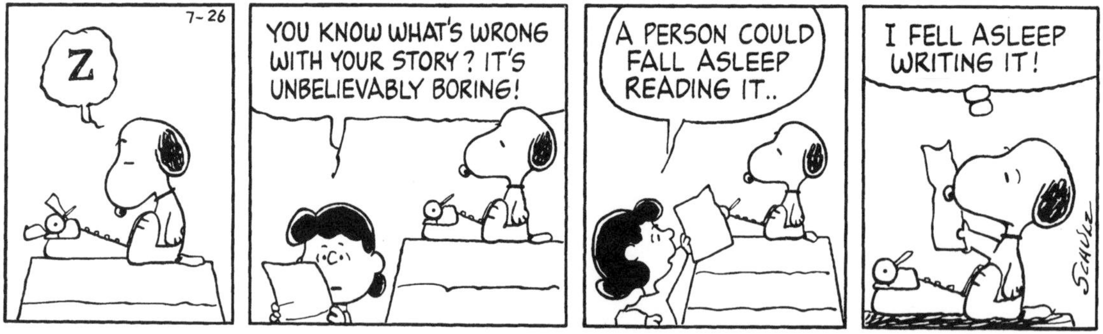
Z
YOU KNOW WHAT'S WRONG WITH YOUR STORY? IT'S UNBELIEVABLY BORING!
A PERSON COULD FALL ASLEEP READING IT..
I FELL ASLEEP WRITING IT!

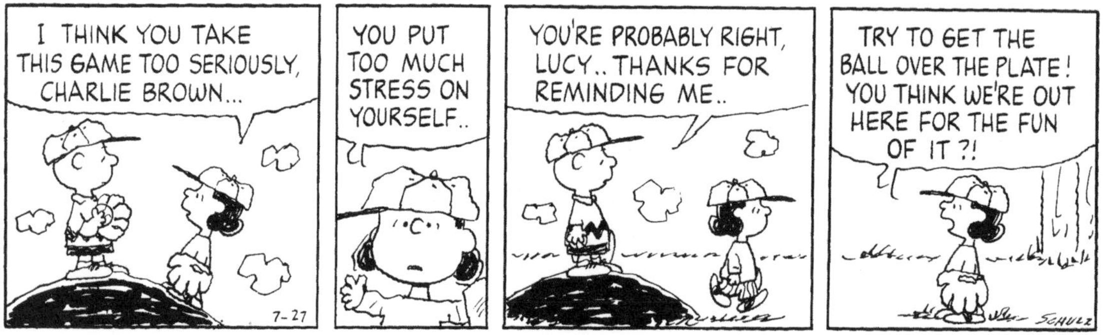
I THINK YOU TAKE THIS GAME TOO SERIOUSLY, CHARLIE BROWN...
YOU PUT TOO MUCH STRESS ON YOURSELF..
YOU'RE PROBABLY RIGHT, LUCY.. THANKS FOR REMINDING ME..
TRY TO GET THE BALL OVER THE PLATE! YOU THINK WE'RE OUT HERE FOR THE FUN OF IT?!

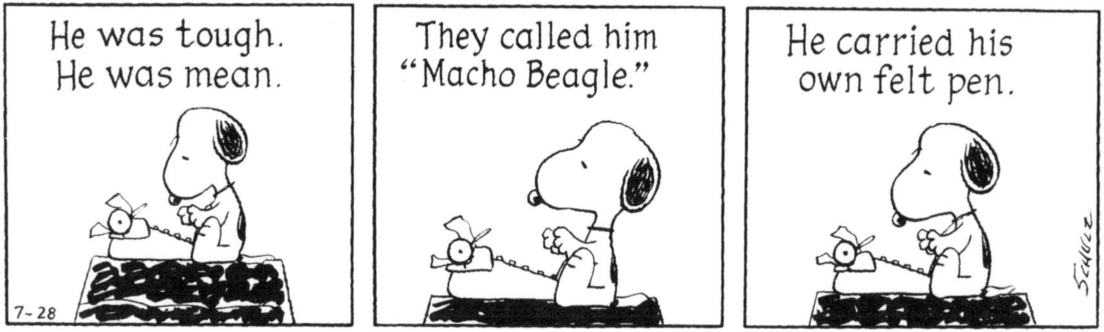
He was tough. He was mean.
They called him "Macho Beagle."
He carried his own felt pen.

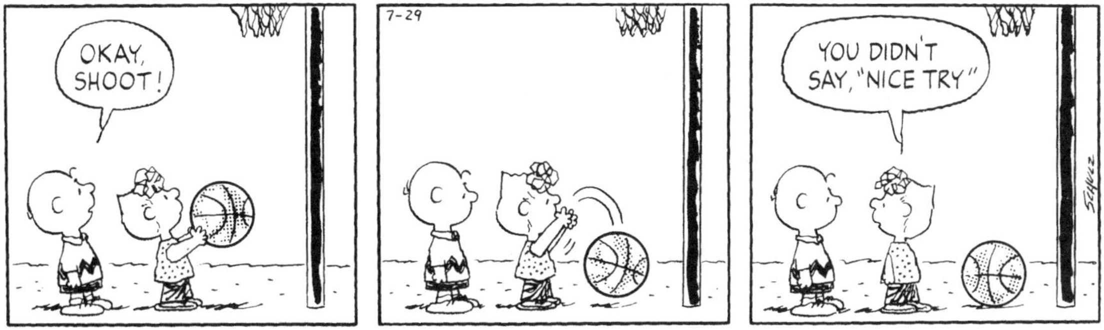
OKAY, SHOOT!
7-29
YOU DIDN'T SAY, "NICE TRY"
SCHULZ

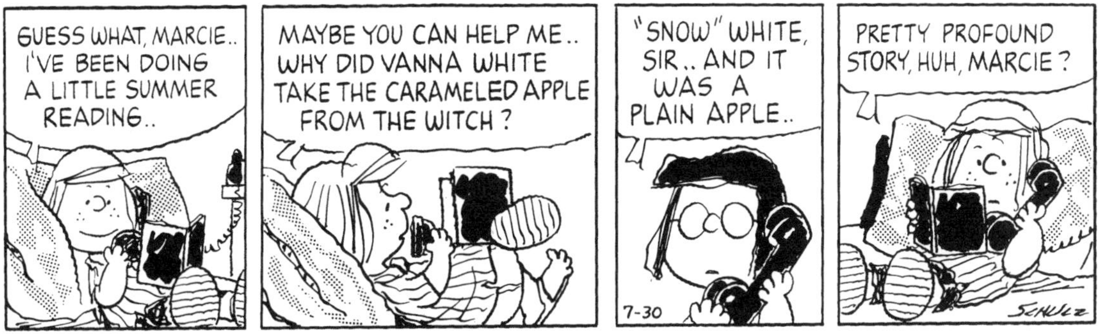
GUESS WHAT, MARCIE.. I'VE BEEN DOING A LITTLE SUMMER READING..
MAYBE YOU CAN HELP ME.. WHY DID VANNA WHITE TAKE THE CARAMELED APPLE FROM THE WITCH?
"SNOW" WHITE, SIR.. AND IT WAS A PLAIN APPLE..
7-30
PRETTY PROFOUND STORY, HUH, MARCIE?
SCHULZ

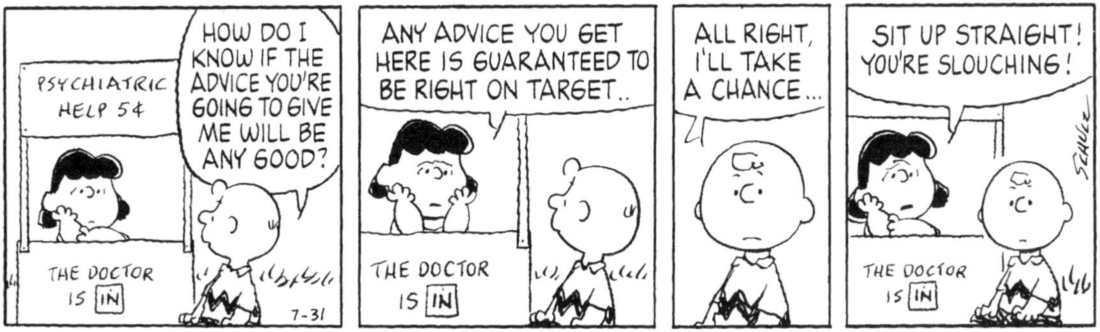
PSYCHIATRIC HELP 5¢
HOW DO I KNOW IF THE ADVICE YOU'RE GOING TO GIVE ME WILL BE ANY GOOD?
THE DOCTOR IS IN
7-31
ANY ADVICE YOU GET HERE IS GUARANTEED TO BE RIGHT ON TARGET..
THE DOCTOR IS IN
ALL RIGHT, I'LL TAKE A CHANCE...
SIT UP STRAIGHT! YOU'RE SLOUCHING!
SCHULZ
THE DOCTOR IS IN

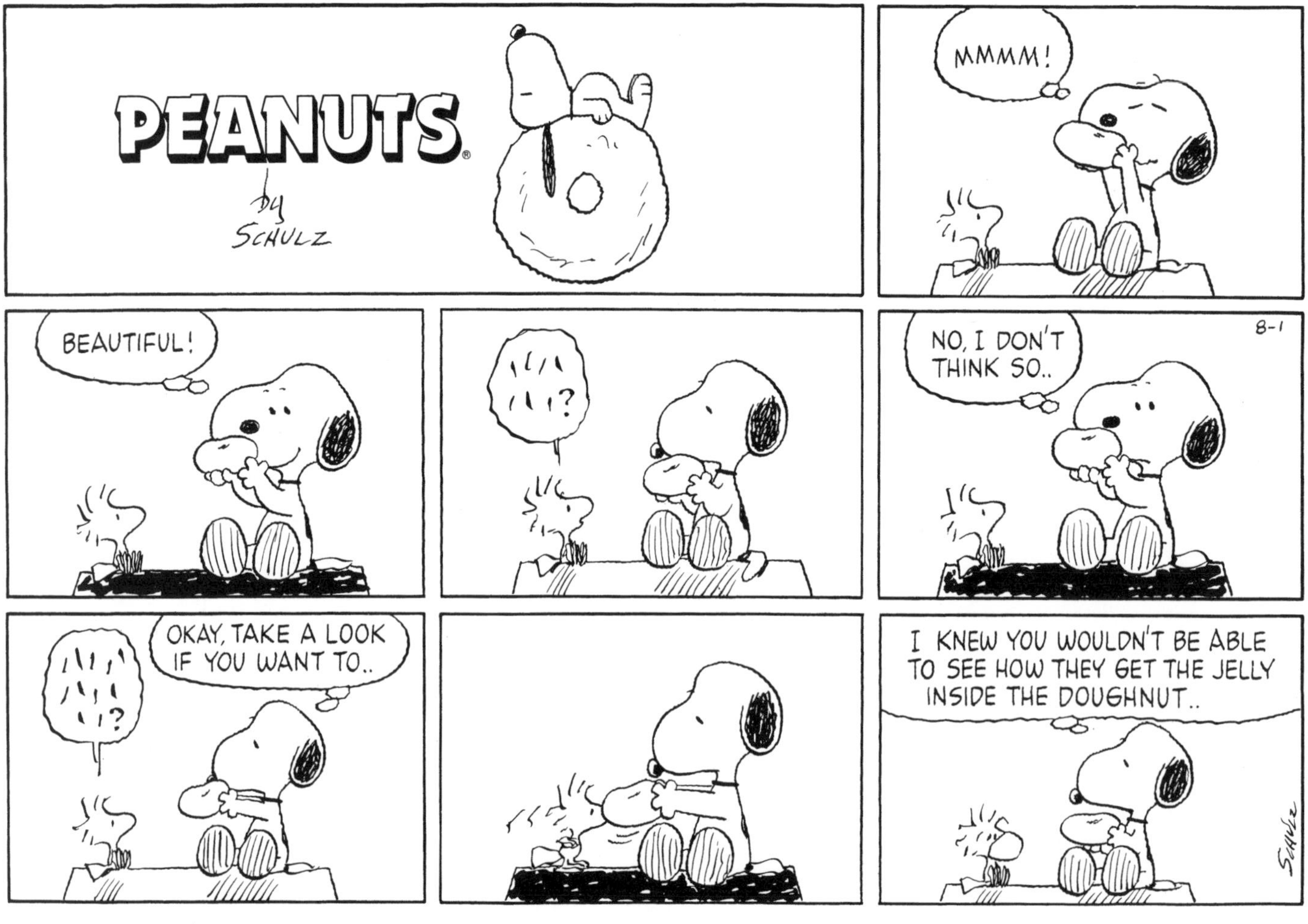
PEANUTS
by SCHULZ
MMMM!
BEAUTIFUL!
?
8-1
NO, I DON'T THINK SO..
?
OKAY, TAKE A LOOK IF YOU WANT TO..
I KNEW YOU WOULDN'T BE ABLE TO SEE HOW THEY GET THE JELLY INSIDE THE DOUGHNUT..
SCHULZ

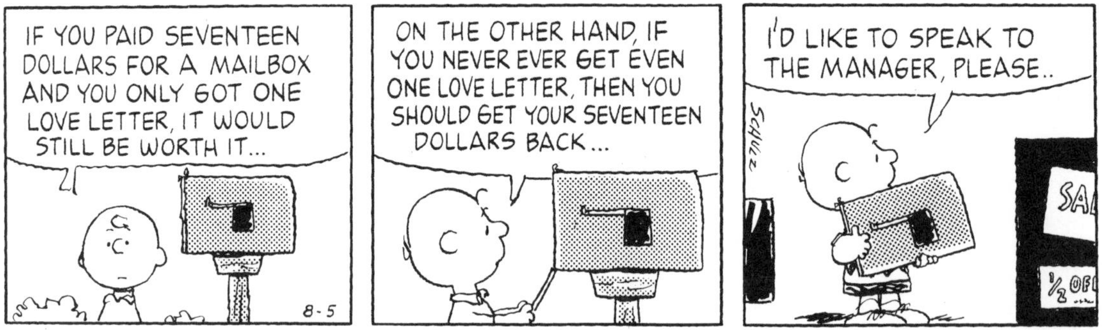
IF YOU PAID SEVENTEEN DOLLARS FOR A MAILBOX AND YOU ONLY GOT ONE LOVE LETTER, IT WOULD STILL BE WORTH IT...
ON THE OTHER HAND, IF YOU NEVER EVER GET EVEN ONE LOVE LETTER, THEN YOU SHOULD GET YOUR SEVENTEEN DOLLARS BACK...
I'D LIKE TO SPEAK TO THE MANAGER, PLEASE..
8-5
SCHULZ

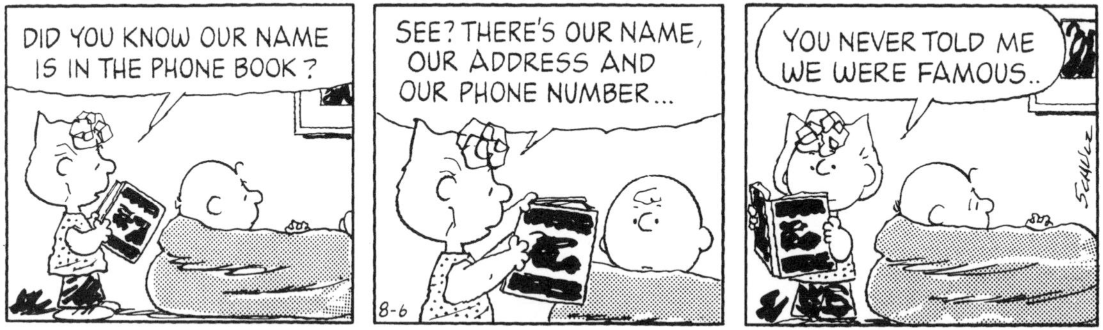
DID YOU KNOW OUR NAME IS IN THE PHONE BOOK?
SEE? THERE'S OUR NAME, OUR ADDRESS AND OUR PHONE NUMBER...
YOU NEVER TOLD ME WE WERE FAMOUS..
8-6
SCHULZ

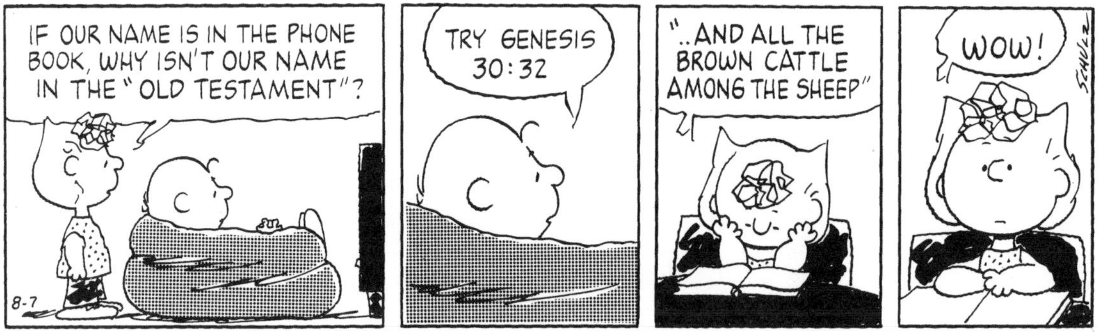
IF OUR NAME IS IN THE PHONE BOOK, WHY ISN'T OUR NAME IN THE "OLD TESTAMENT"?
TRY GENESIS 30:32
"..AND ALL THE BROWN CATTLE AMONG THE SHEEP"
WOW!
8-7
SCHULZ

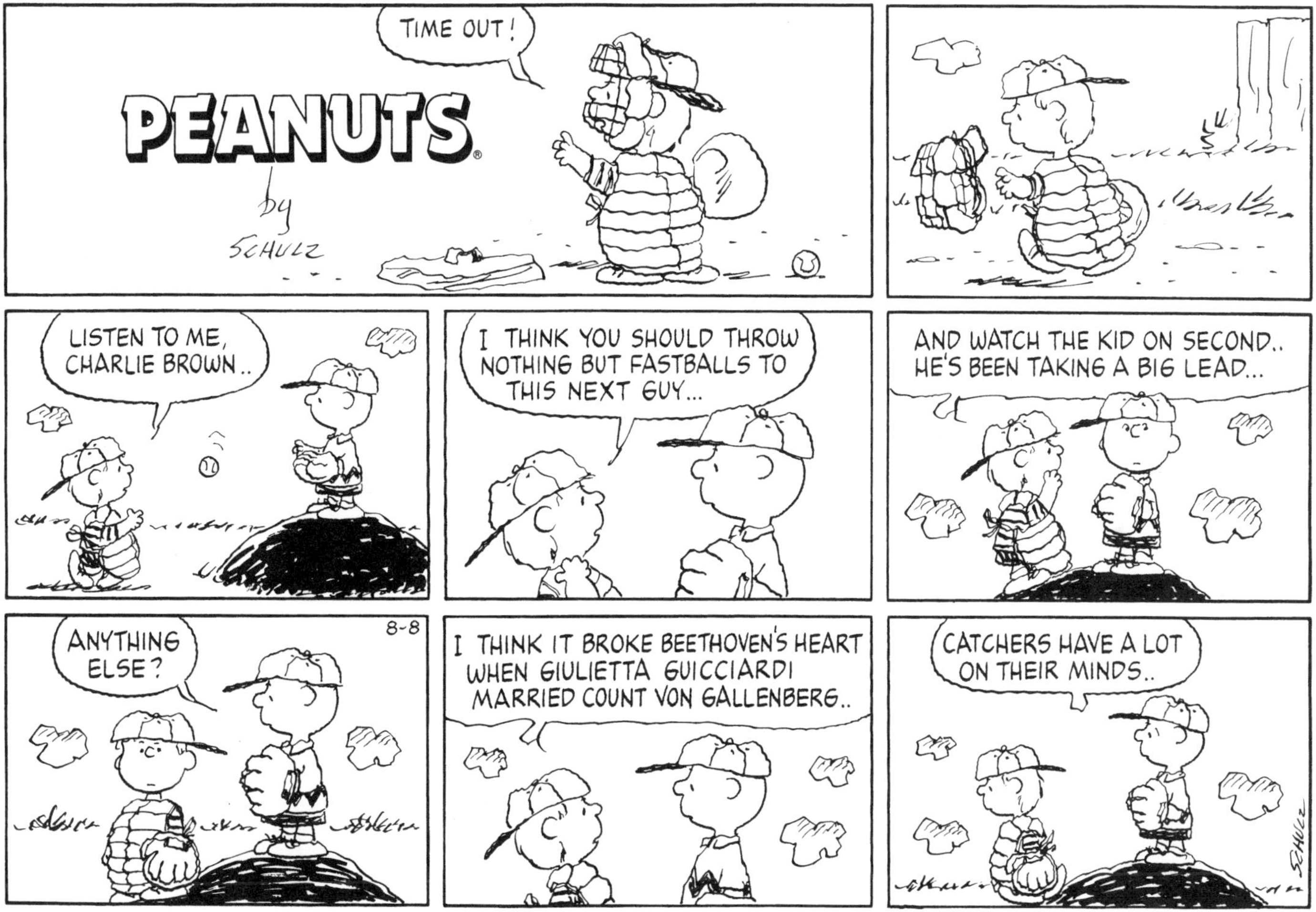
TIME OUT!
PEANUTS®
by SCHULZ
LISTEN TO ME, CHARLIE BROWN..
I THINK YOU SHOULD THROW NOTHING BUT FASTBALLS TO THIS NEXT GUY...
AND WATCH THE KID ON SECOND.. HE'S BEEN TAKING A BIG LEAD...
8-8
ANYTHING ELSE?
I THINK IT BROKE BEETHOVEN'S HEART WHEN GIULIETTA GUICCIARDI MARRIED COUNT VON GALLENBERG..
CATCHERS HAVE A LOT ON THEIR MINDS..
SCHULZ

YOU ARE MY YOUNGER BROTHER AND I AM YOUR OLDER SISTER, AND THAT'S THE WAY IT'S GOING TO BE ALL THE DAYS OF YOUR LIFE..

..AND DON'T TELL ME YOU NEVER THINK ABOUT IT..

8-9

THE SUN IS IN YOUR EYES?

WELL, PUT ON SOME SUNGLASSES, OR WEAR A HAT OR SIT UNDER AN UMBRELLA..

..OR DO ALL THREE..

8-10

YES, MA'AM..DO YOU HAVE ANY BOOKS HERE IN YOUR LIBRARY WHERE A DOG TAKES OVER THE WHOLE WORLD?

8-11

WELL, I THINK NOW YOU'VE GOT ONE..

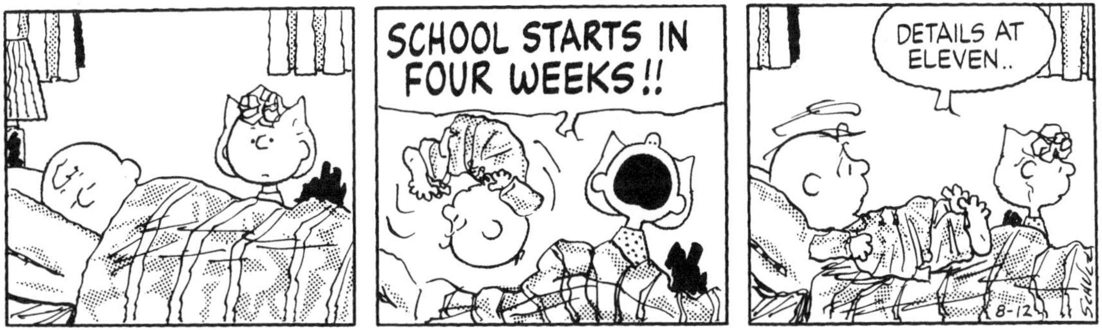

SCHOOL STARTS IN FOUR WEEKS!!
DETAILS AT ELEVEN..
8-12
SCHULZ

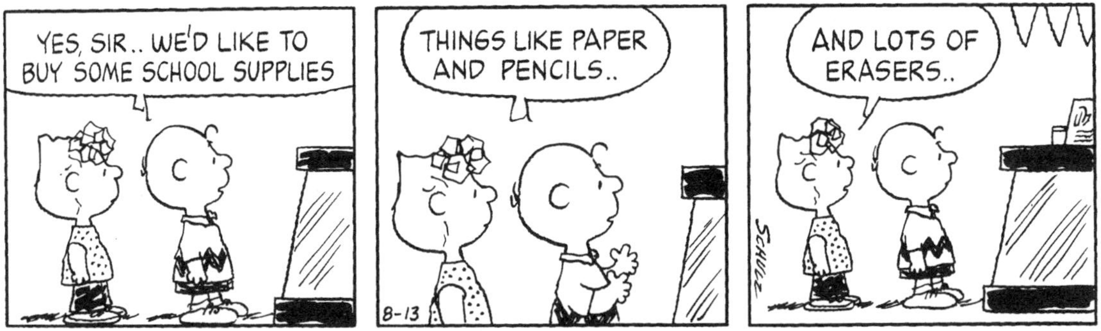

YES, SIR.. WE'D LIKE TO BUY SOME SCHOOL SUPPLIES
THINGS LIKE PAPER AND PENCILS..
8-13
AND LOTS OF ERASERS..
SCHULZ

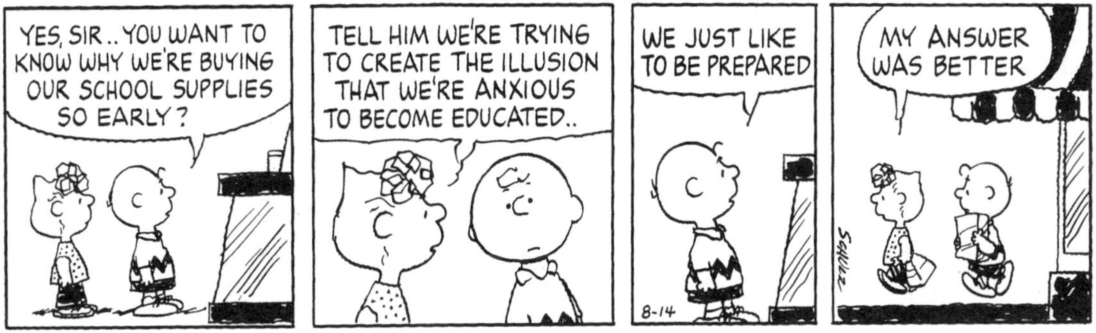

YES, SIR.. YOU WANT TO KNOW WHY WE'RE BUYING OUR SCHOOL SUPPLIES SO EARLY?
TELL HIM WE'RE TRYING TO CREATE THE ILLUSION THAT WE'RE ANXIOUS TO BECOME EDUCATED..
WE JUST LIKE TO BE PREPARED
8-14
MY ANSWER WAS BETTER
SCHULZ

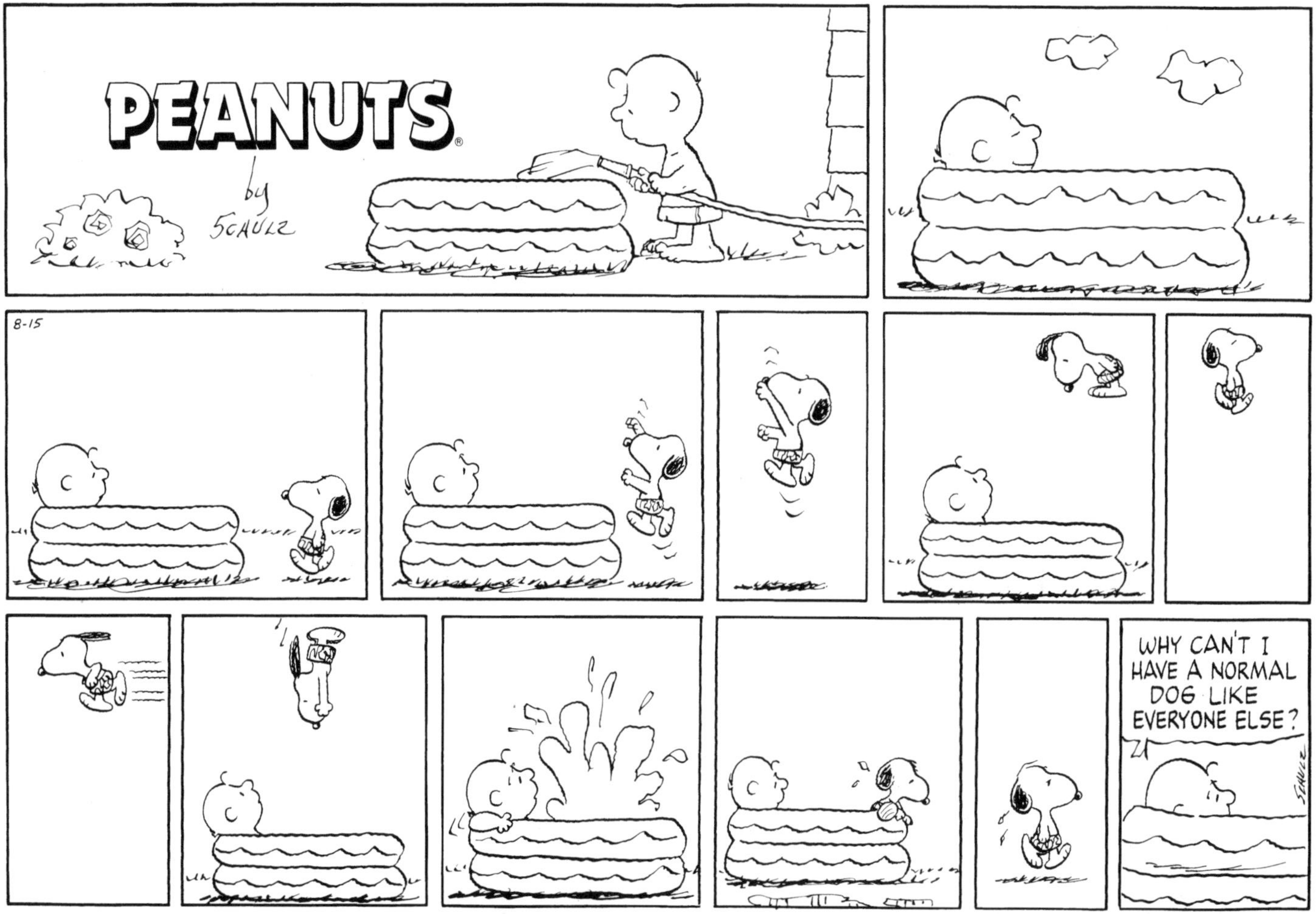
PEANUTS®
by SCHULZ
8-15
WHY CAN'T I HAVE A NORMAL DOG LIKE EVERYONE ELSE?
SCHULZ

NOW, GET OUT THERE IN RIGHT FIELD, AND CONCENTRATE!

THINK ABOUT WHAT YOU'RE DOING..

8-16

KEEP YOUR MIND ON THE GAME..

KEEP YOUR HEAD OUT OF THE CLOUDS..

ROYANNE! WHAT A SURPRISE!

I NEED TO TALK TO YOU, CHARLES..DO YOU HAVE TIME TO GO GET A CHOCOLATE SUNDAE?

8-17

OKAY, ROYANNE, WHAT'S UP?

DO YOU LIKE ME, CHARLES?

OH, GOOD GRIEF!

I HAVE TO TELL YOU SOMETHING, CHARLES.. BUT FIRST, I WANT TO KNOW IF YOU LIKE ME...

WELL, SURE, I LIKE YOU, ROYANNE.. BUT I DON'T REALLY KNOW YOU.. I MEAN, OUR TEAM PLAYED YOUR TEAM A COUPLE OF TIMES..

AND, OF COURSE, I HIT THOSE TWO HOME RUNS, AND..

8-18

THAT'S WHAT I HAVE TO CONFESS, CHARLES..I COULD HAVE STRUCK YOU OUT IF I HAD WANTED TO!

PEANUTS by SCHULZ

I THINK THAT'S HER HOUSE THERE..

HI, CHUCK! THANKS FOR BRINGING YOUR DOG OVER..

MY DAD AND I ARE GOING TO BE GONE OVERNIGHT SO WE NEED A WATCHDOG TO GUARD THE HOUSE..

NOW, AROUND HERE IS THE BACKDOOR...

AND THIS IS THE ENTRANCE TO THE GARAGE..IF ANYONE COMES AROUND, HE SHOULD BARK LIKE MAD!

8-22

IT'LL PROBABLY BE BEST IF HE JUST STANDS GUARD HERE AT THE FRONT OF THE HOUSE, AND...

Z

Z

YOU SURE KNOW HOW TO GET OUT OF THINGS, DON'T YOU?

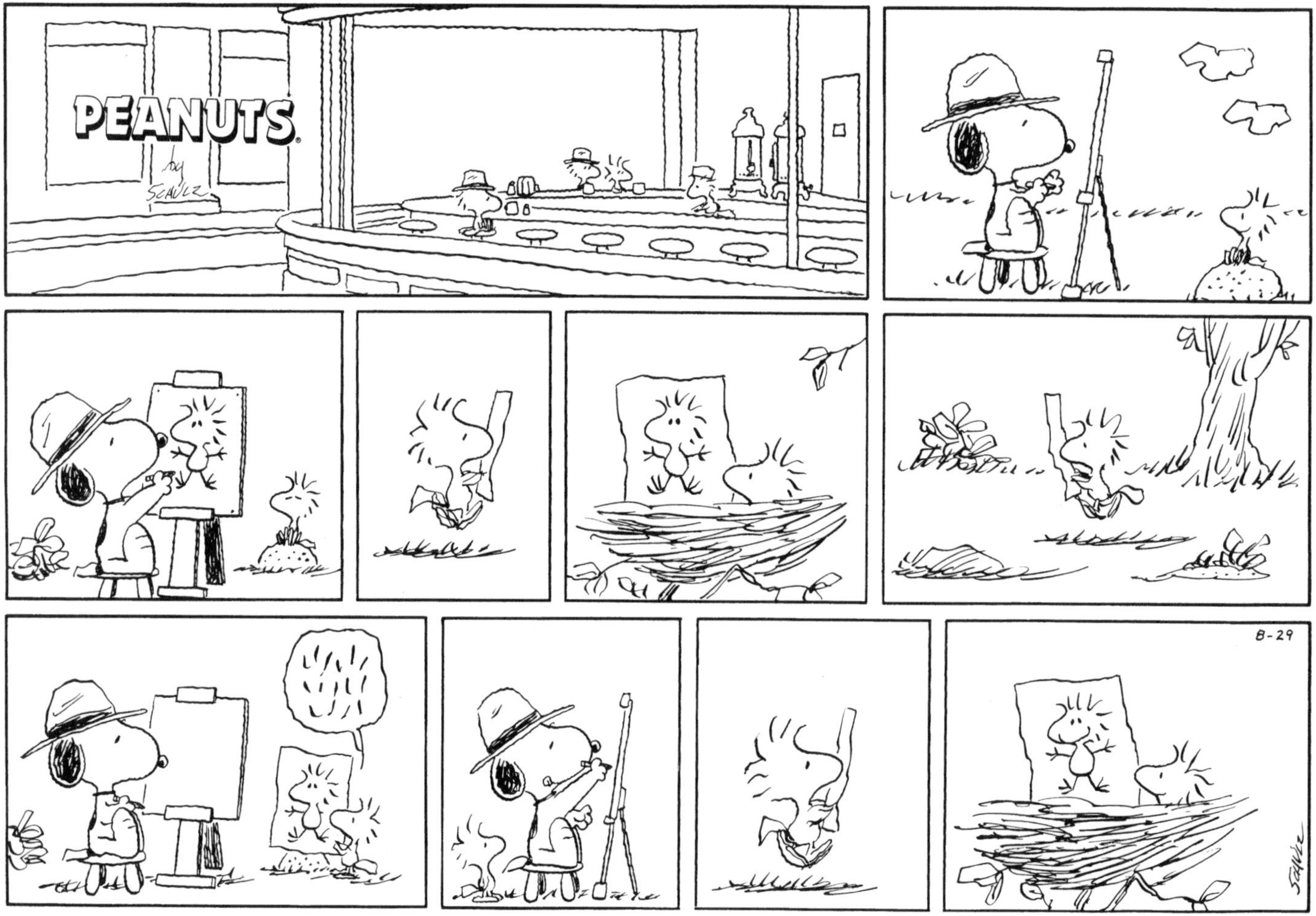
PEANUTS
by SCHULZ
8-29
SCHULZ

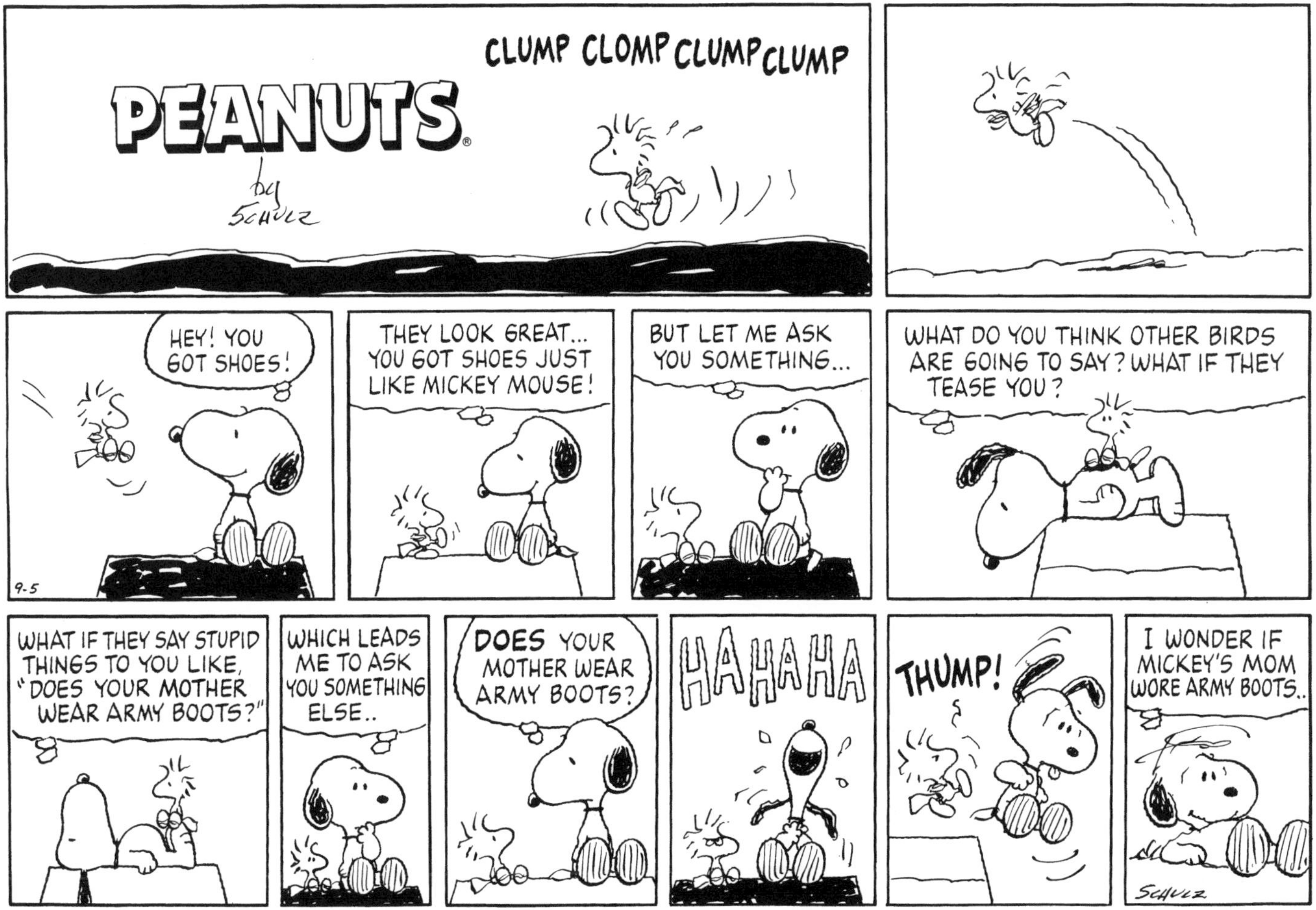

PEANUTS
by SCHULZ
CLUMP CLOMP CLUMP CLUMP
HEY! YOU GOT SHOES!
9-5
THEY LOOK GREAT... YOU GOT SHOES JUST LIKE MICKEY MOUSE!
BUT LET ME ASK YOU SOMETHING...
WHAT DO YOU THINK OTHER BIRDS ARE GOING TO SAY? WHAT IF THEY TEASE YOU?
WHAT IF THEY SAY STUPID THINGS TO YOU LIKE, "DOES YOUR MOTHER WEAR ARMY BOOTS?"
WHICH LEADS ME TO ASK YOU SOMETHING ELSE..
DOES YOUR MOTHER WEAR ARMY BOOTS?
HAHAHA
THUMP!
I WONDER IF MICKEY'S MOM WORE ARMY BOOTS..
SCHULZ

SCHOOL STARTS TOMORROW!!

WOULD YOU RECOGNIZE THE PRINCIPAL IF YOU MET HIM ON THE STREET?! BE READY! BE READY!

AFTER I GRADUATE FROM SCHOOL, WILL I BE A BETTER PERSON?

PROBABLY.. A GOOD EDUCATION IS VERY IMPORTANT

THAT'S RIGHT.. LEARNING ALWAYS MAKES YOU A BETTER PERSON..

UNLESS YOU DON'T HAVE A DOG..

Z

YES, MA'AM.. I'M AWAKE!

DO I HAVE ANYTHING TO TELL THE CLASS? YES, MA'AM..

THERE'S A SPIDER ON THE CEILING..

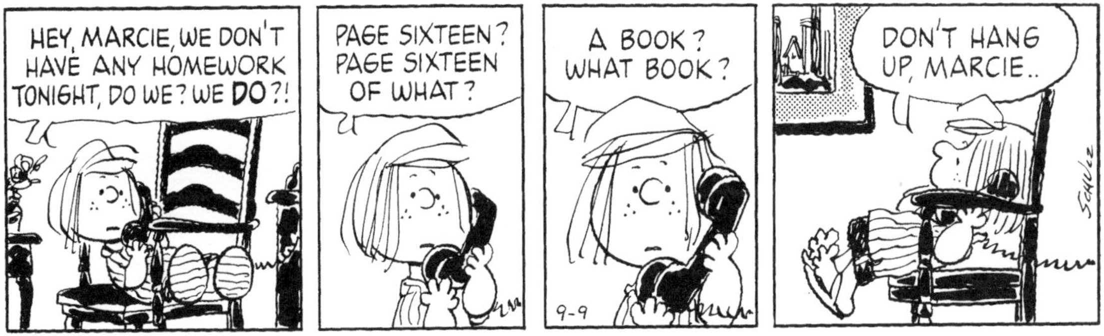
HEY, MARCIE, WE DON'T HAVE ANY HOMEWORK TONIGHT, DO WE? WE DO?!
PAGE SIXTEEN? PAGE SIXTEEN OF WHAT?
A BOOK? WHAT BOOK?
DON'T HANG UP, MARCIE..
9-9
SCHULZ

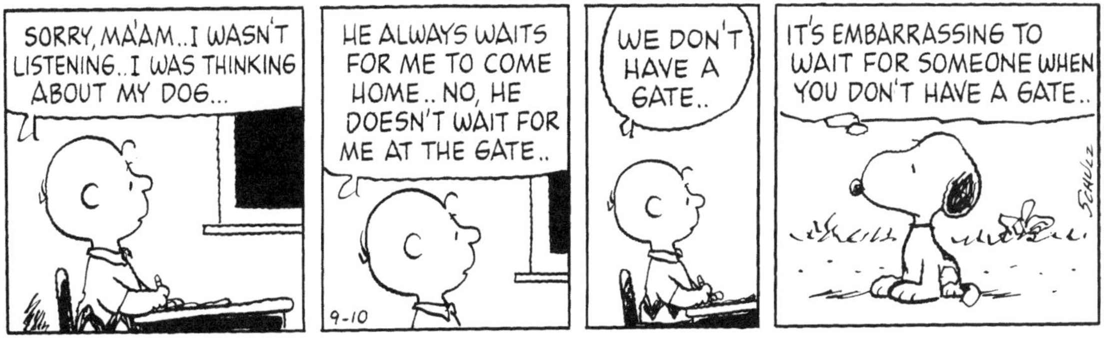
SORRY, MA'AM..I WASN'T LISTENING..I WAS THINKING ABOUT MY DOG...
HE ALWAYS WAITS FOR ME TO COME HOME.. NO, HE DOESN'T WAIT FOR ME AT THE GATE..
WE DON'T HAVE A GATE..
IT'S EMBARRASSING TO WAIT FOR SOMEONE WHEN YOU DON'T HAVE A GATE..
9-10
SCHULZ

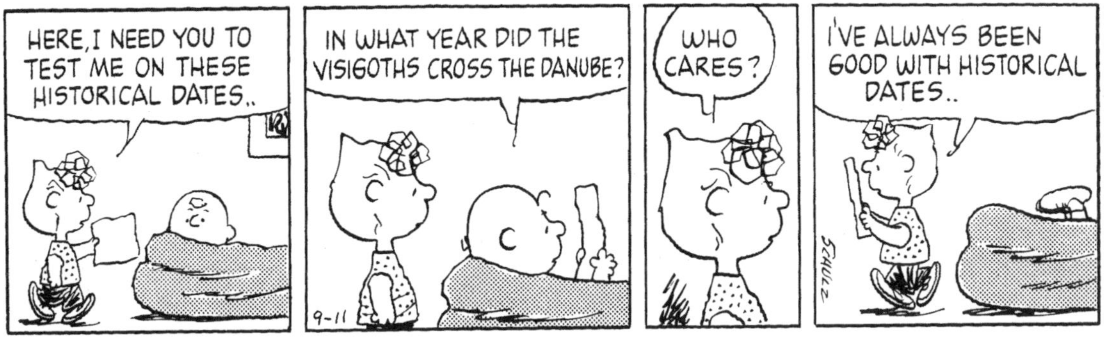
HERE, I NEED YOU TO TEST ME ON THESE HISTORICAL DATES..
IN WHAT YEAR DID THE VISIGOTHS CROSS THE DANUBE?
WHO CARES?
I'VE ALWAYS BEEN GOOD WITH HISTORICAL DATES..
9-11
SCHULZ

YOU'LL PRAY FOR ME? WHY? I'LL PRAY FOR MYSELF!

"CALL NOW FOR BEST SEATS!"... BEST SEATS FOR WHAT?

"STAY TUNED FOR THE WEATHER AND TRAFFIC REPORT!" WHAT DO THEY MEAN, STAY TUNED?

I WASN'T EVEN LISTENING! WHAT DO I NEED A TRAFFIC REPORT FOR? I DON'T HAVE A CAR!

TEN DOLLARS?! THEY WANT ME TO SEND TEN DOLLARS FOR A TAPE OF THEIR PROGRAM? I DIDN'T EVEN LIKE THEIR PROGRAM!

9-12

AND LOOK THERE! HE WANTS ME TO SEND HIM FIFTY DOLLARS SO HE WON'T GO OFF THE AIR! WHAT DO I CARE IF HE GOES OFF? ALL HE DOES IS TALK!

THERE! NOW YOU DON'T HAVE TO DO ANY OF THOSE THINGS..

CLICK!

WHEW! WHAT A RELIEF! THANK YOU, BIG BROTHER..

YOU SHOULD HAVE BEEN AN ATTORNEY

BING BONG ♪♫

9-13

FOOTBALL TIME AGAIN, CHUCK!

GO STRAIGHT DOWN THE FIELD, MARCIE, CUT LEFT, AND I'LL HIT YOU..

9-14

HIT ME WITH WHAT?

I'LL RUN DOWN THE FIELD, MARCIE, AND YOU THROW ME THE BALL..

9-15

?

MARCIE! WHERE DID YOU GO?!

AFTER YOU RAN DOWN THE FIELD, I SUDDENLY FELT VERY LONELY..

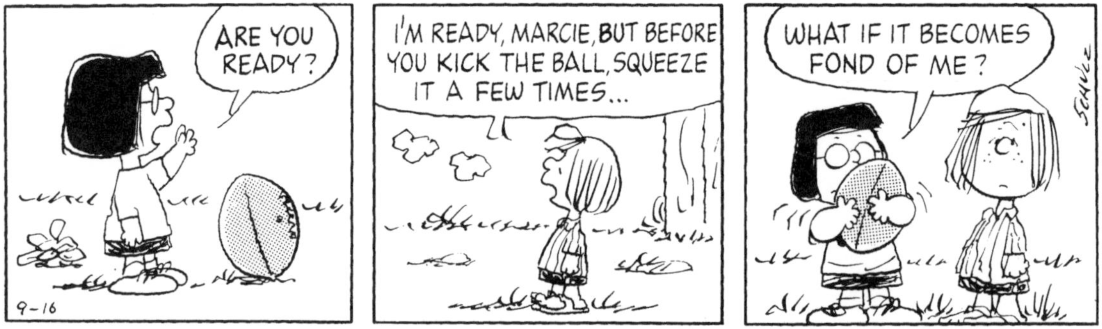
ARE YOU READY?
I'M READY, MARCIE, BUT BEFORE YOU KICK THE BALL, SQUEEZE IT A FEW TIMES...
WHAT IF IT BECOMES FOND OF ME?

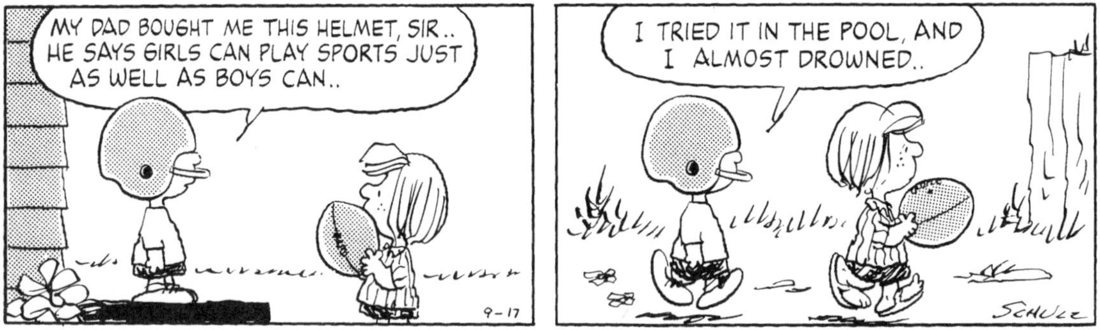
MY DAD BOUGHT ME THIS HELMET, SIR.. HE SAYS GIRLS CAN PLAY SPORTS JUST AS WELL AS BOYS CAN..
I TRIED IT IN THE POOL, AND I ALMOST DROWNED..

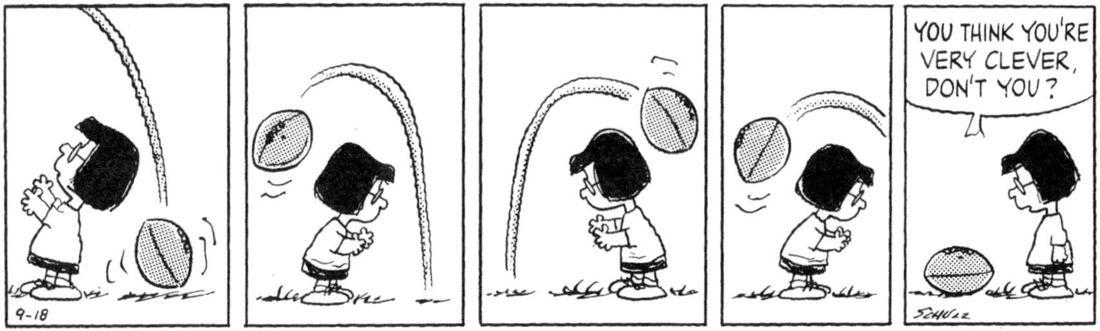
YOU THINK YOU'RE VERY CLEVER, DON'T YOU?

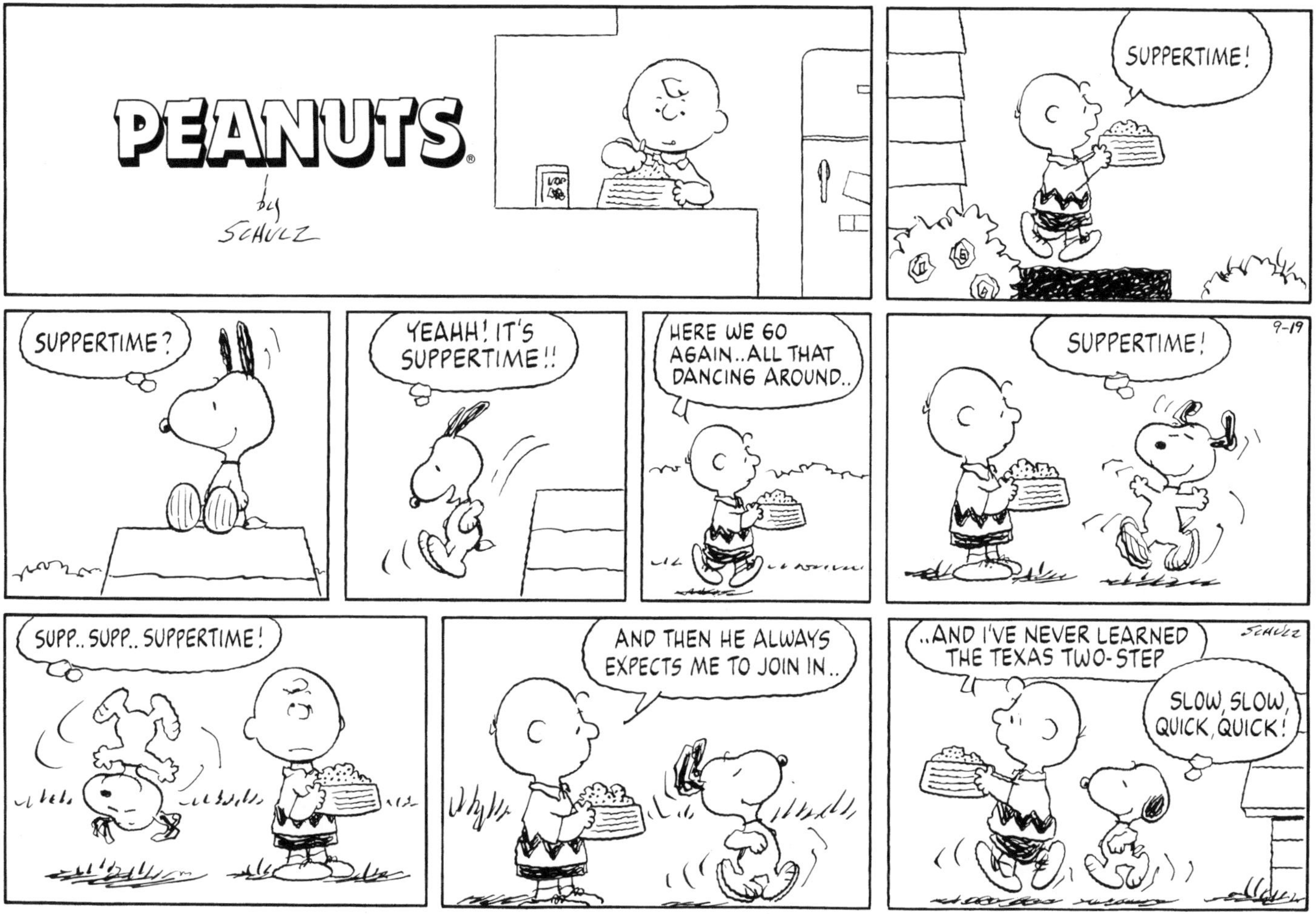
PEANUTS®
by SCHULZ
SUPPERTIME!
SUPPERTIME?
YEAHH! IT'S SUPPERTIME!!
HERE WE GO AGAIN..ALL THAT DANCING AROUND..
9-19
SUPPERTIME!
SUPP.. SUPP.. SUPPERTIME!
AND THEN HE ALWAYS EXPECTS ME TO JOIN IN..
SCHULZ
..AND I'VE NEVER LEARNED THE TEXAS TWO-STEP
SLOW, SLOW, QUICK, QUICK!

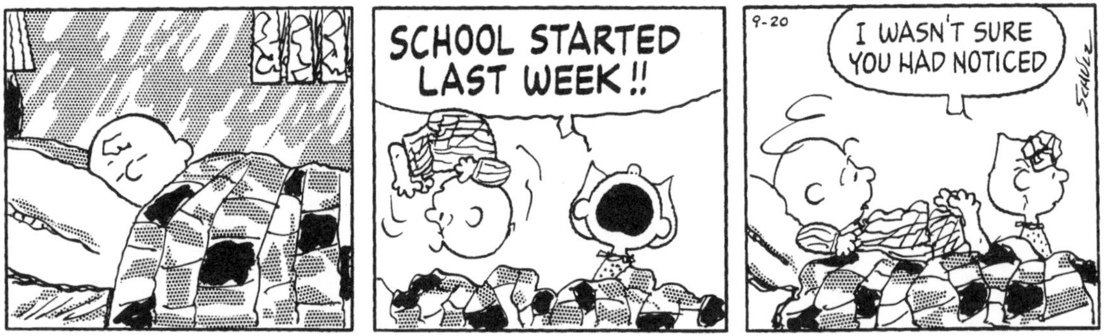
SCHOOL STARTED LAST WEEK !!
I WASN'T SURE YOU HAD NOTICED

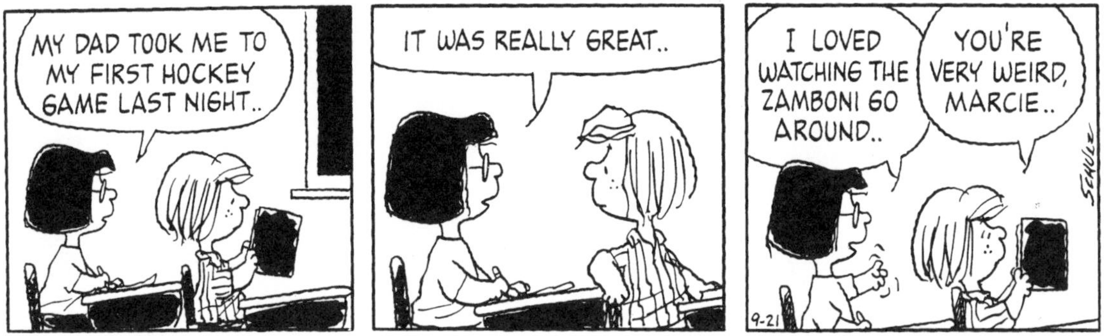
MY DAD TOOK ME TO MY FIRST HOCKEY GAME LAST NIGHT..
IT WAS REALLY GREAT..
I LOVED WATCHING THE ZAMBONI GO AROUND..
YOU'RE VERY WEIRD, MARCIE..

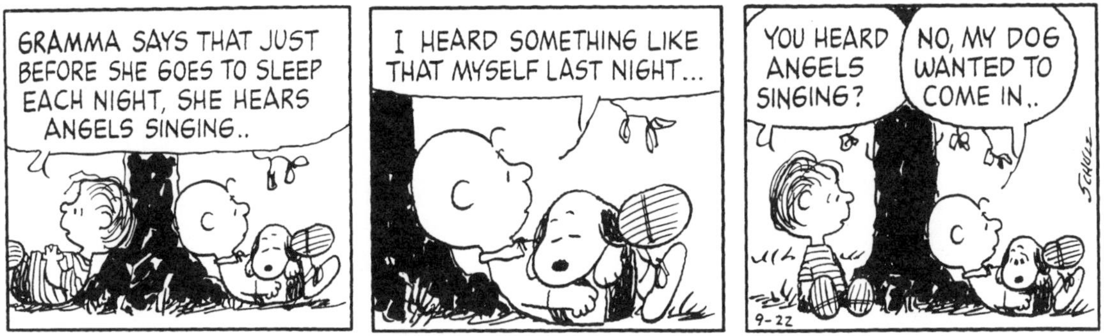
GRAMMA SAYS THAT JUST BEFORE SHE GOES TO SLEEP EACH NIGHT, SHE HEARS ANGELS SINGING..
I HEARD SOMETHING LIKE THAT MYSELF LAST NIGHT...
YOU HEARD ANGELS SINGING?
NO, MY DOG WANTED TO COME IN..

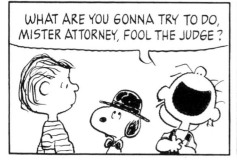

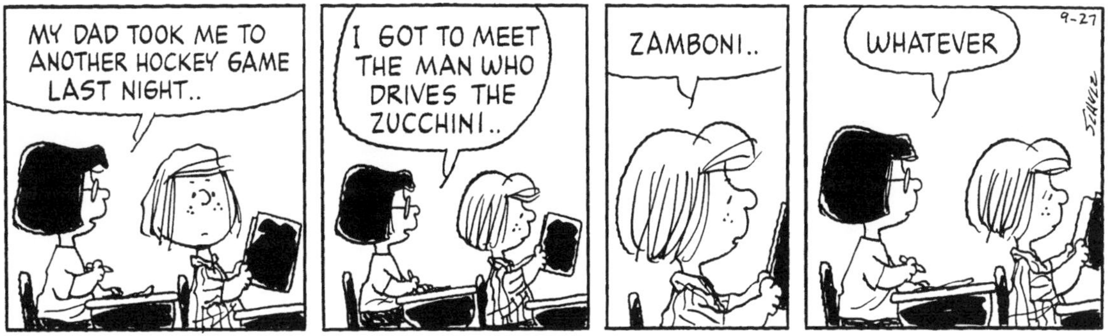
9-27
MY DAD TOOK ME TO ANOTHER HOCKEY GAME LAST NIGHT..
I GOT TO MEET THE MAN WHO DRIVES THE ZUCCHINI..
ZAMBONI..
WHATEVER
SCHULZ

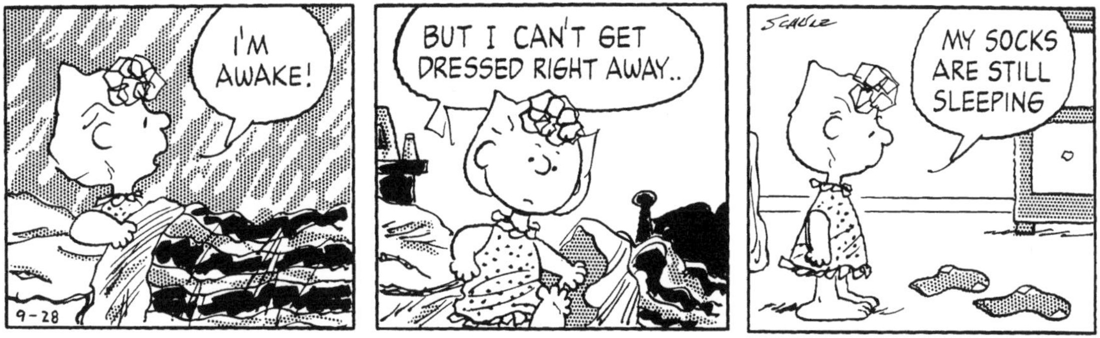
I'M AWAKE!
9-28
BUT I CAN'T GET DRESSED RIGHT AWAY..
SCHULZ
MY SOCKS ARE STILL SLEEPING

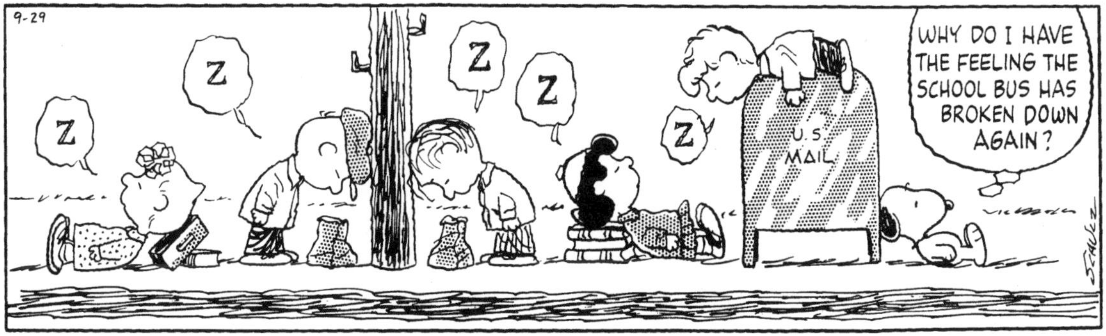
9-29
Z
Z
Z
Z
Z
U.S. MAIL
WHY DO I HAVE THE FEELING THE SCHOOL BUS HAS BROKEN DOWN AGAIN?
SCHULZ

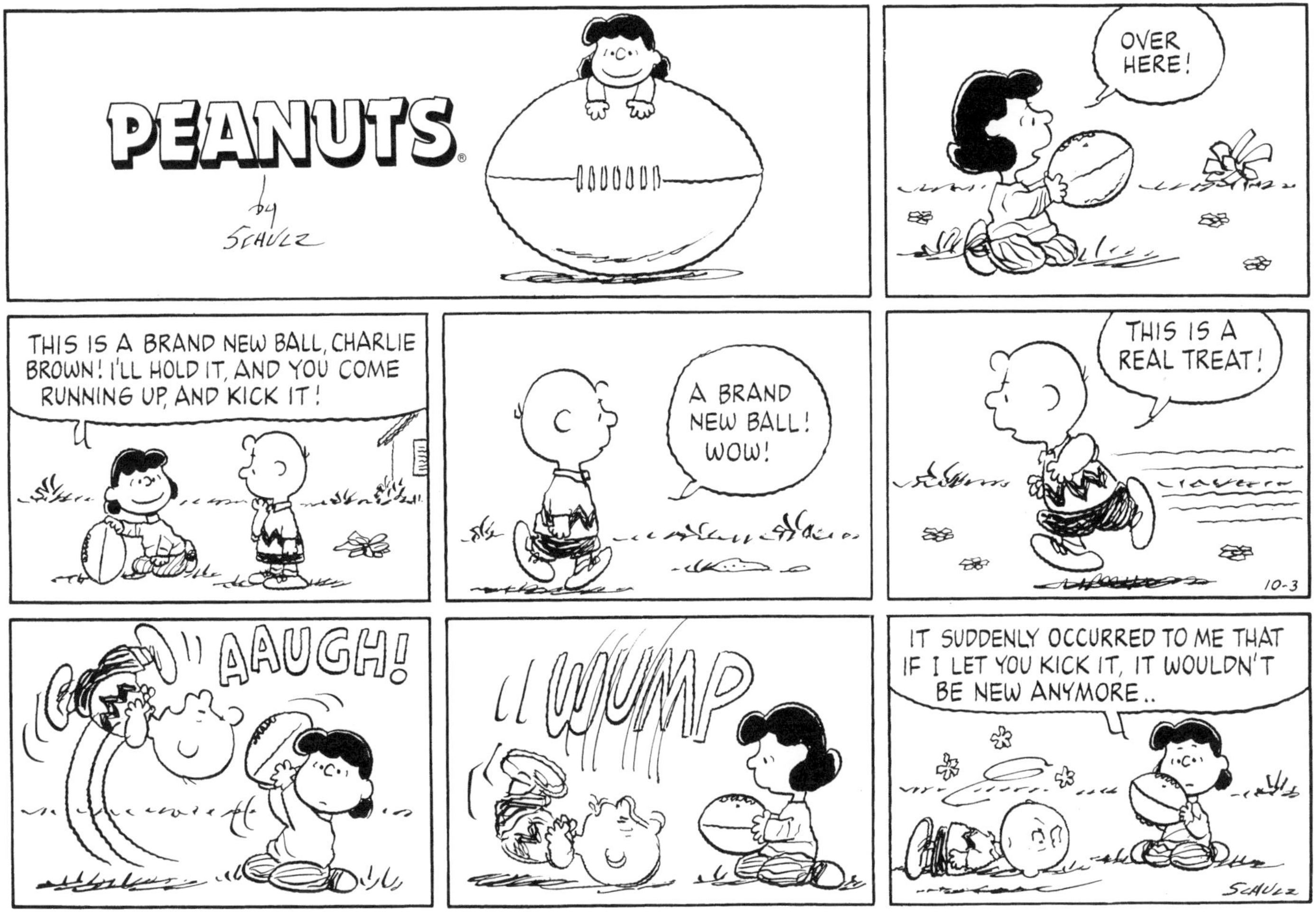
PEANUTS
by SCHULZ
OVER HERE!
THIS IS A BRAND NEW BALL, CHARLIE BROWN! I'LL HOLD IT, AND YOU COME RUNNING UP, AND KICK IT!
A BRAND NEW BALL! WOW!
THIS IS A REAL TREAT!
10-3
AAUGH!
WUMP
IT SUDDENLY OCCURRED TO ME THAT IF I LET YOU KICK IT, IT WOULDN'T BE NEW ANYMORE..
SCHULZ

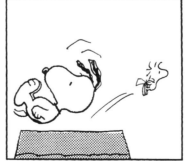

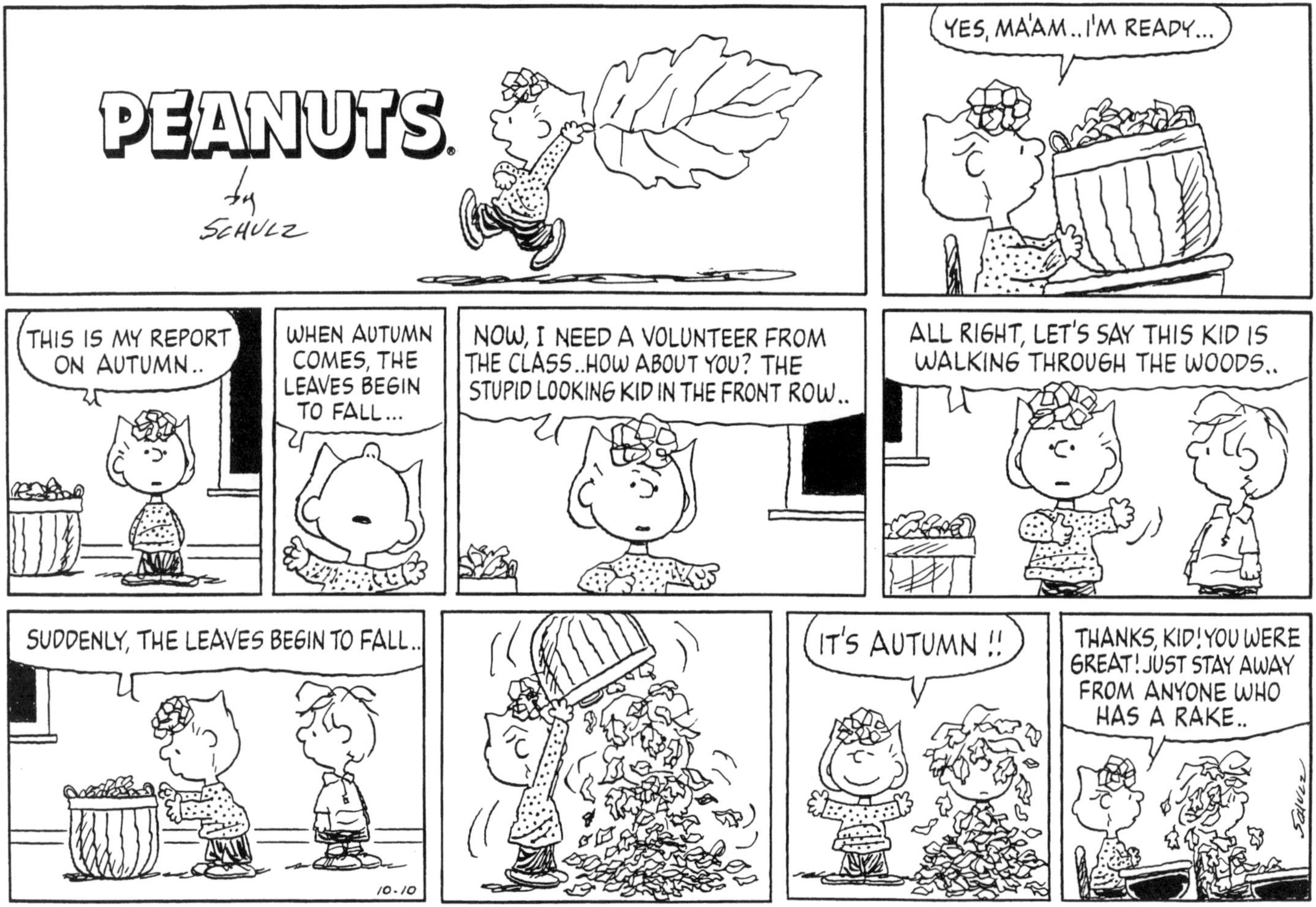

PEANUTS
by SCHULZ
YES, MA'AM..I'M READY...
THIS IS MY REPORT ON AUTUMN..
WHEN AUTUMN COMES, THE LEAVES BEGIN TO FALL...
NOW, I NEED A VOLUNTEER FROM THE CLASS..HOW ABOUT YOU? THE STUPID LOOKING KID IN THE FRONT ROW..
ALL RIGHT, LET'S SAY THIS KID IS WALKING THROUGH THE WOODS..
SUDDENLY, THE LEAVES BEGIN TO FALL..
10-10
IT'S AUTUMN !!
THANKS, KID! YOU WERE GREAT! JUST STAY AWAY FROM ANYONE WHO HAS A RAKE..
SCHULZ

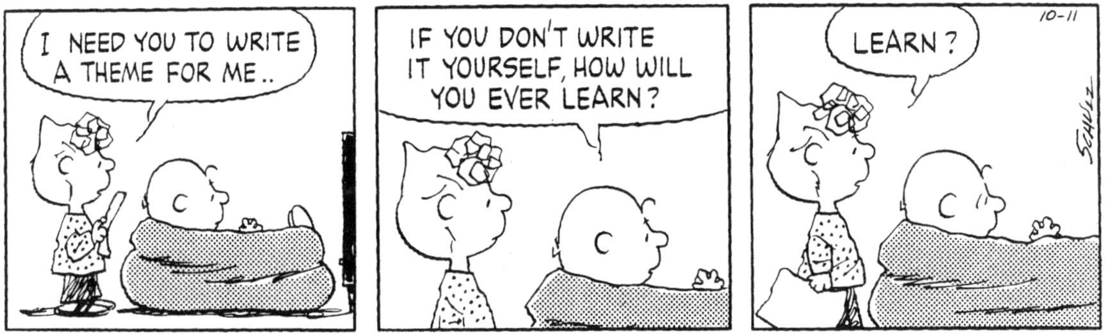
I NEED YOU TO WRITE A THEME FOR ME..
IF YOU DON'T WRITE IT YOURSELF, HOW WILL YOU EVER LEARN?
10-11
LEARN?
SCHULZ

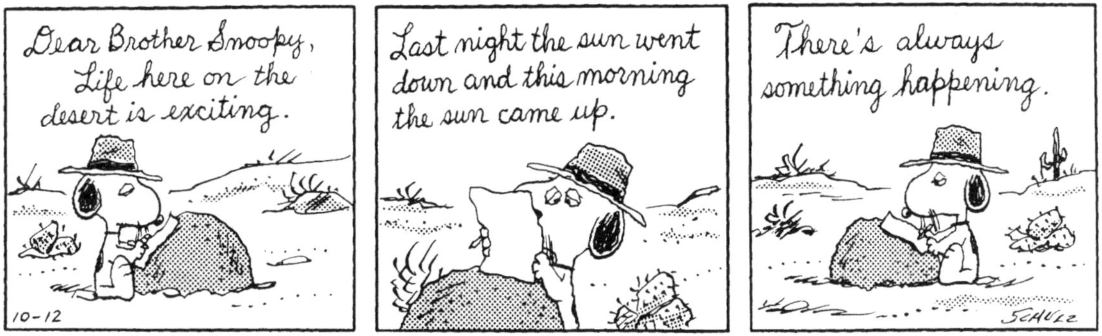
Dear Brother Snoopy,
Life here on the desert is exciting.
10-12
Last night the sun went down and this morning the sun came up.
There's always something happening.
SCHULZ

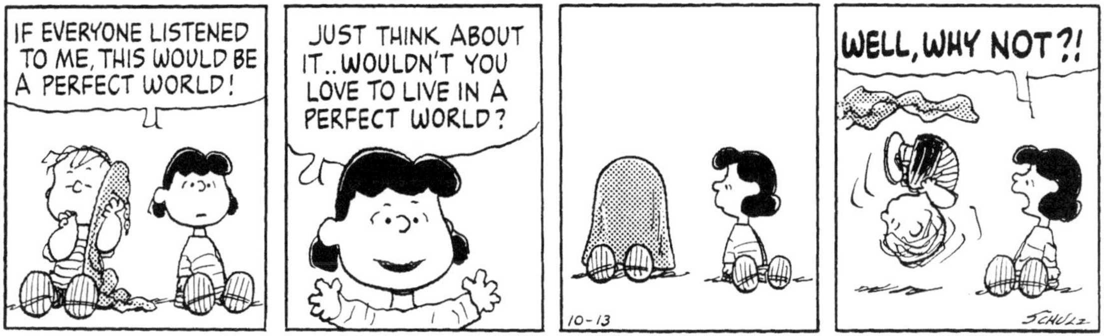
IF EVERYONE LISTENED TO ME, THIS WOULD BE A PERFECT WORLD!
JUST THINK ABOUT IT.. WOULDN'T YOU LOVE TO LIVE IN A PERFECT WORLD?
10-13
WELL, WHY NOT?!
SCHULZ

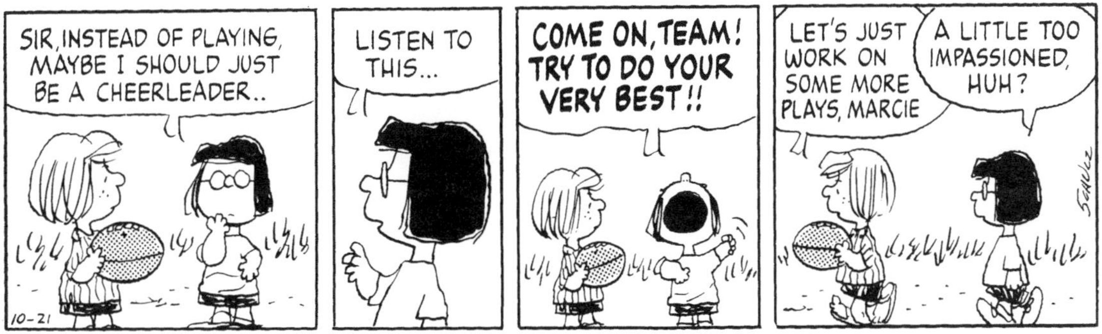
SIR, INSTEAD OF PLAYING, MAYBE I SHOULD JUST BE A CHEERLEADER..
LISTEN TO THIS...
COME ON, TEAM! TRY TO DO YOUR VERY BEST!!
LET'S JUST WORK ON SOME MORE PLAYS, MARCIE
A LITTLE TOO IMPASSIONED, HUH?
SCHULZ
10-21

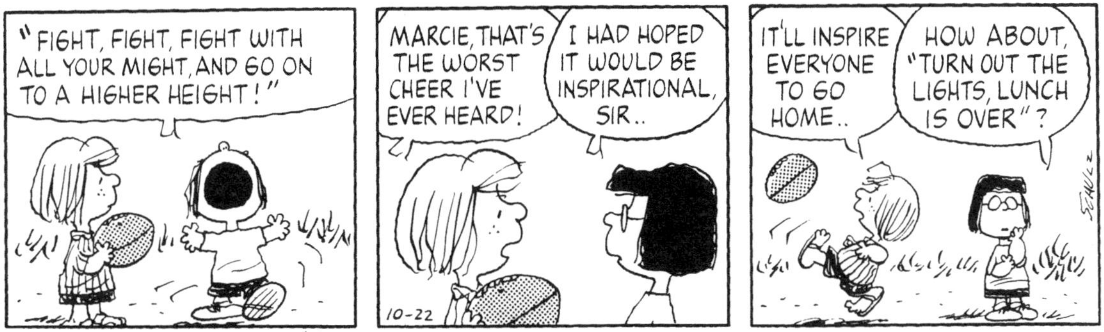
"FIGHT, FIGHT, FIGHT WITH ALL YOUR MIGHT, AND GO ON TO A HIGHER HEIGHT!"
MARCIE, THAT'S THE WORST CHEER I'VE EVER HEARD!
I HAD HOPED IT WOULD BE INSPIRATIONAL, SIR..
IT'LL INSPIRE EVERYONE TO GO HOME..
HOW ABOUT, "TURN OUT THE LIGHTS, LUNCH IS OVER"?
SCHULZ
10-22

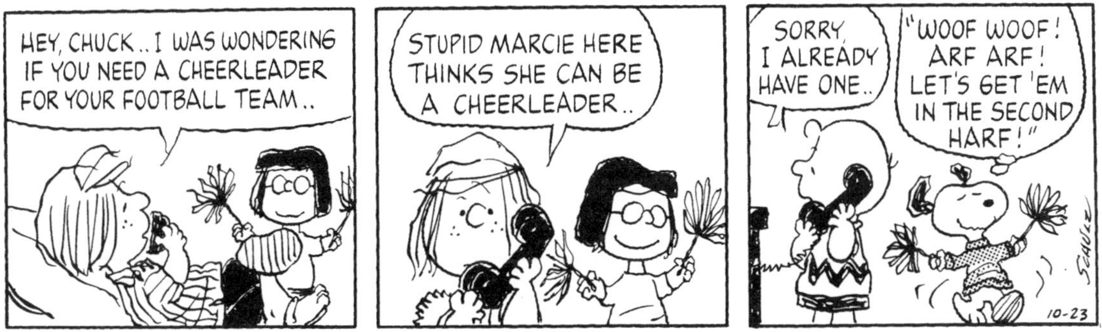
HEY, CHUCK.. I WAS WONDERING IF YOU NEED A CHEERLEADER FOR YOUR FOOTBALL TEAM..
STUPID MARCIE HERE THINKS SHE CAN BE A CHEERLEADER..
SORRY, I ALREADY HAVE ONE..
"WOOF WOOF! ARF ARF! LET'S GET 'EM IN THE SECOND HARF!"
SCHULZ
10-23

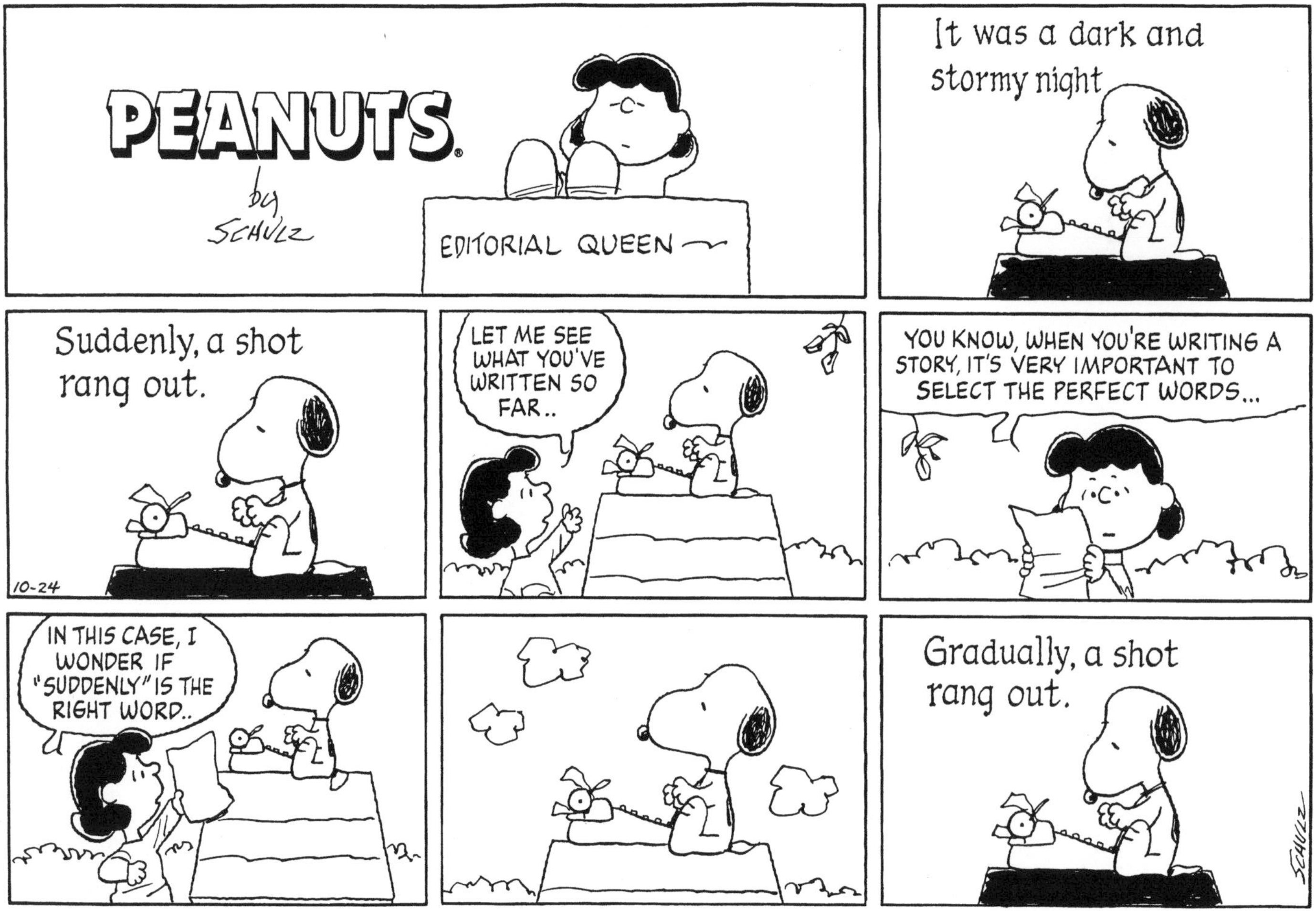
PEANUTS
by SCHULZ
EDITORIAL QUEEN
It was a dark and stormy night
Suddenly, a shot rang out.
10-24
LET ME SEE WHAT YOU'VE WRITTEN SO FAR..
YOU KNOW, WHEN YOU'RE WRITING A STORY, IT'S VERY IMPORTANT TO SELECT THE PERFECT WORDS...
IN THIS CASE, I WONDER IF "SUDDENLY" IS THE RIGHT WORD..
Gradually, a shot rang out.
SCHULZ

PEANUTS

by Schulz

NOW WHAT?

EXPLAIN TO ME WHAT I'M DOING OUT HERE..

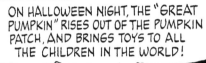

ON HALLOWEEN NIGHT, THE "GREAT PUMPKIN" RISES OUT OF THE PUMPKIN PATCH, AND BRINGS TOYS TO ALL THE CHILDREN IN THE WORLD!

JUST THINK..IF HE CHOOSES THIS PUMPKIN PATCH, YOU AND I WILL BE HERE TO SEE HIM!

10-31

LOOK! THERE HE IS! IT'S THE "GREAT PUMPKIN"!

THAT'S NOT THE "GREAT PUMPKIN"... THAT'S A DOG HOLDING A PUMPKIN ON A STICK!

EXPLAIN TO ME AGAIN WHAT I'M DOING OUT HERE..

TRICK OR TREAT!

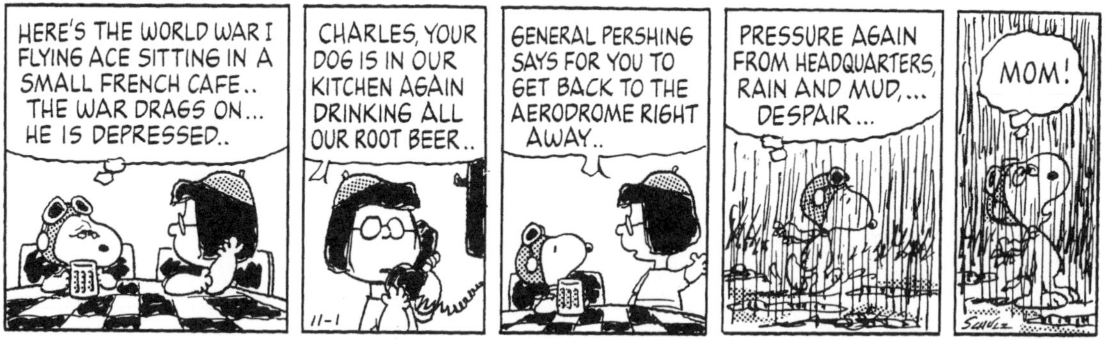
HERE'S THE WORLD WAR I FLYING ACE SITTING IN A SMALL FRENCH CAFE.. THE WAR DRAGS ON... HE IS DEPRESSED..
CHARLES, YOUR DOG IS IN OUR KITCHEN AGAIN DRINKING ALL OUR ROOT BEER..
11-1
GENERAL PERSHING SAYS FOR YOU TO GET BACK TO THE AERODROME RIGHT AWAY..
PRESSURE AGAIN FROM HEADQUARTERS, RAIN AND MUD,... DESPAIR...
MOM!
SCHULZ

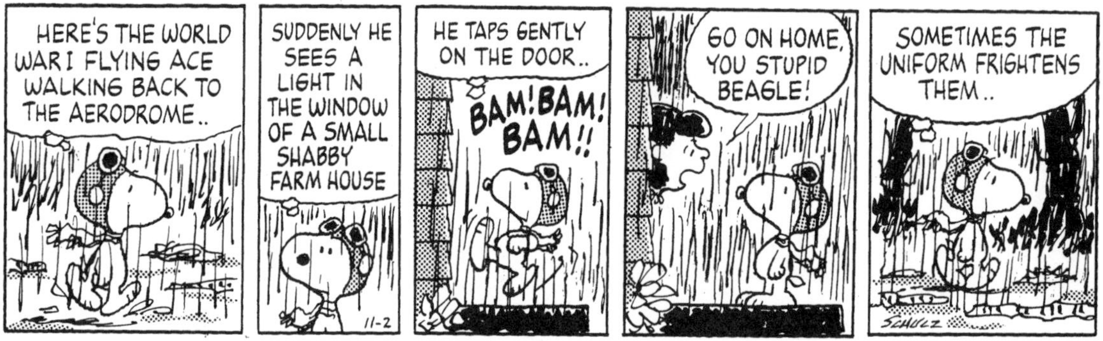
HERE'S THE WORLD WAR I FLYING ACE WALKING BACK TO THE AERODROME..
SUDDENLY HE SEES A LIGHT IN THE WINDOW OF A SMALL SHABBY FARM HOUSE
11-2
HE TAPS GENTLY ON THE DOOR..
BAM! BAM! BAM!!
GO ON HOME, YOU STUPID BEAGLE!
SOMETIMES THE UNIFORM FRIGHTENS THEM..
SCHULZ

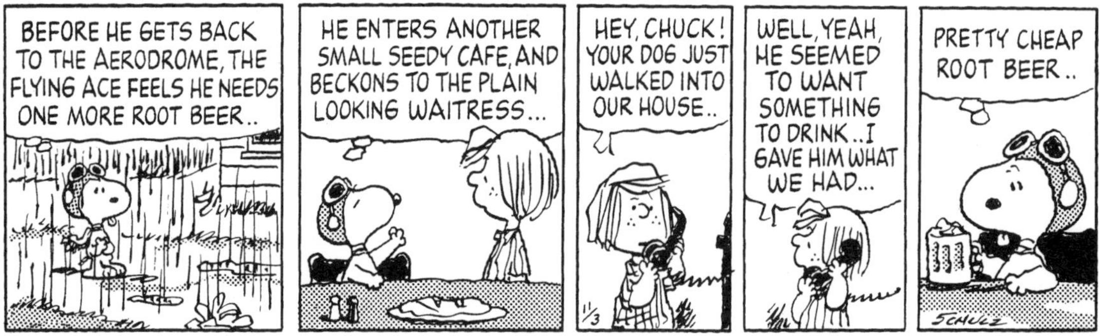
BEFORE HE GETS BACK TO THE AERODROME, THE FLYING ACE FEELS HE NEEDS ONE MORE ROOT BEER..
HE ENTERS ANOTHER SMALL SEEDY CAFE, AND BECKONS TO THE PLAIN LOOKING WAITRESS...
HEY, CHUCK! YOUR DOG JUST WALKED INTO OUR HOUSE..
11/3
WELL, YEAH, HE SEEMED TO WANT SOMETHING TO DRINK.. I GAVE HIM WHAT WE HAD...
PRETTY CHEAP ROOT BEER..
SCHULZ

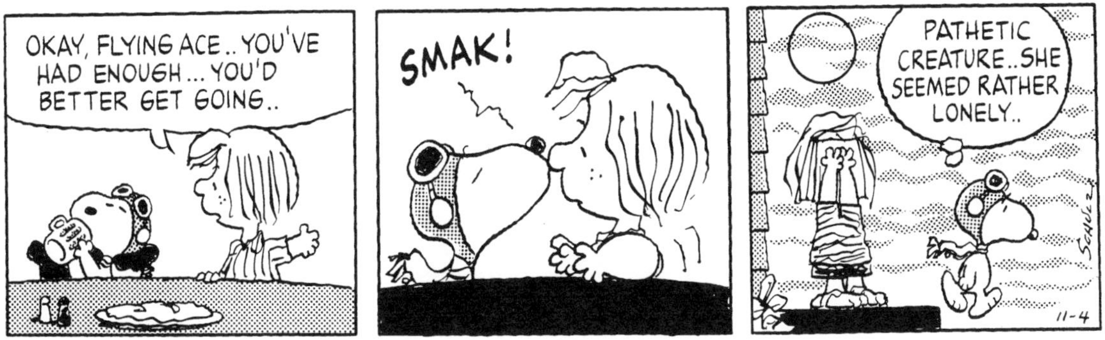
OKAY, FLYING ACE.. YOU'VE HAD ENOUGH... YOU'D BETTER GET GOING..
SMAK!
PATHETIC CREATURE..SHE SEEMED RATHER LONELY..
11-4

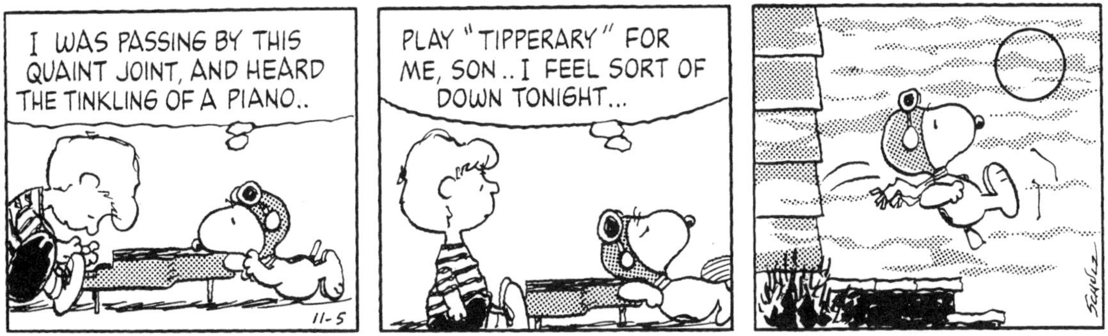
I WAS PASSING BY THIS QUAINT JOINT, AND HEARD THE TINKLING OF A PIANO..
11-5
PLAY "TIPPERARY" FOR ME, SON.. I FEEL SORT OF DOWN TONIGHT...

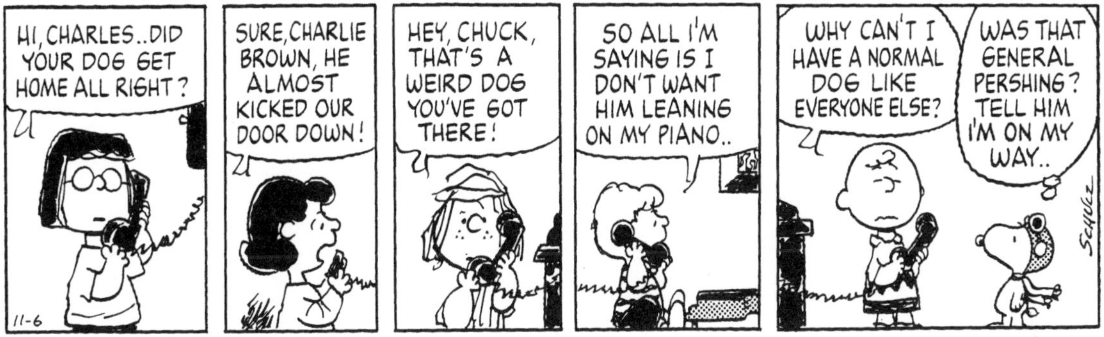
HI, CHARLES..DID YOUR DOG GET HOME ALL RIGHT?
11-6
SURE, CHARLIE BROWN, HE ALMOST KICKED OUR DOOR DOWN!
HEY, CHUCK, THAT'S A WEIRD DOG YOU'VE GOT THERE!
SO ALL I'M SAYING IS I DON'T WANT HIM LEANING ON MY PIANO..
WHY CAN'T I HAVE A NORMAL DOG LIKE EVERYONE ELSE?
WAS THAT GENERAL PERSHING? TELL HIM I'M ON MY WAY..

 IT IS DAWN.. HERE'S THE WORLD WAR I FLYING ACE WALKING ONTO THE AERODROME

11-8

 HE CLIMBS INTO THE COCKPIT OF HIS SOPWITH CAMEL, AND ADJUSTS THE SUTTON HARNESS...

 NOW, THE EARLY MORNING QUIET IS SHATTERED BY THE ROAR OF THE 110 HP LE RHÔNE ENGINE!

 SOME PEOPLE HAVE DOGS WHO BARK A LOT, OR DIG HOLES IN THE GARDEN, OR...

 HERE'S THE WORLD WAR I FLYING ACE SEARCHING THE SKY FOR HIS ENEMY, THE RED BARON..

 SUDDENLY, OUT OF NOWHERE, A HAIL OF BULLETS RIPS THE FABRIC OF HIS SOPWITH CAMEL!

 WITH UNBELIEVABLE SKILL HE GUIDES THE STRICKEN CRAFT BACK TO THE AERODROME

 FEARING A FIERY EXPLOSION, HE LEAPS FROM THE COCKPIT!

 WHAT'S A SUPPER DISH DOING ON THE RUNWAY?!

11-9

 WHY DOES YOUR DOG STAND IN THE BACKYARD JUST STARING AT HIS DOGHOUSE?

 THAT STUPID RED BARON..LOOK WHAT HE DID TO MY PLANE...

11-10

ON VETERANS DAY I ALWAYS GO OVER TO BILL MAULDIN'S HOUSE TO QUAFF A FEW ROOT BEERS..

11-11

BILL KNEW MY HERO, AUDIE MURPHY...

I'VE TOLD BILL HOW I MET CAPTAIN HARRY TRUMAN IN FRANCE...

BUT BILL NEVER BELIEVES ME..

ARE YOU THROUGH WITH THE SPORTS SECTION?

WHY? YOU DON'T KNOW ANYTHING ABOUT SPORTS..

IS THERE AN "ANYTHING" SECTION FOR SOMEONE WHO DOESN'T KNOW ANYTHING ABOUT ANYTHING?

11-12

SOMETIMES, I LIE AWAKE AT NIGHT, AND I ASK, "WHY ME?"

11-13

THEN A VOICE ANSWERS, "NOTHING PERSONAL.. YOUR NAME JUST HAPPENED TO COME UP.."

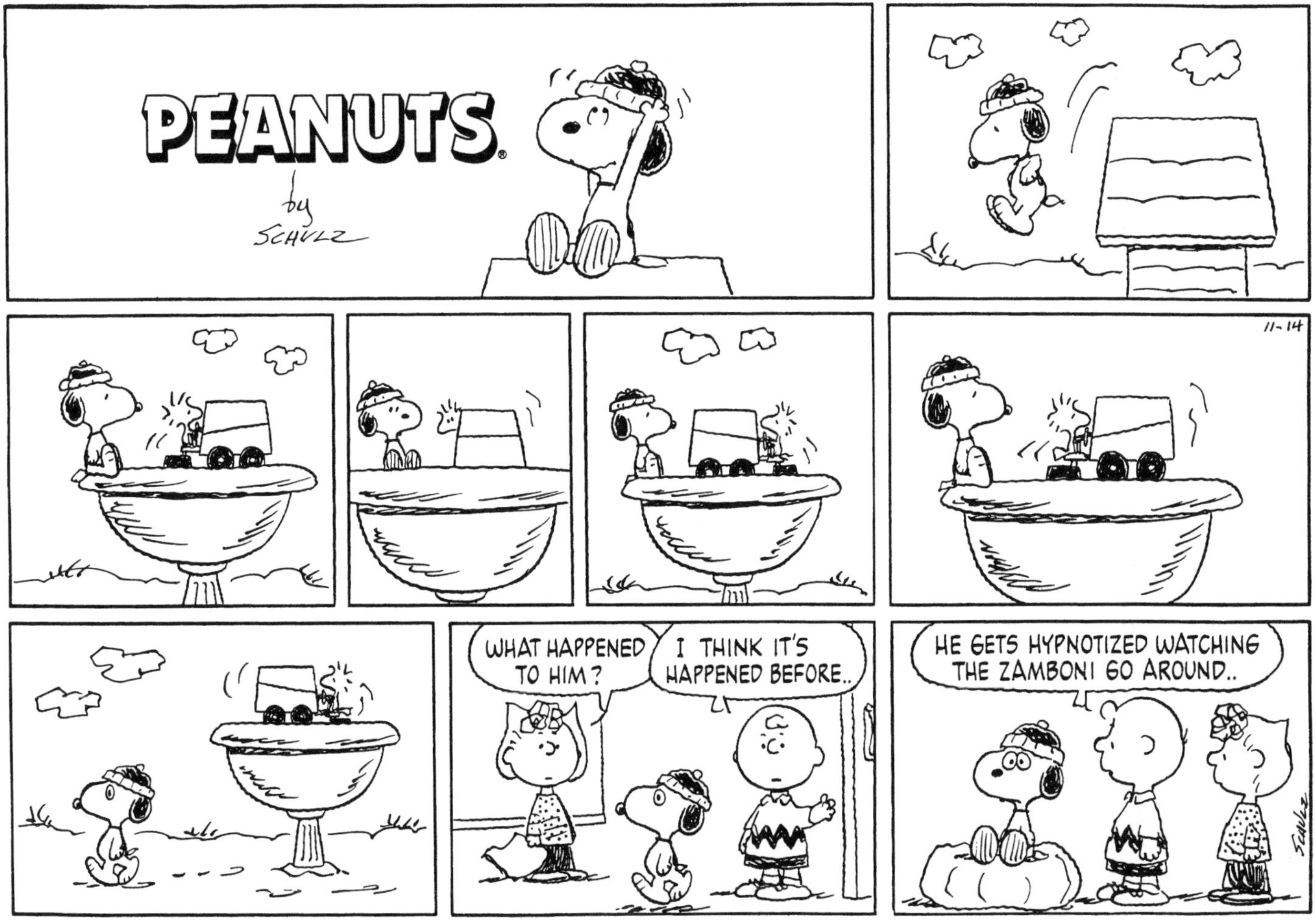
PEANUTS
by SCHULZ
11-14
WHAT HAPPENED TO HIM?
I THINK IT'S HAPPENED BEFORE..
HE GETS HYPNOTIZED WATCHING THE ZAMBONI GO AROUND..
SCHULZ

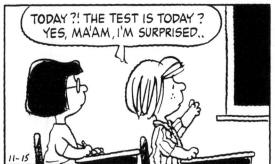

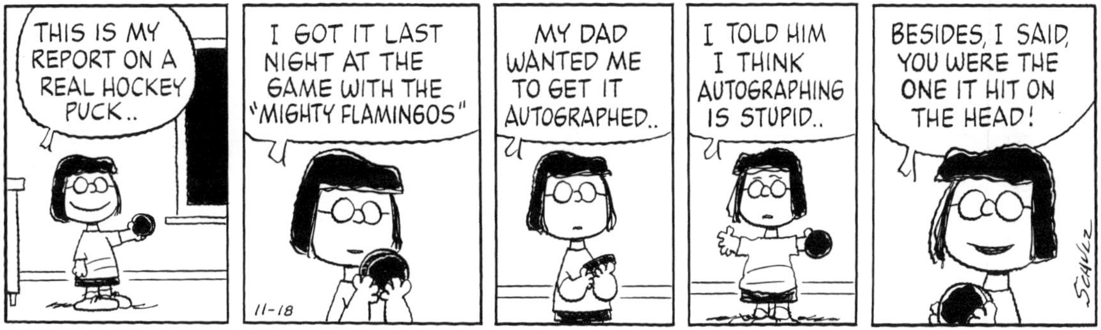
THIS IS MY REPORT ON A REAL HOCKEY PUCK..
I GOT IT LAST NIGHT AT THE GAME WITH THE "MIGHTY FLAMINGOS"
11-18
MY DAD WANTED ME TO GET IT AUTOGRAPHED..
I TOLD HIM I THINK AUTOGRAPHING IS STUPID..
BESIDES, I SAID, YOU WERE THE ONE IT HIT ON THE HEAD!
SCHULZ

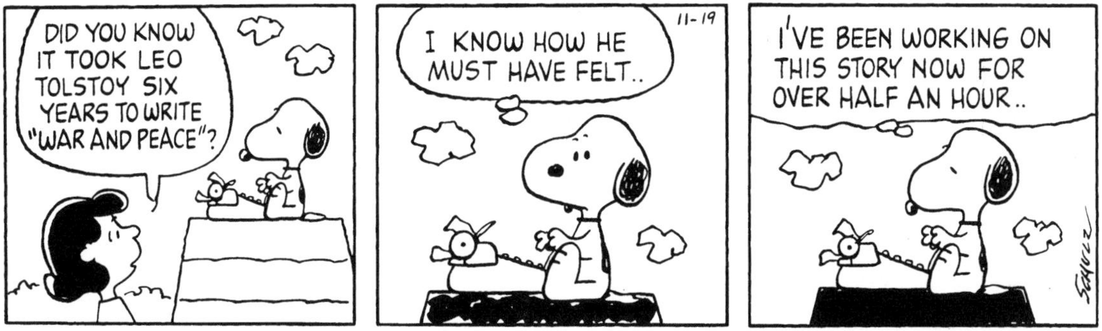
DID YOU KNOW IT TOOK LEO TOLSTOY SIX YEARS TO WRITE "WAR AND PEACE"?
11-19
I KNOW HOW HE MUST HAVE FELT..
I'VE BEEN WORKING ON THIS STORY NOW FOR OVER HALF AN HOUR..
SCHULZ

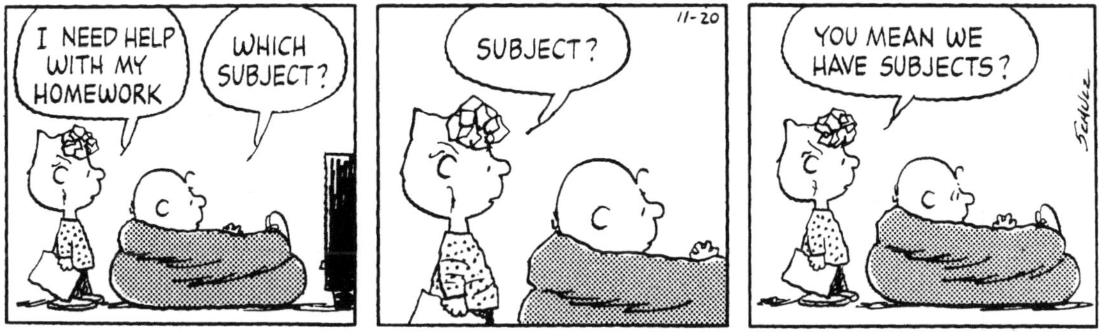
I NEED HELP WITH MY HOMEWORK
WHICH SUBJECT?
11-20
SUBJECT?
YOU MEAN WE HAVE SUBJECTS?
SCHULZ

I'VE DECIDED TO SPEND THE REST OF MY LIFE LOOKING FOR "THE BIG ROCK CANDY MOUNTAIN"

11-22

I DIDN'T FIND IT TODAY, BUT MAYBE I'LL FIND IT TOMORROW..

IF YOU REALLY WANT SOMETHING IN THIS LIFE, YOU HAVE TO BE DETERMINED!

IF I DON'T FIND IT TOMORROW, I THINK I'LL QUIT LOOKING..

SCHULZ

11-23
HAS THE SCHOOL BUS COME YET?

WHY DON'T YOU OPEN YOUR EYES AND SEE FOR YOURSELF?

IT'S TOO EARLY IN THE MORNING TO GO TO ALL THAT TROUBLE..

Schulz

YES, MA'AM, I WALKED TO SCHOOL IN THE RAIN..

11-24

YES, MA'AM.. MY WET HAIR IS DRIPPING ON THE DESK, AND THE WATER SEEMS TO BE RUNNING DOWN THE AISLE...

Schulz

NO, MA'AM, IT'S THE KIDS BEHIND ME WHO ARE MAKING THE LITTLE PAPER SAILBOATS..

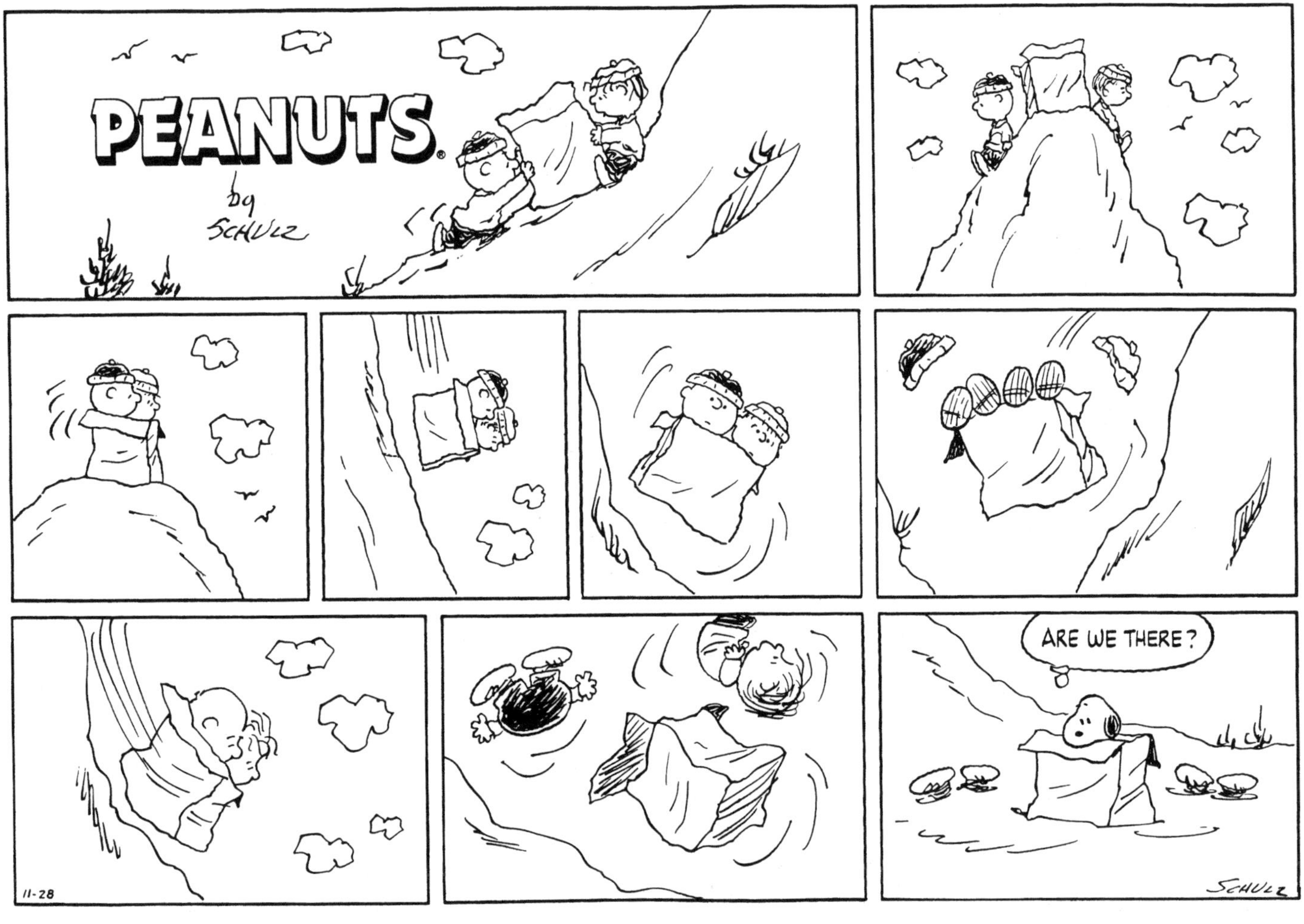
PEANUTS
by SCHULZ
11-28
ARE WE THERE?
SCHULZ

I WONDER IF THEY HAVE FRACTIONS IN HEAVEN..

NO FRACTIONS, SIR..NO DECIMALS, EITHER...

HOW ABOUT COMMAS?

THERE HAVE TO BE COMMAS, SIR.. WE CAN'T AVOID THEM

11-29

ETERNITY'S GOING TO BE LONGER THAN I THOUGHT..

WELL, I'LL BE! THIS IS THE SAME LITTLE BUG I SAW OVER ON THE PLAYGROUND TWO DAYS AGO..

11-30

HOW DO YOU KNOW?

I HAVE A GOOD MEMORY FOR FACES

CAN YOU SEE THE SCHOOL BUS?

NOT YET

I'VE CHANGED MY MIND.. I DON'T THINK I'LL GET ON THE BUS..

WHY NOT?

12-1

MY LUNCH JUST WENT HOME..

1993

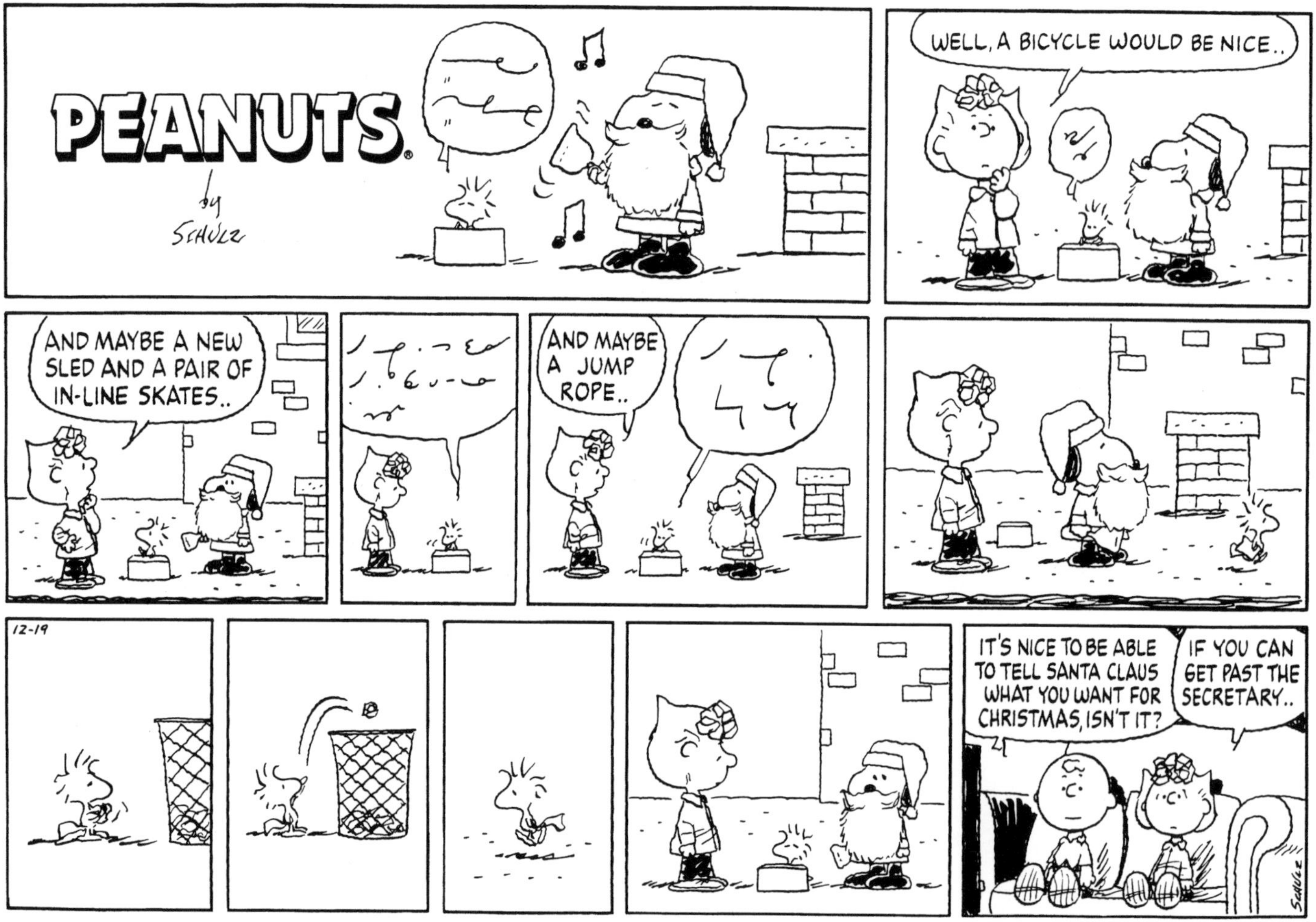
PEANUTS
by SCHULZ
WELL, A BICYCLE WOULD BE NICE..
AND MAYBE A NEW SLED AND A PAIR OF IN-LINE SKATES..
AND MAYBE A JUMP ROPE..
12-19
IT'S NICE TO BE ABLE TO TELL SANTA CLAUS WHAT YOU WANT FOR CHRISTMAS, ISN'T IT?
IF YOU CAN GET PAST THE SECRETARY..
SCHULZ

ONE OF THE GREAT JOYS IN LIFE IS SLIDING ON AN ICY SIDEWALK..

12-20

JOE 'ICE FOLLIES'..

YES, MA'AM..IT'S COLD OUTSIDE...

12-21

I'D LIKE AN ICE CREAM CONE, PLEASE

DO YOU MIND MITTEN MONEY? THIS IS SOME MONEY THAT'S BEEN IN MY MITTEN SINCE LAST WINTER..

ONE MORE QUESTION..

HOW DO YOU EAT ICE CREAM THROUGH A WOOLEN SCARF?

WHERE'S MY BIG FURRY HAT?

HAS ANYONE SEEN MY BIG FURRY HAT?

12-22

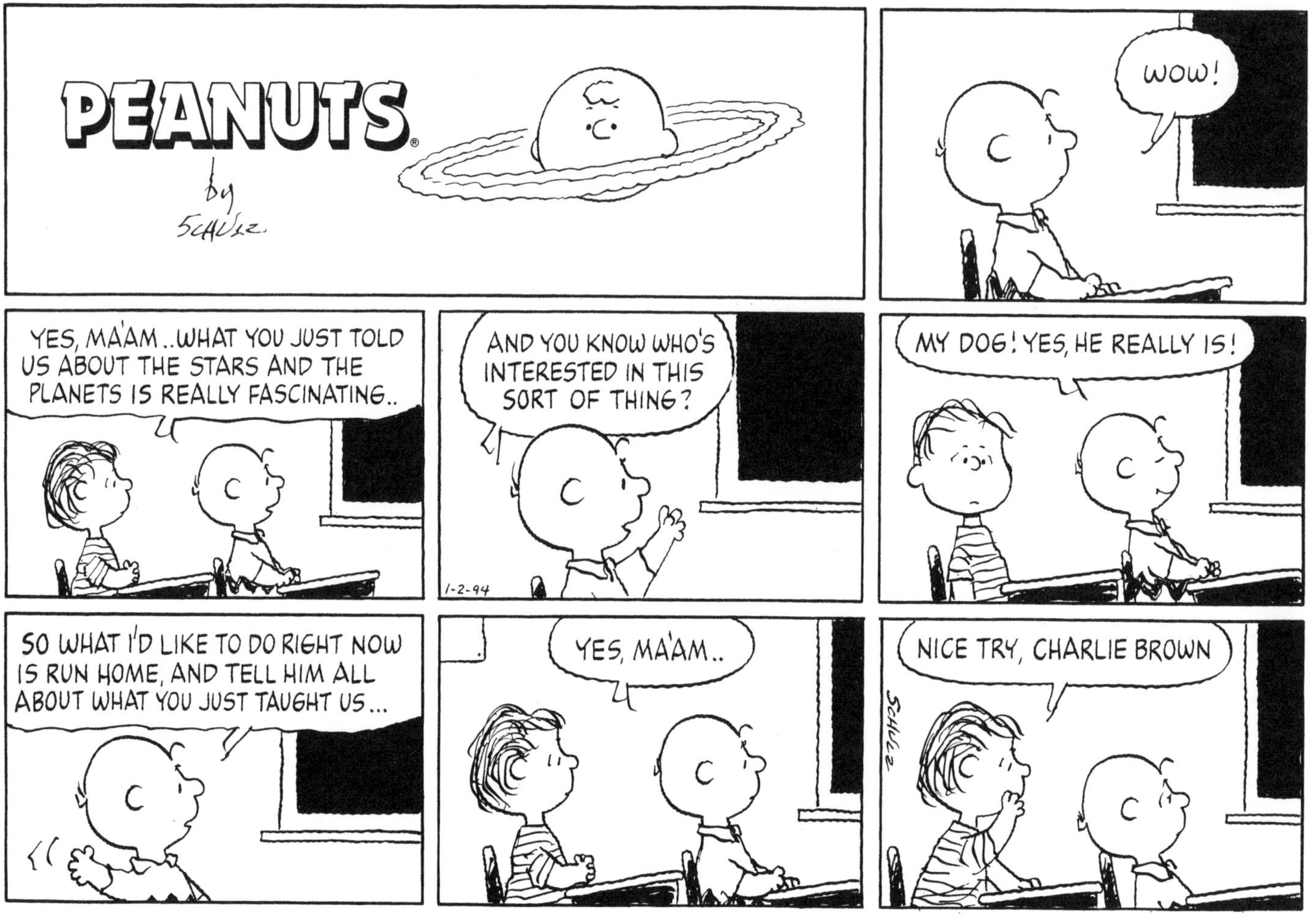
PEANUTS®
by SCHULZ
WOW!
YES, MA'AM..WHAT YOU JUST TOLD US ABOUT THE STARS AND THE PLANETS IS REALLY FASCINATING..
AND YOU KNOW WHO'S INTERESTED IN THIS SORT OF THING?
1-2-94
MY DOG! YES, HE REALLY IS!
SO WHAT I'D LIKE TO DO RIGHT NOW IS RUN HOME, AND TELL HIM ALL ABOUT WHAT YOU JUST TAUGHT US...
YES, MA'AM..
SCHULZ
NICE TRY, CHARLIE BROWN

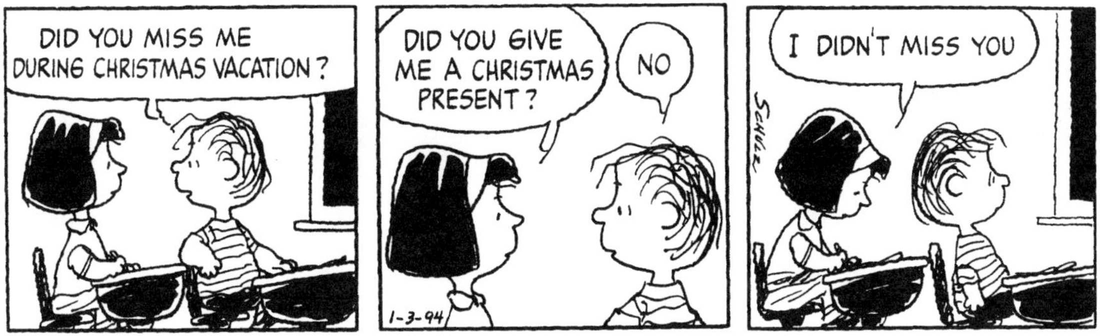
DID YOU MISS ME DURING CHRISTMAS VACATION?
DID YOU GIVE ME A CHRISTMAS PRESENT?
NO
I DIDN'T MISS YOU
SCHULZ
1-3-94

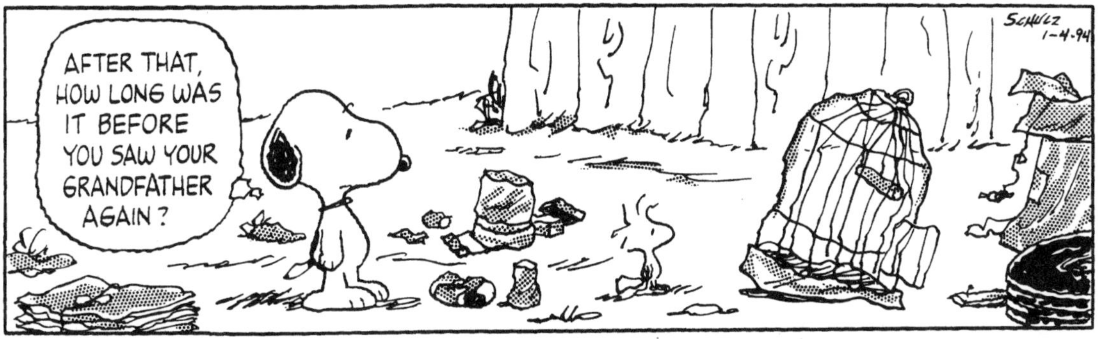
SCHULZ 1-4-94
AFTER THAT, HOW LONG WAS IT BEFORE YOU SAW YOUR GRANDFATHER AGAIN?

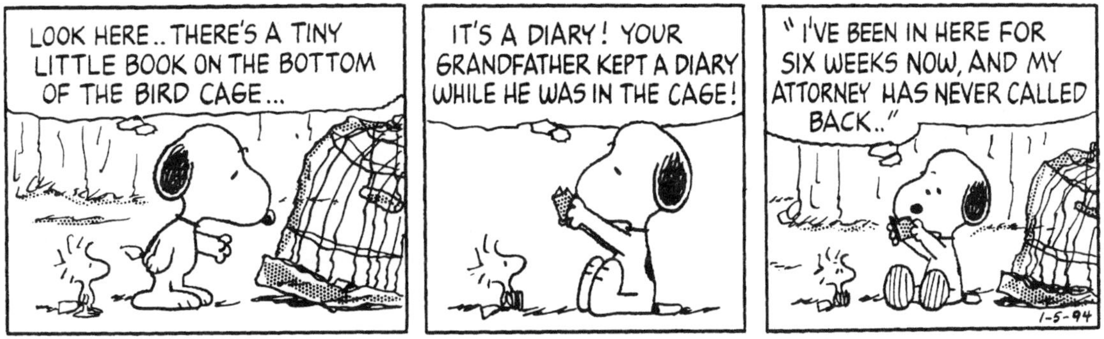
LOOK HERE.. THERE'S A TINY LITTLE BOOK ON THE BOTTOM OF THE BIRD CAGE...
IT'S A DIARY! YOUR GRANDFATHER KEPT A DIARY WHILE HE WAS IN THE CAGE!
"I'VE BEEN IN HERE FOR SIX WEEKS NOW, AND MY ATTORNEY HAS NEVER CALLED BACK.."
1-5-94

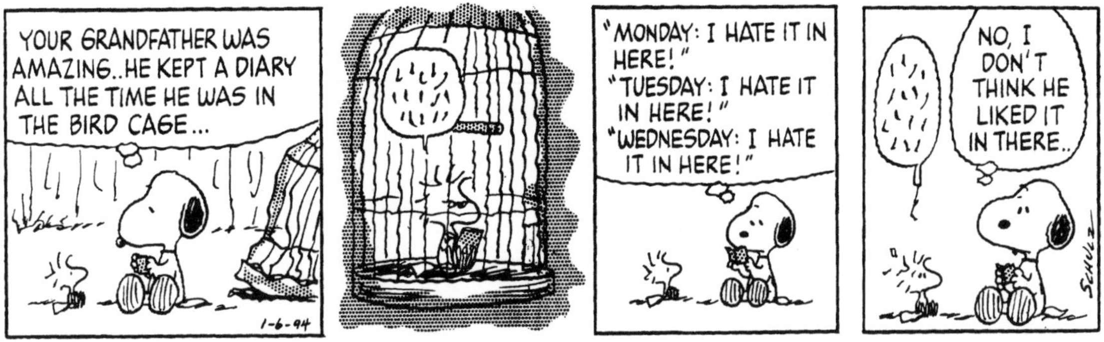
YOUR GRANDFATHER WAS AMAZING..HE KEPT A DIARY ALL THE TIME HE WAS IN THE BIRD CAGE...
1-6-94
"MONDAY: I HATE IT IN HERE!"
"TUESDAY: I HATE IT IN HERE!"
"WEDNESDAY: I HATE IT IN HERE!"
NO, I DON'T THINK HE LIKED IT IN THERE..
SCHULZ

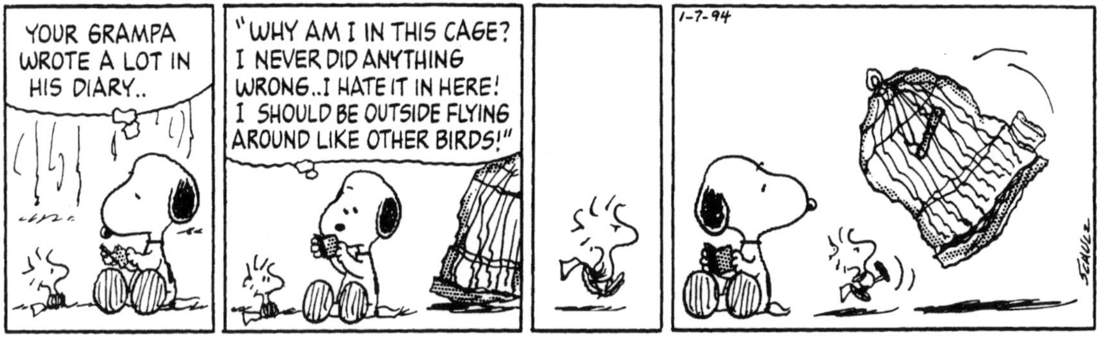
YOUR GRAMPA WROTE A LOT IN HIS DIARY..
"WHY AM I IN THIS CAGE? I NEVER DID ANYTHING WRONG..I HATE IT IN HERE! I SHOULD BE OUTSIDE FLYING AROUND LIKE OTHER BIRDS!"
1-7-94
SCHULZ

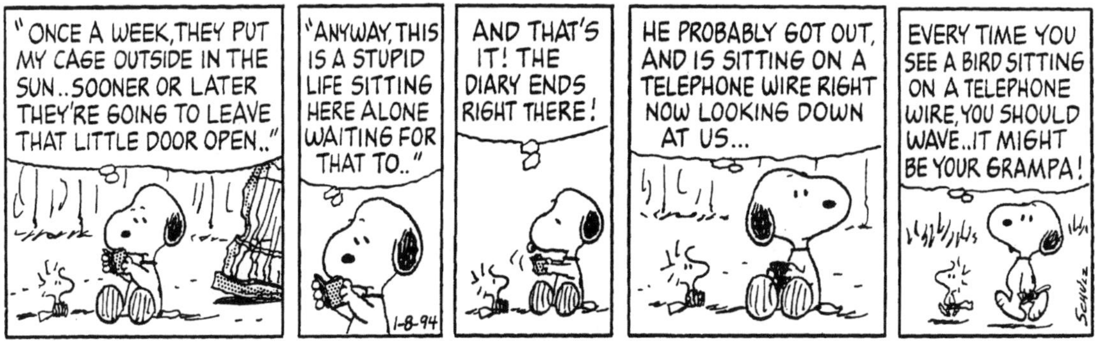
"ONCE A WEEK, THEY PUT MY CAGE OUTSIDE IN THE SUN..SOONER OR LATER THEY'RE GOING TO LEAVE THAT LITTLE DOOR OPEN.."
"ANYWAY, THIS IS A STUPID LIFE SITTING HERE ALONE WAITING FOR THAT TO.."
1-8-94
AND THAT'S IT! THE DIARY ENDS RIGHT THERE!
HE PROBABLY GOT OUT, AND IS SITTING ON A TELEPHONE WIRE RIGHT NOW LOOKING DOWN AT US...
EVERY TIME YOU SEE A BIRD SITTING ON A TELEPHONE WIRE, YOU SHOULD WAVE..IT MIGHT BE YOUR GRAMPA!
SCHULZ

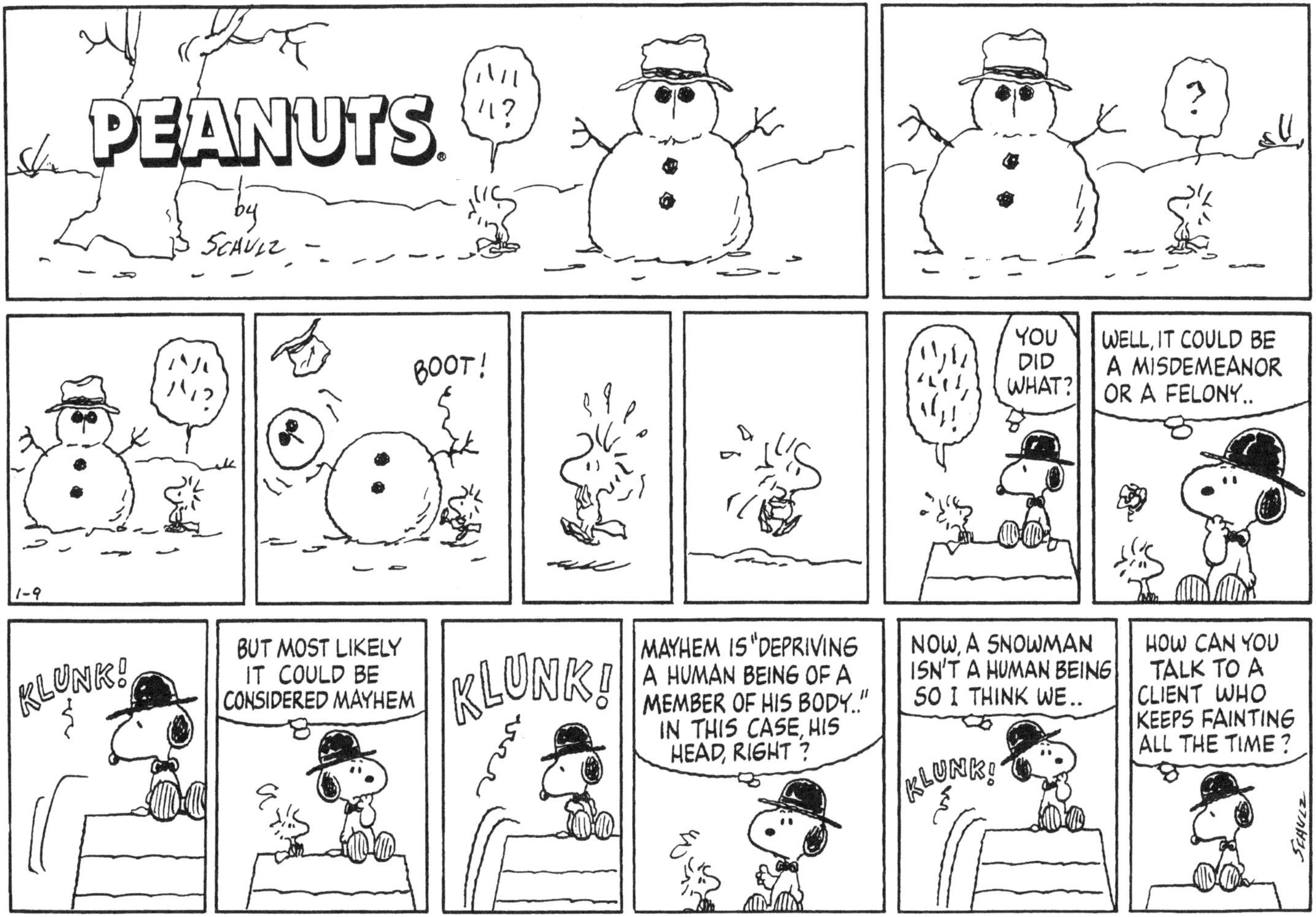
PEANUTS
by SCHULZ
BOOT!
1-9
YOU DID WHAT?
WELL, IT COULD BE A MISDEMEANOR OR A FELONY..
KLUNK!
BUT MOST LIKELY IT COULD BE CONSIDERED MAYHEM
KLUNK!
MAYHEM IS "DEPRIVING A HUMAN BEING OF A MEMBER OF HIS BODY.." IN THIS CASE, HIS HEAD, RIGHT ?
NOW, A SNOWMAN ISN'T A HUMAN BEING SO I THINK WE..
KLUNK!
HOW CAN YOU TALK TO A CLIENT WHO KEEPS FAINTING ALL THE TIME ?
SCHULZ

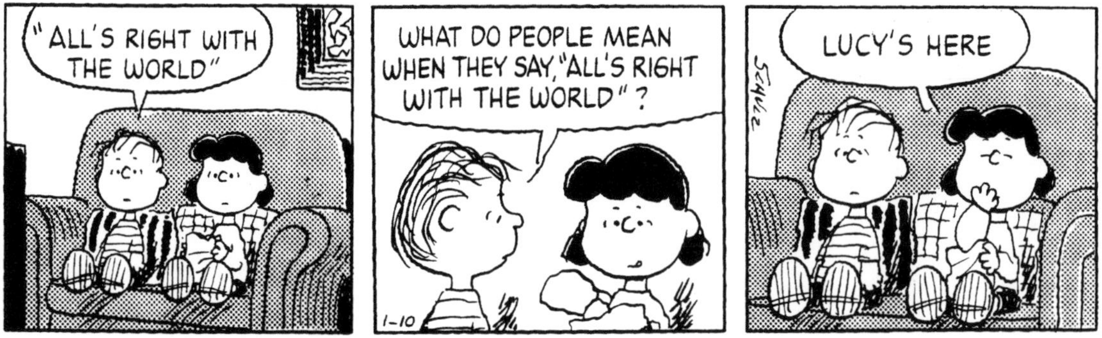
"ALL'S RIGHT WITH THE WORLD"
WHAT DO PEOPLE MEAN WHEN THEY SAY, "ALL'S RIGHT WITH THE WORLD" ?
LUCY'S HERE

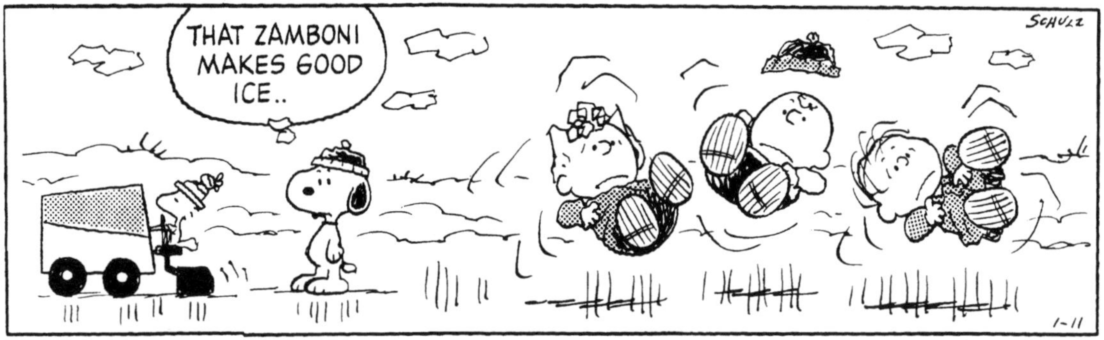
THAT ZAMBONI MAKES GOOD ICE..

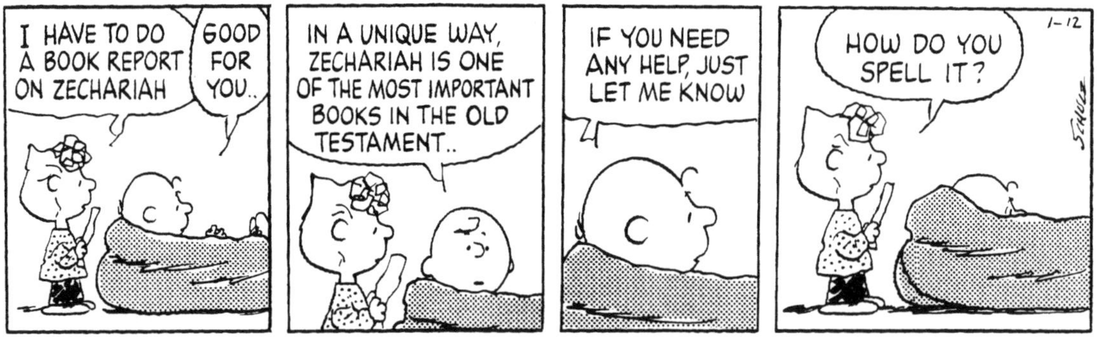
I HAVE TO DO A BOOK REPORT ON ZECHARIAH
GOOD FOR YOU..
IN A UNIQUE WAY, ZECHARIAH IS ONE OF THE MOST IMPORTANT BOOKS IN THE OLD TESTAMENT..
IF YOU NEED ANY HELP, JUST LET ME KNOW
HOW DO YOU SPELL IT?

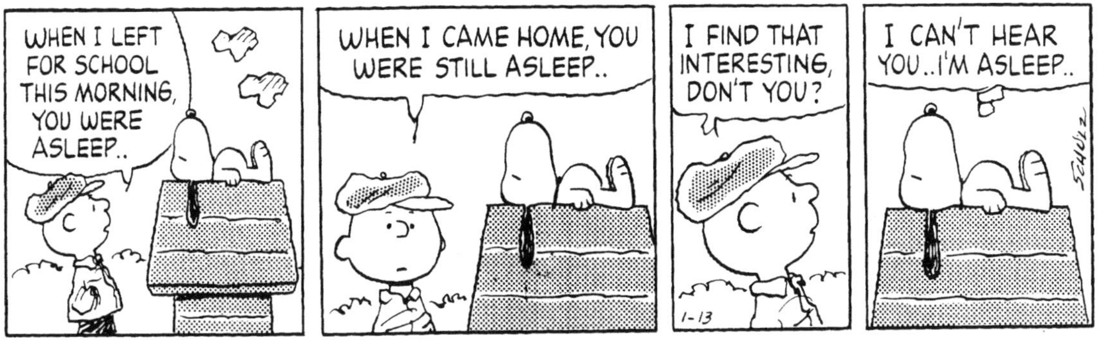
WHEN I LEFT FOR SCHOOL THIS MORNING, YOU WERE ASLEEP..
WHEN I CAME HOME, YOU WERE STILL ASLEEP..
I FIND THAT INTERESTING, DON'T YOU?
1-13
I CAN'T HEAR YOU..I'M ASLEEP..
SCHULZ

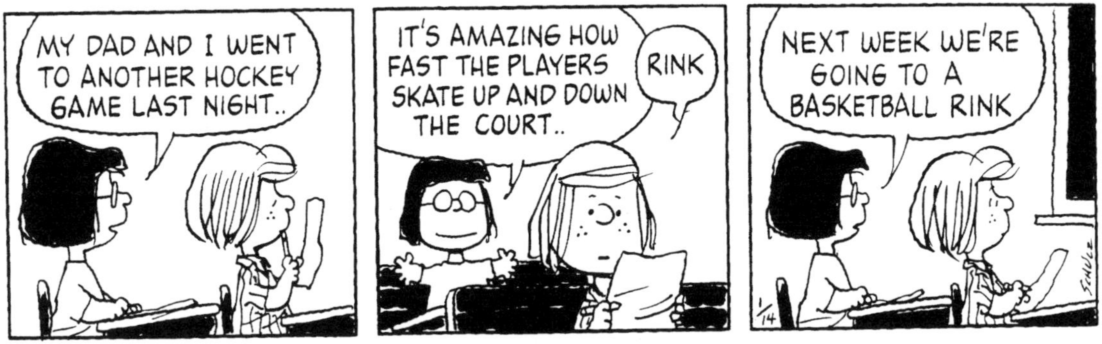
MY DAD AND I WENT TO ANOTHER HOCKEY GAME LAST NIGHT..
IT'S AMAZING HOW FAST THE PLAYERS SKATE UP AND DOWN THE COURT..
RINK
NEXT WEEK WE'RE GOING TO A BASKETBALL RINK
1/14
SCHULZ

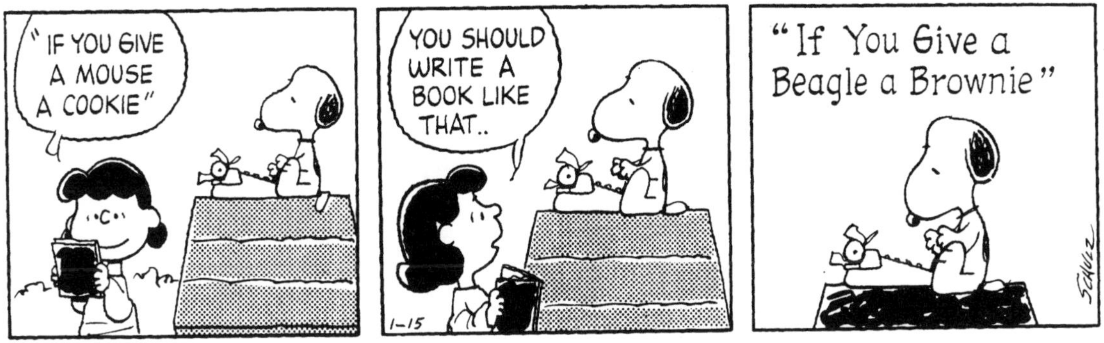
"IF YOU GIVE A MOUSE A COOKIE"
YOU SHOULD WRITE A BOOK LIKE THAT..
1-15
"If You Give a Beagle a Brownie"
SCHULZ

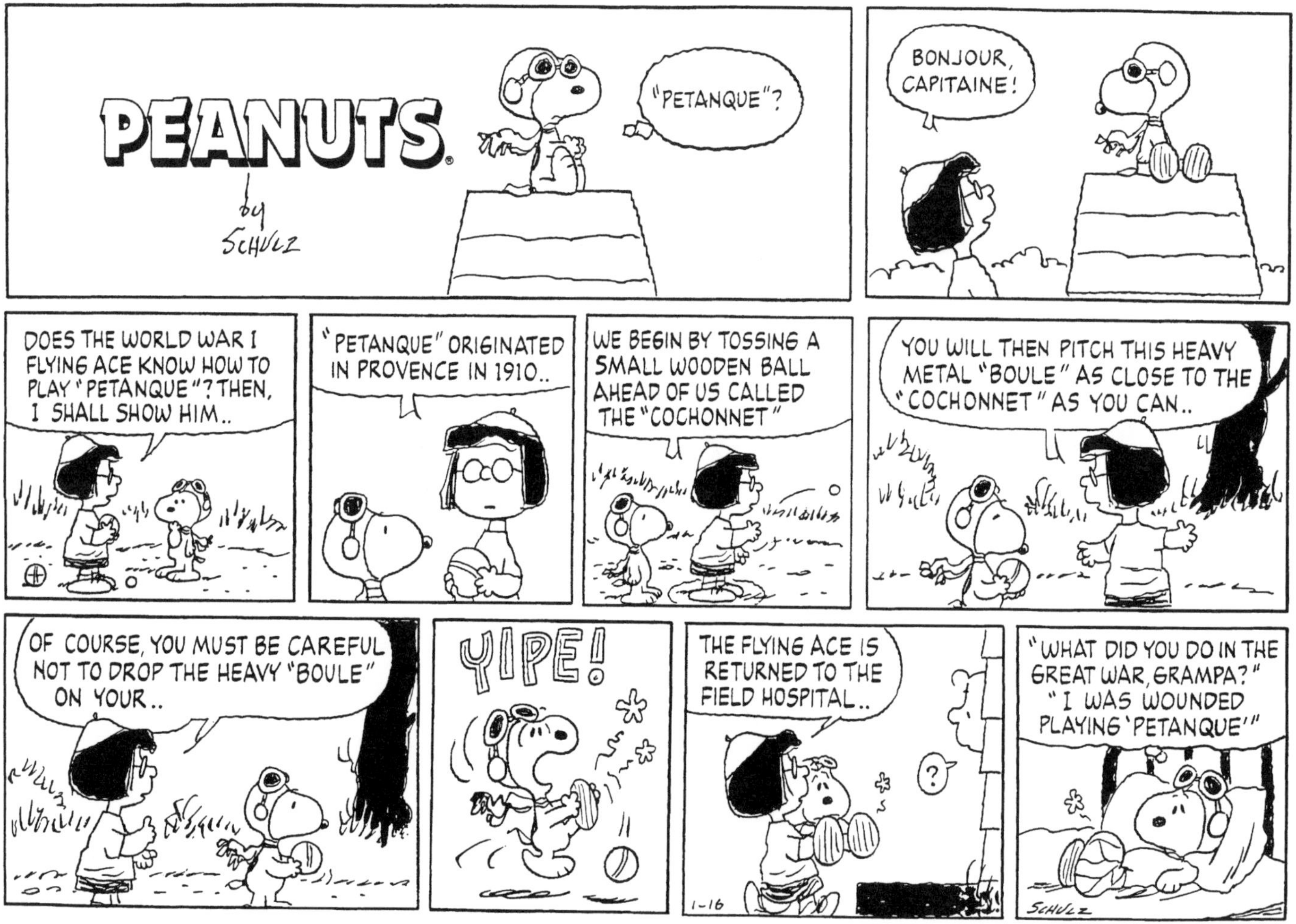
PEANUTS
by SCHULZ
"PETANQUE"?
BONJOUR, CAPITAINE!
DOES THE WORLD WAR I FLYING ACE KNOW HOW TO PLAY "PETANQUE"? THEN, I SHALL SHOW HIM..
"PETANQUE" ORIGINATED IN PROVENCE IN 1910..
WE BEGIN BY TOSSING A SMALL WOODEN BALL AHEAD OF US CALLED THE "COCHONNET"
YOU WILL THEN PITCH THIS HEAVY METAL "BOULE" AS CLOSE TO THE "COCHONNET" AS YOU CAN..
OF COURSE, YOU MUST BE CAREFUL NOT TO DROP THE HEAVY "BOULE" ON YOUR..
YIPE!
THE FLYING ACE IS RETURNED TO THE FIELD HOSPITAL..
?
1-16
"WHAT DID YOU DO IN THE GREAT WAR, GRAMPA?" "I WAS WOUNDED PLAYING 'PETANQUE'"
SCHULZ

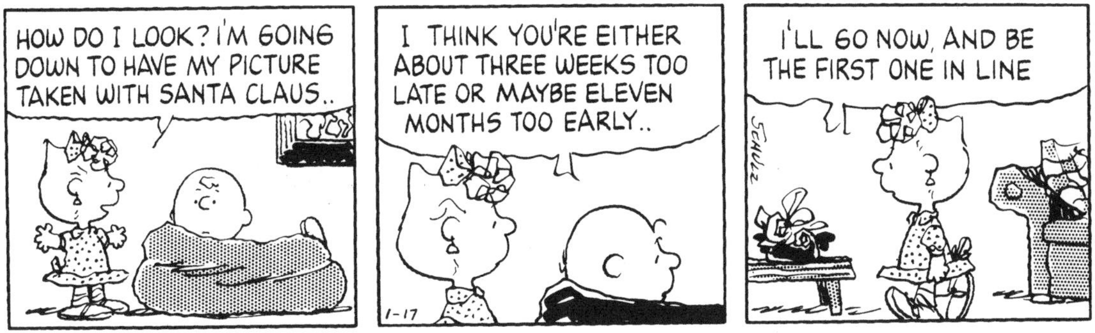
HOW DO I LOOK? I'M GOING DOWN TO HAVE MY PICTURE TAKEN WITH SANTA CLAUS..
I THINK YOU'RE EITHER ABOUT THREE WEEKS TOO LATE OR MAYBE ELEVEN MONTHS TOO EARLY..
I'LL GO NOW, AND BE THE FIRST ONE IN LINE
SCHULZ
1-17

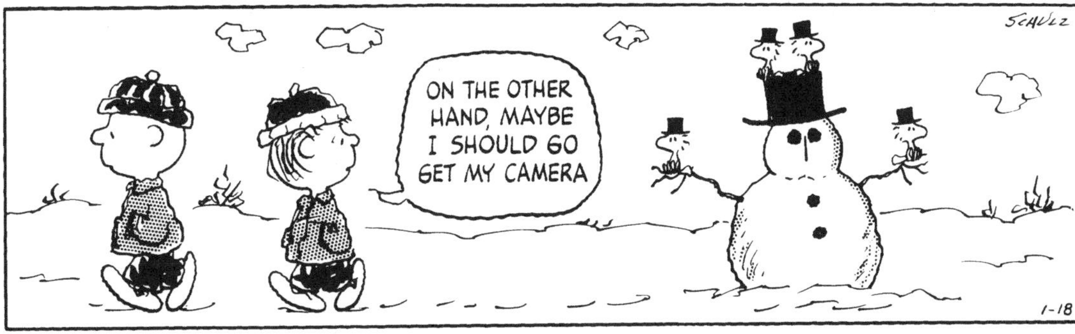
ON THE OTHER HAND, MAYBE I SHOULD GO GET MY CAMERA
SCHULZ
1-18

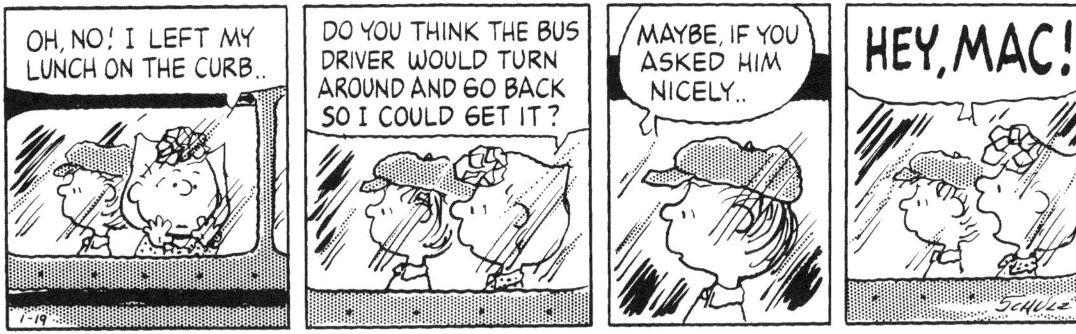
OH, NO! I LEFT MY LUNCH ON THE CURB..
DO YOU THINK THE BUS DRIVER WOULD TURN AROUND AND GO BACK SO I COULD GET IT?
MAYBE, IF YOU ASKED HIM NICELY..
HEY, MAC!
SCHULZ
1-19

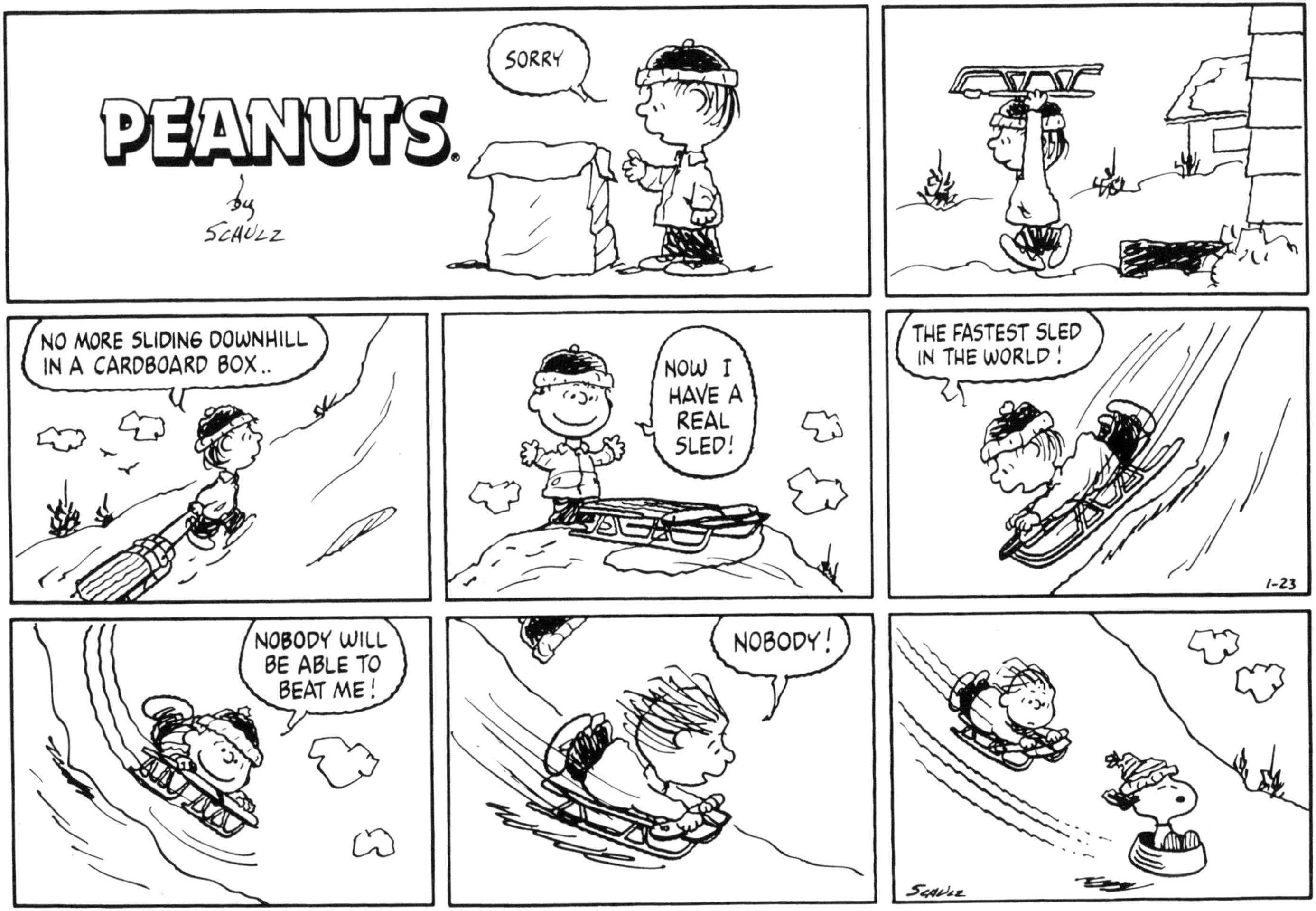
PEANUTS
by SCHULZ
SORRY
NO MORE SLIDING DOWNHILL IN A CARDBOARD BOX..
NOW I HAVE A REAL SLED!
THE FASTEST SLED IN THE WORLD!
1-23
NOBODY WILL BE ABLE TO BEAT ME!
NOBODY!
SCHULZ

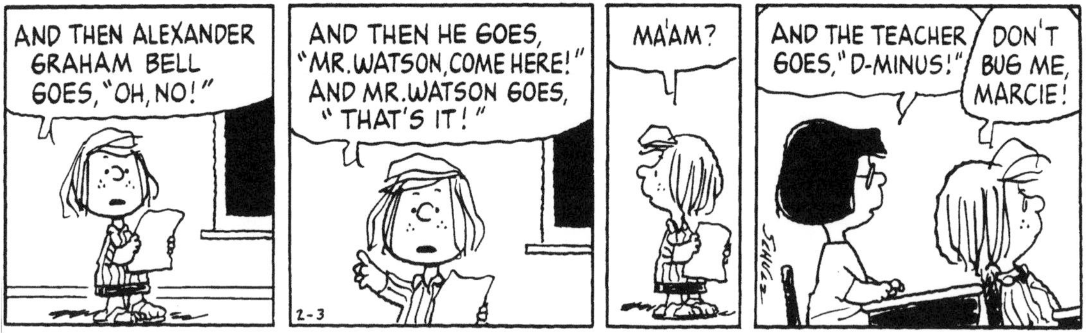
AND THEN ALEXANDER GRAHAM BELL GOES, "OH, NO!"
AND THEN HE GOES, "MR. WATSON, COME HERE!" AND MR. WATSON GOES, "THAT'S IT!"
2-3
MA'AM?
AND THE TEACHER GOES, "D-MINUS!"
DON'T BUG ME, MARCIE!

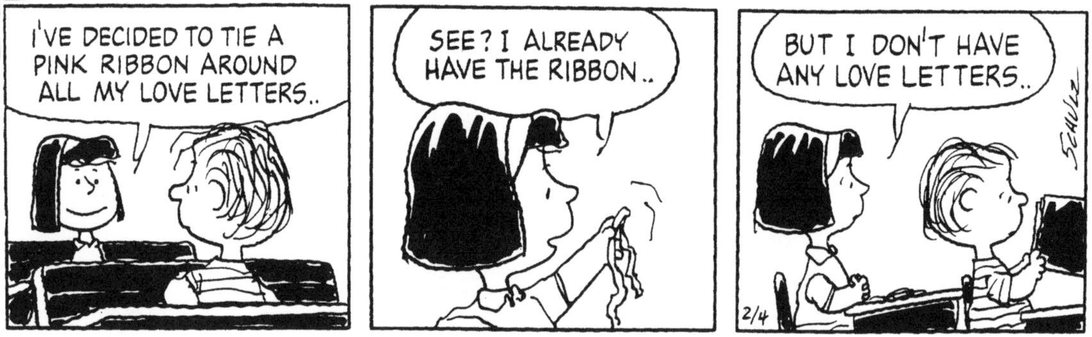
I'VE DECIDED TO TIE A PINK RIBBON AROUND ALL MY LOVE LETTERS..
SEE? I ALREADY HAVE THE RIBBON..
BUT I DON'T HAVE ANY LOVE LETTERS..
2/4

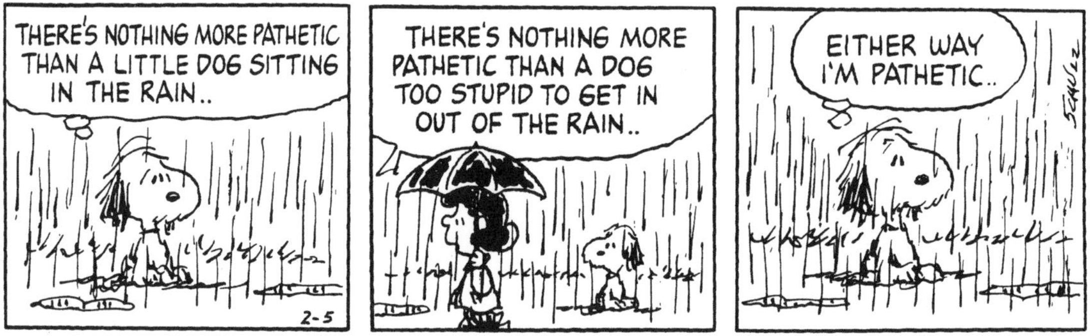
THERE'S NOTHING MORE PATHETIC THAN A LITTLE DOG SITTING IN THE RAIN..
2-5
THERE'S NOTHING MORE PATHETIC THAN A DOG TOO STUPID TO GET IN OUT OF THE RAIN..
EITHER WAY I'M PATHETIC..

HOMEMADE VALENTINES

I NEED A VALENTINE THAT WILL IMPRESS THIS GIRL I LIKE..

FOR THE ♡ IN YOUR LIFE

THEN YOU'LL WANT THIS SUPER POTENT VALENTINE!

POTENT?

IT'LL SWEEP HER OFF HER FEET! IT'LL KNOCK HER SOCKS OFF!

ALL RIGHT, I'LL TAKE IT!

FOR THE ♡

2-6

GOOD..IF YOU COME AROUND NEXT FRIDAY, YOU CAN PICK IT UP..

FRIDAY?! WHY CAN'T I HAVE IT NOW?

FOR THE ♡

IT'S TOO POTENT...

FOR THE ♡

THERE'S A FIVE-DAY WAITING PERIOD!

FOR THE ♡ IN YOUR LIFE

SOMETIMES I LIE AWAKE AT NIGHT, AND I ASK, "WHY AM I HERE?"

THEN A VOICE ANSWERS, "WHY? WHERE DO YOU WANT TO BE?"

I GUESS I LEAD KIND OF A SIMPLE LIFE..

BUT YOU KNOW WHAT I NEVER HAVE TO WORRY ABOUT?

2-8

LEAVING MY KEYS IN THE CAR..

I'M GOING IN TO TOWN TO BUY VALENTINES FOR ALL THE GIRLS WHO LOVE ME..

I SHOULD BE BACK IN TEN SECONDS..

2-9

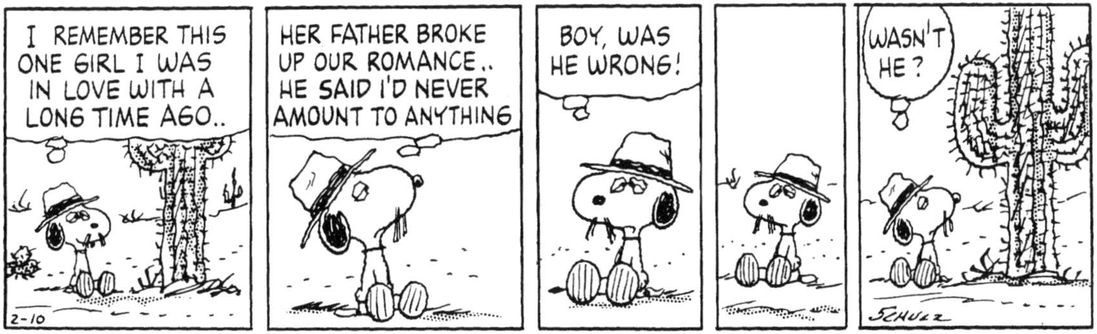
I REMEMBER THIS ONE GIRL I WAS IN LOVE WITH A LONG TIME AGO..
2-10
HER FATHER BROKE UP OUR ROMANCE.. HE SAID I'D NEVER AMOUNT TO ANYTHING
BOY, WAS HE WRONG!
WASN'T HE ?
SCHULZ

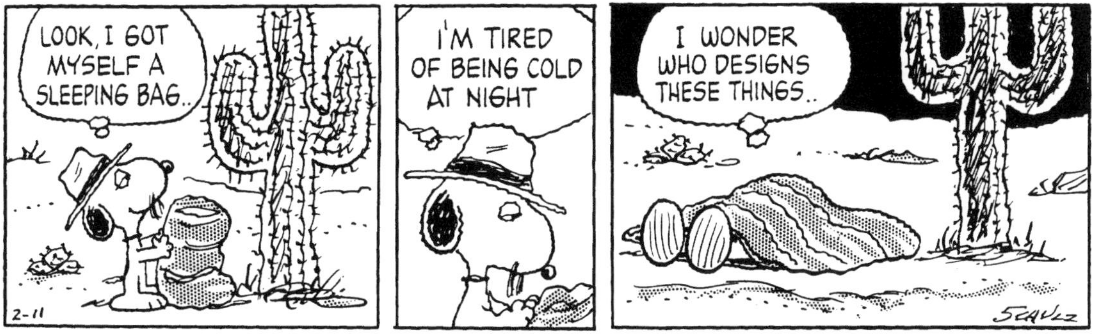
LOOK, I GOT MYSELF A SLEEPING BAG..
2-11
I'M TIRED OF BEING COLD AT NIGHT
I WONDER WHO DESIGNS THESE THINGS..
SCHULZ

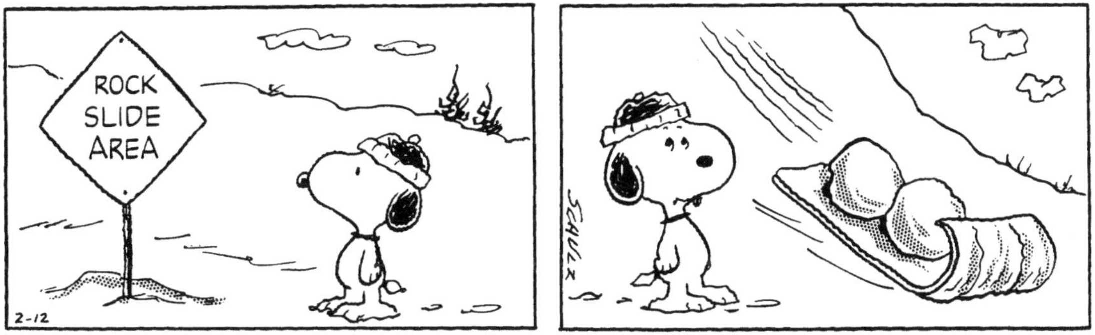
ROCK SLIDE AREA
2-12
SCHULZ

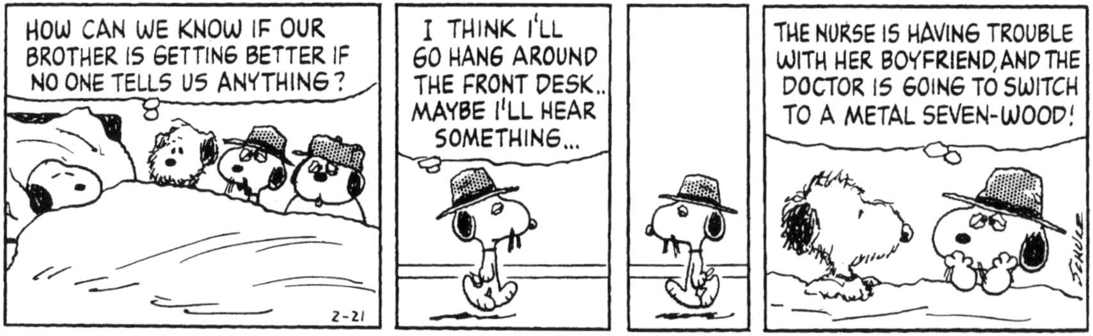
HOW CAN WE KNOW IF OUR BROTHER IS GETTING BETTER IF NO ONE TELLS US ANYTHING?
2-21
I THINK I'LL GO HANG AROUND THE FRONT DESK.. MAYBE I'LL HEAR SOMETHING...
THE NURSE IS HAVING TROUBLE WITH HER BOYFRIEND, AND THE DOCTOR IS GOING TO SWITCH TO A METAL SEVEN-WOOD!
SCHULZ

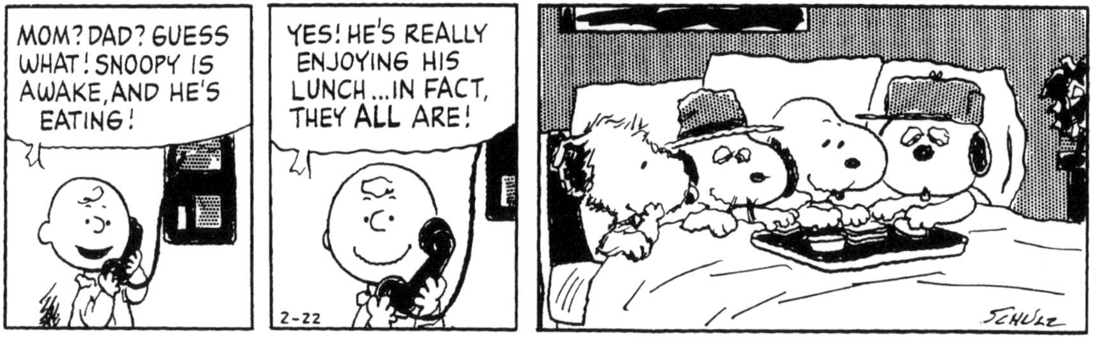
MOM? DAD? GUESS WHAT! SNOOPY IS AWAKE, AND HE'S EATING!
YES! HE'S REALLY ENJOYING HIS LUNCH... IN FACT, THEY ALL ARE!
2-22
SCHULZ

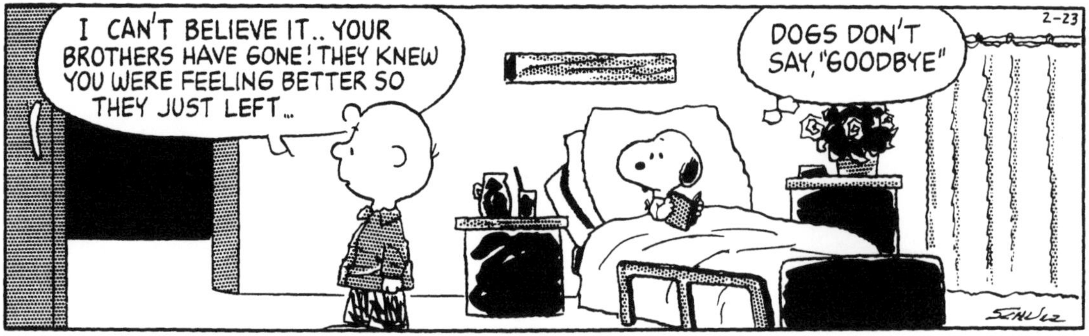
I CAN'T BELIEVE IT.. YOUR BROTHERS HAVE GONE! THEY KNEW YOU WERE FEELING BETTER SO THEY JUST LEFT...
DOGS DON'T SAY, "GOODBYE"
2-23
SCHULZ

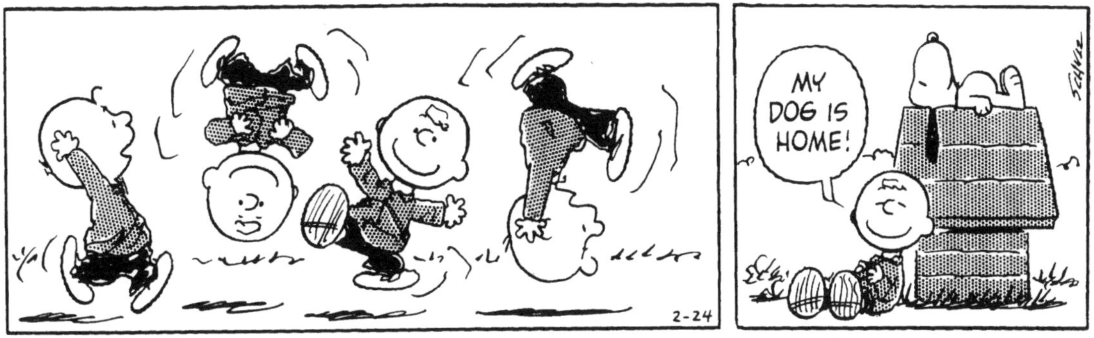
MY DOG IS HOME!
2-24
SCHULZ

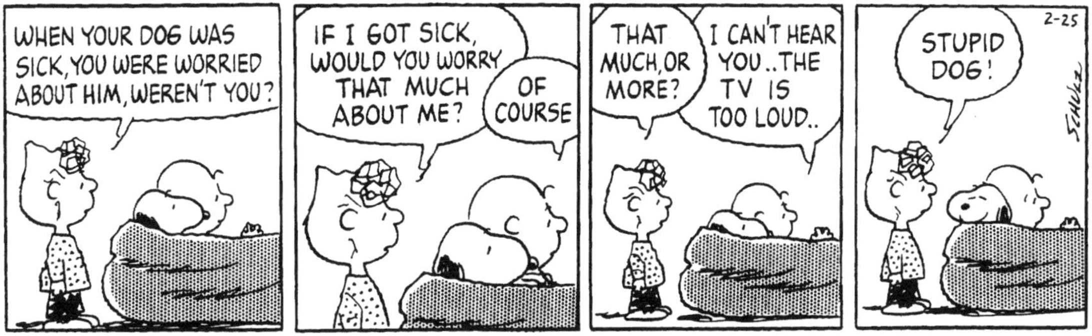
WHEN YOUR DOG WAS SICK, YOU WERE WORRIED ABOUT HIM, WEREN'T YOU?
IF I GOT SICK, WOULD YOU WORRY THAT MUCH ABOUT ME?
OF COURSE
THAT MUCH, OR MORE?
I CAN'T HEAR YOU..THE TV IS TOO LOUD..
STUPID DOG!
2-25
SCHULZ

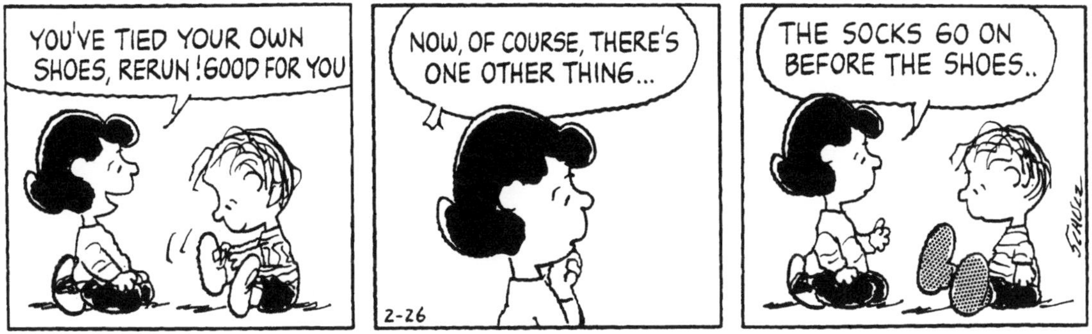
YOU'VE TIED YOUR OWN SHOES, RERUN! GOOD FOR YOU
NOW, OF COURSE, THERE'S ONE OTHER THING...
2-26
THE SOCKS GO ON BEFORE THE SHOES..
SCHULZ

MARCIE, I DON'T UNDERSTAND THE PROBLEM ON PAGE 362..

THERE IS NO PROBLEM ON PAGE 362, SIR... THAT'S THE INDEX..

PRETTY TRICKY, MA'AM!

2-28

TELL MY TEACHER TO BRING THE CLASS TO OUR HOUSE TODAY, AND WE CAN STUDY HERE IN MY ROOM..

3-1

SHE SAID IS IT ALL RIGHT TO BRING THE PRINCIPAL, TOO, AND ALL THE MEMBERS OF THE SCHOOL BOARD?

IT WOULD HAVE BEEN PRETTY CROWDED..

WAKE UP! IT'S A PERFECT DAY FOR CHASING RABBITS!

3-2

WHAT ARE YOU DOING?

YOU DON'T CATCH RABBITS BY HANDING OUT LITERATURE..

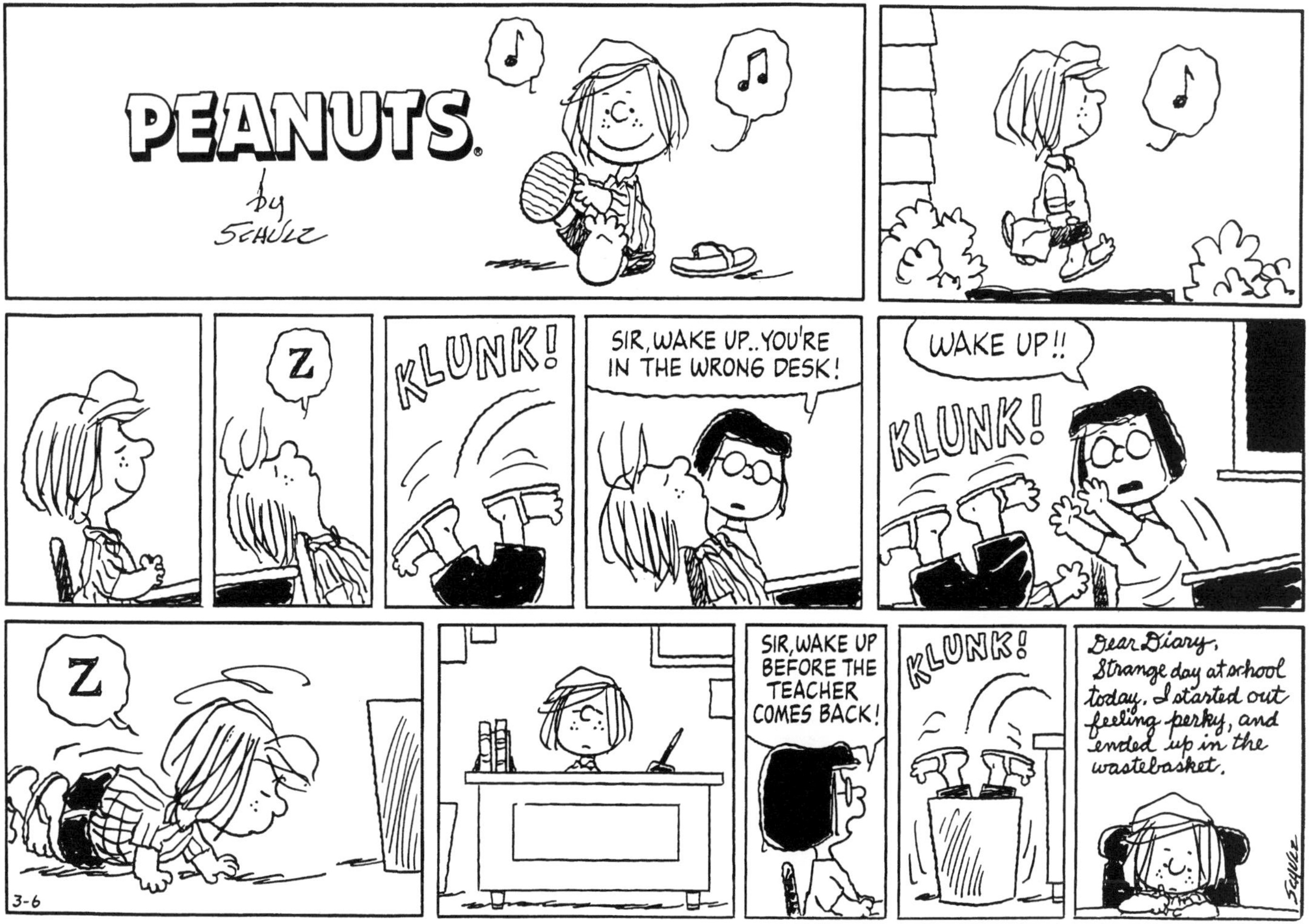
PEANUTS
by SCHULZ
Z
KLUNK!
SIR, WAKE UP.. YOU'RE IN THE WRONG DESK!
WAKE UP!!
KLUNK!
Z
3-6
SIR, WAKE UP BEFORE THE TEACHER COMES BACK!
KLUNK!
Dear Diary, Strange day at school today. I started out feeling perky, and ended up in the wastebasket.
SCHULZ

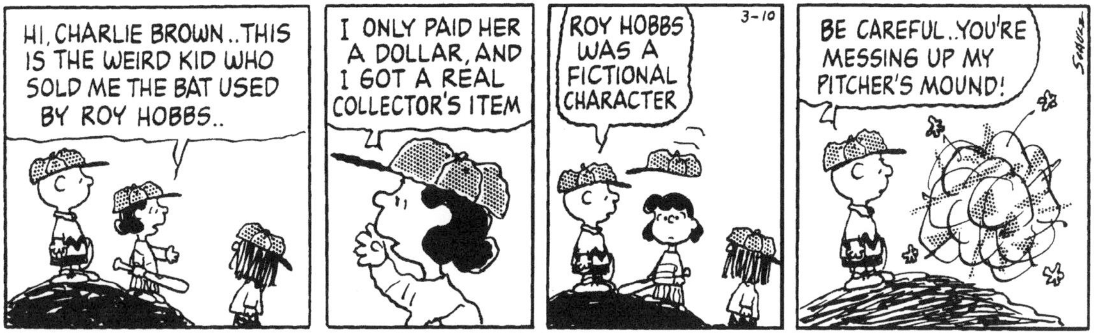
HI, CHARLIE BROWN..THIS IS THE WEIRD KID WHO SOLD ME THE BAT USED BY ROY HOBBS..
I ONLY PAID HER A DOLLAR, AND I GOT A REAL COLLECTOR'S ITEM
ROY HOBBS WAS A FICTIONAL CHARACTER
3-10
BE CAREFUL..YOU'RE MESSING UP MY PITCHER'S MOUND!

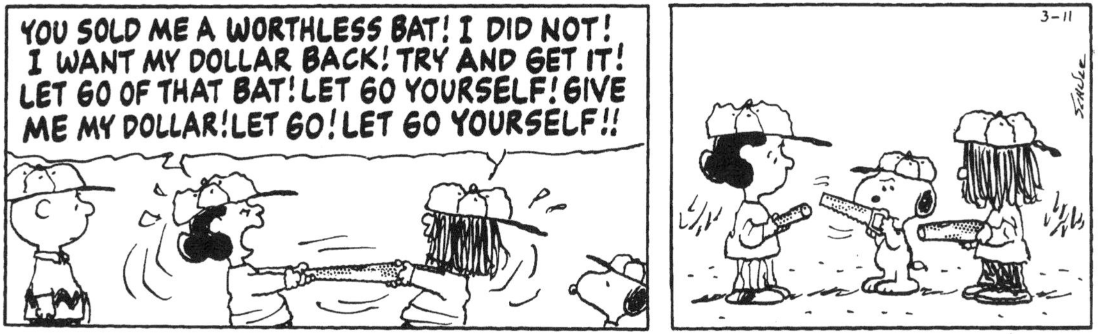
YOU SOLD ME A WORTHLESS BAT! I DID NOT! I WANT MY DOLLAR BACK! TRY AND GET IT! LET GO OF THAT BAT! LET GO YOURSELF! GIVE ME MY DOLLAR! LET GO! LET GO YOURSELF!!
3-11

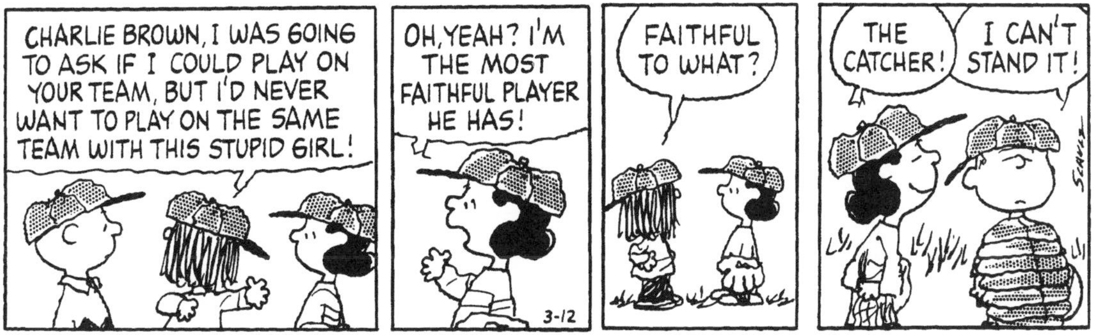
CHARLIE BROWN, I WAS GOING TO ASK IF I COULD PLAY ON YOUR TEAM, BUT I'D NEVER WANT TO PLAY ON THE SAME TEAM WITH THIS STUPID GIRL!
OH, YEAH? I'M THE MOST FAITHFUL PLAYER HE HAS!
3-12
FAITHFUL TO WHAT?
THE CATCHER!
I CAN'T STAND IT!

PEANUTS. by SCHULZ

MY PITCHER'S MOUND LOOKS GREAT..

IT'S GOING TO BE A GOOD SEASON, CHARLIE BROWN!

OUR OL' BACKSTOP SEEMS TO BE IN GOOD SHAPE..

HOW ABOUT THE OUTFIELD?

ALL MOWED, CHARLIE BROWN..IT'S BEAUTIFUL!

AND WE'VE RAKED THE INFIELD SO IT LOOKS BETTER THAN EVER..

3-20

THEN ALL WE HAVE TO WORRY ABOUT IS THE SOUND SYSTEM..

THE SOUND SYSTEM?

THIS YEAR LET'S TRY TO GET THE BALL OVER THE PLATE, YOU BLOCKHEAD!

THE SOUND SYSTEM IS STILL WORKING..

I'M SORRY, MA'AM, IF MY TEST PAPER IS A LITTLE HARD TO READ...

I HAD TROUBLE WRITING IT BECAUSE THERE WAS SOMETHING ON MY DESK..

3-21

A HEAD!

Z

HEY, CHUCK..I NEED YOUR HELP WITH A SCHOOL ASSIGNMENT

WE HAVE TO INTERVIEW A BUSINESSMAN..WHAT DOES YOUR DAD DO?

A BARBER? ASK HIM IF THAT'S A BUSINESS..

3-22

AN ART? WELL, I GUESS THAT'LL BE ALL RIGHT..

EXCUSE ME.. IS THIS A BARBER SHOP?

SIR, MY NAME IS PATRICIA.. I'M A FRIEND OF YOUR SON, CHUCK, THE WEIRD KID...

ANYWAY, I'M HERE TO INTERVIEW YOU FOR A SCHOOL ASSIGNMENT

3-23

NO, YOU GO AHEAD AND CUT HAIR..I'LL JUST STAND HERE AND WATCH...

PEANUTS by SCHULZ

THIS HAS BEEN A LONG UPHILL CLIMB..

BUT IT WAS WORTH IT, WASN'T IT?

OF COURSE, NOW WE HAVE THAT LITTLE PROBLEM OF GETTING DOWN..

3-27

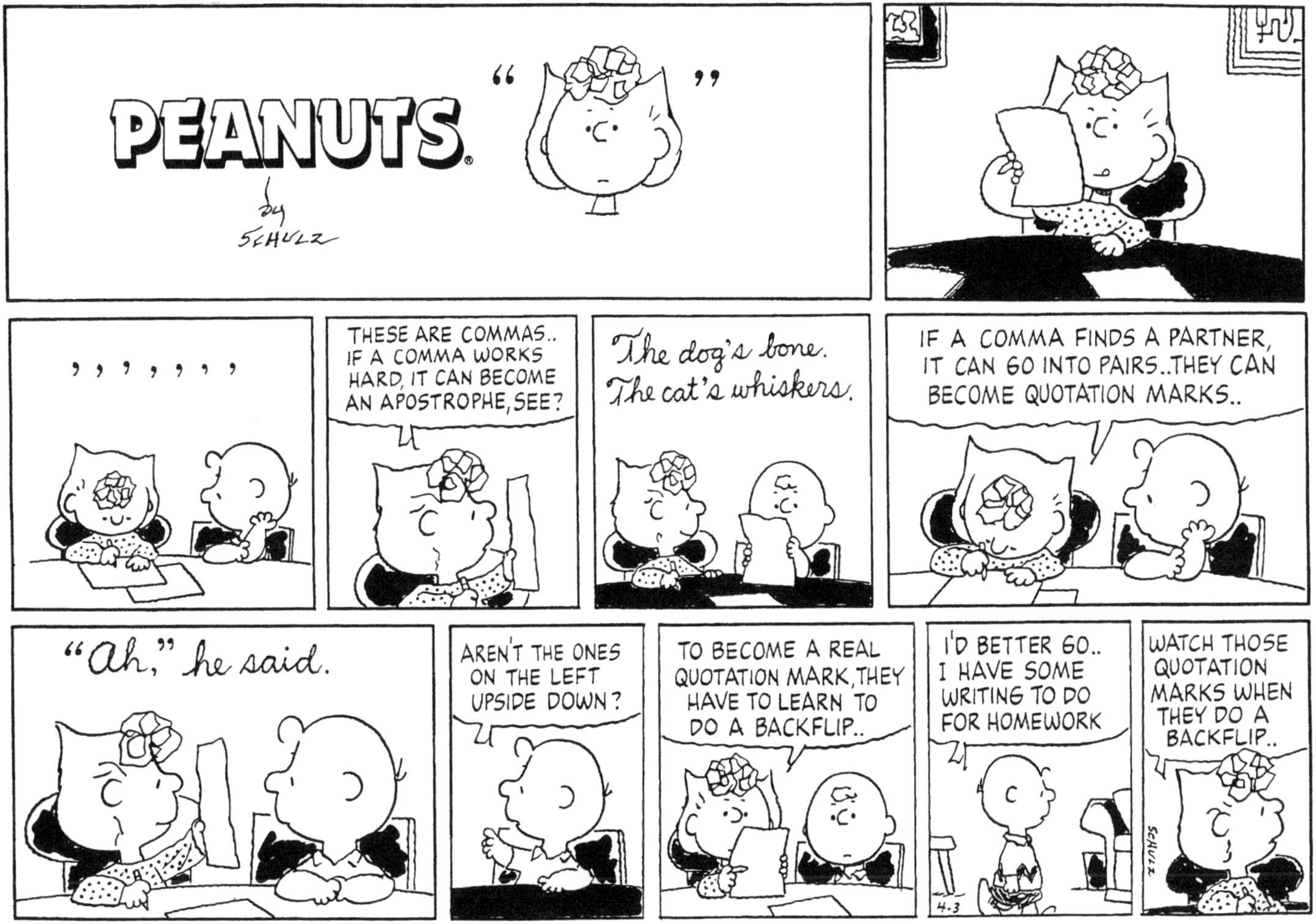
PEANUTS
" "
by SCHULZ
, , , , , , ,
THESE ARE COMMAS.. IF A COMMA WORKS HARD, IT CAN BECOME AN APOSTROPHE, SEE?
The dog's bone. The cat's whiskers.
IF A COMMA FINDS A PARTNER, IT CAN GO INTO PAIRS..THEY CAN BECOME QUOTATION MARKS..
"Ah," he said.
AREN'T THE ONES ON THE LEFT UPSIDE DOWN?
TO BECOME A REAL QUOTATION MARK, THEY HAVE TO LEARN TO DO A BACKFLIP..
I'D BETTER GO.. I HAVE SOME WRITING TO DO FOR HOMEWORK
4-3
SCHULZ
WATCH THOSE QUOTATION MARKS WHEN THEY DO A BACKFLIP..

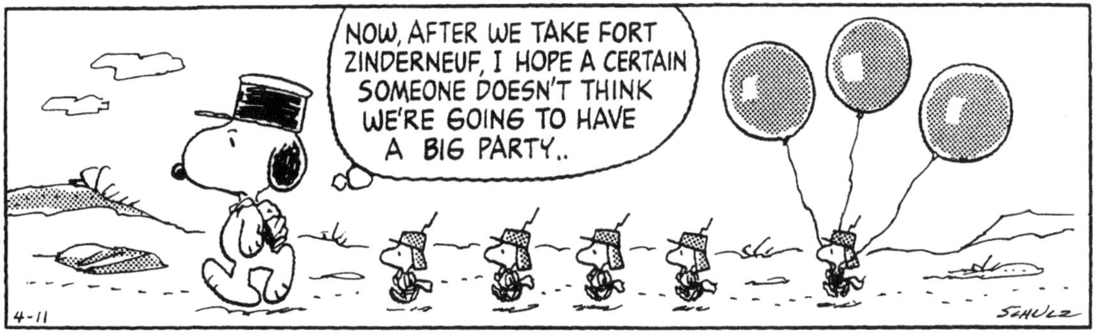
NOW, AFTER WE TAKE FORT ZINDERNEUF, I HOPE A CERTAIN SOMEONE DOESN'T THINK WE'RE GOING TO HAVE A BIG PARTY..

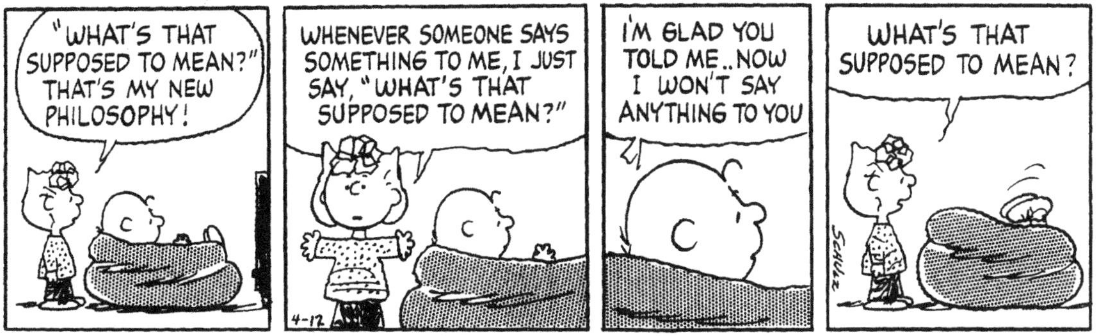
"WHAT'S THAT SUPPOSED TO MEAN?" THAT'S MY NEW PHILOSOPHY!
WHENEVER SOMEONE SAYS SOMETHING TO ME, I JUST SAY, "WHAT'S THAT SUPPOSED TO MEAN?"
I'M GLAD YOU TOLD ME..NOW I WON'T SAY ANYTHING TO YOU
WHAT'S THAT SUPPOSED TO MEAN?

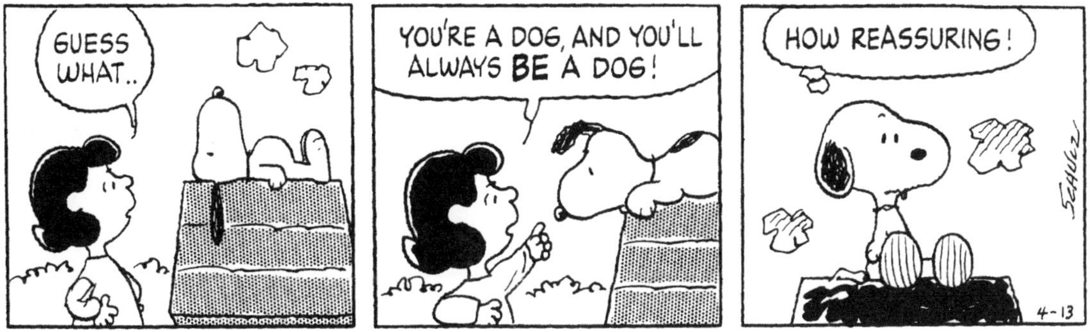
GUESS WHAT..
YOU'RE A DOG, AND YOU'LL ALWAYS BE A DOG!
HOW REASSURING!

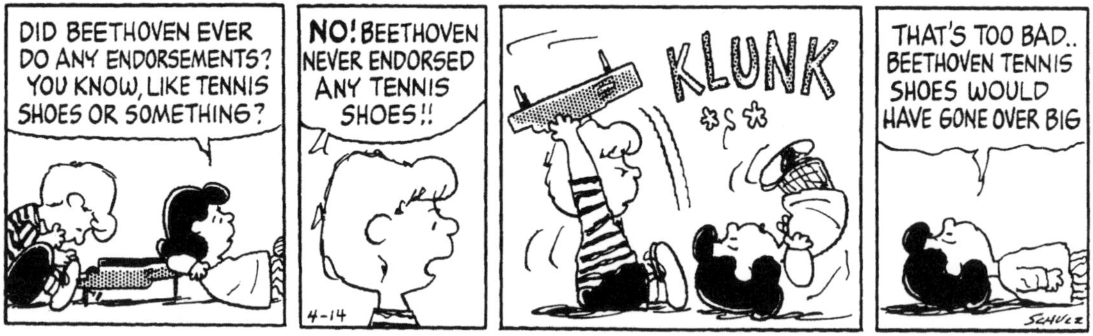
DID BEETHOVEN EVER DO ANY ENDORSEMENTS? YOU KNOW, LIKE TENNIS SHOES OR SOMETHING?
NO! BEETHOVEN NEVER ENDORSED ANY TENNIS SHOES!!
4-14
KLUNK
THAT'S TOO BAD.. BEETHOVEN TENNIS SHOES WOULD HAVE GONE OVER BIG
SCHULZ

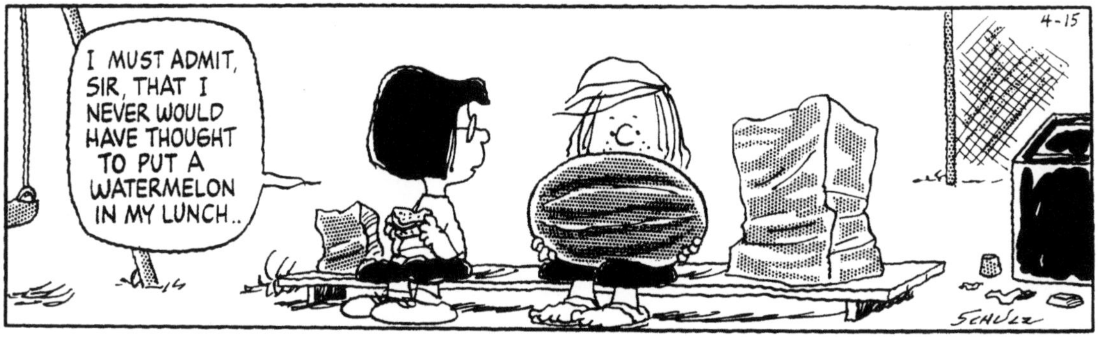
4-15
I MUST ADMIT, SIR, THAT I NEVER WOULD HAVE THOUGHT TO PUT A WATERMELON IN MY LUNCH..
SCHULZ

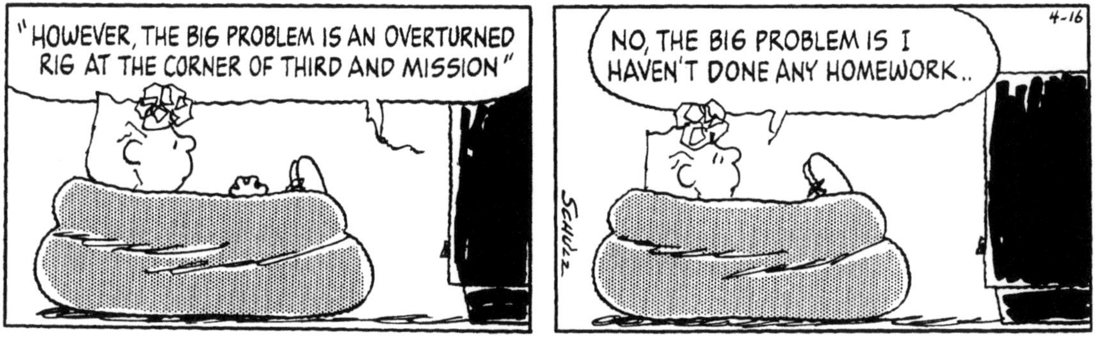
"HOWEVER, THE BIG PROBLEM IS AN OVERTURNED RIG AT THE CORNER OF THIRD AND MISSION"
SCHULZ
4-16
NO, THE BIG PROBLEM IS I HAVEN'T DONE ANY HOMEWORK..

OKAY, THERE'S FORT ZINDERNEUF! I NEED ONE VOLUNTEER TO GO AHEAD, AND DEMAND THEIR SURRENDER..

4-18

GOOD! IF THEY SURRENDER, THEY CAN HAVE A BALLOON

YESTERDAY I STOOD HERE IN THE RAIN FOR TEN MINUTES WAITING FOR THE SCHOOL BUS..

AFTER I GOT TO SCHOOL, YOU KNOW WHAT I LEARNED? I LEARNED HOW WIDE THE MISSISSIPPI RIVER IS..

I STOOD IN THE RAIN FOR TEN MINUTES TO LEARN HOW WIDE THE MISSISSIPPI RIVER IS!

HOW WIDE IS THE MISSISSIPPI RIVER?

I FORGOT

4-20

NEVER TRY TO KISS SOMEBODY THROUGH A CATCHER'S MASK!

CLICK!

I HAVE PHOTOS OF ALL MY SUPPER DISHES..

DO YOU WANT ONE FOR YOUR WALLET?

I KNOW THE ANSWER! I KNOW THE ANSWER!

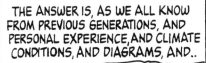

THE ANSWER IS, AS WE ALL KNOW FROM PREVIOUS GENERATIONS, AND PERSONAL EXPERIENCE, AND CLIMATE CONDITIONS, AND DIAGRAMS, AND..

SIX!

YES, THE ANSWER IS SIX..

OKAY, SAY, "BIRDSEED"

ARE YOU
PADDLING
UPSTREAM OR
DOWNSTREAM?

5-5

SORRY..
I DIDN'T
MEAN TO
CONFUSE
YOU..

I THINK SNOOPY
WOULD ENJOY
GETTING A
LETTER FROM US

WE DON'T
KNOW HOW
TO WRITE,
DO WE?

NO, REMEMBER
WHAT I USED
TO TELL YOU?

WHAT
WAS
THAT?

OBEDIENCE SCHOOL WAS A
WASTE OF TIME!

5-6

BE
CAREFUL..

5-7

IF YOU PADDLE TO THE
EDGE OF THE EARTH, YOU
MIGHT FALL OFF..

I'M DESPERATELY IN NEED OF HELP WITH MY HOMEWORK..

ALL RIGHT, BUT YOU'RE GOING TO HAVE TO PAY ATTENTION..

NOW, IN THIS FIRST PROBLEM, THE..

I HATE PAYING ATTENTION..

5/12

HEY, PITCHER! YOU WANT SOME ADVICE?

5-13

WHAT KIND OF ADVICE COULD A PITCHER GET FROM AN OUTFIELDER?

YOU NEED A HAIRCUT!

I HEAR YOU JUST LOST ANOTHER CASE..

IN THE OLD DAYS, WHEN AN ATTORNEY LOST A CASE, HE'D REND HIS GARMENTS..

5-14

NOWADAYS WE JUST KICK OUR HAT!

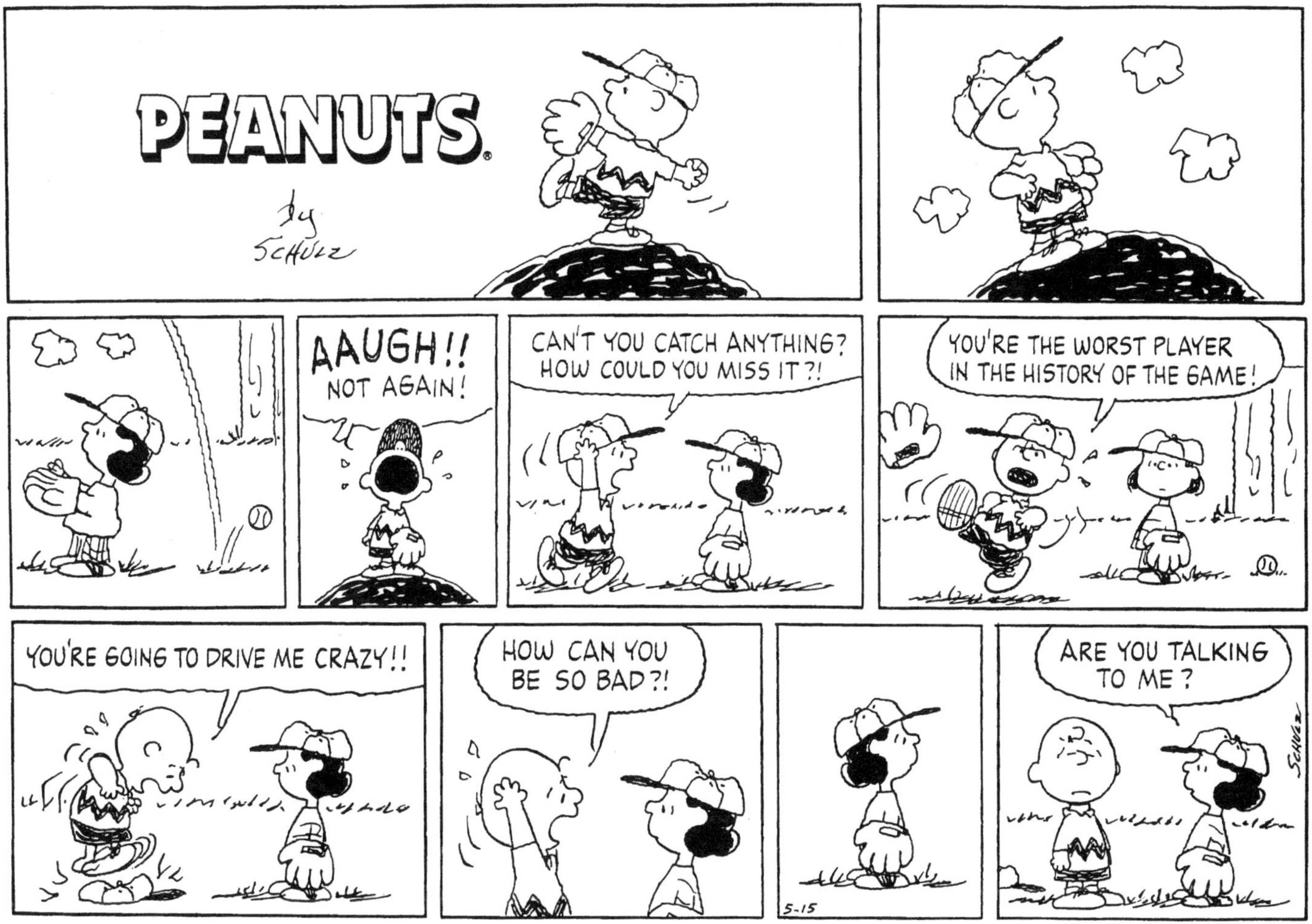
PEANUTS®
by SCHULZ
AAUGH!! NOT AGAIN!
CAN'T YOU CATCH ANYTHING? HOW COULD YOU MISS IT?!
YOU'RE THE WORST PLAYER IN THE HISTORY OF THE GAME!
YOU'RE GOING TO DRIVE ME CRAZY!!
HOW CAN YOU BE SO BAD?!
5-15
ARE YOU TALKING TO ME?
SCHULZ

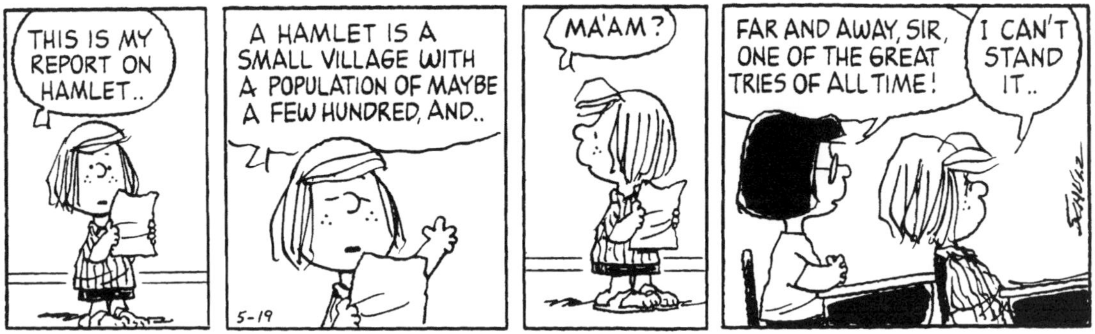
THIS IS MY REPORT ON HAMLET..
A HAMLET IS A SMALL VILLAGE WITH A POPULATION OF MAYBE A FEW HUNDRED, AND..
5-19
MA'AM?
FAR AND AWAY, SIR, ONE OF THE GREAT TRIES OF ALL TIME!
I CAN'T STAND IT..

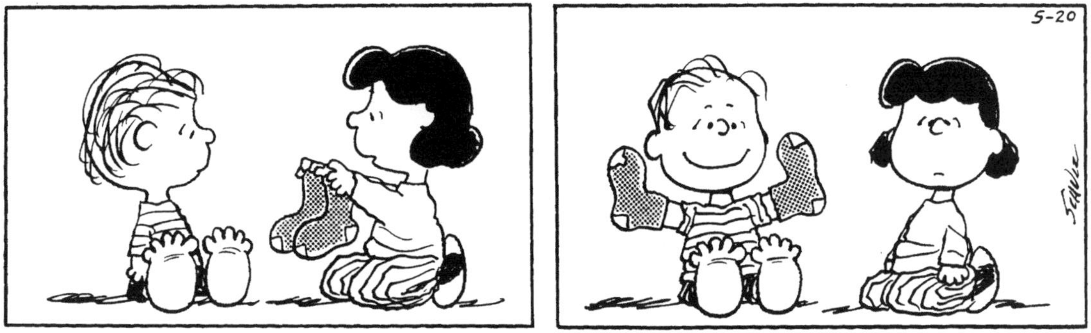
5-20

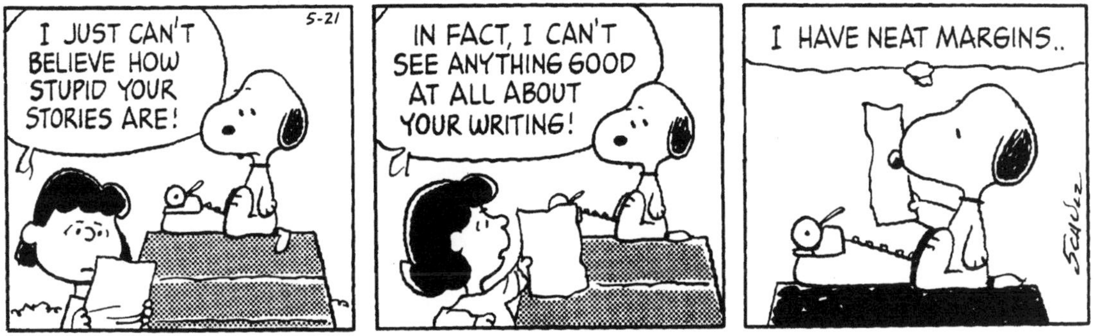
5-21
I JUST CAN'T BELIEVE HOW STUPID YOUR STORIES ARE!
IN FACT, I CAN'T SEE ANYTHING GOOD AT ALL ABOUT YOUR WRITING!
I HAVE NEAT MARGINS..

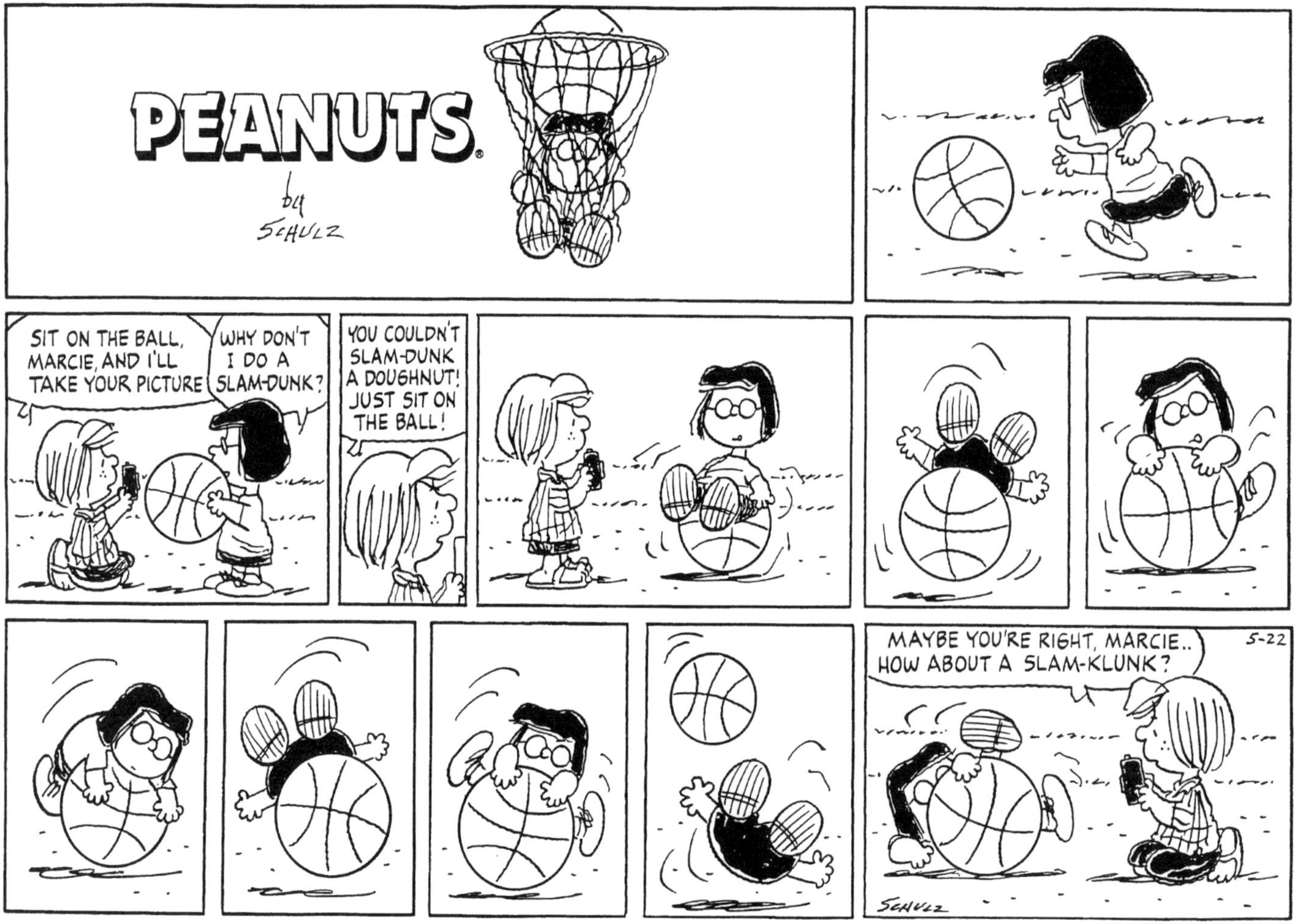
PEANUTS
by SCHULZ
SIT ON THE BALL, MARCIE, AND I'LL TAKE YOUR PICTURE
WHY DON'T I DO A SLAM-DUNK?
YOU COULDN'T SLAM-DUNK A DOUGHNUT! JUST SIT ON THE BALL!
MAYBE YOU'RE RIGHT, MARCIE.. HOW ABOUT A SLAM-KLUNK?
5-22
SCHULZ

5-23

SMALLEST DESERT I'VE EVER SEEN..

5-24

WELL, DID YOU ENJOY THE BOOK?

I DON'T KNOW..I SLEPT ALL THE WAY THROUGH IT..

I NEED HELP WITH MY HOMEWORK

AGAIN?

YOU KNOW, I'M NOT ALWAYS GOING TO BE AROUND TO HELP YOU..

HOW OLD DO YOU THINK YOU'RE GOING TO BE BEFORE YOU WON'T NEED ME ANYMORE?

EIGHTY!

5-25

1994   *Page 219*

PEANUTS.

LET ME EXPLAIN..

THE DOCTOR IS IN

PSYCHIATRIC HELP 5¢

THE DOCTOR IS IN

IT'S A RELAXING TECHNIQUE

I WANT YOU TO PICTURE YOURSELF STANDING IN A BEAUTIFUL MEADOW

IMAGINE THE SOFT RAYS OF THE SUN PENETRATING YOUR WHOLE BODY..

THEN TRY TO IMAGINE THE MOST WONDERFUL GENTLE BREEZE CARESSING YOUR UPTURNED FACE..

CAN YOU DO THAT, CHARLIE BROWN?

THE DOCTOR IS IN

5-29

YOU'RE STANDING OUT IN THIS BEAUTIFUL MEADOW..WHAT ARE YOU THINKING?

IT'S ONLY THE FIRST INNING, AND THE OTHER TEAM HAS ALREADY SCORED FORTY RUNS!

THE DOCTOR

SOME PRETTY BIG ONES IN THERE, HUH?

5-30

ROOM SERVICE!

5-31

WELL, DO YOU THINK YOU'LL GET A GOOD REPORT CARD THIS YEAR?

A WHAT?

A REPORT CARD.. YOU KNOW, GRADES.. "A, B, C, D"...

SOME SCHOOLS JUST GIVE "SATISFACTORY" OR "UNSATISFACTORY"

HOW ABOUT, "THANKS FOR BEING HERE"?

PEANUTS

ANOTHER ROOT BEER, PLEASE..

THIS IS MY REPORT ON "D-DAY," JUNE 6, 1944..

FIFTY YEARS AGO THE ALLIES WERE POISED TO BEGIN THE INVASION OF NORMANDY..

NO ONE, HOWEVER, KNEW WHEN THAT DAY WOULD BE..

NO ONE BUT AN UNKNOWN SOLDIER SITTING IN A TINY PUB DRINKING ROOT BEER WHO CAME TO A STARTLING CONCLUSION..

"FELDMARSCHALL" ROMMEL IS IN CHARGE OF DEFENDING THE BEACHES OF NORMANDY..

BUT HIS WIFE'S BIRTHDAY IS JUNE 6 !! HE'S SURE TO GO HOME FOR HER BIRTHDAY! HE WON'T BE IN NORMANDY !!

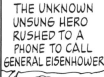

THE UNKNOWN UNSUNG HERO RUSHED TO A PHONE TO CALL GENERAL EISENHOWER

"D-DAY HAS TO BE JUNE 6 !

SPEAKING IN CODE, THE SIMPLE SOLDIER MADE A PHONE CALL THAT CHANGED THE COURSE OF HISTORY..

6-5

WOOF!

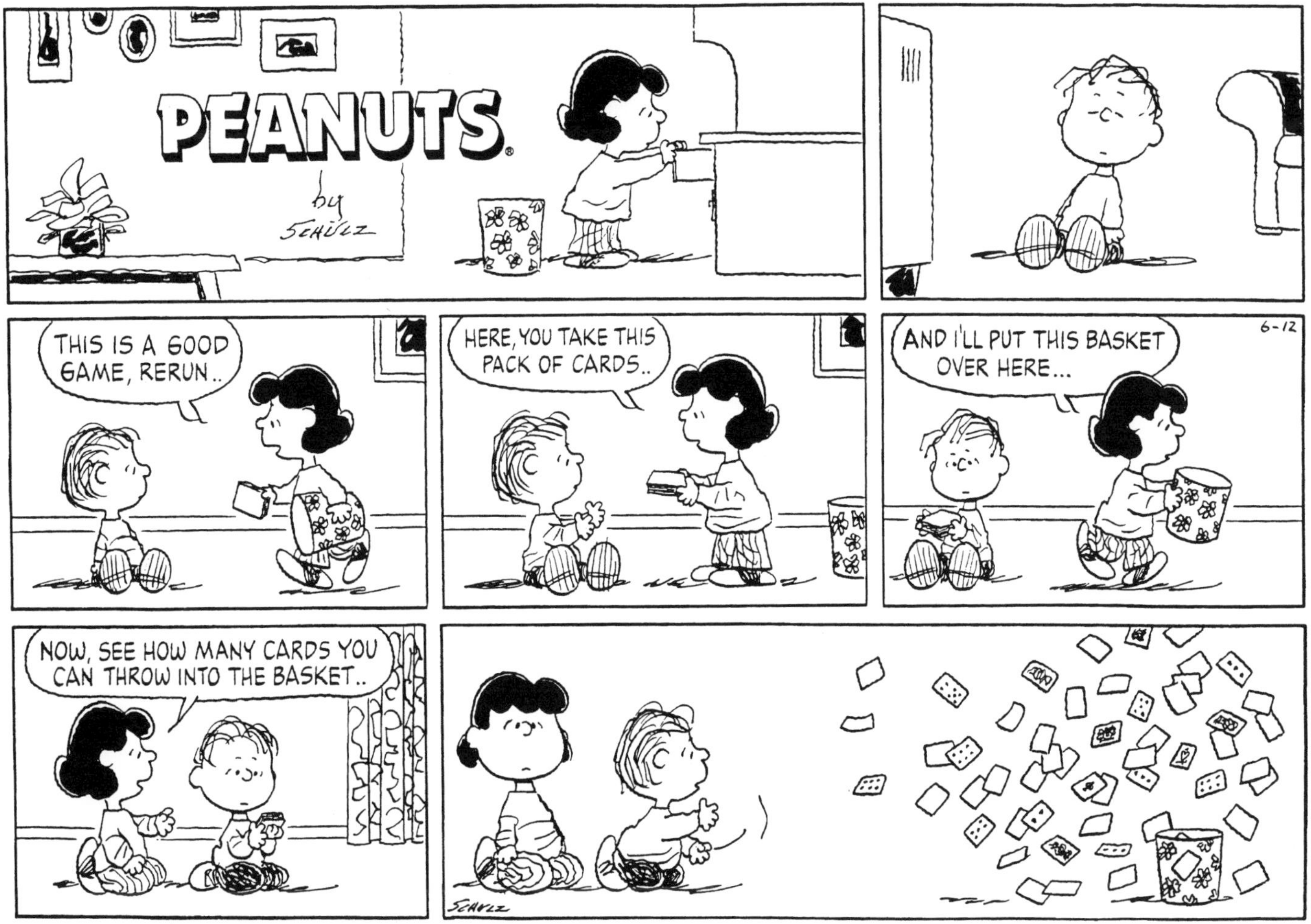
PEANUTS
by SCHULZ
THIS IS A GOOD GAME, RERUN..
HERE, YOU TAKE THIS PACK OF CARDS..
AND I'LL PUT THIS BASKET OVER HERE...
6-12
NOW, SEE HOW MANY CARDS YOU CAN THROW INTO THE BASKET..
SCHULZ

ARE YOU AND YOUR DOG GOING TO CAMP THIS SUMMER, CHARLIE BROWN?

I DON'T KNOW.. I'M NEVER QUITE SURE HOW HE FEELS ABOUT IT...

I'D RATHER GO TO AFRICA, AND GET EATEN BY AN ELEPHANT..

MAYBE WE SHOULD GO TO SUMMER CAMP AFTER ALL.. I'VE BEEN LOOKING AT THIS BROCHURE...

THEY HAVE TEN CABINS, AND EACH CABIN HAS SIX BUNK BEDS..

SURE, AND THE DOG SLEEPS ON THE FLOOR..

OKAY, SNOOPY, WE'RE ALL SET TO GO!

WOW! ARE YOU SURE YOU'RE BRINGING ENOUGH STUFF?

I'M GLAD YOU REMINDED ME.. I FORGOT MY BOWLING BALL!

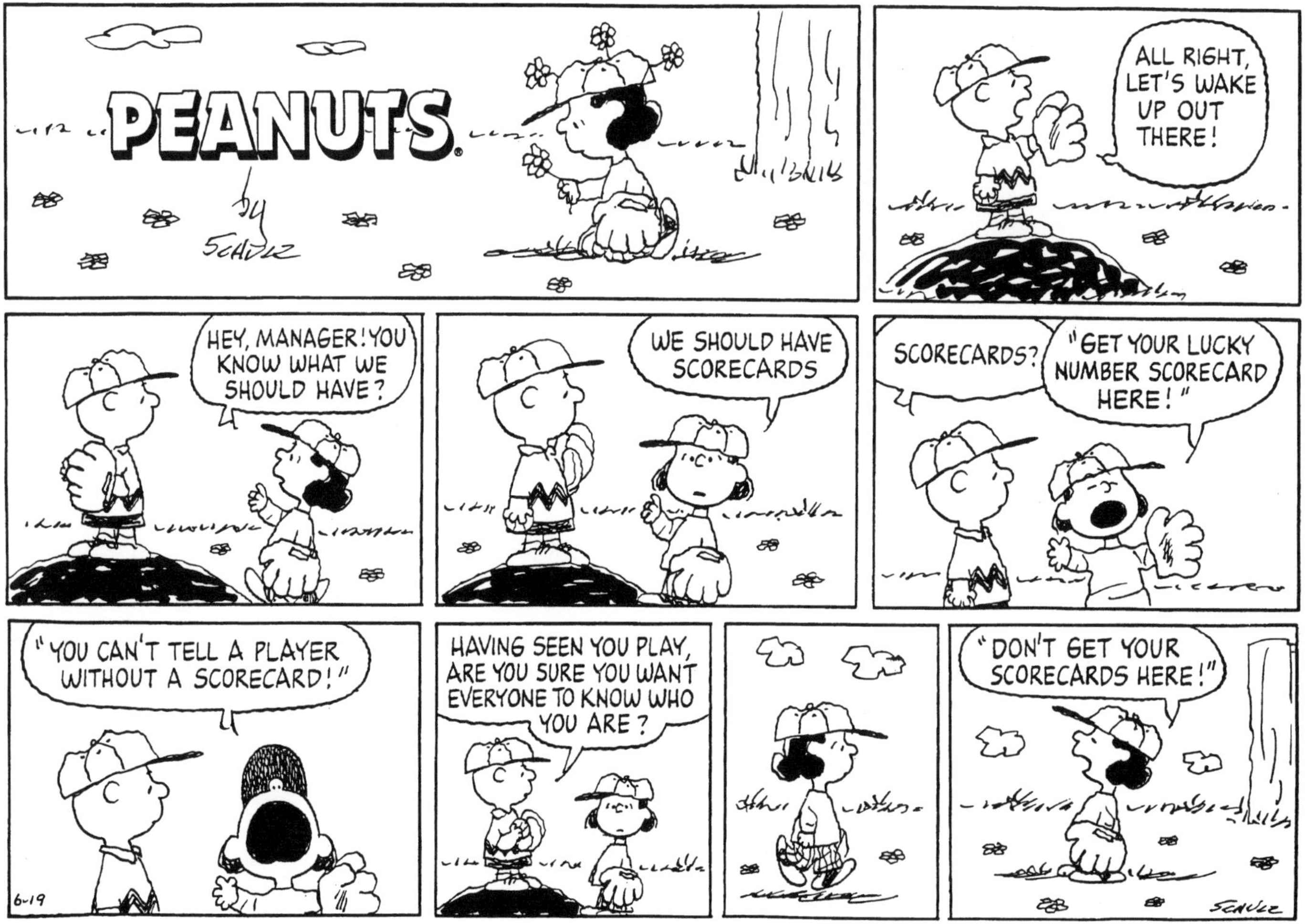
PEANUTS
by SCHULZ
ALL RIGHT, LET'S WAKE UP OUT THERE!
HEY, MANAGER! YOU KNOW WHAT WE SHOULD HAVE?
WE SHOULD HAVE SCORECARDS
SCORECARDS?
"GET YOUR LUCKY NUMBER SCORECARD HERE!"
"YOU CAN'T TELL A PLAYER WITHOUT A SCORECARD!"
HAVING SEEN YOU PLAY, ARE YOU SURE YOU WANT EVERYONE TO KNOW WHO YOU ARE?
"DON'T GET YOUR SCORECARDS HERE!"
6-19
SCHULZ

SNOOPY! SWIMMING LESSONS DOWN IN THE LAKE RIGHT AWAY!

AREN'T YOU GOING TO UNPACK?

6-23

I TOLD THE COUNSELOR THAT YOU HAVE A LOT OF WRITING EXPERIENCE SO THEY WANT YOU TO EDIT THE CAMP NEWSPAPER..

Well, gang, this has been a great week at camp, right?

Personally, I would rather have gone to Africa and been eaten by an elephant.

6-24

THE BEST PART OF GOING TO CAMP IS THE BUS RIDE HOME..

I HAVE TO ASK YOU AGAIN..YOU DIDN'T FORGET YOUR BOWLING BALL, DID YOU?

6-25

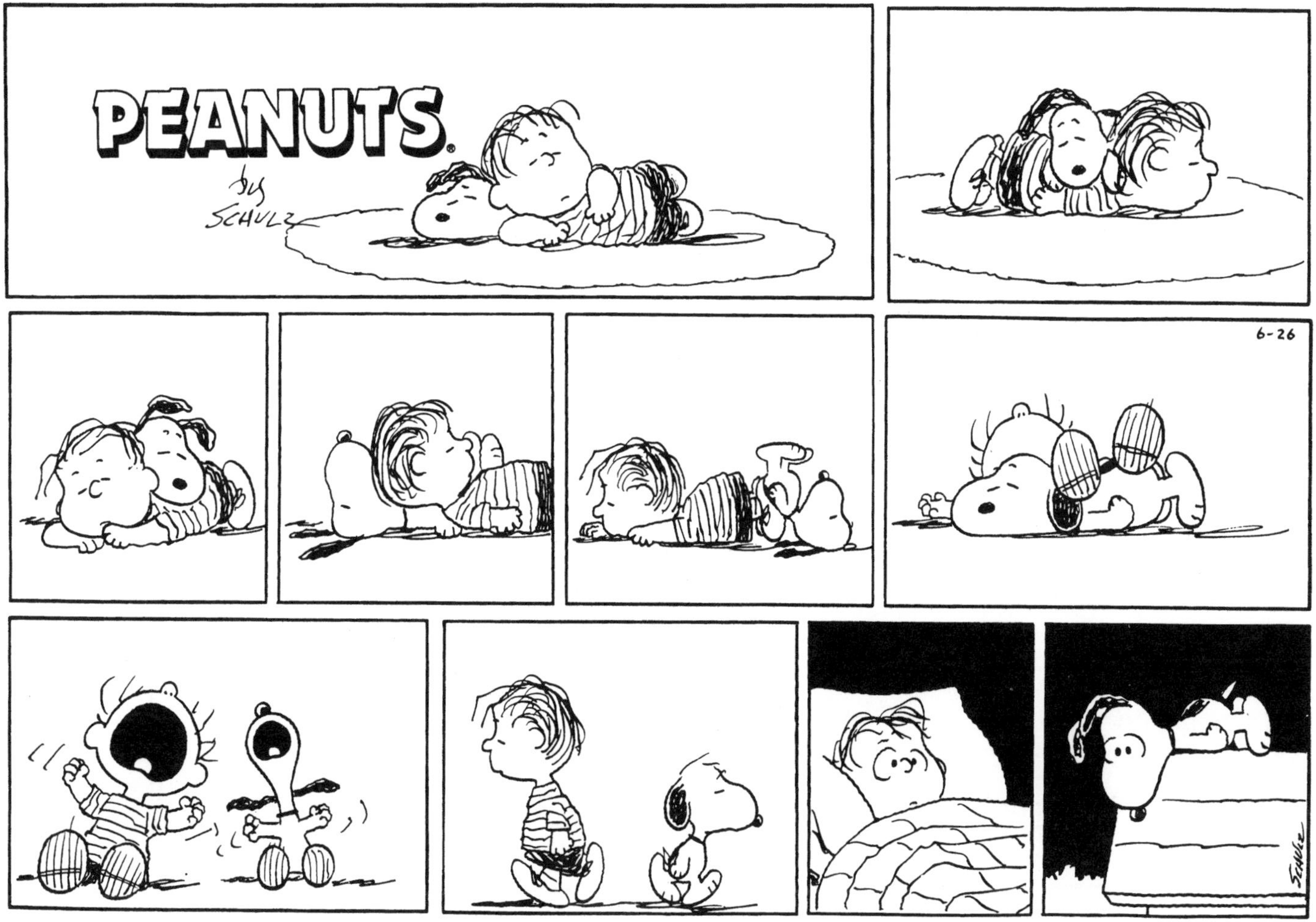
PEANUTS
by SCHULZ
6-26
SCHULZ

OKAY, I TIED MY OWN SHOES...NOW WHAT?

NOW, YOU CAN WALK, OR RUN, OR JUMP, OR DO ANYTHING YOU WANT..

YOU MEAN I DON'T HAVE TO GET PERMISSION?

HI! MY NAME IS RERUN..I'VE NEVER BEEN TO THIS PLAYGROUND BEFORE..

I CAN TIE MY OWN SHOES!

MOM!

WOODSTOCK ALWAYS TELLS SUCH SAD STORIES..

☼ SNIF ☼

DOGS DON'T HAVE HANDKERCHIEFS

1994

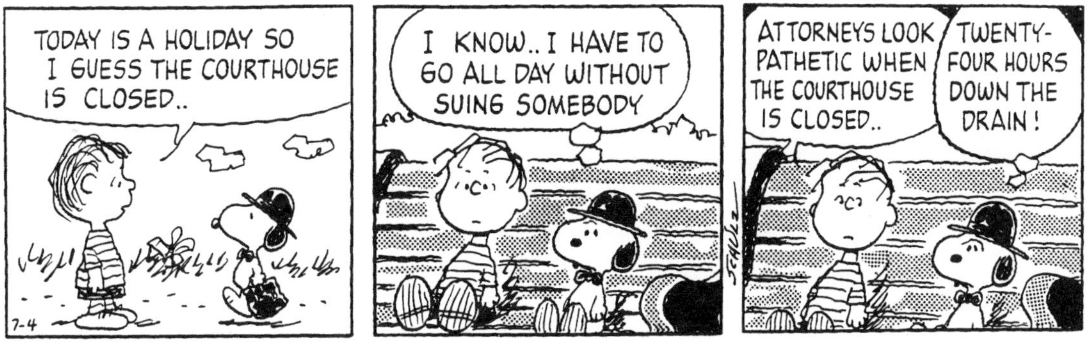
TODAY IS A HOLIDAY SO I GUESS THE COURTHOUSE IS CLOSED..
7-4
I KNOW.. I HAVE TO GO ALL DAY WITHOUT SUING SOMEBODY
ATTORNEYS LOOK PATHETIC WHEN THE COURTHOUSE IS CLOSED..
TWENTY-FOUR HOURS DOWN THE DRAIN!

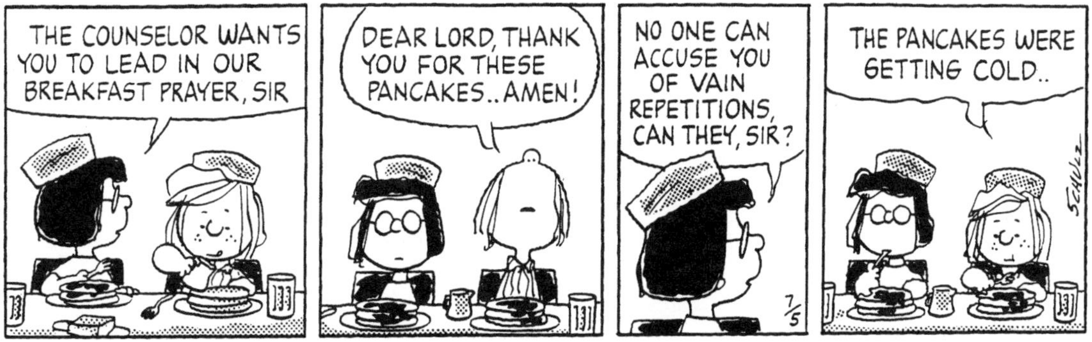
THE COUNSELOR WANTS YOU TO LEAD IN OUR BREAKFAST PRAYER, SIR
DEAR LORD, THANK YOU FOR THESE PANCAKES.. AMEN!
NO ONE CAN ACCUSE YOU OF VAIN REPETITIONS, CAN THEY, SIR?
7/5
THE PANCAKES WERE GETTING COLD..

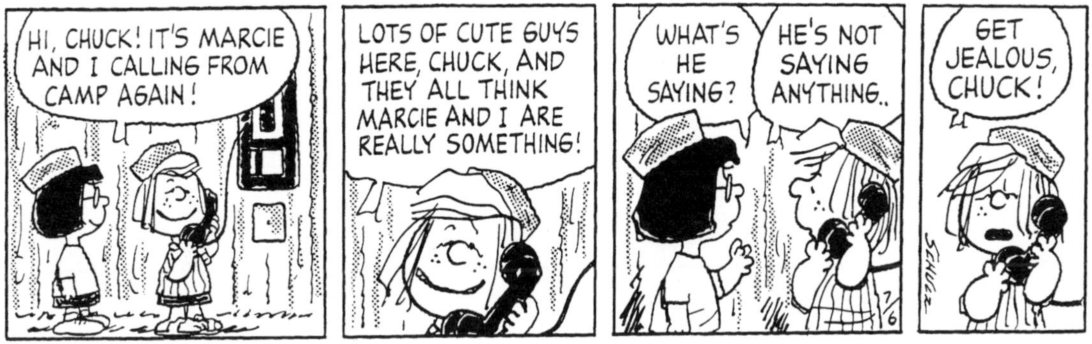
HI, CHUCK! IT'S MARCIE AND I CALLING FROM CAMP AGAIN!
LOTS OF CUTE GUYS HERE, CHUCK, AND THEY ALL THINK MARCIE AND I ARE REALLY SOMETHING!
WHAT'S HE SAYING?
HE'S NOT SAYING ANYTHING..
7/6
GET JEALOUS, CHUCK!

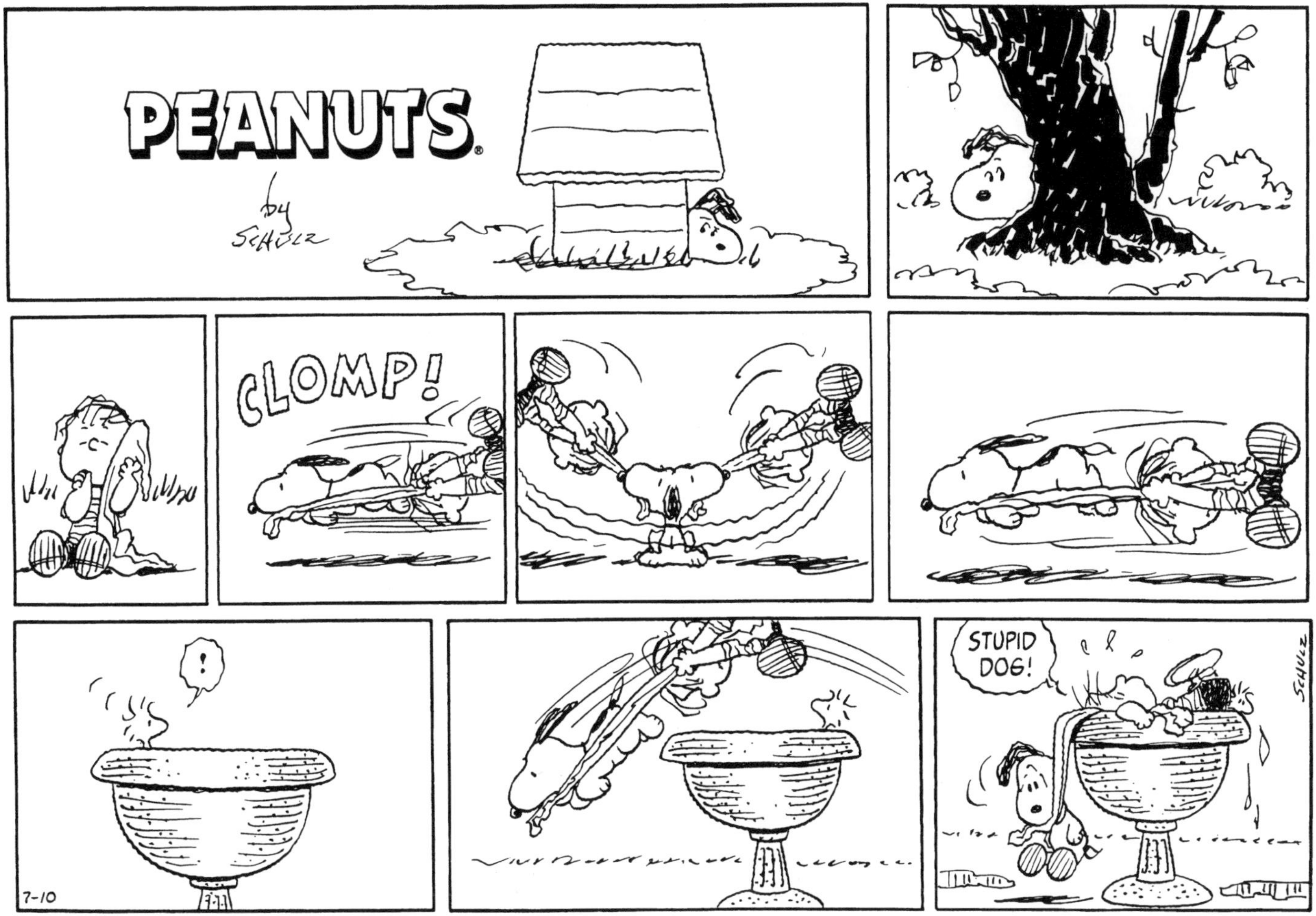
PEANUTS
by SCHULZ
CLOMP!
!
STUPID DOG!
SCHULZ
7-10

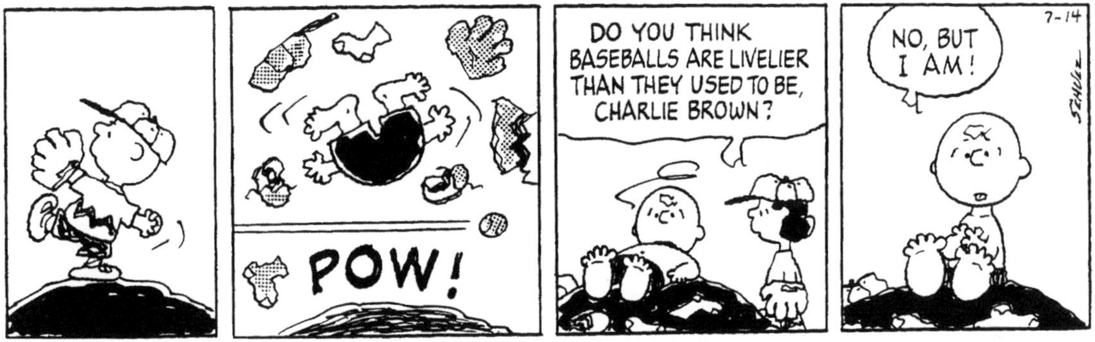
POW!
DO YOU THINK BASEBALLS ARE LIVELIER THAN THEY USED TO BE, CHARLIE BROWN?
NO, BUT I AM!
7-14

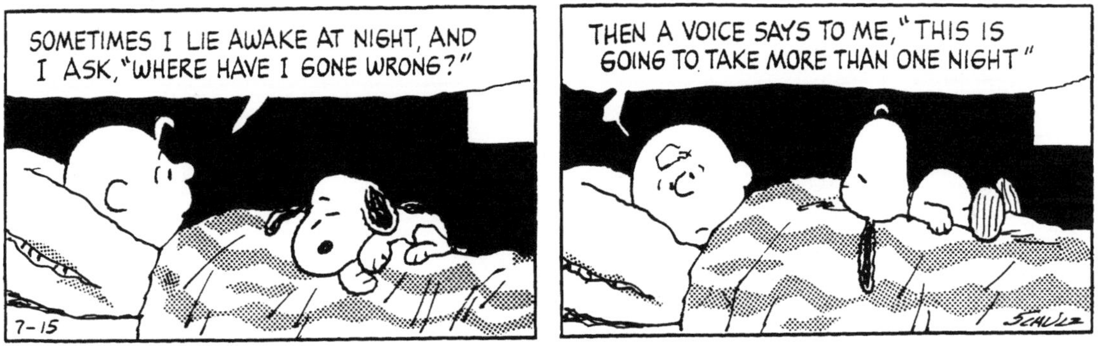
SOMETIMES I LIE AWAKE AT NIGHT, AND I ASK, "WHERE HAVE I GONE WRONG?"
THEN A VOICE SAYS TO ME, "THIS IS GOING TO TAKE MORE THAN ONE NIGHT"
7-15

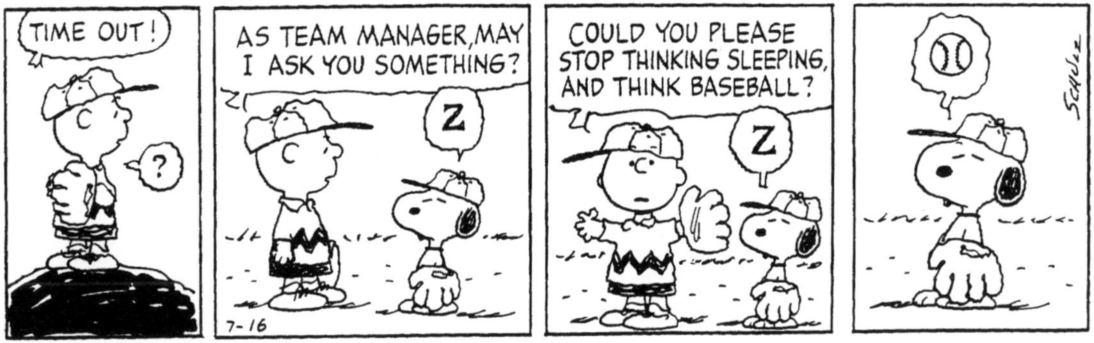
TIME OUT!
?
AS TEAM MANAGER, MAY I ASK YOU SOMETHING?
Z
COULD YOU PLEASE STOP THINKING SLEEPING, AND THINK BASEBALL?
Z
7-16

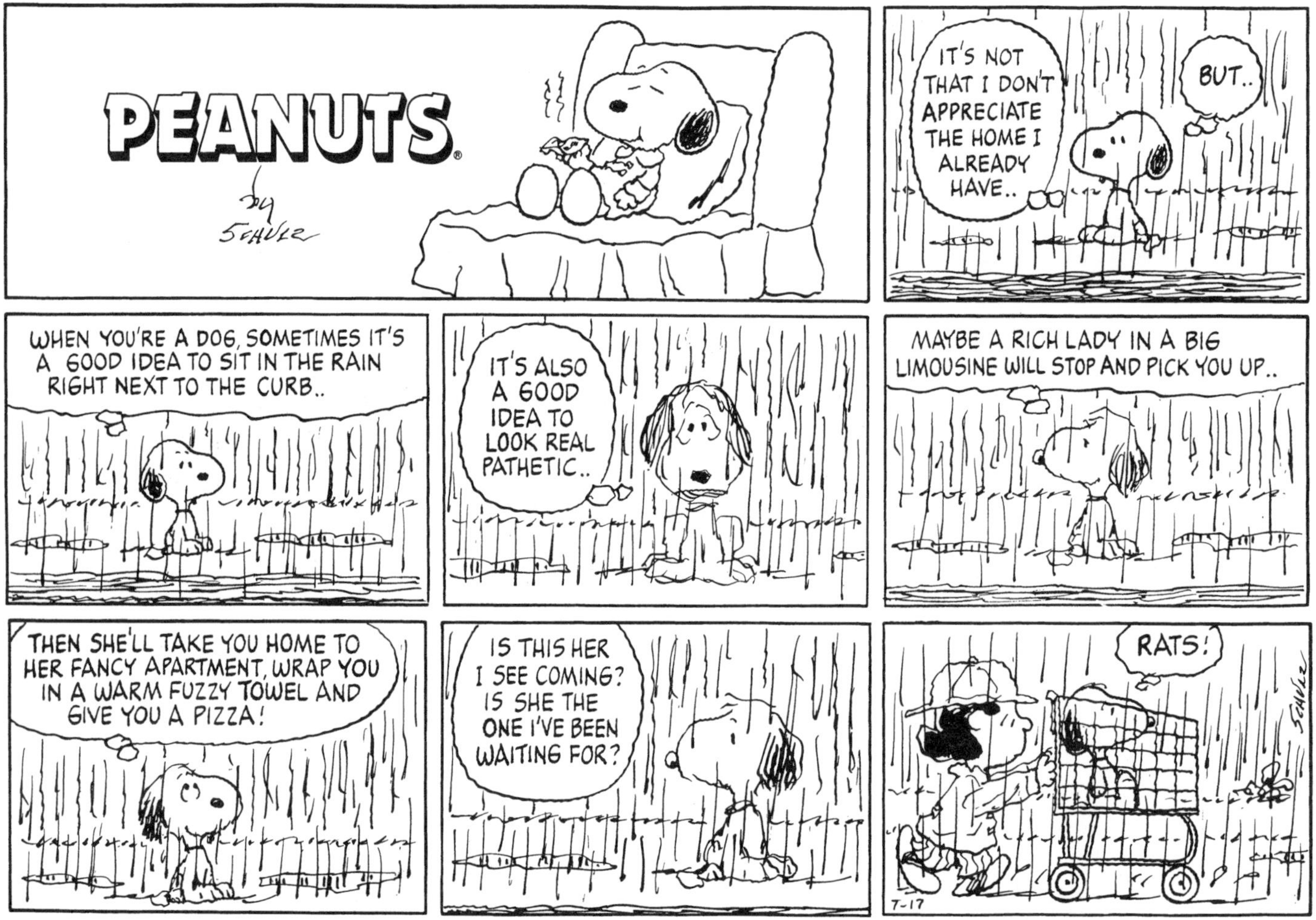
PEANUTS
by SCHULZ
IT'S NOT THAT I DON'T APPRECIATE THE HOME I ALREADY HAVE..
BUT..
WHEN YOU'RE A DOG, SOMETIMES IT'S A GOOD IDEA TO SIT IN THE RAIN RIGHT NEXT TO THE CURB..
IT'S ALSO A GOOD IDEA TO LOOK REAL PATHETIC..
MAYBE A RICH LADY IN A BIG LIMOUSINE WILL STOP AND PICK YOU UP..
THEN SHE'LL TAKE YOU HOME TO HER FANCY APARTMENT, WRAP YOU IN A WARM FUZZY TOWEL AND GIVE YOU A PIZZA!
IS THIS HER I SEE COMING? IS SHE THE ONE I'VE BEEN WAITING FOR?
RATS!
SCHULZ
7-17

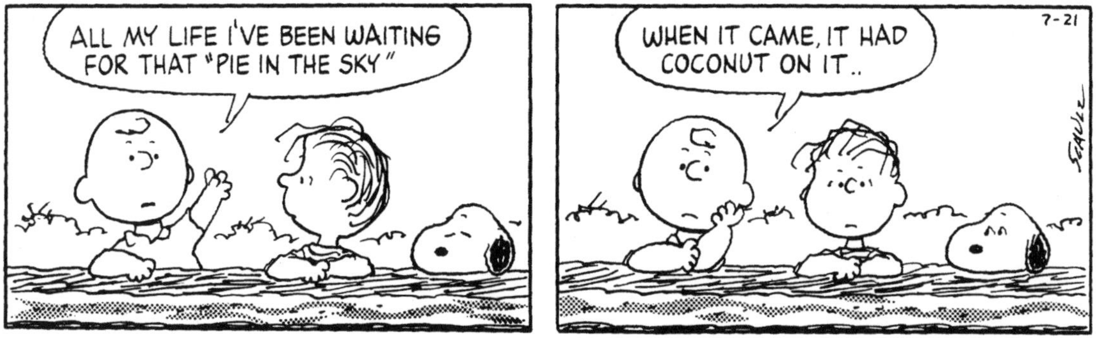
ALL MY LIFE I'VE BEEN WAITING FOR THAT "PIE IN THE SKY"
7-21
WHEN IT CAME, IT HAD COCONUT ON IT..
SCHULZ

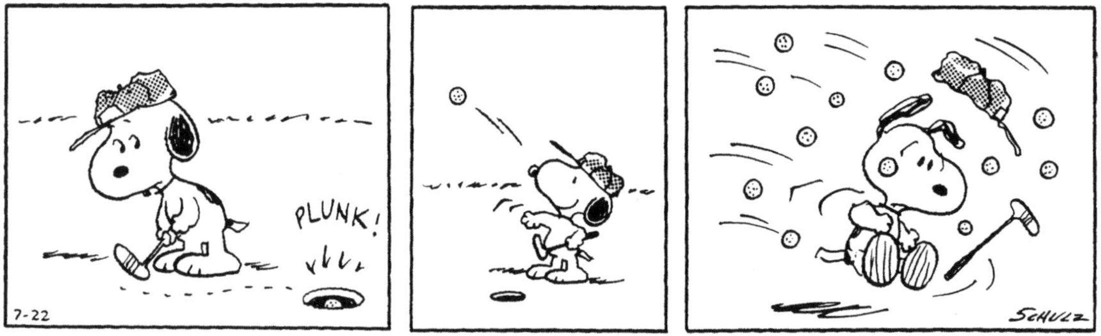
PLUNK!
7-22
SCHULZ

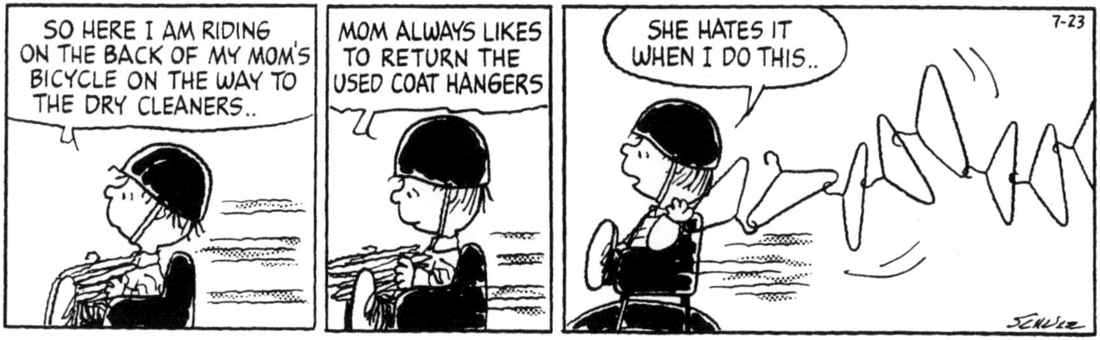
SO HERE I AM RIDING ON THE BACK OF MY MOM'S BICYCLE ON THE WAY TO THE DRY CLEANERS..
MOM ALWAYS LIKES TO RETURN THE USED COAT HANGERS
7-23
SHE HATES IT WHEN I DO THIS..
SCHULZ

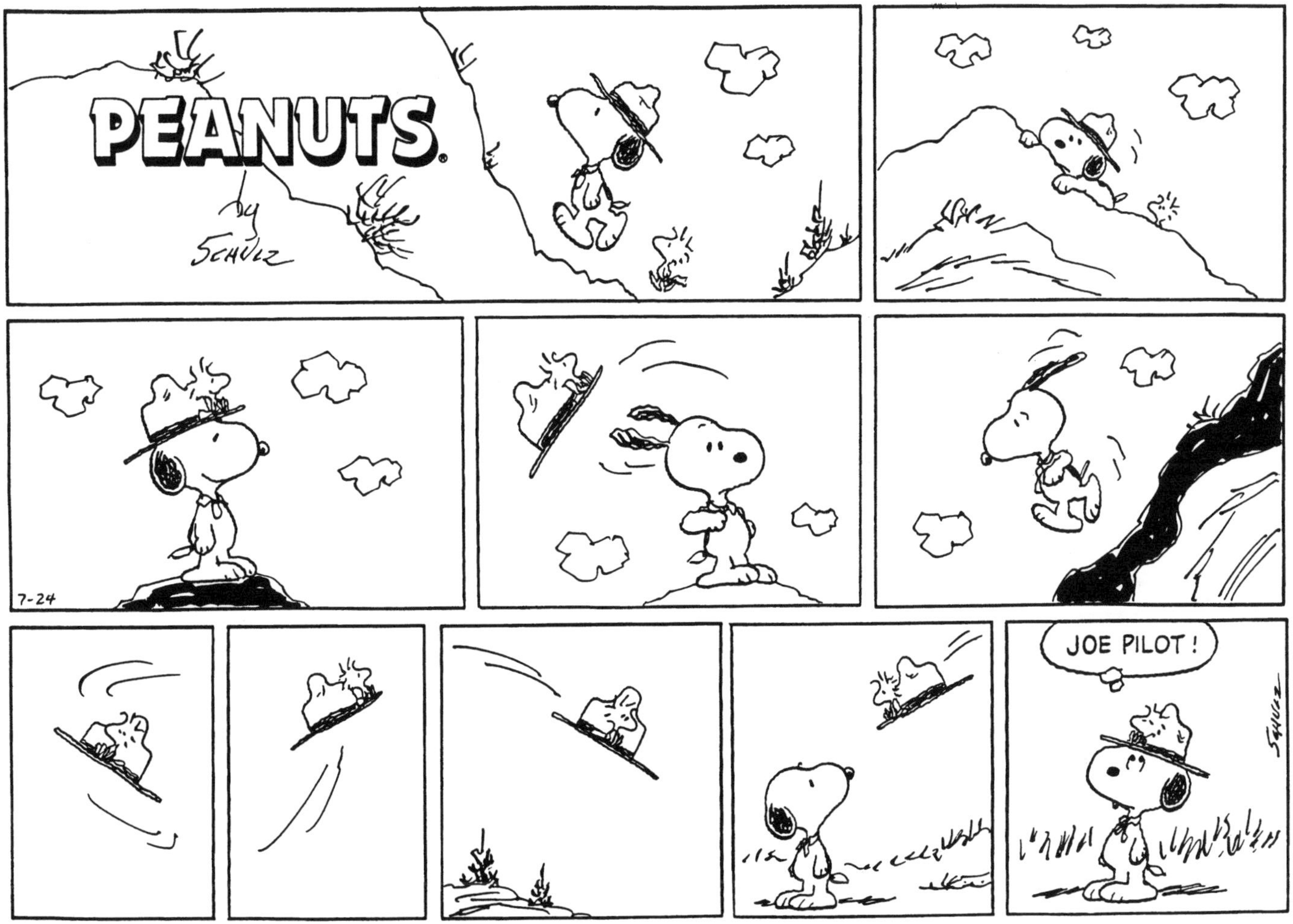
PEANUTS
by SCHULZ
7-24
JOE PILOT!
SCHULZ

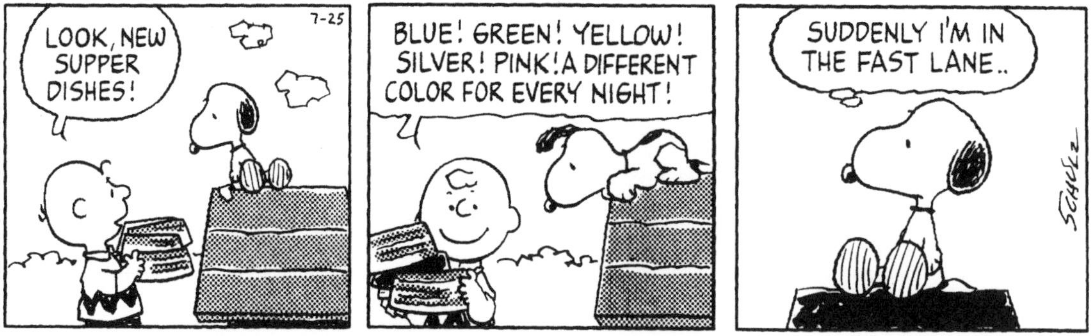
7-25
LOOK, NEW SUPPER DISHES!
BLUE! GREEN! YELLOW! SILVER! PINK! A DIFFERENT COLOR FOR EVERY NIGHT!
SUDDENLY I'M IN THE FAST LANE..
SCHULZ

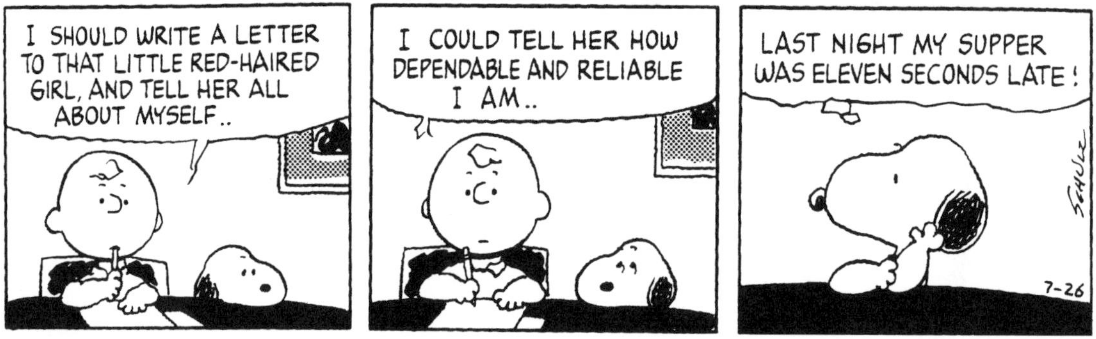
I SHOULD WRITE A LETTER TO THAT LITTLE RED-HAIRED GIRL, AND TELL HER ALL ABOUT MYSELF..
I COULD TELL HER HOW DEPENDABLE AND RELIABLE I AM..
LAST NIGHT MY SUPPER WAS ELEVEN SECONDS LATE!
SCHULZ
7-26

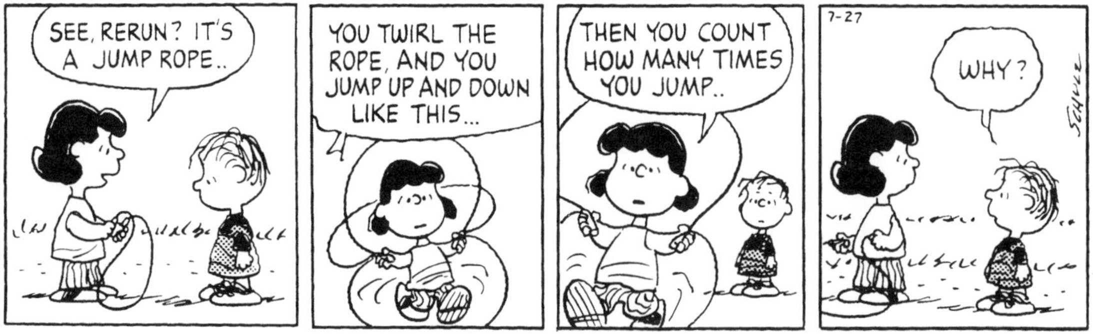
SEE, RERUN? IT'S A JUMP ROPE..
YOU TWIRL THE ROPE, AND YOU JUMP UP AND DOWN LIKE THIS...
THEN YOU COUNT HOW MANY TIMES YOU JUMP..
7-27
WHY?
SCHULZ

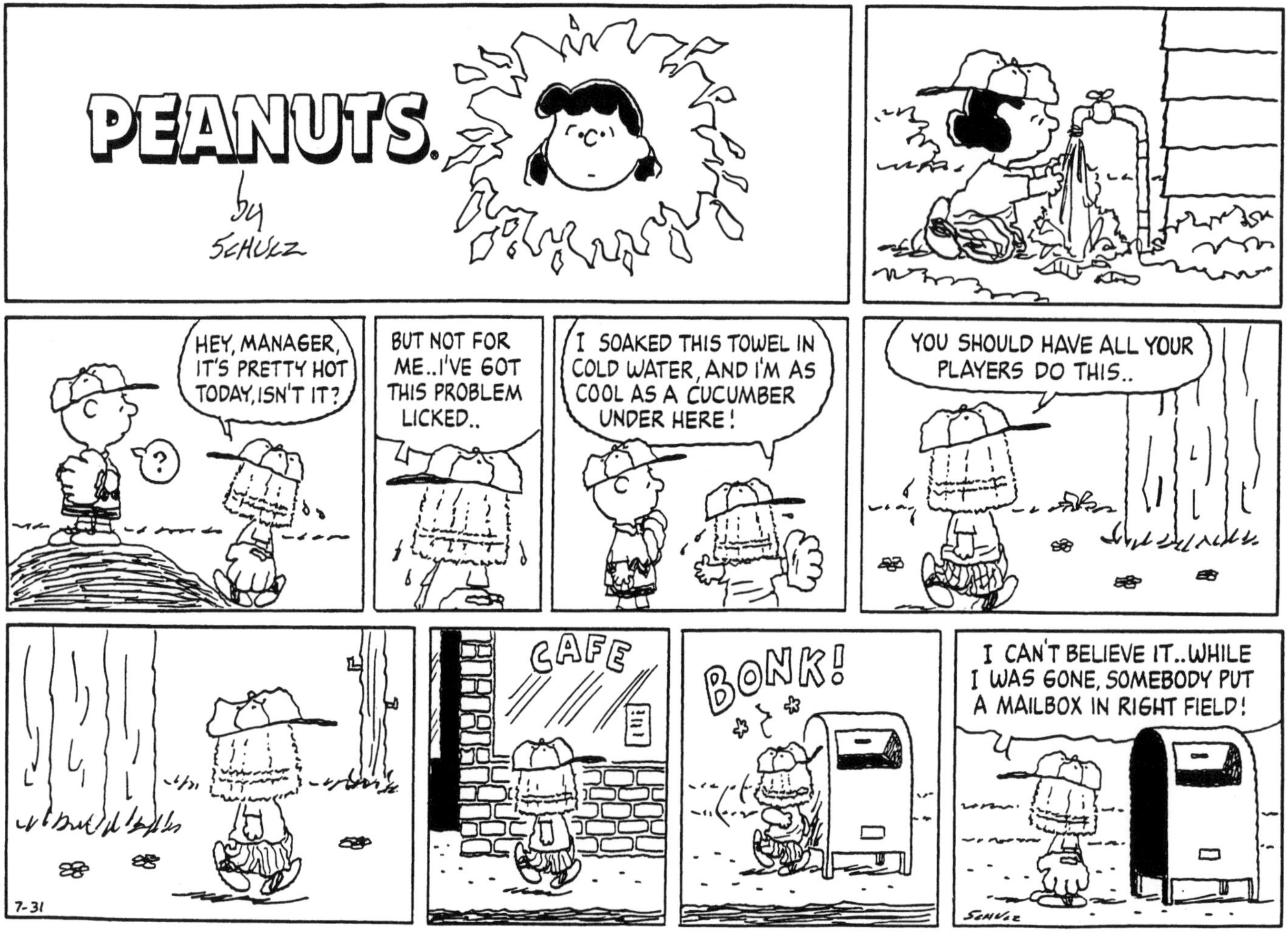
PEANUTS
by SCHULZ
HEY, MANAGER, IT'S PRETTY HOT TODAY, ISN'T IT?
?
BUT NOT FOR ME..I'VE GOT THIS PROBLEM LICKED..
I SOAKED THIS TOWEL IN COLD WATER, AND I'M AS COOL AS A CUCUMBER UNDER HERE!
YOU SHOULD HAVE ALL YOUR PLAYERS DO THIS..
7-31
CAFE
BONK!
I CAN'T BELIEVE IT..WHILE I WAS GONE, SOMEBODY PUT A MAILBOX IN RIGHT FIELD!
SCHULZ

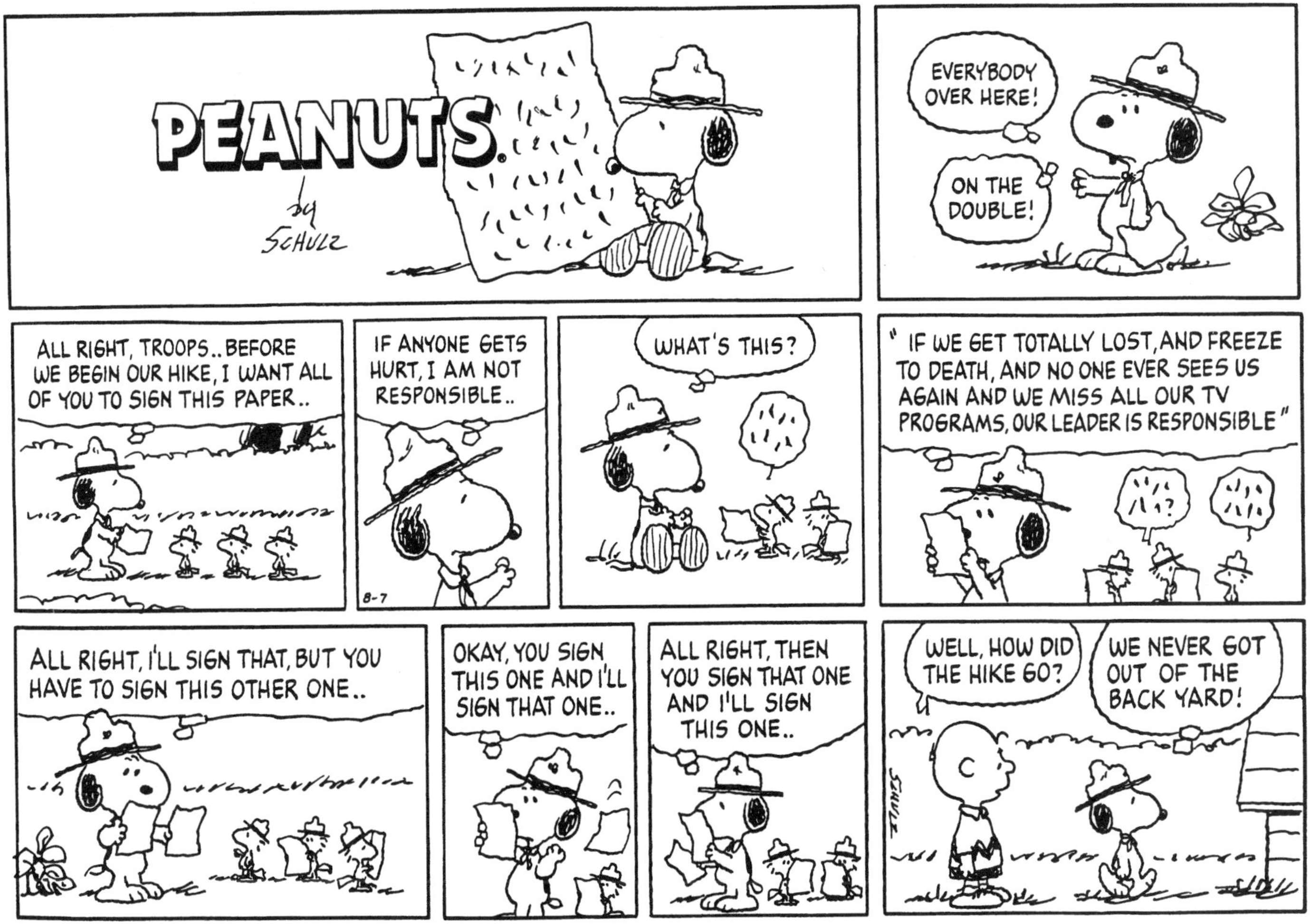
PEANUTS
by SCHULZ
EVERYBODY OVER HERE!
ON THE DOUBLE!
ALL RIGHT, TROOPS.. BEFORE WE BEGIN OUR HIKE, I WANT ALL OF YOU TO SIGN THIS PAPER..
IF ANYONE GETS HURT, I AM NOT RESPONSIBLE..
8-7
WHAT'S THIS?
" IF WE GET TOTALLY LOST, AND FREEZE TO DEATH, AND NO ONE EVER SEES US AGAIN AND WE MISS ALL OUR TV PROGRAMS, OUR LEADER IS RESPONSIBLE "
ALL RIGHT, I'LL SIGN THAT, BUT YOU HAVE TO SIGN THIS OTHER ONE..
OKAY, YOU SIGN THIS ONE AND I'LL SIGN THAT ONE..
ALL RIGHT, THEN YOU SIGN THAT ONE AND I'LL SIGN THIS ONE..
WELL, HOW DID THE HIKE GO?
WE NEVER GOT OUT OF THE BACK YARD!
SCHULZ

HI, CHUCK..SORRY TO WAKE YOU UP, BUT I COULDN'T SLEEP..

I'VE HAD A LOT ON MY MIND LATELY...

I LIKE TO TALK TO YOU BECAUSE YOU'RE ALWAYS A GOOD LISTENER..

8-11

SORRY I CALLED YOU SO LATE LAST NIGHT, CHUCK.. I GUESS I TALKED YOUR HEAD OFF, HUH?

SOMETIMES I CAN'T SLEEP, AND I NEED TO TALK.. I LOVE TO TALK..

SOMETIMES I JUST NEED SOMEONE TO TALK TO..

8-12

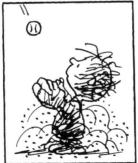

8-13

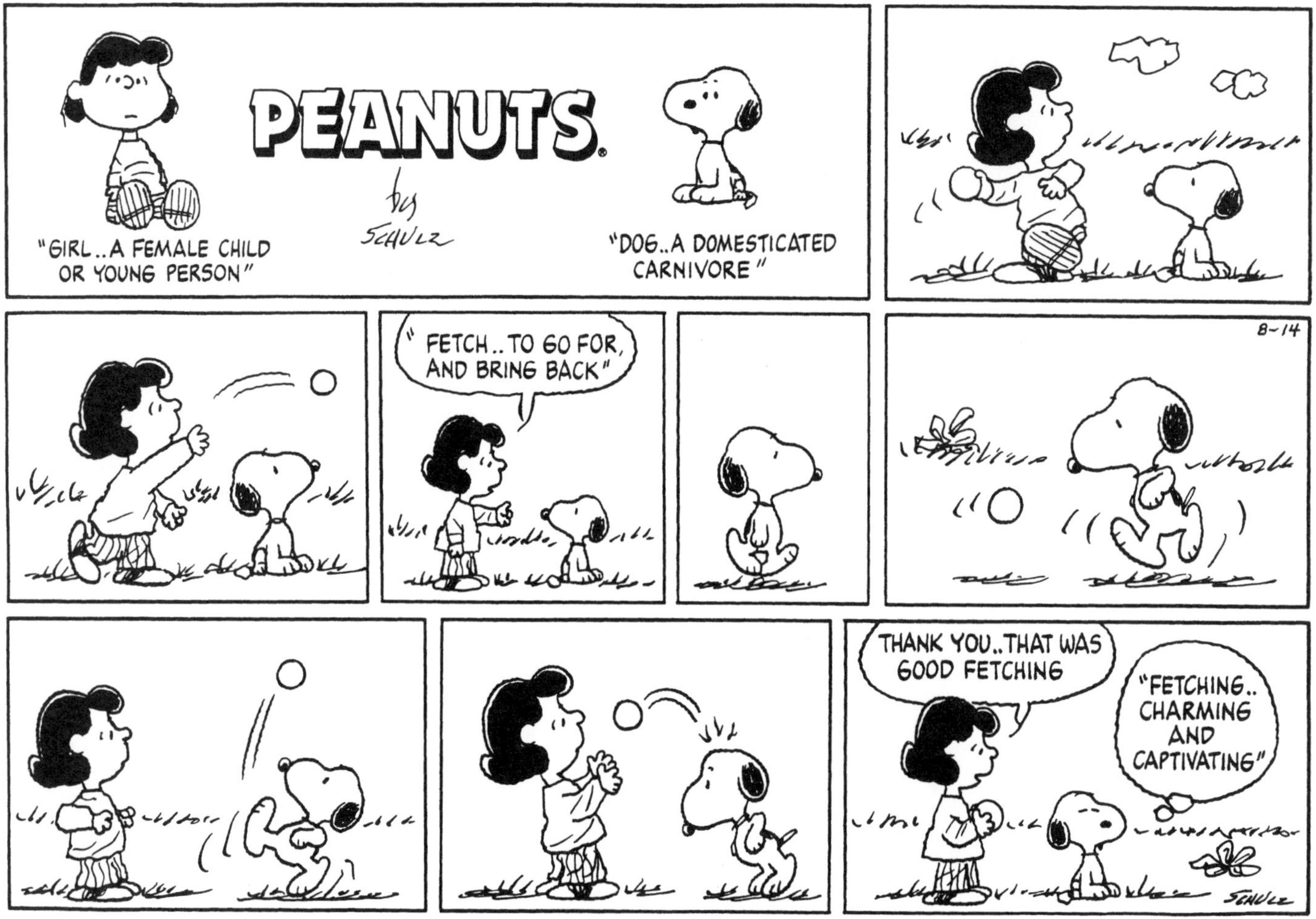
PEANUTS
by SCHULZ
"GIRL..A FEMALE CHILD OR YOUNG PERSON"
"DOG..A DOMESTICATED CARNIVORE"
"FETCH..TO GO FOR, AND BRING BACK"
8-14
THANK YOU..THAT WAS GOOD FETCHING
"FETCHING.. CHARMING AND CAPTIVATING"
SCHULZ

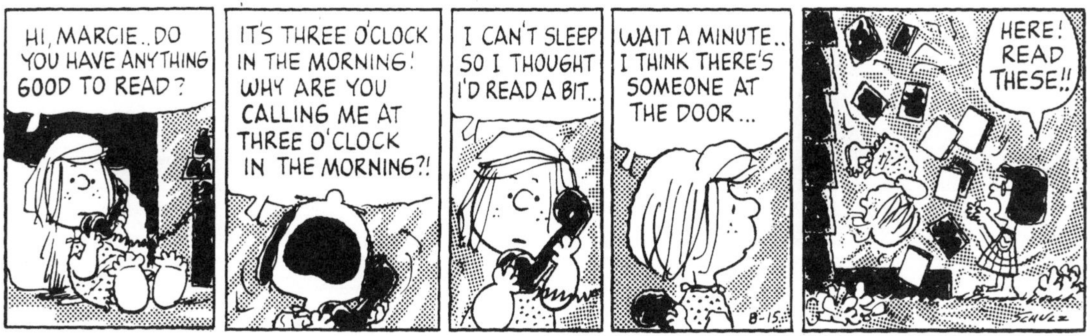
HI, MARCIE.. DO YOU HAVE ANYTHING GOOD TO READ?
IT'S THREE O'CLOCK IN THE MORNING! WHY ARE YOU CALLING ME AT THREE O'CLOCK IN THE MORNING?!
I CAN'T SLEEP SO I THOUGHT I'D READ A BIT..
WAIT A MINUTE.. I THINK THERE'S SOMEONE AT THE DOOR...
8-15
HERE! READ THESE!!
SCHULZ

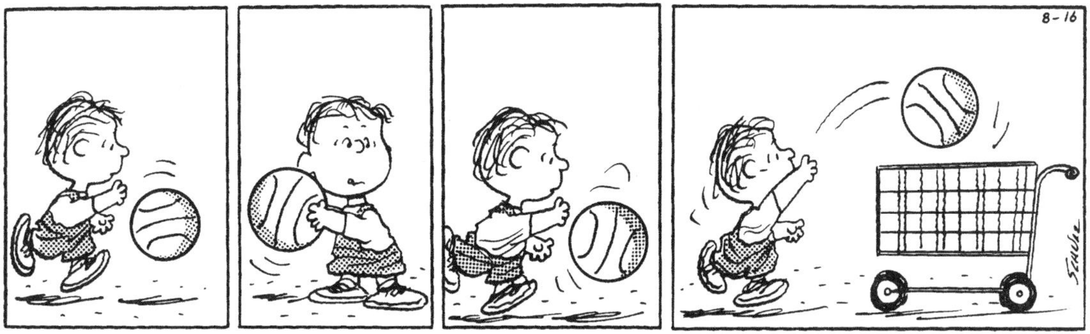
8-16
SCHULZ

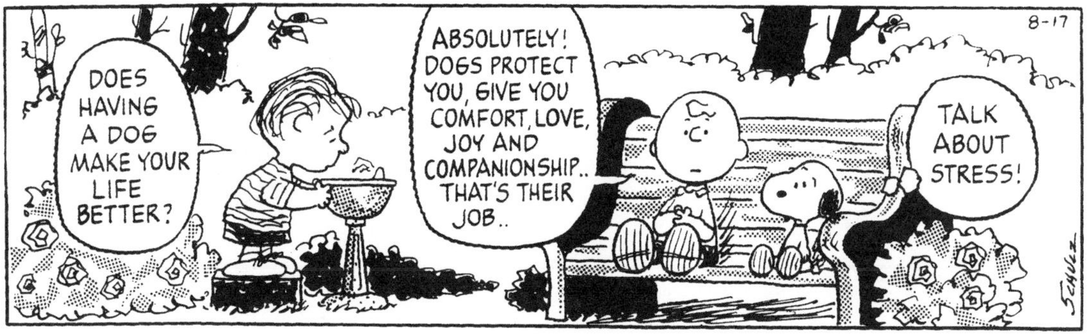
8-17
DOES HAVING A DOG MAKE YOUR LIFE BETTER?
ABSOLUTELY! DOGS PROTECT YOU, GIVE YOU COMFORT, LOVE, JOY AND COMPANIONSHIP.. THAT'S THEIR JOB..
TALK ABOUT STRESS!
SCHULZ

I DIDN'T SLEEP WELL LAST NIGHT.. I COULDN'T GET COMFORTABLE..

..AND SOME PENCILS, SOME PAPER, A PEN AND A LOOSE-LEAF BINDER..

CAN YOU THINK OF ANYTHING ELSE I MIGHT NEED FOR SCHOOL?

ASK HIM IF HE SELLS BRAINS..

IGNORE HER, SIR.. SHE'S EXCESSIVELY WEIRD!

OKAY, LITTLE BROTHER, RUN OUT TO THE KITCHEN, AND GET ME A GLASS OF WATER..

WHY SHOULD I?

TO KEEP FROM GETTING POUNDED ON THE HEAD!

BROTHER HARASSMENT!!

PEANUTS.

by
SCHULZ

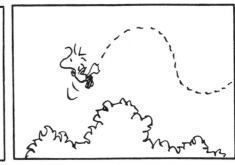

REMOTE CONTROLLED WOODSTOCK..

YOU SHOULD WRITE ABOUT SOMETHING PLEASANT

WRITE SOMETHING THAT YOU KNOW WILL MAKE EVERYONE HAPPY..

The cat left the room.

DON'T BE DISCOURAGED.. I'M NEW AT THIS..

SEE? YOU HAVE FIVE TOES ON THIS FOOT AND FIVE TOES ON THAT FOOT..

IT'S A TIE!

IF THERE'S A PLAY-OFF, I'M IN TROUBLE..

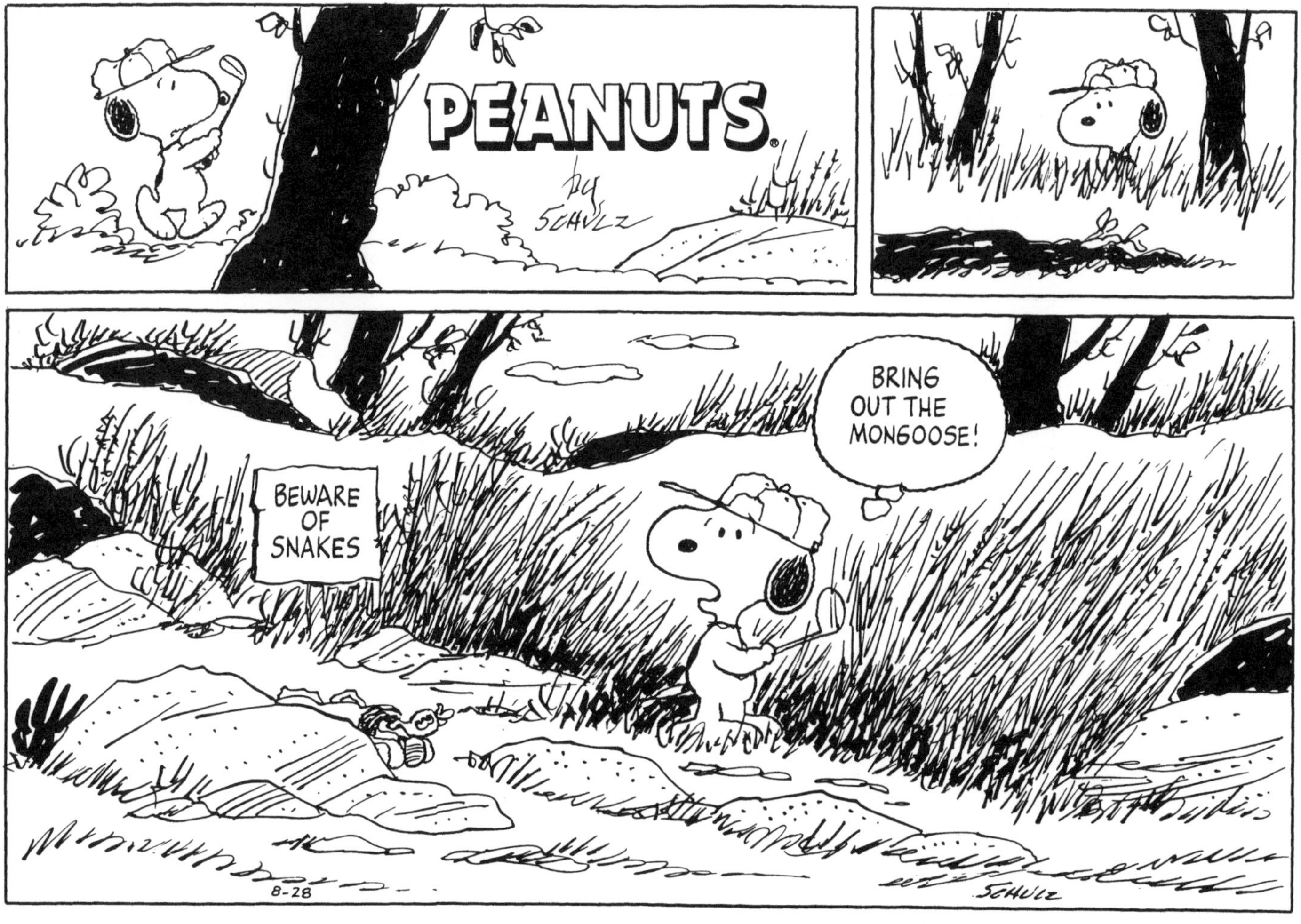
PEANUTS
by SCHULZ
BEWARE OF SNAKES
BRING OUT THE MONGOOSE!
8-28
SCHULZ

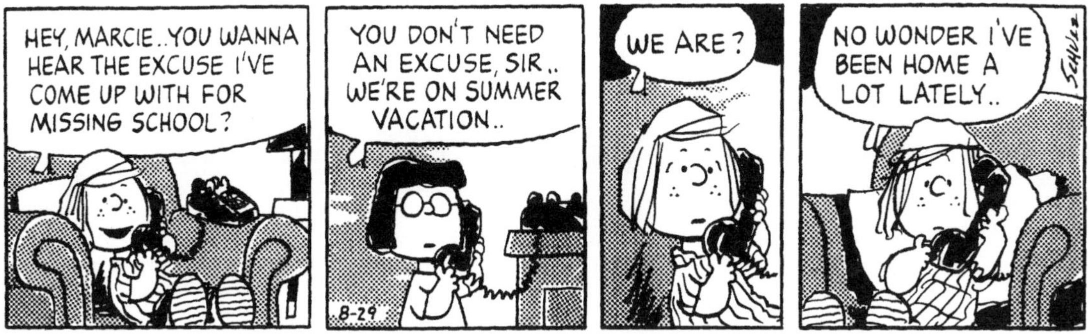
HEY, MARCIE..YOU WANNA HEAR THE EXCUSE I'VE COME UP WITH FOR MISSING SCHOOL?
YOU DON'T NEED AN EXCUSE, SIR.. WE'RE ON SUMMER VACATION..
8-29
WE ARE?
NO WONDER I'VE BEEN HOME A LOT LATELY..
SCHULZ

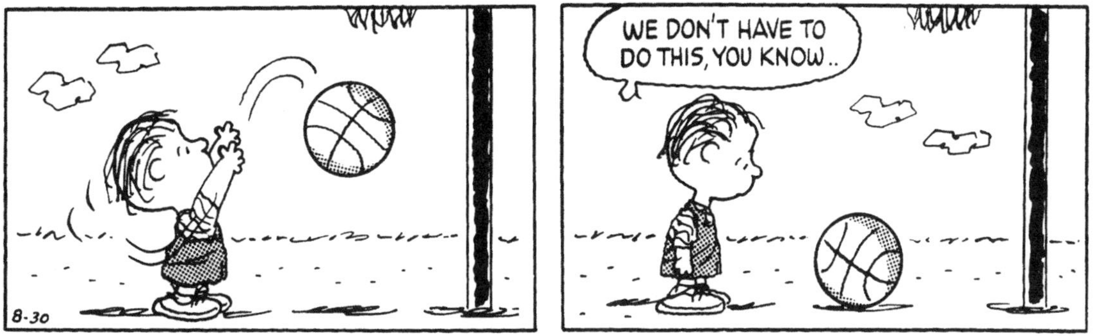
8-30
WE DON'T HAVE TO DO THIS, YOU KNOW..

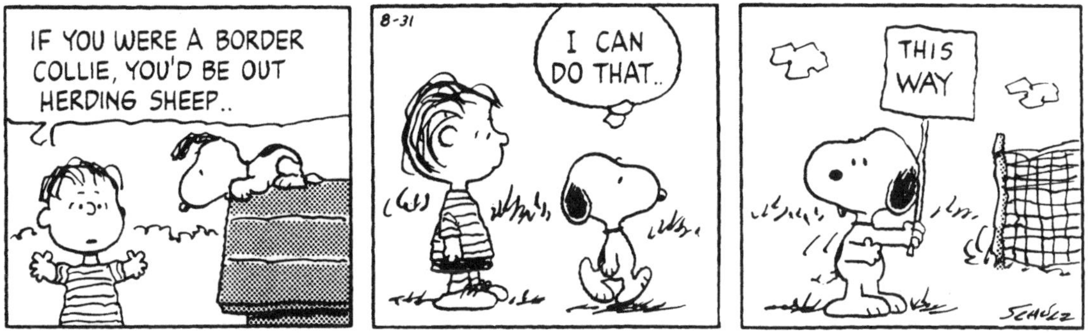
IF YOU WERE A BORDER COLLIE, YOU'D BE OUT HERDING SHEEP..
8-31
I CAN DO THAT..
THIS WAY
SCHULZ

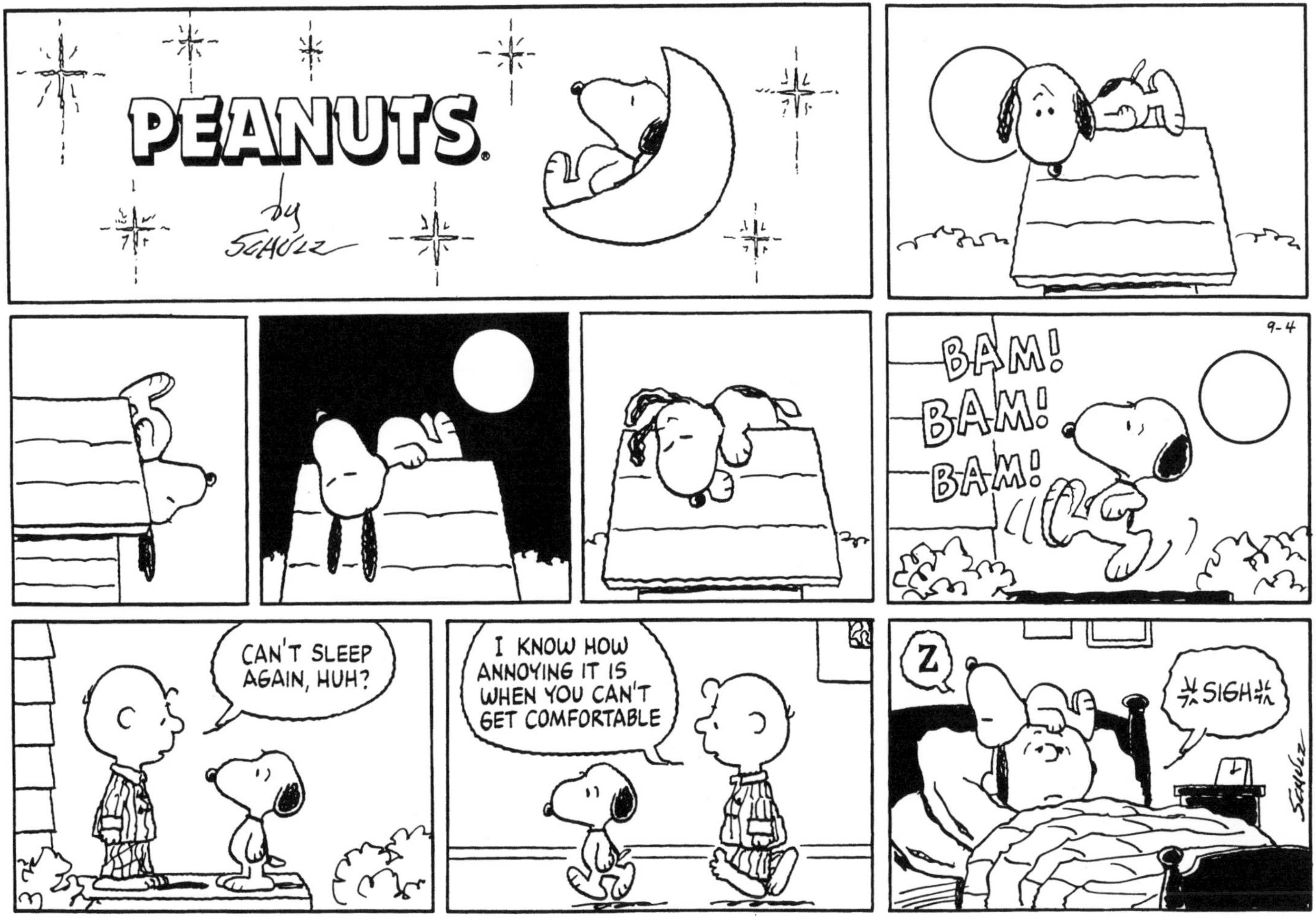
PEANUTS
by SCHULZ
9-4
BAM!
BAM!
BAM!
CAN'T SLEEP AGAIN, HUH?
I KNOW HOW ANNOYING IT IS WHEN YOU CAN'T GET COMFORTABLE
Z
SIGH
SCHULZ

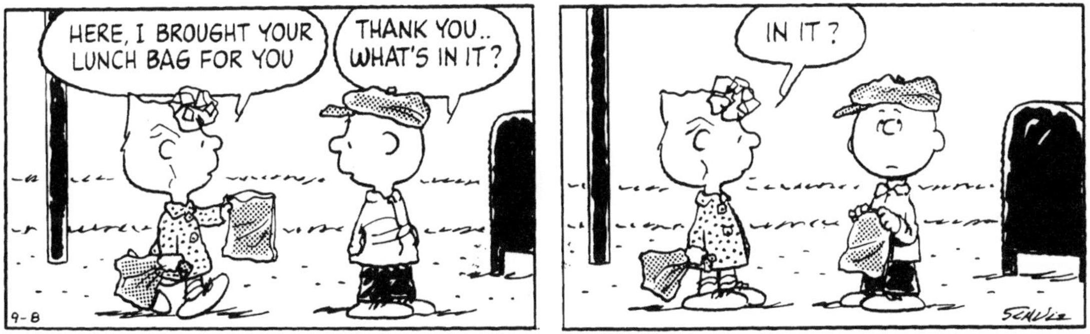
HERE, I BROUGHT YOUR LUNCH BAG FOR YOU
THANK YOU.. WHAT'S IN IT?
IN IT?
9-8
SCHULZ

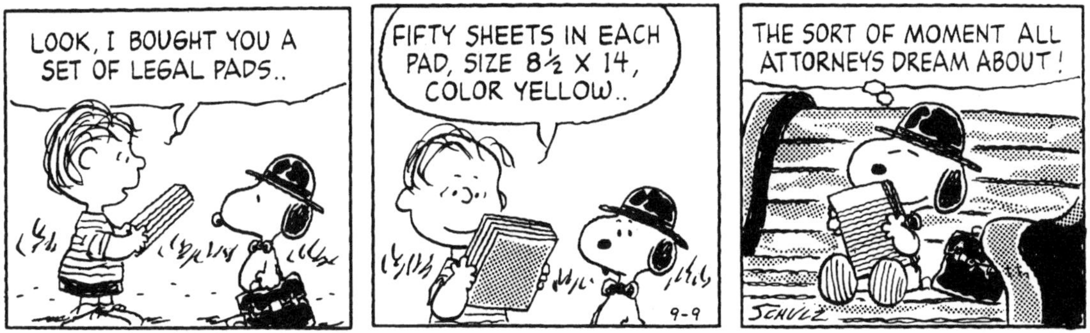
LOOK, I BOUGHT YOU A SET OF LEGAL PADS..
FIFTY SHEETS IN EACH PAD, SIZE 8½ X 14, COLOR YELLOW..
THE SORT OF MOMENT ALL ATTORNEYS DREAM ABOUT!
9-9
SCHULZ

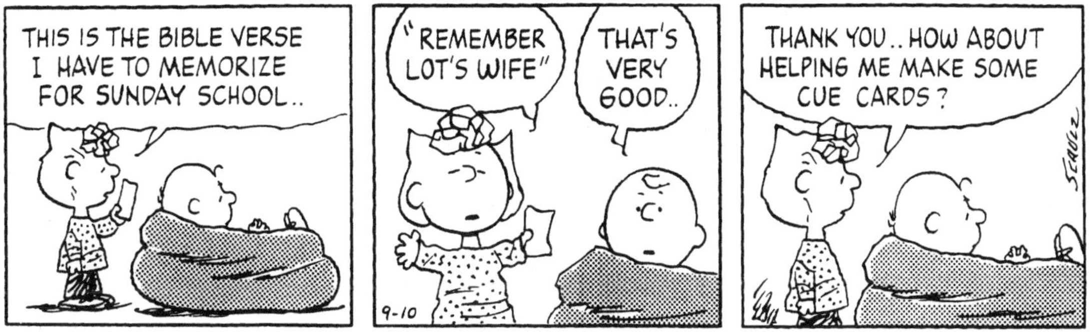
THIS IS THE BIBLE VERSE I HAVE TO MEMORIZE FOR SUNDAY SCHOOL..
"REMEMBER LOT'S WIFE"
THAT'S VERY GOOD..
THANK YOU.. HOW ABOUT HELPING ME MAKE SOME CUE CARDS?
9-10
SCHULZ

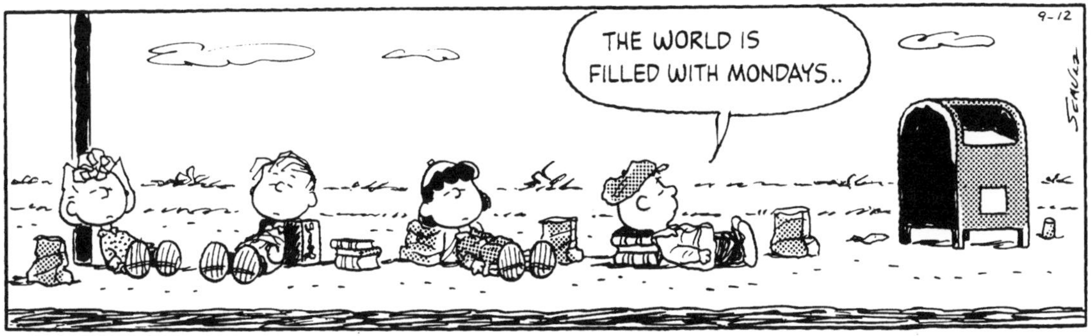
9-12
THE WORLD IS FILLED WITH MONDAYS..
SCHULZ

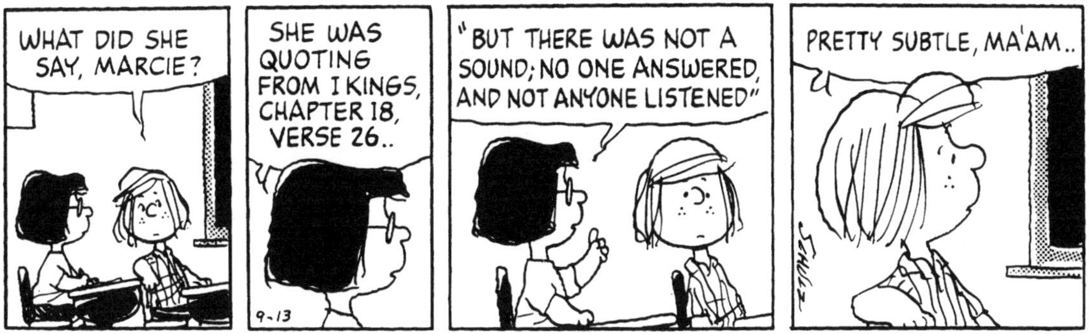
WHAT DID SHE SAY, MARCIE?
SHE WAS QUOTING FROM I KINGS, CHAPTER 18, VERSE 26..
9-13
"BUT THERE WAS NOT A SOUND; NO ONE ANSWERED, AND NOT ANYONE LISTENED"
SCHULZ
PRETTY SUBTLE, MA'AM..

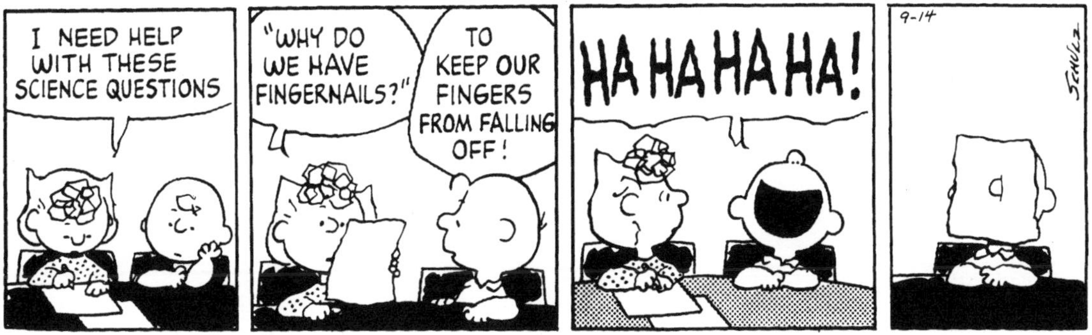
I NEED HELP WITH THESE SCIENCE QUESTIONS
"WHY DO WE HAVE FINGERNAILS?"
TO KEEP OUR FINGERS FROM FALLING OFF!
HA HA HA HA!
9-14
SCHULZ

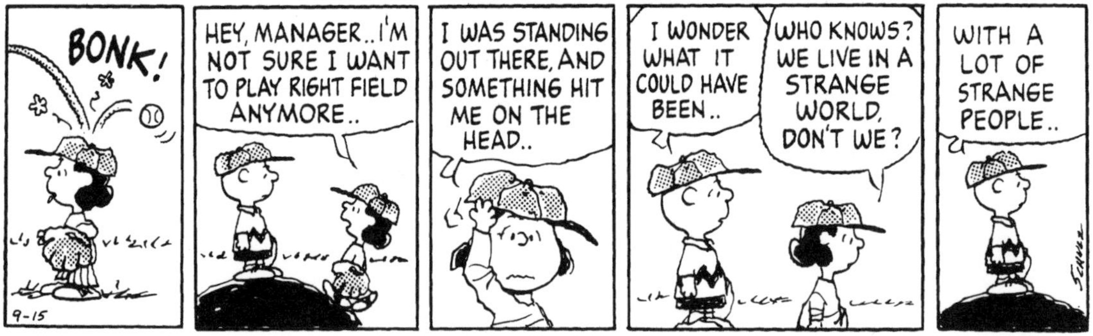
9-15
BONK!
HEY, MANAGER.. I'M NOT SURE I WANT TO PLAY RIGHT FIELD ANYMORE..
I WAS STANDING OUT THERE, AND SOMETHING HIT ME ON THE HEAD..
I WONDER WHAT IT COULD HAVE BEEN..
WHO KNOWS? WE LIVE IN A STRANGE WORLD, DON'T WE?
WITH A LOT OF STRANGE PEOPLE..

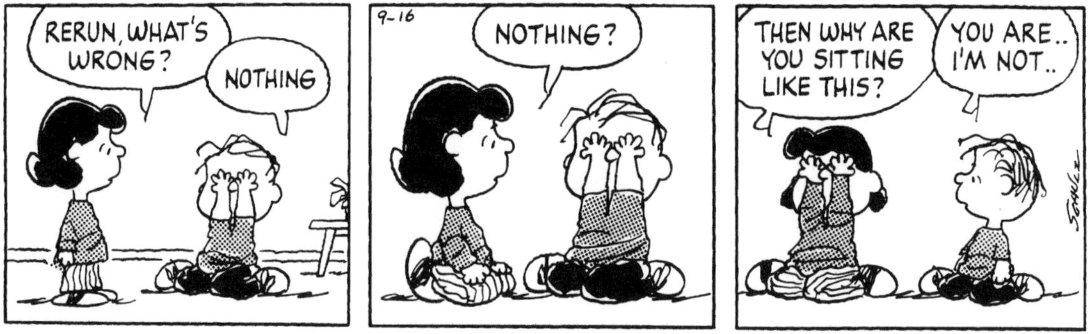
RERUN, WHAT'S WRONG?
NOTHING
9-16
NOTHING?
THEN WHY ARE YOU SITTING LIKE THIS?
YOU ARE.. I'M NOT..

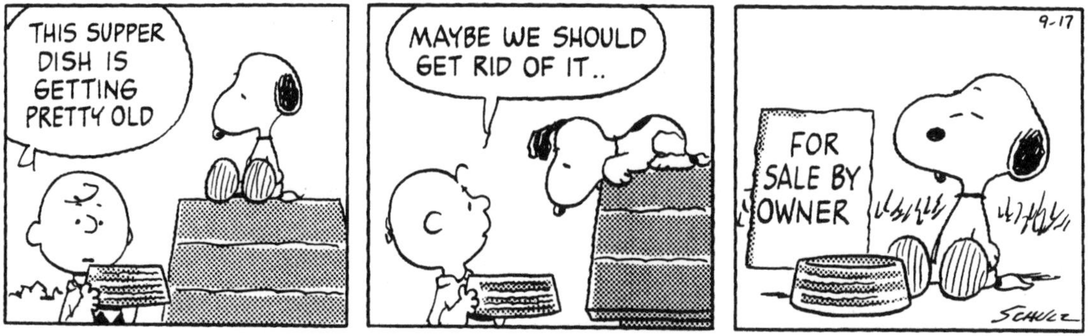
THIS SUPPER DISH IS GETTING PRETTY OLD
MAYBE WE SHOULD GET RID OF IT..
9-17
FOR SALE BY OWNER

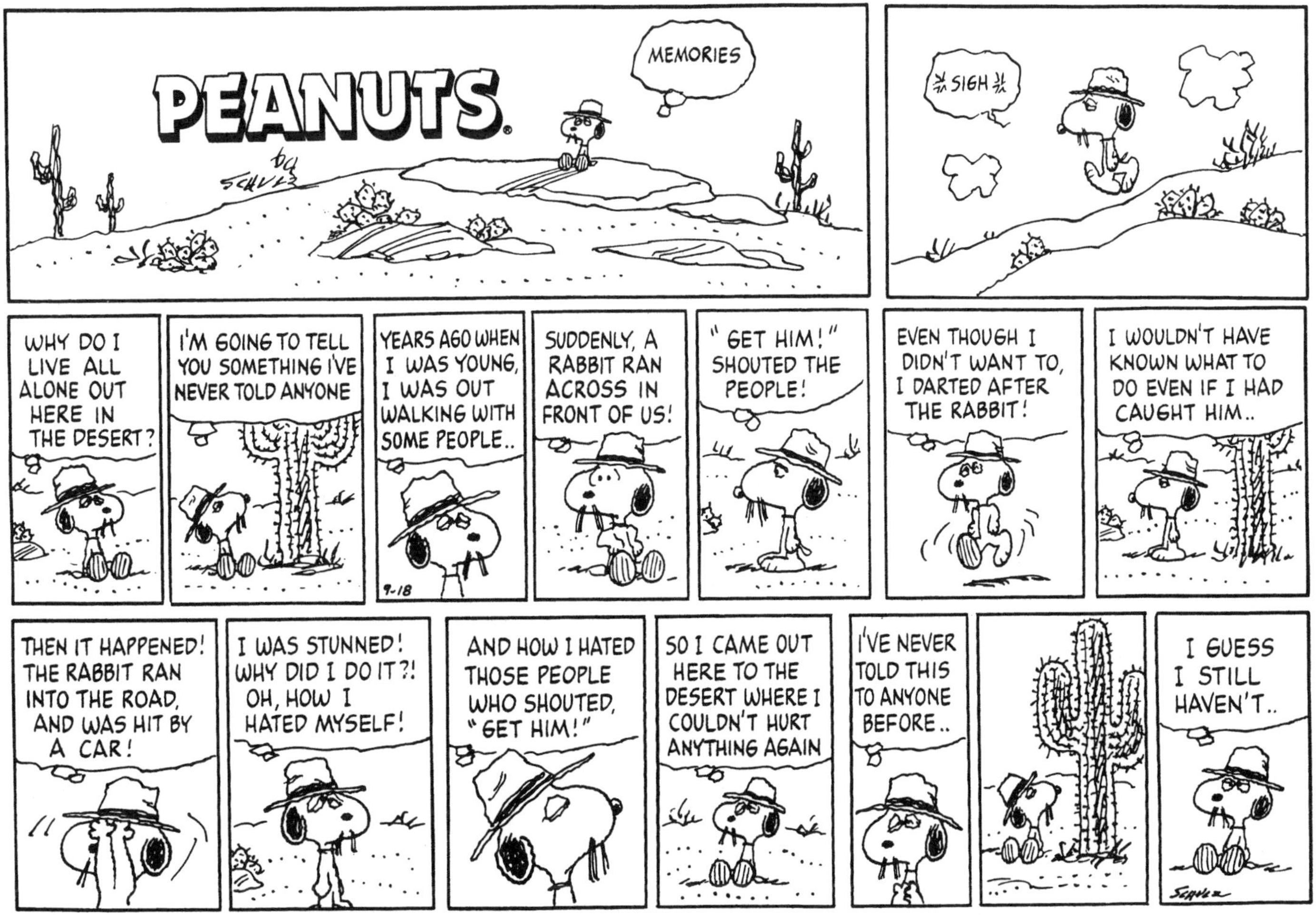
PEANUTS
by SCHULZ
MEMORIES
SIGH
WHY DO I LIVE ALL ALONE OUT HERE IN THE DESERT?
I'M GOING TO TELL YOU SOMETHING I'VE NEVER TOLD ANYONE
YEARS AGO WHEN I WAS YOUNG, I WAS OUT WALKING WITH SOME PEOPLE..
9-18
SUDDENLY, A RABBIT RAN ACROSS IN FRONT OF US!
"GET HIM!" SHOUTED THE PEOPLE!
EVEN THOUGH I DIDN'T WANT TO, I DARTED AFTER THE RABBIT!
I WOULDN'T HAVE KNOWN WHAT TO DO EVEN IF I HAD CAUGHT HIM..
THEN IT HAPPENED! THE RABBIT RAN INTO THE ROAD, AND WAS HIT BY A CAR!
I WAS STUNNED! WHY DID I DO IT?! OH, HOW I HATED MYSELF!
AND HOW I HATED THOSE PEOPLE WHO SHOUTED, "GET HIM!"
SO I CAME OUT HERE TO THE DESERT WHERE I COULDN'T HURT ANYTHING AGAIN
I'VE NEVER TOLD THIS TO ANYONE BEFORE..
I GUESS I STILL HAVEN'T..
SCHULZ

PEANUTS by SCHULZ

PSST..SIR, DON'T GO TO SLEEP...

Z

I'M AWAKE! GENTLEMEN, START YOUR ENGINES!

SIR, WHY DID YOU SAY, "GENTLEMEN, START YOUR ENGINES!"?

I DIDN'T SAY, "GENTLEMEN, START YOUR ENGINES!"

YES, YOU SAID, "I'M AWAKE! GENTLEMEN, START YOUR ENGINES!"

MARCIE, YOU ARE SO WEIRD!

Z

GENTLEMEN, START YOUR ENGINES!

I REMEMBER NOW.. IT'S WHAT THEY SAY TO BEGIN THE RACE..

YOU WIN THE WEIRD RACE, MARCIE

PRINCIPAL'S OFFICE

9-25

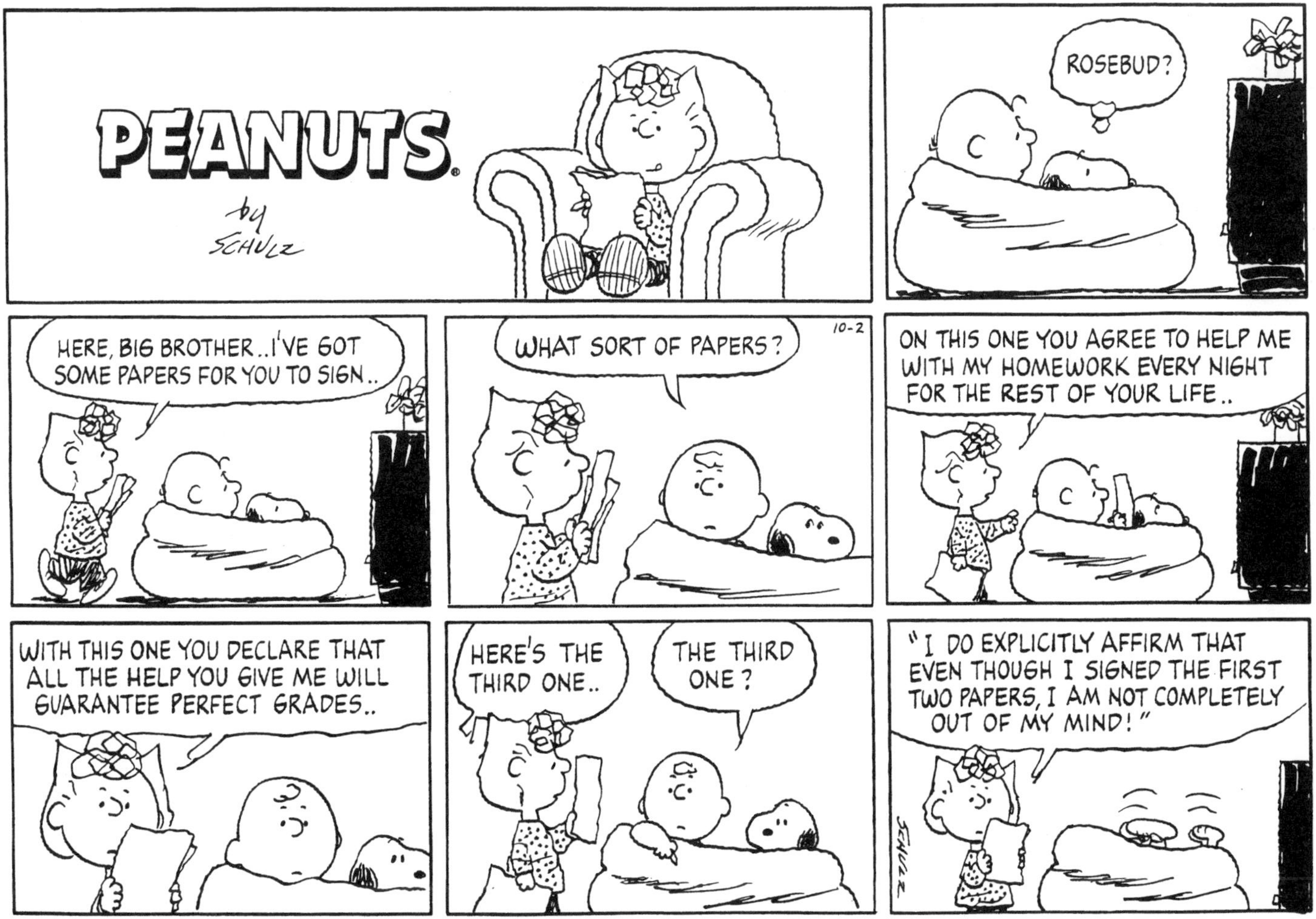
PEANUTS
by SCHULZ
ROSEBUD?
HERE, BIG BROTHER..I'VE GOT SOME PAPERS FOR YOU TO SIGN..
WHAT SORT OF PAPERS?
10-2
ON THIS ONE YOU AGREE TO HELP ME WITH MY HOMEWORK EVERY NIGHT FOR THE REST OF YOUR LIFE..
WITH THIS ONE YOU DECLARE THAT ALL THE HELP YOU GIVE ME WILL GUARANTEE PERFECT GRADES..
HERE'S THE THIRD ONE..
THE THIRD ONE?
"I DO EXPLICITLY AFFIRM THAT EVEN THOUGH I SIGNED THE FIRST TWO PAPERS, I AM NOT COMPLETELY OUT OF MY MIND!"
SCHULZ

DO WE HAVE ANY MARBLES?

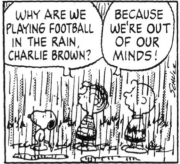

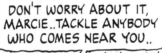

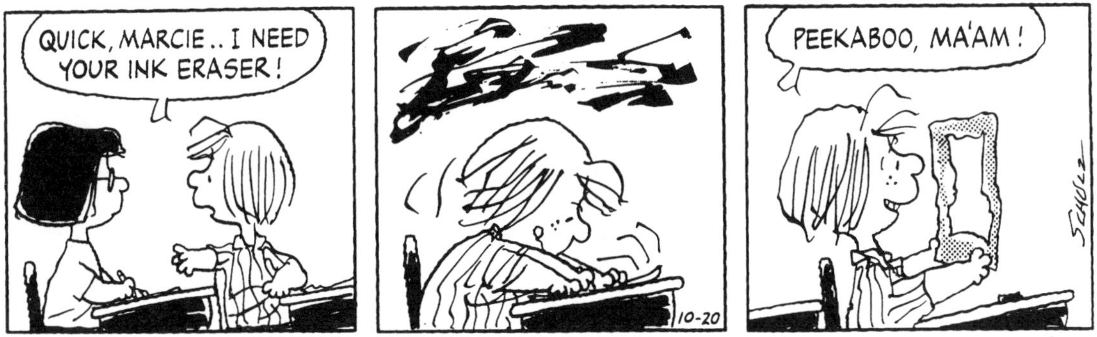
QUICK, MARCIE.. I NEED YOUR INK ERASER!
10-20
PEEKABOO, MA'AM!

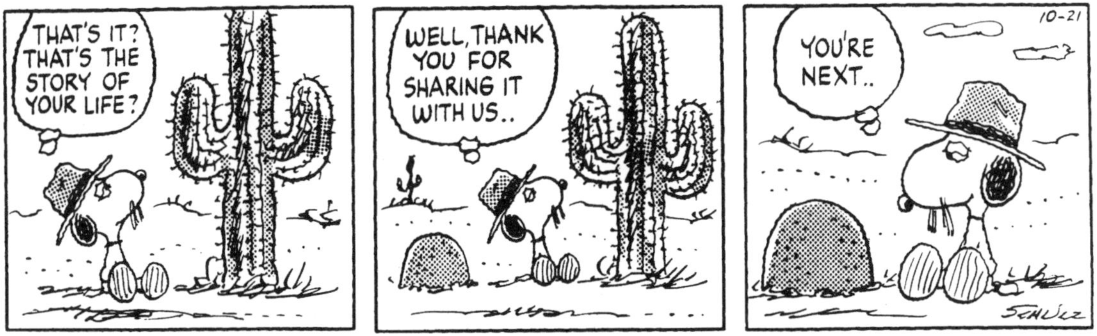
THAT'S IT? THAT'S THE STORY OF YOUR LIFE?
WELL, THANK YOU FOR SHARING IT WITH US..
10-21
YOU'RE NEXT..

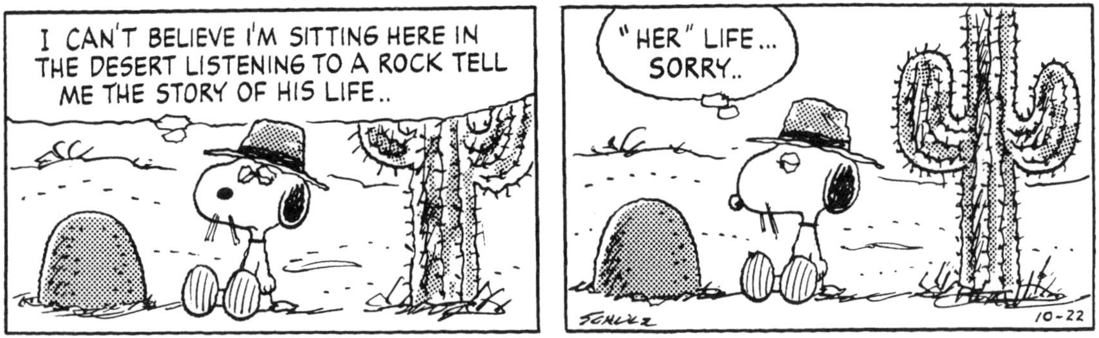
I CAN'T BELIEVE I'M SITTING HERE IN THE DESERT LISTENING TO A ROCK TELL ME THE STORY OF HIS LIFE..
"HER" LIFE... SORRY..
10-22

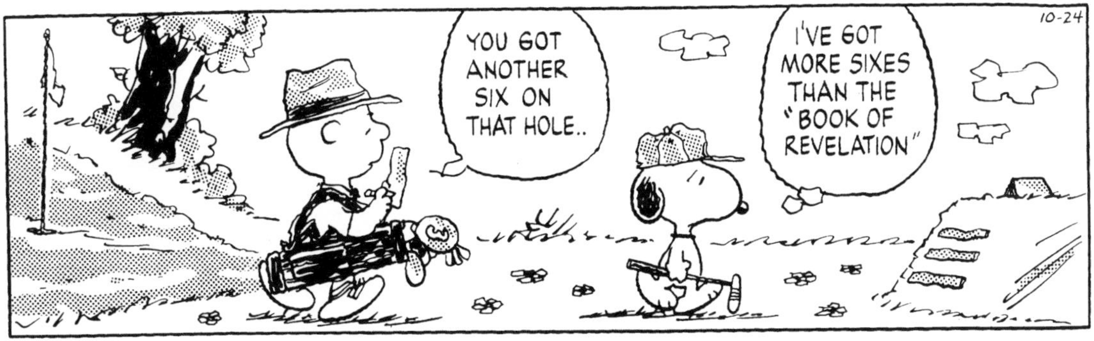
YOU GOT ANOTHER SIX ON THAT HOLE..
I'VE GOT MORE SIXES THAN THE "BOOK OF REVELATION"

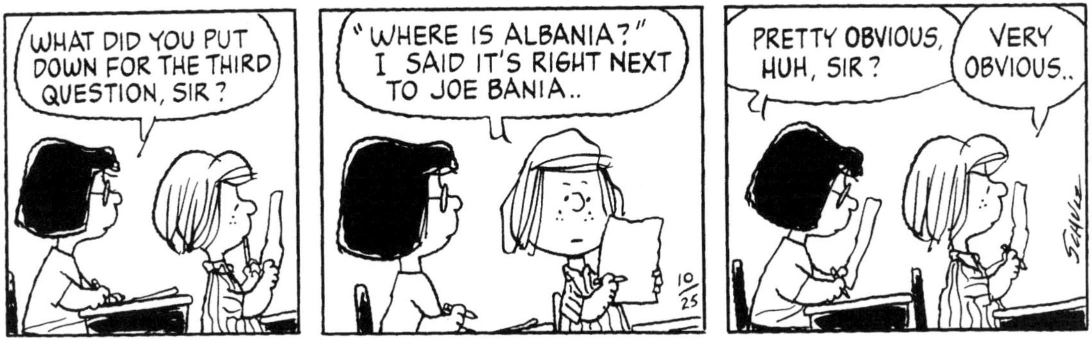
WHAT DID YOU PUT DOWN FOR THE THIRD QUESTION, SIR?
"WHERE IS ALBANIA?" I SAID IT'S RIGHT NEXT TO JOE BANIA..
PRETTY OBVIOUS, HUH, SIR?
VERY OBVIOUS..

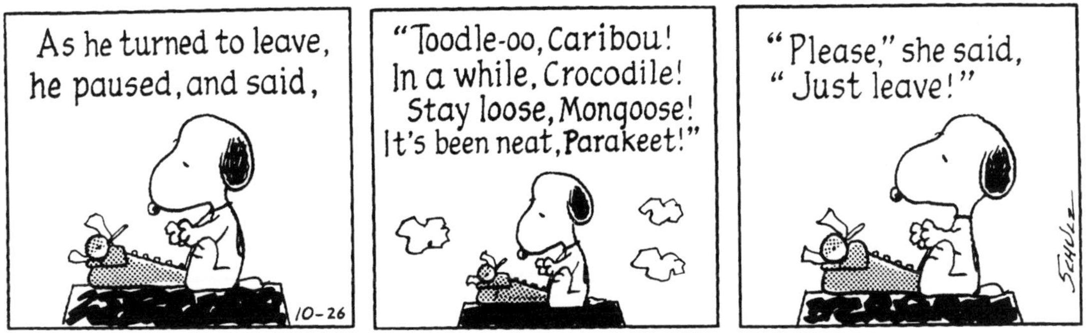
As he turned to leave, he paused, and said,
"Toodle-oo, Caribou! In a while, Crocodile! Stay loose, Mongoose! It's been neat, Parakeet!"
"Please," she said, "Just leave!"

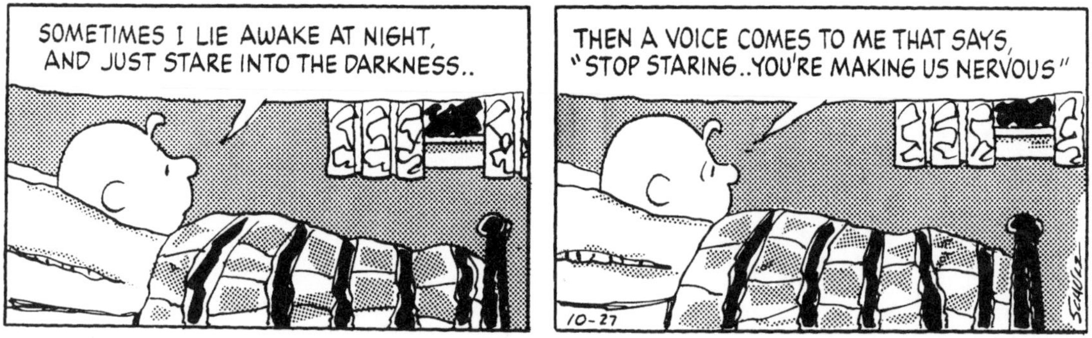
SOMETIMES I LIE AWAKE AT NIGHT, AND JUST STARE INTO THE DARKNESS..
THEN A VOICE COMES TO ME THAT SAYS, "STOP STARING..YOU'RE MAKING US NERVOUS"
10-27

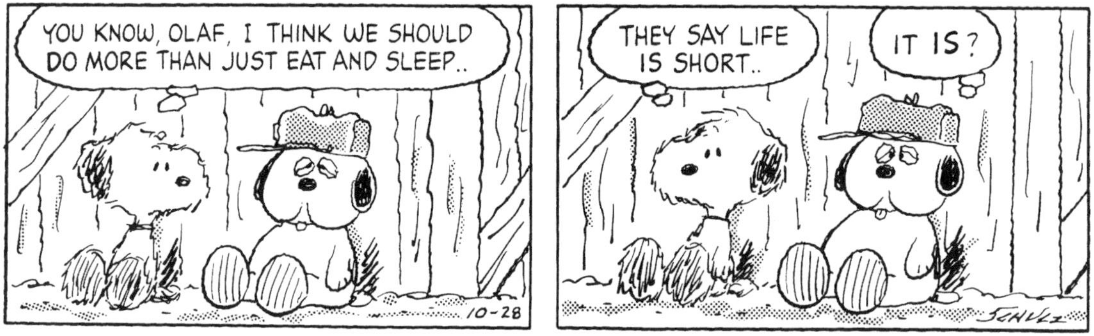
YOU KNOW, OLAF, I THINK WE SHOULD DO MORE THAN JUST EAT AND SLEEP..
10-28
THEY SAY LIFE IS SHORT..
IT IS?

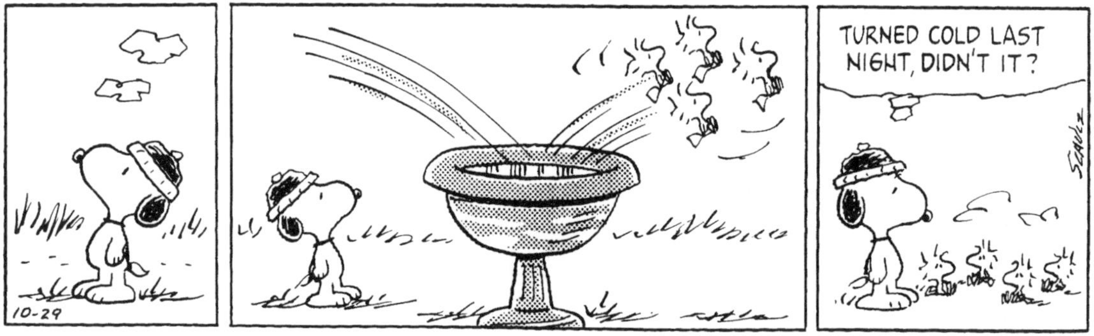
10-29
TURNED COLD LAST NIGHT, DIDN'T IT?

WINTER IS COMING..

A SHARPNESS IN THE AIR.. SMOKE RISING FROM CHIMNEYS...

THE SOUND OF THE ZAMBONI..

11-10

I FAILED A BIG TEST TODAY.. ALL THE TRUES WERE FALSE AND ALL THE FALSES WERE TRUE..

THAT'S LIFE.. ALL THE TRUES ARE FALSE AND ALL THE FALSES ARE TRUE

11-11

LIFE IS PROBABLY EASIER IF YOU'RE A DOG..

THAT'S TRUE.. OR IS IT FALSE?

WHAT ARE YOU EATING?

A NEW BREAKFAST CEREAL..

I LIKE THE NAME..

"FLAKEY THINGS"?

11/12

PEANUTS by Schulz

EVERYTHING LOOKS GOOD..

WHAT ARE YOU GOING TO HAVE, MARCIE?

I DON'T KNOW.. MAYBE JUST A HOT DOG...

I THINK I'LL HAVE A TUNA FISH SANDWICH..

THAT'S REDUNDANT, SIR

11-13

WHAT'S REDUNDANT?

"TUNA FISH" IS REDUNDANT

YOU KNOW, I THINK YOU'RE RIGHT.. THANKS FOR TELLING ME..

I'LL HAVE A FISH SANDWICH!

PEANUTS by SCHULZ

NO, IT'S MORE OF A "GOBBLE GOBBLE"

ANYWAY, IT'S FOUR MORE DAYS..

THEY CALL IT "THANKSGIVING"

AND THEY EAT BIRDS! CAN YOU BELIEVE IT?!

WHY WOULD ANYONE WANT TO EAT A BIRD?

THAT'S GOOD..THEY'LL NEVER BOTHER AN ATTORNEY..

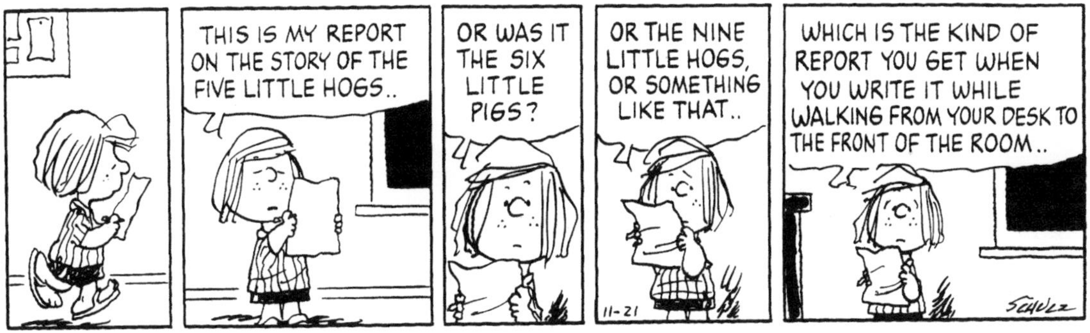
THIS IS MY REPORT ON THE STORY OF THE FIVE LITTLE HOGS..
OR WAS IT THE SIX LITTLE PIGS?
OR THE NINE LITTLE HOGS, OR SOMETHING LIKE THAT..
WHICH IS THE KIND OF REPORT YOU GET WHEN YOU WRITE IT WHILE WALKING FROM YOUR DESK TO THE FRONT OF THE ROOM..

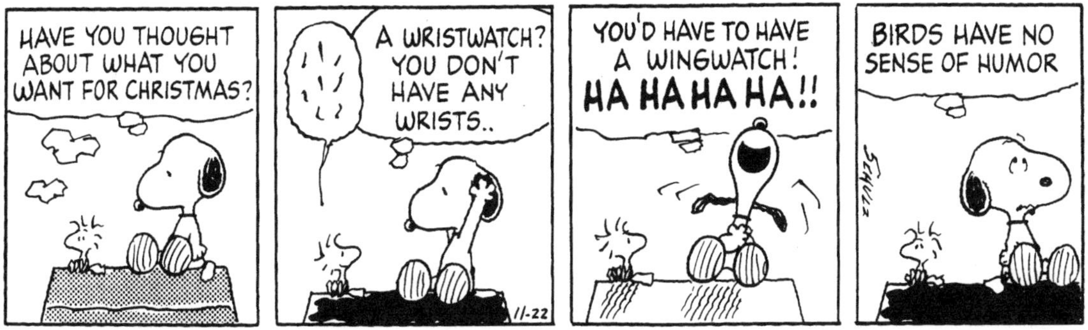
HAVE YOU THOUGHT ABOUT WHAT YOU WANT FOR CHRISTMAS?
A WRISTWATCH? YOU DON'T HAVE ANY WRISTS..
YOU'D HAVE TO HAVE A WINGWATCH! HA HA HA HA!!
BIRDS HAVE NO SENSE OF HUMOR

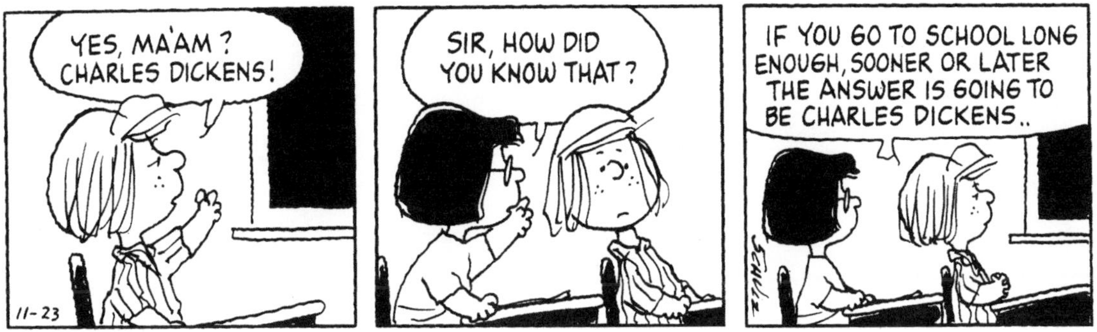
YES, MA'AM? CHARLES DICKENS!
SIR, HOW DID YOU KNOW THAT?
IF YOU GO TO SCHOOL LONG ENOUGH, SOONER OR LATER THE ANSWER IS GOING TO BE CHARLES DICKENS..

Panel 1: ASK YOUR DOG IF HE WANTS TO COME OUT AND PLAY..

Panel 2: 12-1

Panel 4: I DON'T KNOW MY SOCIAL SECURITY NUMBER

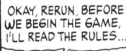

Panel 5: OKAY, RERUN, BEFORE WE BEGIN THE GAME, I'LL READ THE RULES...

Panel 6: I LOVE THE RULES! YOU CAN'T PLAY A GAME UNLESS YOU KNOW THE RULES!

Panel 7: YOU NEED RULES TO BE FAIR.. TO ENJOY ANY GAME A PERSON MUST ALWAYS STRIVE TO BE FAIR! 12-2

Panel 8: GOOD.. NOW THE FIRST THING WE DO IS DECIDE WHO..

Panel 9: I WANT THE RED !!

Panel 10: I'M GONNA WIN! I'M GONNA WIN!

Panel 11: WAIT JUST A MINUTE! IT'S MY TURN!

Panel 12: OKAY, YOUR TURN.. 12-3

Panel 13: Z

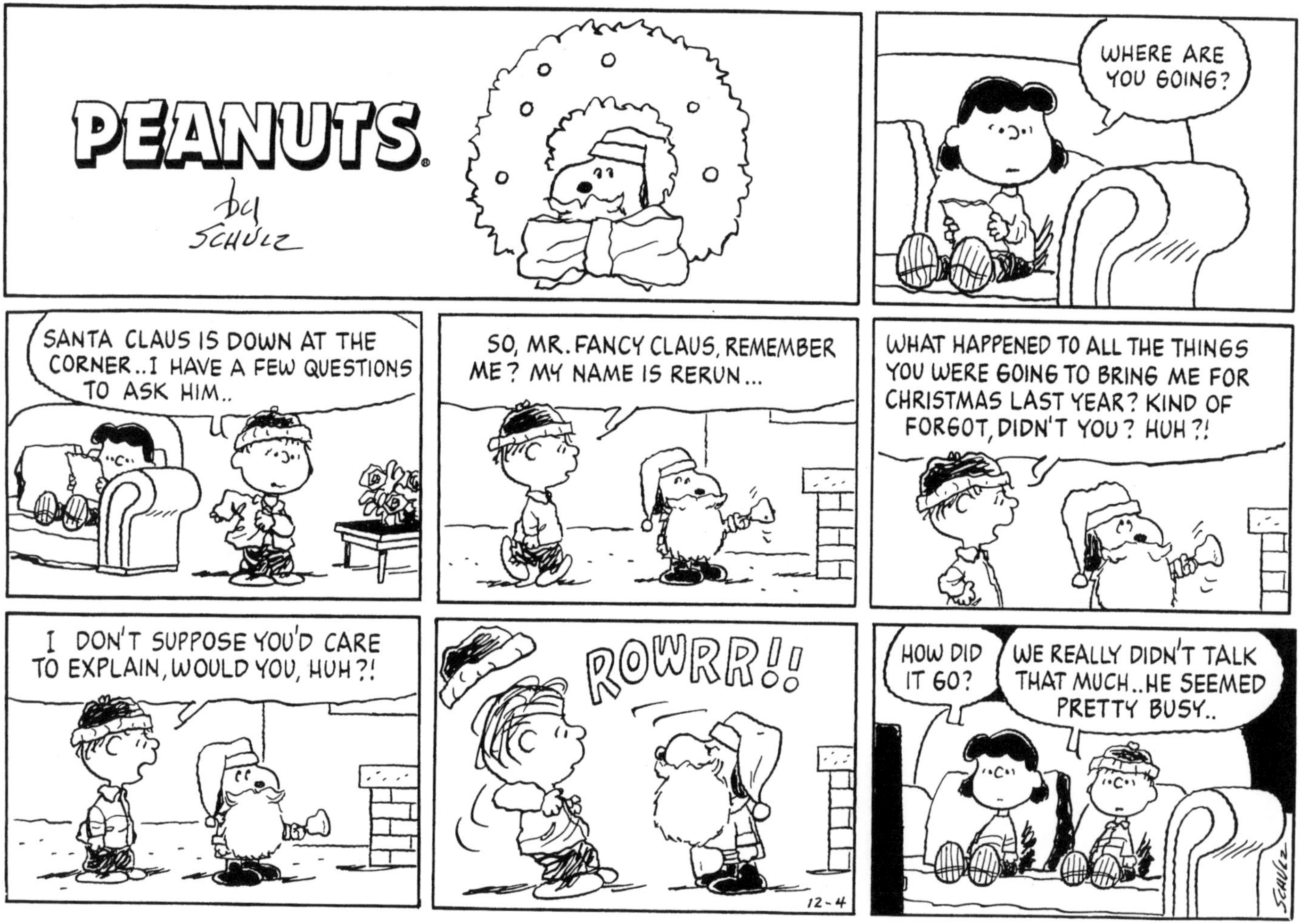
PEANUTS
by SCHULZ
WHERE ARE YOU GOING?
SANTA CLAUS IS DOWN AT THE CORNER..I HAVE A FEW QUESTIONS TO ASK HIM..
SO, MR. FANCY CLAUS, REMEMBER ME? MY NAME IS RERUN...
WHAT HAPPENED TO ALL THE THINGS YOU WERE GOING TO BRING ME FOR CHRISTMAS LAST YEAR? KIND OF FORGOT, DIDN'T YOU? HUH?!
I DON'T SUPPOSE YOU'D CARE TO EXPLAIN, WOULD YOU, HUH?!
ROWRR!!
12-4
HOW DID IT GO?
WE REALLY DIDN'T TALK THAT MUCH..HE SEEMED PRETTY BUSY..
SCHULZ

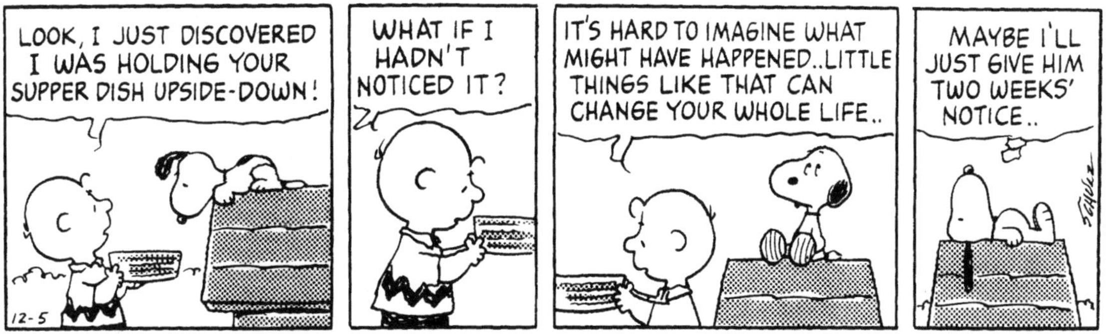
LOOK, I JUST DISCOVERED I WAS HOLDING YOUR SUPPER DISH UPSIDE-DOWN!
WHAT IF I HADN'T NOTICED IT?
IT'S HARD TO IMAGINE WHAT MIGHT HAVE HAPPENED..LITTLE THINGS LIKE THAT CAN CHANGE YOUR WHOLE LIFE..
MAYBE I'LL JUST GIVE HIM TWO WEEKS' NOTICE..
SCHULZ
12-5

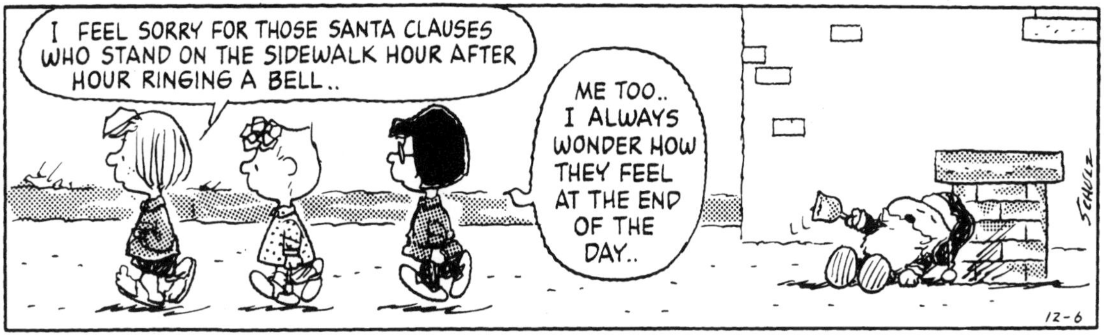
I FEEL SORRY FOR THOSE SANTA CLAUSES WHO STAND ON THE SIDEWALK HOUR AFTER HOUR RINGING A BELL..
ME TOO.. I ALWAYS WONDER HOW THEY FEEL AT THE END OF THE DAY..
SCHULZ
12-6

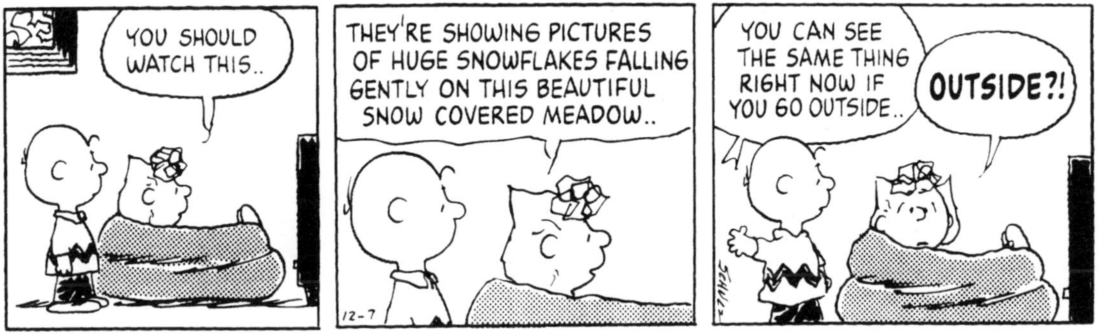
YOU SHOULD WATCH THIS..
THEY'RE SHOWING PICTURES OF HUGE SNOWFLAKES FALLING GENTLY ON THIS BEAUTIFUL SNOW COVERED MEADOW..
YOU CAN SEE THE SAME THING RIGHT NOW IF YOU GO OUTSIDE..
OUTSIDE?!
SCHULZ
12-7

"MEN ARE FROM MARS, WOMEN ARE FROM VENUS"

THAT'S A GOOD TITLE.. YOU SHOULD WRITE A BOOK LIKE THAT..

Dogs Are From Jupiter..Cats Are From the Moon

YOU'RE NOT TICKLISH, I HOPE..

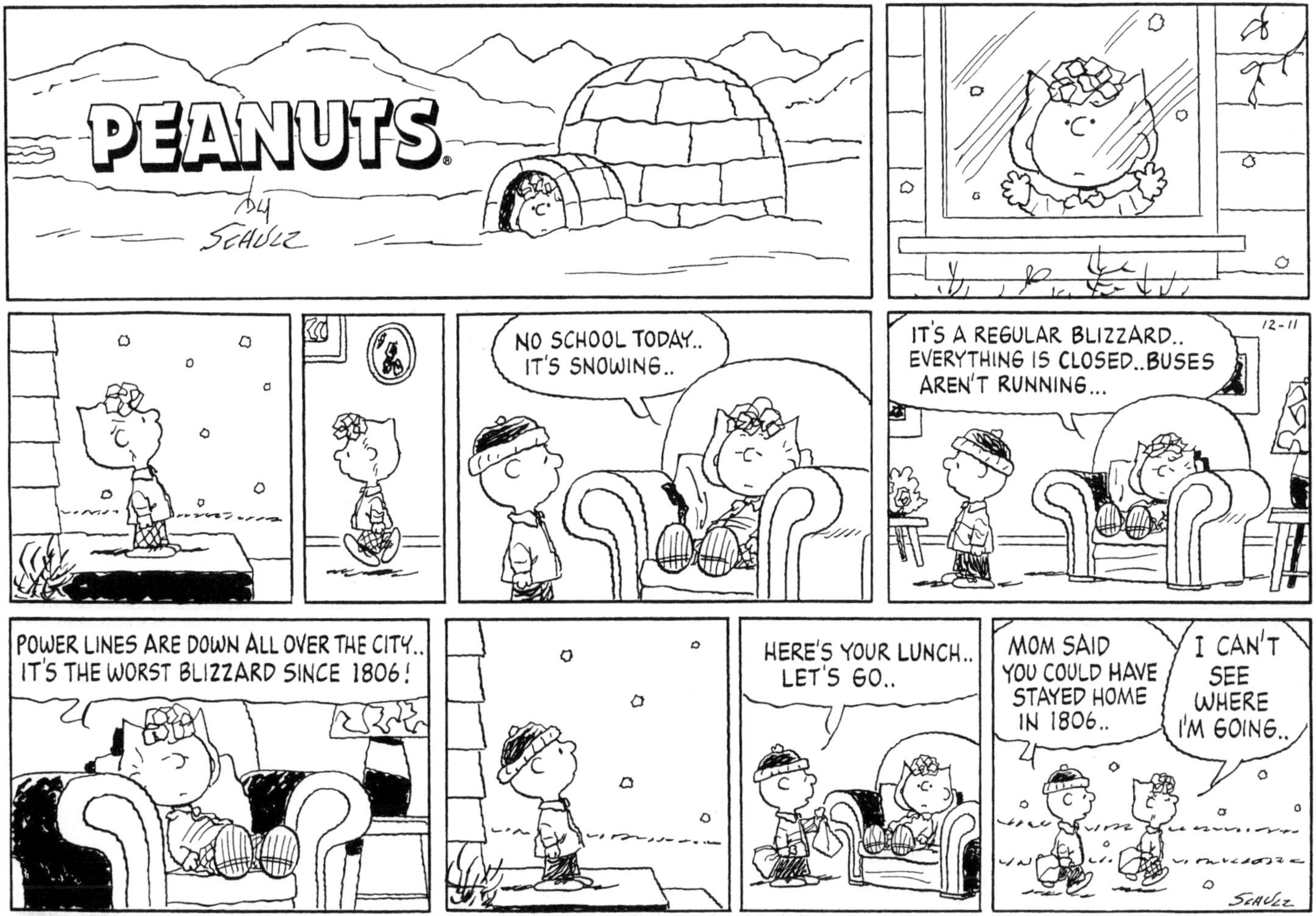
PEANUTS
by SCHULZ
12-11
NO SCHOOL TODAY.. IT'S SNOWING..
IT'S A REGULAR BLIZZARD.. EVERYTHING IS CLOSED..BUSES AREN'T RUNNING...
POWER LINES ARE DOWN ALL OVER THE CITY.. IT'S THE WORST BLIZZARD SINCE 1806!
HERE'S YOUR LUNCH.. LET'S GO..
MOM SAID YOU COULD HAVE STAYED HOME IN 1806..
I CAN'T SEE WHERE I'M GOING..
SCHULZ

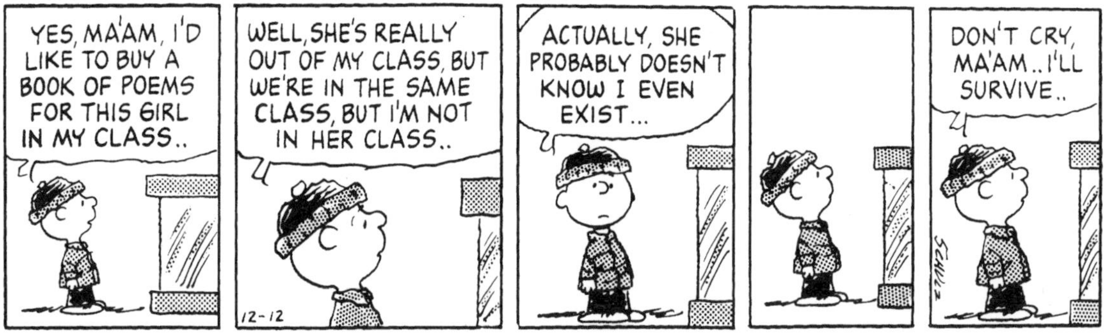
YES, MA'AM, I'D LIKE TO BUY A BOOK OF POEMS FOR THIS GIRL IN MY CLASS..
WELL, SHE'S REALLY OUT OF MY CLASS, BUT WE'RE IN THE SAME CLASS, BUT I'M NOT IN HER CLASS..
12-12
ACTUALLY, SHE PROBABLY DOESN'T KNOW I EVEN EXIST...
DON'T CRY, MA'AM.. I'LL SURVIVE..
SCHULZ

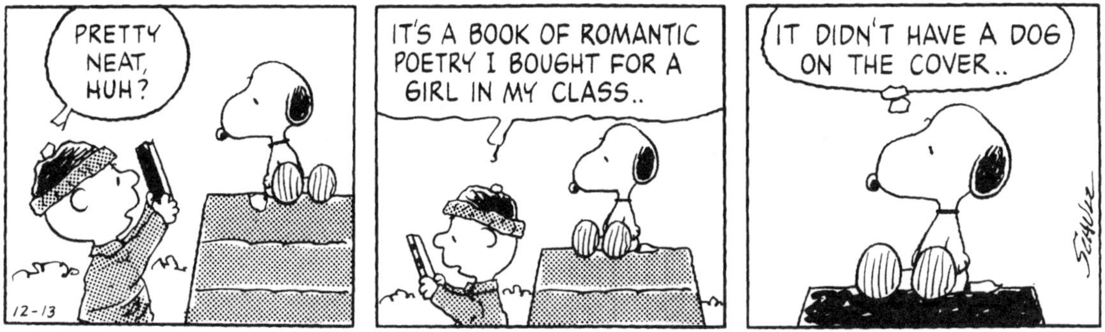
PRETTY NEAT, HUH?
12-13
IT'S A BOOK OF ROMANTIC POETRY I BOUGHT FOR A GIRL IN MY CLASS..
IT DIDN'T HAVE A DOG ON THE COVER..
SCHULZ

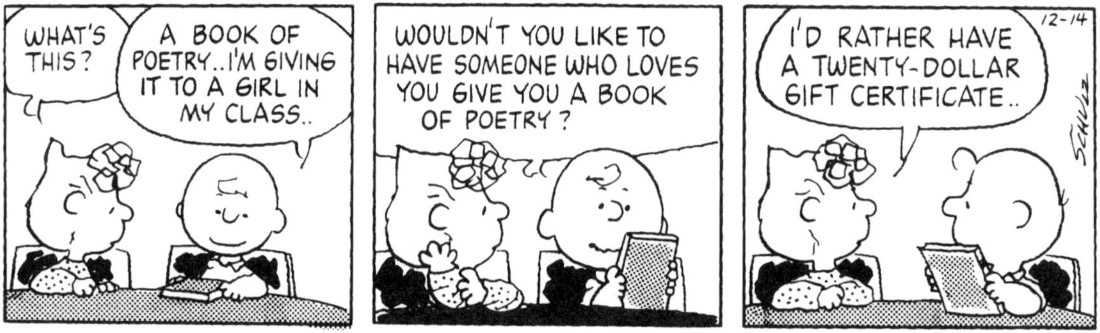
WHAT'S THIS?
A BOOK OF POETRY.. I'M GIVING IT TO A GIRL IN MY CLASS..
WOULDN'T YOU LIKE TO HAVE SOMEONE WHO LOVES YOU GIVE YOU A BOOK OF POETRY?
12-14
I'D RATHER HAVE A TWENTY-DOLLAR GIFT CERTIFICATE..
SCHULZ

DO ME A FAVOR, LINUS.. GO ACROSS THE ROOM, AND GIVE THIS BOOK OF POEMS TO THAT GIRL FOR ME.. I'M TOO SHY...

WHAT WILL I SAY TO HER?

SAY ANYTHING.. JUST BE SMOOTH...

12-15

HERE, DARLING!

SORRY, CHARLIE BROWN.. SHE SAYS SHE DOESN'T CARE FOR POETRY.. SHE SAYS SHE DOESN'T EVEN LIKE TO READ

WHY DON'T YOU GIVE IT TO SOMEONE WHO APPRECIATES POETRY?

" IN A FIELD BY THE RIVER MY LOVE AND I DID STAND "

12-16

YES, MA'AM.. REMEMBER ME?

I WAS IN HERE A FEW DAYS AGO AND BOUGHT A BOOK OF POEMS FOR A GIRL IN MY CLASS..

12-17

SHE DIDN'T LIKE IT... CAN YOU THINK OF ANYTHING ELSE I MIGHT BUY FOR HER?

SOMETHING THAT WOULD REALLY IMPRESS HER, AND MAKE HER LIKE ME MORE THAN ANYONE SHE'S EVER KNOWN..

FOR ABOUT A DOLLAR?

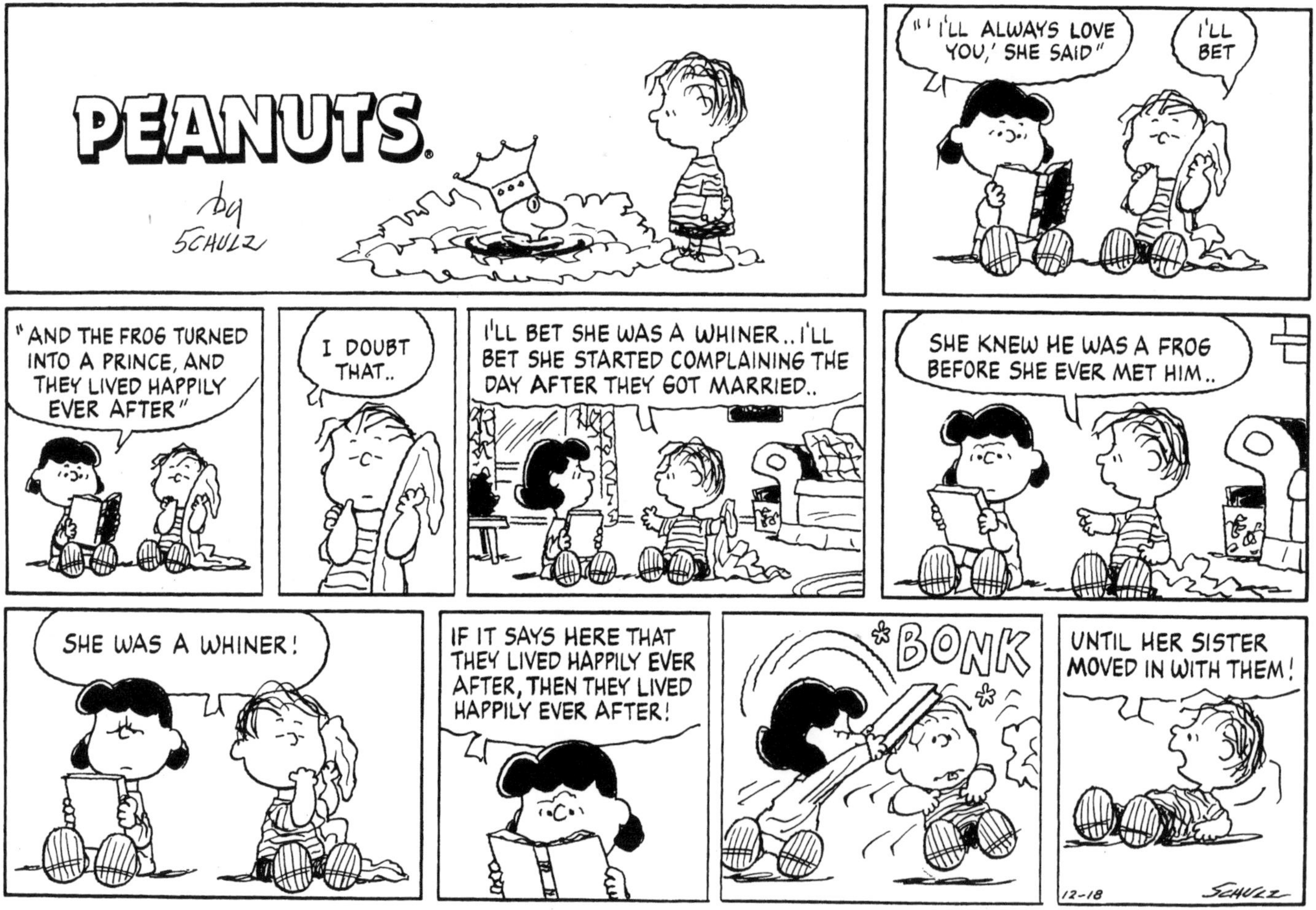
PEANUTS
by SCHULZ
"'I'LL ALWAYS LOVE YOU,' SHE SAID"
I'LL BET
"AND THE FROG TURNED INTO A PRINCE, AND THEY LIVED HAPPILY EVER AFTER"
I DOUBT THAT..
I'LL BET SHE WAS A WHINER.. I'LL BET SHE STARTED COMPLAINING THE DAY AFTER THEY GOT MARRIED..
SHE KNEW HE WAS A FROG BEFORE SHE EVER MET HIM..
SHE WAS A WHINER!
IF IT SAYS HERE THAT THEY LIVED HAPPILY EVER AFTER, THEN THEY LIVED HAPPILY EVER AFTER!
BONK
UNTIL HER SISTER MOVED IN WITH THEM!
12-18
SCHULZ

PEANUTS by Schulz

HERE, I GUESS THIS IS FOR YOU..

A CHRISTMAS PRESENT FROM WOODSTOCK! WOW!

THIS IS EXCITING! I WONDER WHAT IT IS...

BIRDSEED?!

WHAT AM I GOING TO DO WITH A PACKAGE OF BIRDSEED?

WHY GIVE SOMEBODY SOMETHING THEY CAN'T USE?

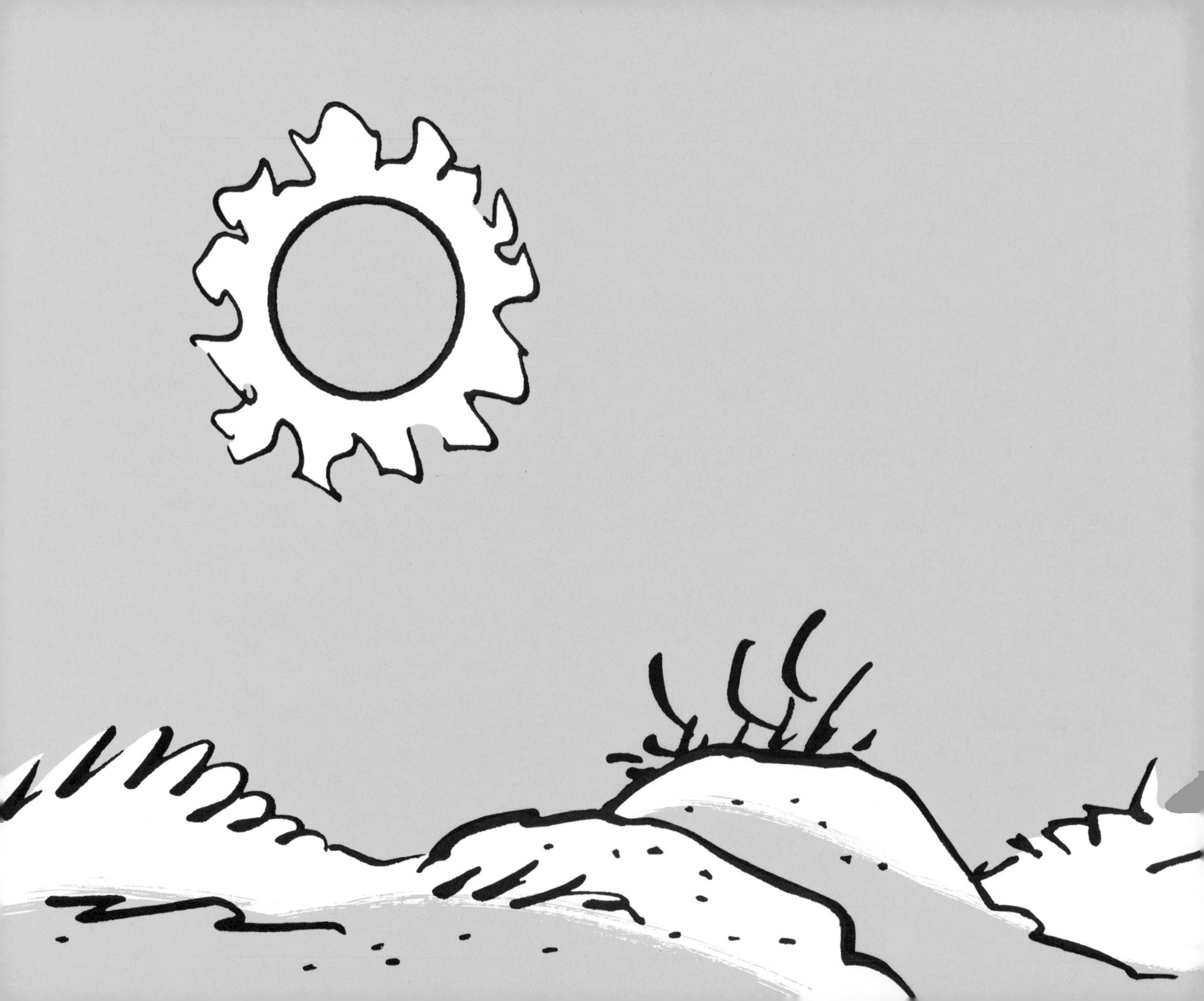

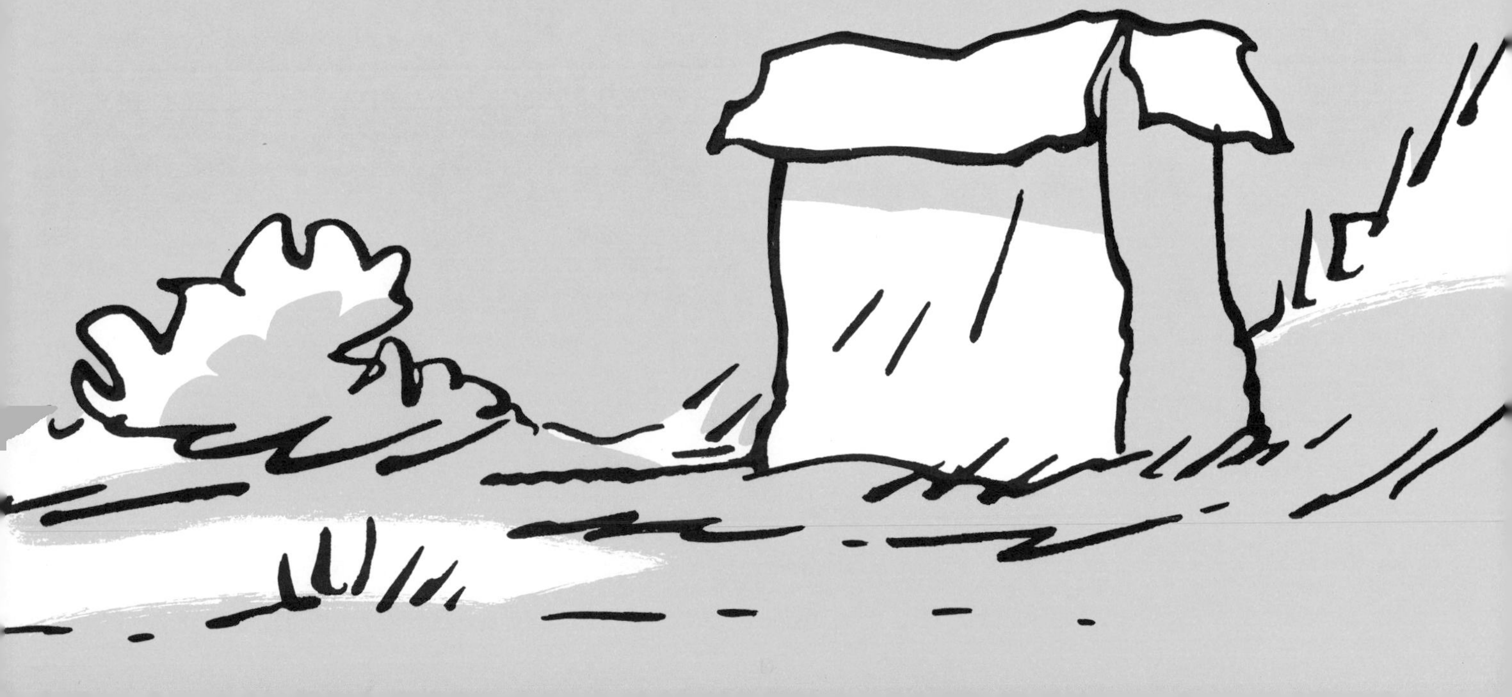

INDEX

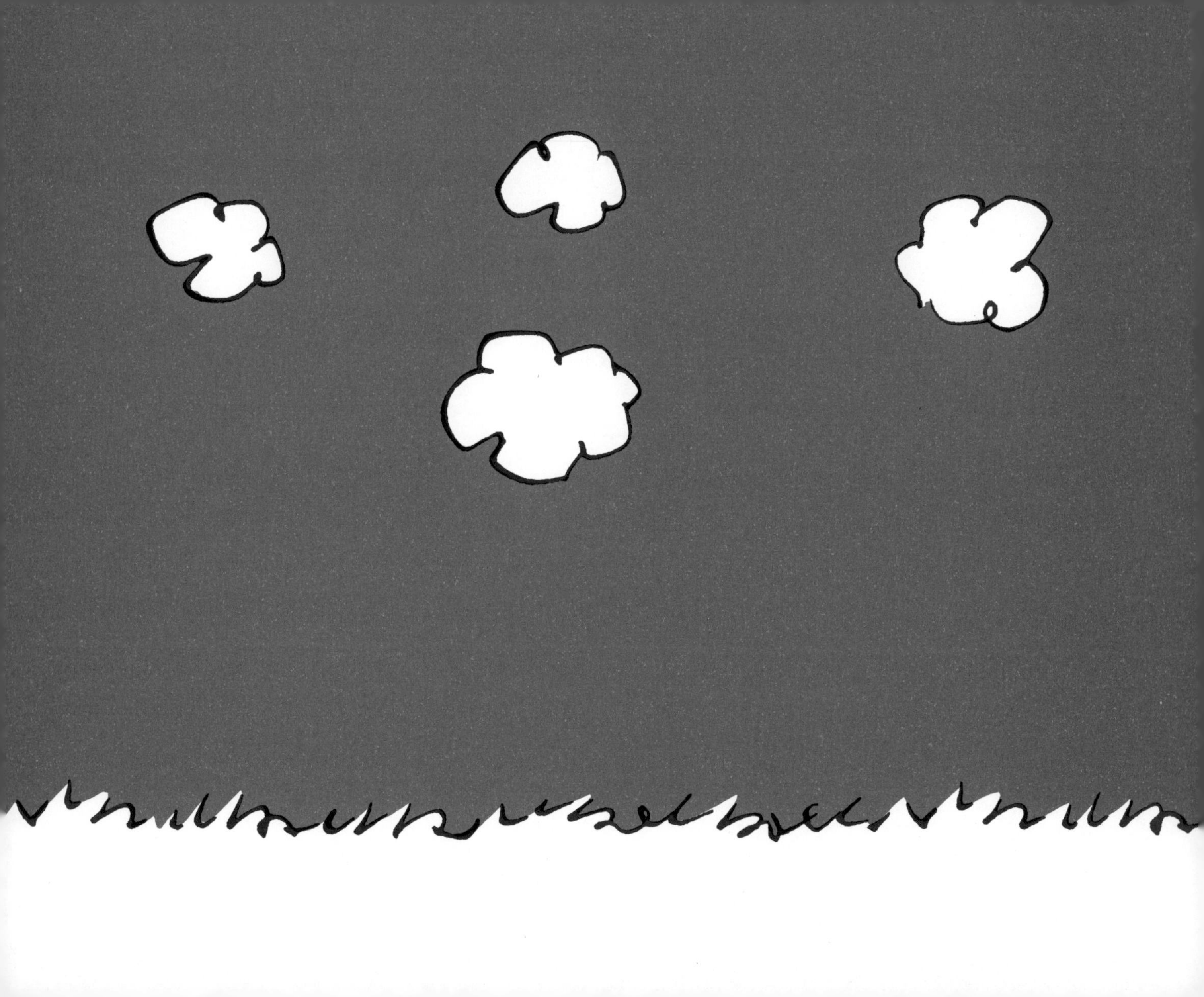

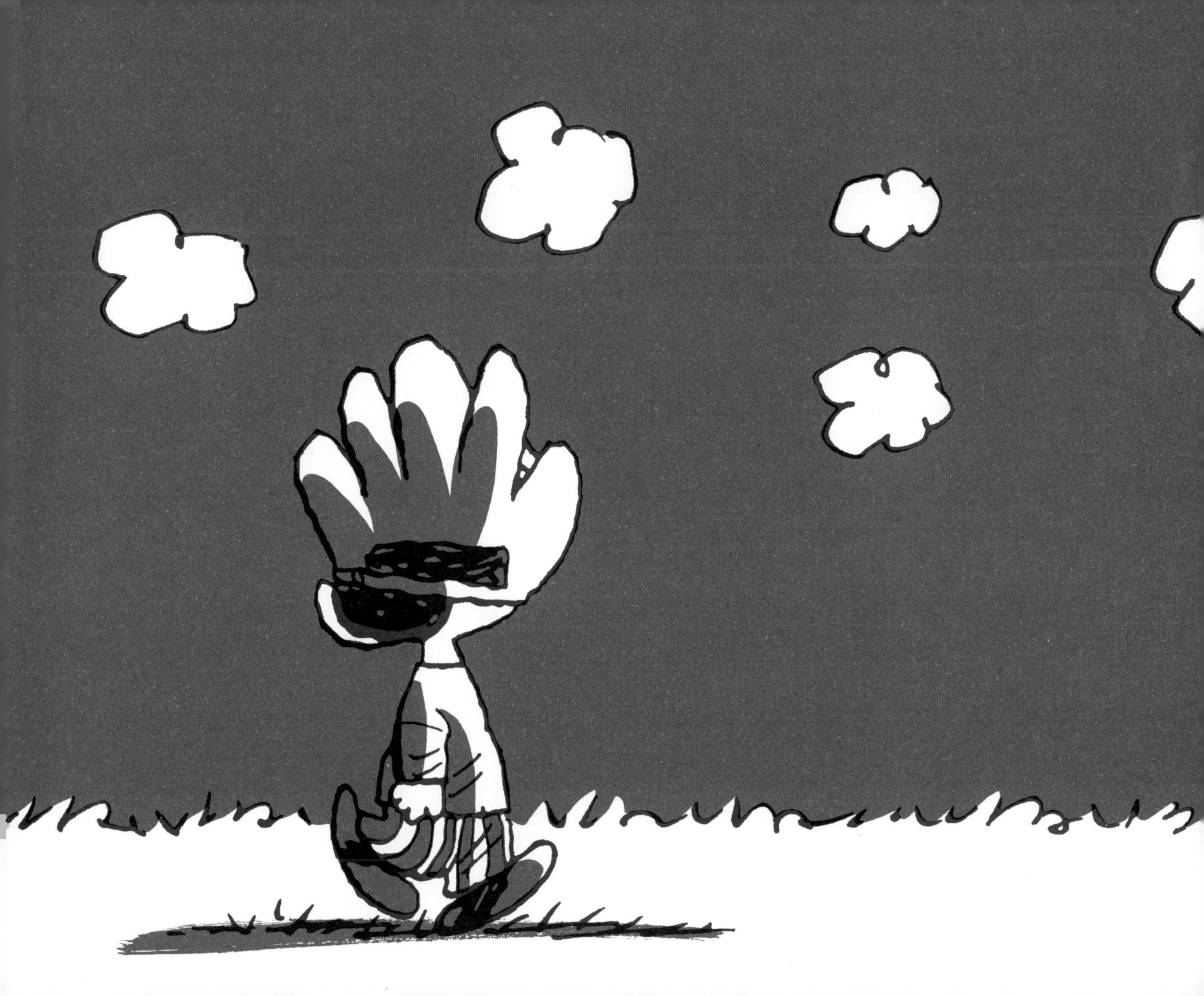

CHARLES M. SCHULZ · 1922 To 2000

Charles M. Schulz was born November 26, 1922, in Minneapolis. His destiny was foreshadowed when an uncle gave him, at the age of two days, the nickname "Sparky" (after the racehorse Spark Plug in the newspaper strip *Barney Google*).

Schulz grew up in St. Paul. By all accounts, he led an unremarkable, albeit sheltered, childhood. He was an only child, close to both parents. His eventual career path was nurtured by his father, who bought four Sunday papers every week — just for the comics.

An outstanding student, he skipped two grades early on, but began to flounder in high school — perhaps not so coincidentally at the same time kids are going through their cruelest, most status-conscious period of socialization. The pain, bitterness, insecurity, and failures chronicled in *Peanuts* appear to have originated from this period of Schulz's life.

Although Schulz enjoyed sports, he also found refuge in solitary activities: reading, drawing, and watching movies. He bought comic books and Big Little Books, pored over the newspaper strips, and copied his favorites — *Buck Rogers*, the Walt Disney characters, *Popeye, Tim Tyler's Luck*. He quickly became a connoisseur; his heroes were Milton Caniff, Roy Crane, Hal Foster, and Alex Raymond.

In his senior year in high school, his mother noticed an ad in a local newspaper for a correspondence school, Federal Schools (later called Art

Instruction Schools). Schulz passed the talent test, completed the course, and began trying, unsuccessfully, to sell gag cartoons to magazines. (His first published drawing was of his dog, Spike, and appeared in a 1937 *Ripley's Believe It or Not!* installment.)

After World War II had ended and Schulz was discharged from the army, he started submitting gag cartoons to the various magazines of the time; his first breakthrough, however, came when an editor at *Timeless Topix* hired him to letter adventure comics. Soon after that, he was hired by his alma mater, Art Instruction, to correct student lessons returned by mail.

Between 1948 and 1950, he succeeded in selling 17 cartoons to the *Saturday Evening Post* — as well as, to the local *St. Paul Pioneer Press*, a weekly comic feature called *Li'l Folks*. It ran in the women's section and paid $10 a week. After writing and drawing the feature for two years, Schulz asked for a better location in the paper or for daily exposure, as well as a raise. When he was turned down on all three counts, he quit.

He started submitting strips to the newspaper syndicates. In the spring of 1950, he received a letter from the United Feature Syndicate, announcing its interest in his submission, *Li'l Folks*. Schulz boarded a train in June for New York City; more interested in doing a strip than a panel, he also brought along the first installments of what would become *Peanuts* — and that was what sold. (The title, which Schulz loathed to his dying day, was imposed by the syndicate). The first *Peanuts* daily appeared October 2, 1950; the first Sunday, January 6, 1952.

Prior to *Peanuts*, the province of the comics page had been that of gags, social and political observation, domestic comedy, soap opera, and various adventure genres. Although *Peanuts* changed, or evolved, during the 50 years Schulz wrote and drew it, it remained, as it began, an anomaly on the comics page — a comic strip about the interior crises of the cartoonist himself. After a painful divorce in 1973 from which he had not yet recovered, Schulz told a reporter, "Strangely, I've drawn better cartoons in the last six months — or as good as I've ever drawn. I don't know how the human mind works." Surely, it was this kind of humility in the face of profoundly irreducible human questions that makes *Peanuts* as universally moving as it is.

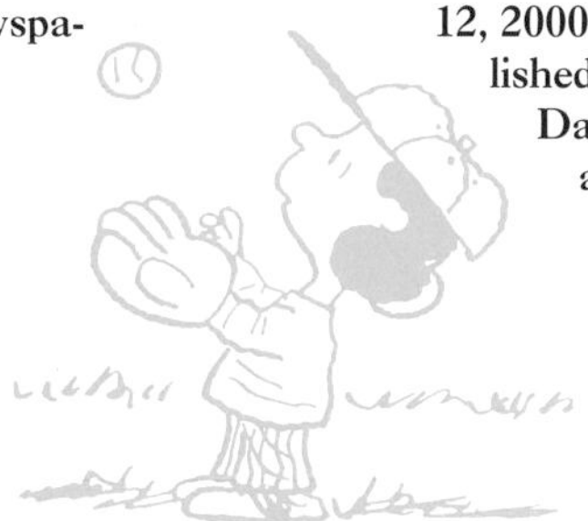

Diagnosed with cancer, Schulz retired from *Peanuts* at the end of 1999. He died on February 12, 2000, the day before his last strip was published (and two days before Valentine's Day) — having completed 17,897 daily and Sunday strips, each and every one fully written, drawn, and lettered entirely by his own hand — an unmatched achievement in comics.

—*Gary Groth*

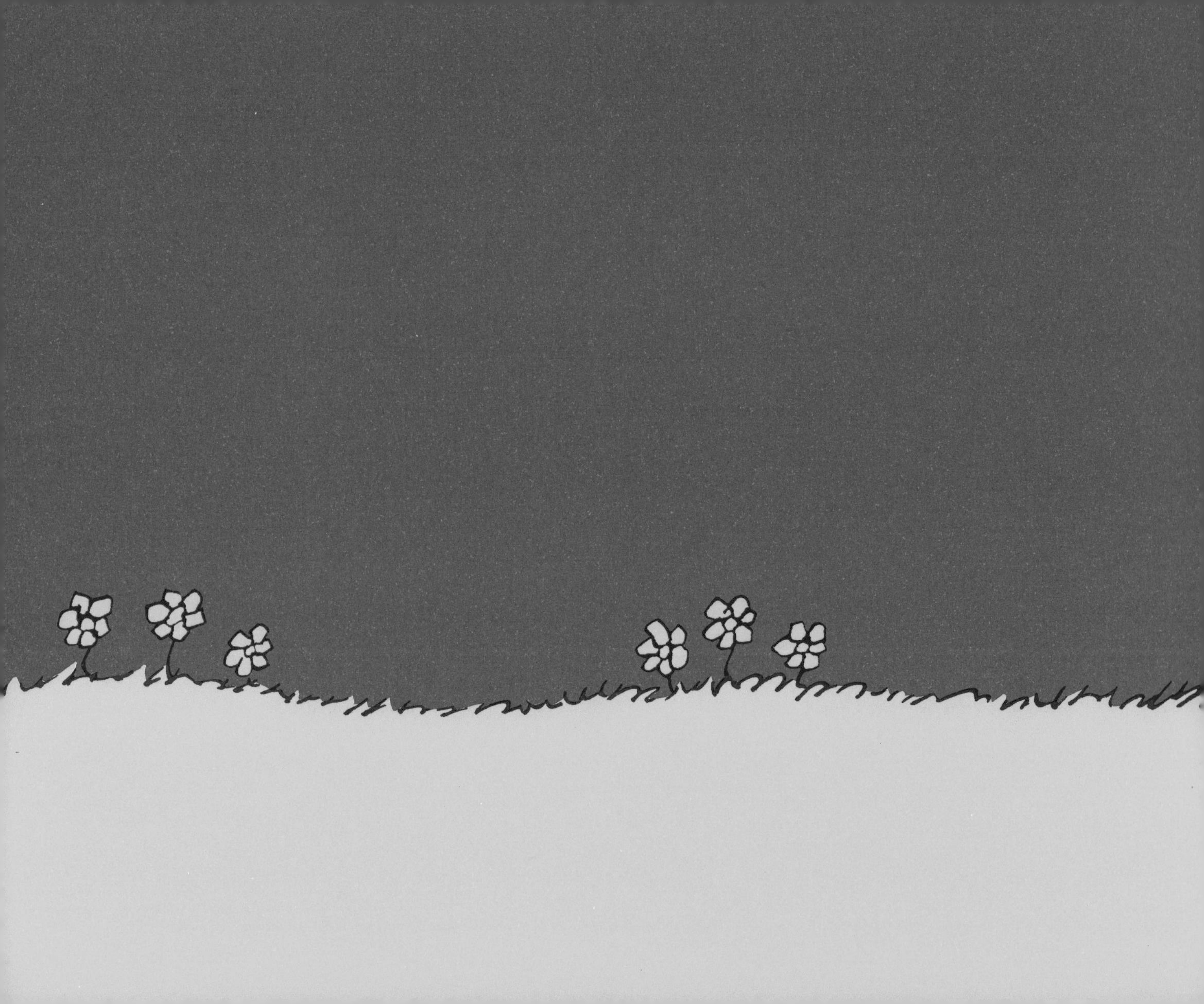

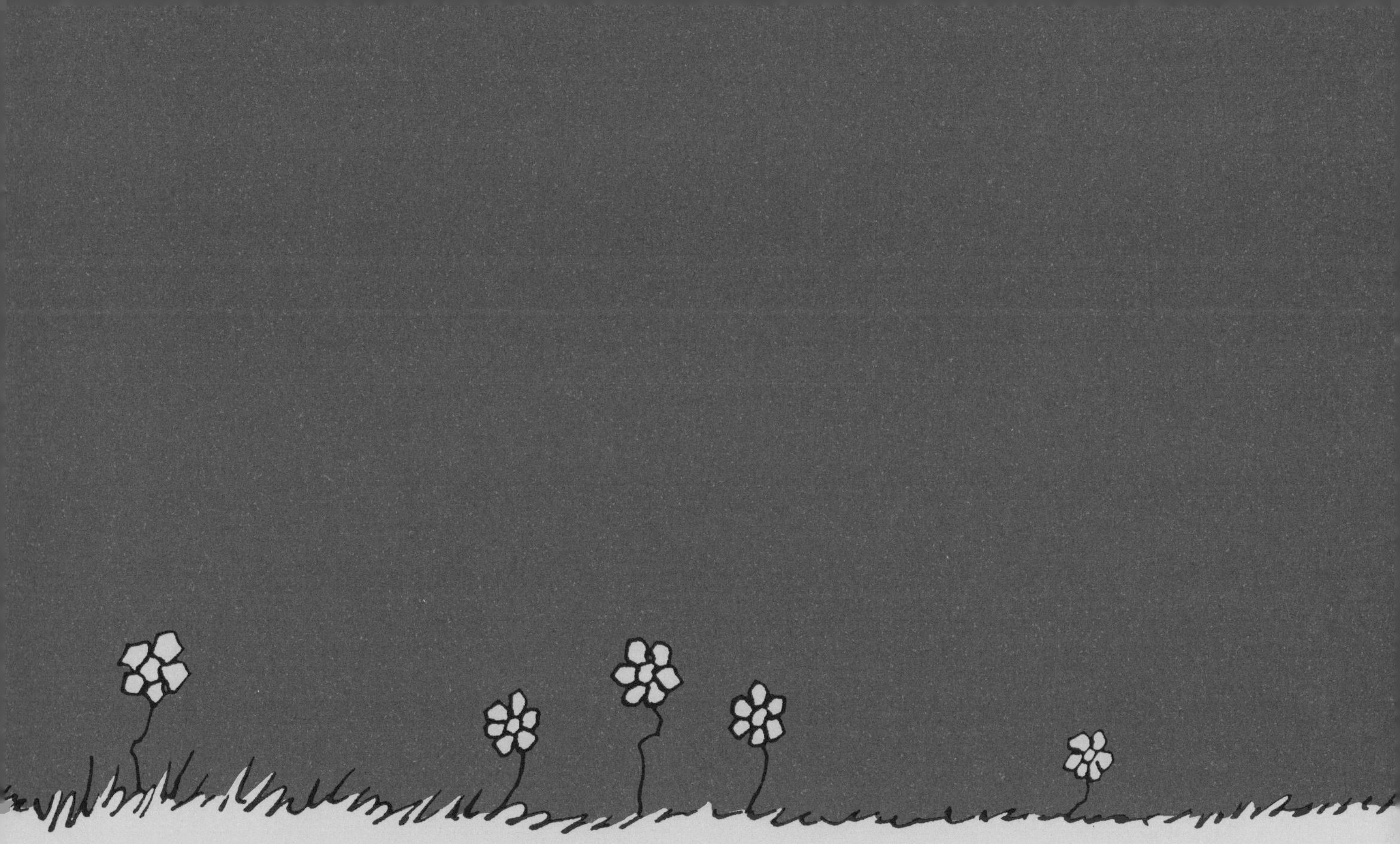

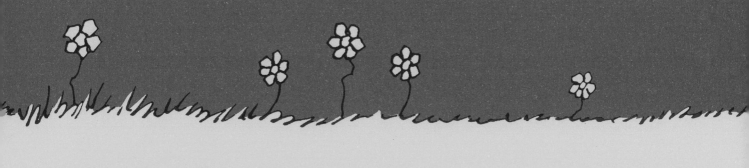

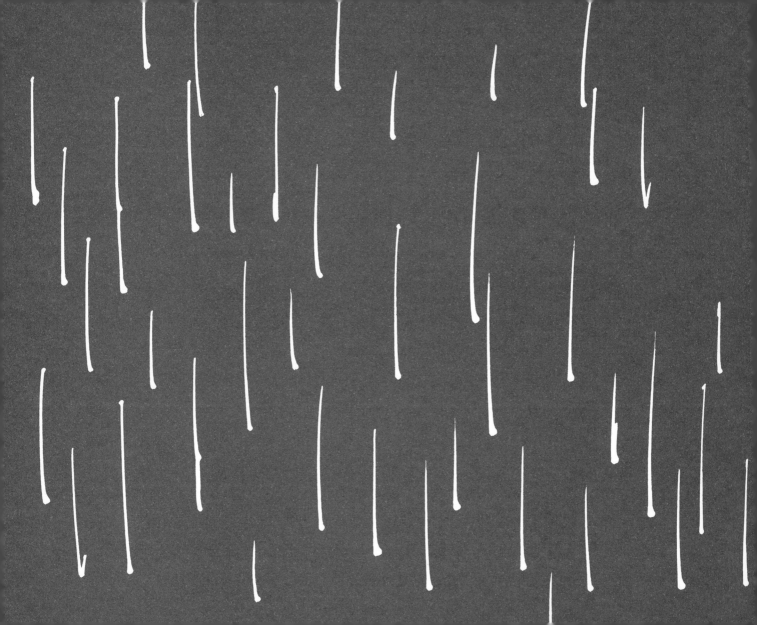

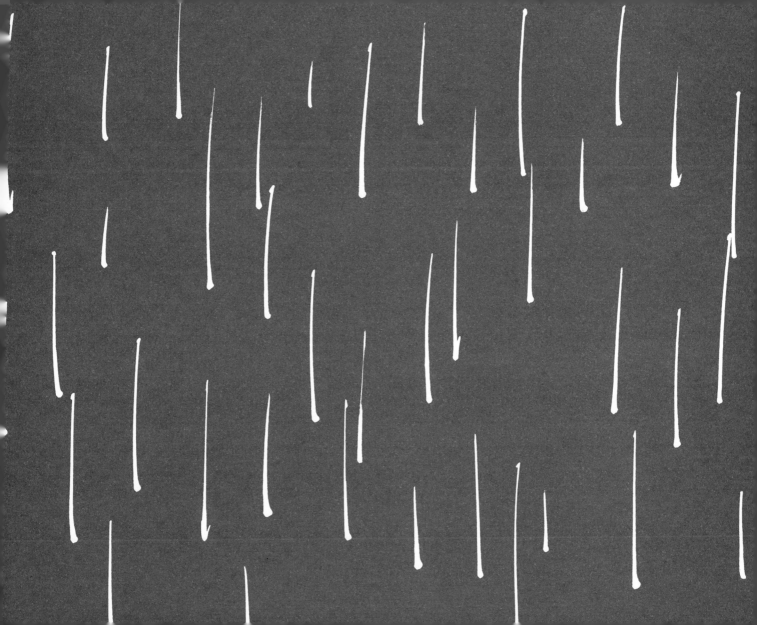

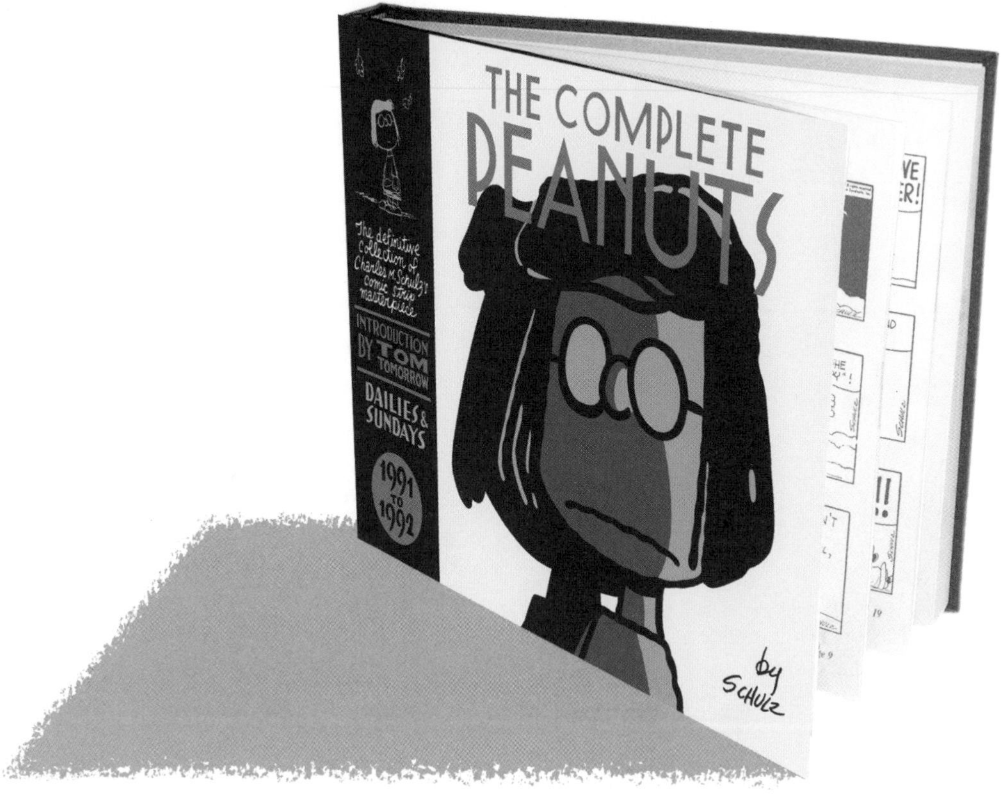
THE COMPLETE PEANUTS
The definitive collection of Charles M. Schulz's comic strip masterpiece
INTRODUCTION BY TOM TOMORROW
DAILIES & SUNDAYS
1991 TO 1992
by SCHULZ

Also available from Canongate *The Complete Peanuts: 1991-1992*

Love takes many shapes and shades in *The Complete Peanuts: 1991-1992*. Charlie Brown's interest in the Little Red-Haired Girl is rekindled; Linus fails to impress Lydia; Sally hoorays for Hollywood; Marcie pines for the World War 1 Flying Ace, who becomes lost in his cups (of root beer); Peppermint Patty and Marcie try to make Charlie Brown choose between them; and Snoopy is dangerously obsessed . . . with cookies.

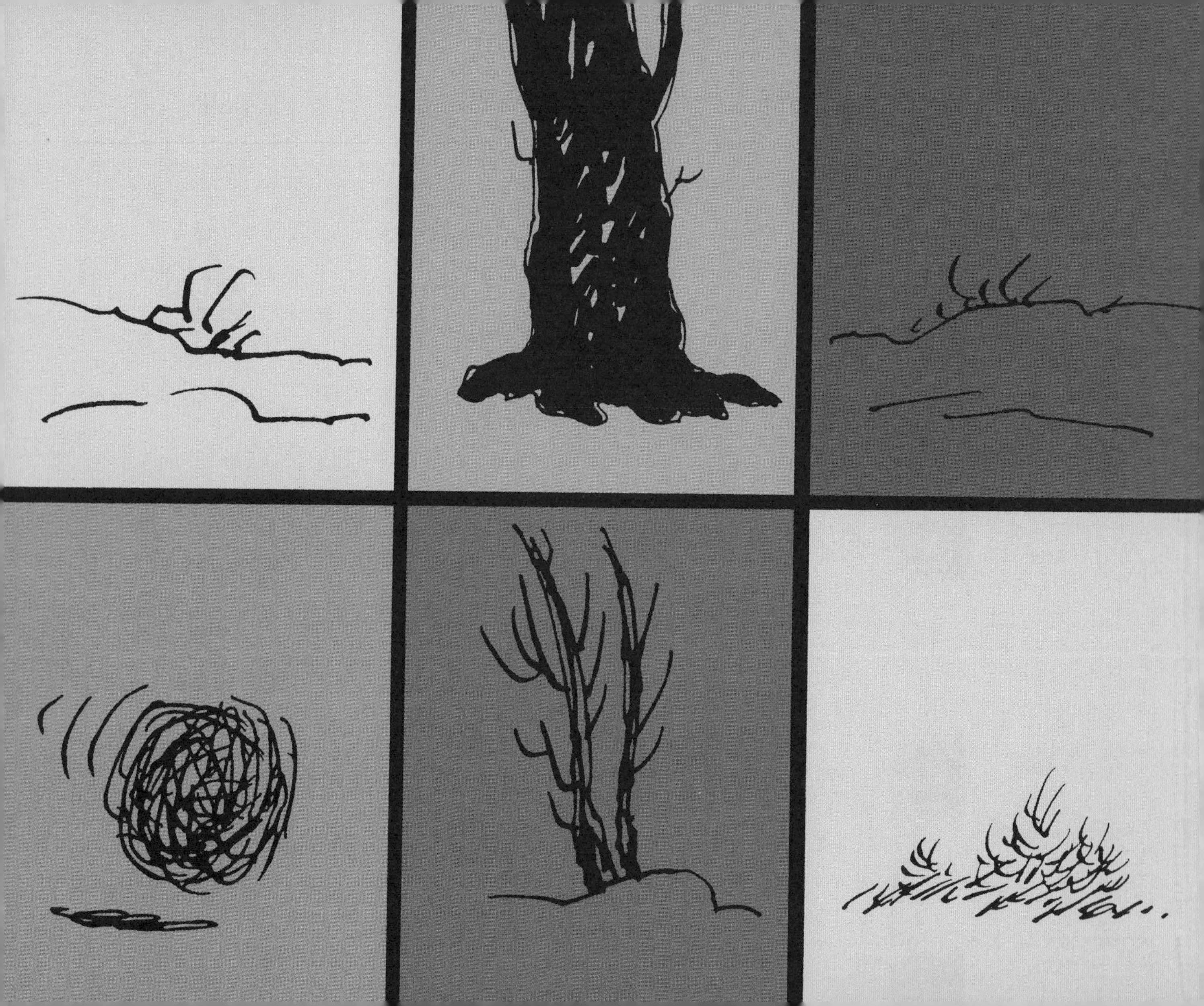